Paratroopers, or *Fallschirmjäger* as they are known in German, were ᴛ⁀ (*Fallschirmtruppe*) of the Luftwaffe during the Second World War. Although the America... Italians, and, to a greater extent, the Russians had experimented with airborne troops, it was the Germans who pioneered vertical envelopment using parachute, glider-borne and air-landed troops to conduct successful airborne operations in the early stages of the war. The man considered as the innovator and father of the German airborne forces was *General* Kurt Student and his vision would add a new dimension to warfare inspiring both the British and Americans to develop their own airborne forces.

The newly raised *Fallschirmjäger* formations took part in airborne and glider operations from April to June 1940 in Norway, Denmark, Belgium and Holland to attack and hold vital airfields, bridges and in one case an impregnable Belgian redoubt in support of ground operations in the west. On 20 May 1941, *Fallschirmjäger* formations would take part in their largest airborne assault of the war, Operation Mercury, the airborne invasion of Crete. Due to the heavy losses incurred during this operation, Hitler vetoed any further large scale airborne operations. With the exception of several small scale parachute and glider missions, *Fallschirmjäger* were mainly utilised as elite infantry for the remainder of the war, fighting on all fronts and often used as a fire brigade to support conventional forces.

This book is the result of several years of written correspondence, telephone interviews and meetings with veteran *Fallschirmjäger* between 1999 and 2006 and contains the memoirs of seventeen pre to mid-war volunteers and one late war conscript. The stories and diaries feature vivid battlefield memories that reflect the reality of war. On the other hand many of the stories convey the lighter-hearted moments or gallows humour that has remained etched in their memories. The one common factor shared by almost all of these men is captivity, whether captured during bitter fighting or surrendering at the end of hostilities. These men and thousands like them would be shipped off to POW camps in the USA, Britain and France until their repatriation, in some cases from several months to several years after the end of the war. Their words provide a fascinating insight into their training, combat, capture and subsequent captivity, creating an important historical record of their military service during the Second World War. Sadly, many of these men have now passed away and oral histories such as these now belong to an ever decreasing number of elderly veterans. There are several excellent publications that utilise extracts from veteran's first-hand accounts to compliment the historical text of a battle or campaign. Rarely do you see a book purely containing veterans' oral histories describing their military experience from their personal perspective and in their own words.

The veterans featured in this book took part in the both the airborne operations and ground campaigns on many fronts during the war from the heat of Crete and Africa to the frozen battle-fields of Russia and East Prussia and from the fields and hedgerows of Normandy to the mountains of Italy. Their words provide a fascinating insight into their training, combat, capture and subsequent captivity, creating an important historical record of their military service during the Second World War.

Greg Way was born in southwest England in 1970. He joined the Royal Navy in 1988 and volunteered for the submarine service, completing his 22 years' service in 2010. Having gained some experience in Naval maritime security and force protection he spent the next eight years working for a private maritime security company providing armed and unarmed protection for merchant ships in the worlds high risk areas. After 30 years in a maritime environment, Gregory decided upon a career change and in late 2018 started work with a global engineering company closer to home. With a lifelong interest in the Second World War, particularly the German military, he became interested in the *Fallschirmtruppe* during the 1990s and by chance in 1998 came into contact with several *Fallschirmjäger* veterans. Having conducted further research, Gregory set up a website in 1999 detailing the exploits of this famous formation and in 2001 he decided to publish the first-hand accounts he had received over the years. The veterans were pleased that their stories could finally be told, in their own words. Gregory currently lives in Plymouth, England with his wife and two children.

FALLSCHIRMJÄGER!

FALLSCHIRMJÄGER!

A Collection of Firsthand Accounts and Diaries by German Paratrooper Veterans from the Second World War

Greg Way

Helion & Company

Helion & Company Limited
Unit 8 Amherst Business Centre
Budbrooke Road
Warwick
CV34 5WE
England
Tel. 01926 499 619
Email: info@helion.co.uk
Website: www.helion.co.uk
Twitter: @helionbooks
blog.helion.co.uk

Published by Helion & Company 2020. Reprinted in paperback 2021
Designed and typeset by Mach 3 Solutions Ltd (www.mach3solutions.co.uk)
Cover designed by Paul Hewitt, Battlefield Design (www.battlefield-design.co.uk)

ISBN 978-1-914059-40-7

British Library Cataloguing-in-Publication Data.
A catalogue record for this book is available from the British Library.

For details of other military history titles published by Helion & Company Limited contact the above
address, or visit our website: http://www.helion.co.uk.

We always welcome receiving book proposals from prospective authors.

This book is dedicated to Josef 'Sepp' Jendryschik.

Sepp was an early member of *Fallschirmjäger Regiment 1* and later an advocate of peace and justice who was eager to see the completion of a book containing firsthand veteran accounts and stories that needed to be told. He sadly passed away in May 2001. In one of his letters, Sepp wrote the following:

>*"Nie wieder, sollen die Waffen gegeneinander erhoben werden!"*
>('Never again, should weapons be raised against each other')

Contents

Foreword

"There is nothing either good or bad but thinking makes it so."
William Shakespeare

This book proves the validity of Shakespeare's wisdom twice over: to Greg Way, whom we owe the immense work of collecting, sorting, arranging and publishing the material, and the expected but still unknown readers, who withstand the temptation to hate the former enemy, to ignore humanity and tolerance. A book about the acting, thinking, feeling and suffering of German *Fallschirmjäger* (paratroopers), narrated in their own words, would be a nonsense, if there would not exist what the world names "very British": fairness and common sense. No foe, but a human being; no malicious joy, but sympathy; no evil wishes, but a helping hand.

Greg Way, also very British, took a keen interest in the history and life of German *Fallschirmjäger*. He did not juggle with preconceived opinions, but made friends with the rare survivors of the war and succeeded in obtaining reports, stories, notes, letters and comments. The translation must have been difficult and included arranging an apparatus of explanations and pointing out essential parts of the soldier's 'lingo'.

The book at hand is deeply human, and if one sniffs ideology it is that of charity and understanding. It represents a big step forward – hate replaced by love and understanding. Looking around at our present world of brutal killing and destruction, we pray for more personalities like Greg Way, who knows what to do: see no enemy but a suffering human being, replace egotism with amiable actions. Set to work by listening to the cries of mortal souls.

How happy we are that William Shakespeare, the 'Ancient Sage', is still understood…

Volker Stutzer
Former journalist, newspaper editor, author and veteran
of Fallschirmjäger Regiment.27

Volker Stutzer at the *Flugtag Oberschleißheim* in 2003. The JU-52 is AZ+JU, a CASA 325 post-war Spanish version of the German wartime aircraft which came to be affectionately known as *Tante Ju* by the paratroops. (Volker Stutzer)

The author with Volker Stutzer during a visit in February 2019. (Oliver Stutzer)

Preface

Paratroopers, or *Fallschirmjäger* as they are called in German, were the elite parachute troops (*Fallschirmtruppe*) of the *Luftwaffe* during the Second World War. Although the Americans and Italians had experimented with airborne troops, it was the Soviets who demonstrated the potential of large-scale parachute drops during the 1930s and created a formidable airborne capability.[1] Amongst the foreign military observers witnessing Soviet airborne manoeuvres in 1935 was Hermann Göring, the future leader of the *Luftwaffe*, who was inspired to create a parachute formation from his own Berlin Police unit.[2] Another German officer who witnessed the Soviet airborne demonstration was the man considered as the innovator and father of the German airborne forces. *General* Kurt Student would pioneer the concept of vertical envelopment and his vision would add a new dimension to warfare, inspiring both the British and Americans to develop their own airborne forces during the early stages of the war.

Following the outbreak of war in September 1939, *Fallschirmjäger* formations received their baptism of fire in Poland albeit in a limited ground role. In 1940, the Fallschirmtruppe took part in several airborne and glider operations between April and June in Norway, Demark, Belgium and Holland, to attack and hold vital airfields, bridges and in one case an impregnable Belgian redoubt in support of ground operations in the West. On 20 May 1941, *Fallschirmjäger* formations would take part in their largest airborne assault of the war, Operation Mercury, the invasion of Crete. Due to the heavy losses sustained during this operation, Hitler vetoed any further large-scale airborne operations. With the exception of several small-scale parachute and glider missions, *Fallschirmjäger* were mainly utilised as elite infantry for the remainder of the war, fighting on all fronts and often used as a fire brigade to support conventional forces. By the end of hostilities in May 1945, it is estimated that upwards of 250,000 men had served as volunteer or conscripted *Fallschirmjäger* during the war, with almost 60,000 killed and 8,000 men listed as missing; however, these statistics are very difficult to determine accurately and can no longer be reliably researched.[3]

The exploits of German airborne troops have interested me for the best part of two decades. In the mid-90s, I read a 1973 military modelling magazine featuring an article written by Brian Molloy about the German *Fallschirmjäger* of the Second World War. The magazine featured photos of men wearing short-rimmed helmets and thigh-length smocks taking part in the assault on the

---

1   Although the Soviets had amassed a considerable airborne force, they conducted only a handful of parachute operations on the Eastern Front after the German invasion in June 1941. One notable operation was conducted in January and February 1942 in the central sector between Vyazma and Yukhnov, involving several thousand Soviet paratroopers. Many of these operations were unsuccessful. See Taylor, pp.202–17.

2   The Army established its own *Fallschirm-Infanterie Kompanie* (and later a *Bataillon*) on 1 April 1937, which was transferred to the Luftwaffe on 1 January 1939 as II/FJR1. See Peters, p.113.

3   Stimpel, p.446, states that there are no reliable statistics on losses. The daily reports from the Quartermaster General of the *Luftwaffe* high command and other statistics are too patchy. The number of losses in 1944 to February 1945 are, in his opinion, too low. In 1944 alone, losses of 95,084 were reported, among them about 55,000 dead, missing or captured soldiers. How many deaths resulted from the 40,000 wounded is unknown. The MIA (missing in action) statistics come from the BDF (*Bund Deutscher Fallschirmjäger*, the Association of German Paratroopers) and cases are still being investigated by the *Suchdienst* (Search Service).

General der Flieger Student arriving at Diepholz in north-west Germany in early 1942 to conduct an award ceremony for *II/FJR2*. This *Bataillon* had suffered heavy casualties on the island of Crete several months earlier. (Karl Jörger)

fort at Eben Emael, the invasion of Crete and the defence of Monte Cassino. I decided to further research this military formation.

What intrigued me about the *Fallschirmjäger* was their *esprit de corps*, the pride, honour and mutual loyalty displayed by these airborne warriors and the fact that until the summer of 1944, their ranks were made up purely of volunteers. They came to be known as the Green Devils and were renowned for their courageous offensive feats and tenacious defence, fighting with chivalry and honour, being respected by those who encountered them in combat. In 1998, I was fortunate enough to come into contact with several high-profile *Fallschirmjäger* veterans who had been recipients of the *Ritterkreuz*, and they in turn put me in contact with other men who they knew from their veteran associations. These men provided some invaluable information regarding their military service, and over the next seven years I made contact with more rank and file veterans, most of whom were more than happy to share their stories and anecdotes from the war. Many veterans were surprised as to why an Englishman would be interested in the stories of a former foe! Understandably, a handful of veterans were wary of my approach and declined to take part, and in some cases they just wanted the war to remain a part of their past.

The father of the German airborne forces, *General* Kurt Arthur Benno Student. (Karl Jörger)

After conducting further research, I decided to develop a website and forum as there were very few sites dedicated to the German paratroops at that time. The website attracted military enthusiasts and collectors, many of whom contributed written and photographic material. Having collated more and more written testimonies, I pondered over the creation of a book in order to share the fascinating accounts and documents that I now had in my possession. I wrote to the veterans and informed them of my idea; it was warmly welcomed and many were eager to see their material published as a permanent record of their wartime experiences from their perspective and in their own words. Unfortunately, in 2006, my Naval career took me away for extended periods, and with the additional workload and a young family I had to put the book on hold. During this time I lost contact with many veterans who had sadly passed away in the meantime.

In late 2017, I found out about the passing of three veterans whom I had formed a special relationship with over a decade earlier. I felt guilty that I had not fulfilled my promise to publish their wartime experiences. All of my correspondence and notes were unboxed and reviewed, and I began to collate the written accounts to ensure that these experiences could be shared. This book is a compilation of firsthand accounts and diary extracts from a small cross-section of rank and file

Austrian-born Heini Breitfuß as a *Jäger* in 1942. He served with *FJR5* in Tunisia and *FJR16 Ost* in Lithuania. The photo epitomises the image of the *Fallschirmjäger*, with the distinctive helmet and jump smock. (Wilfried Diehl)

German paratroopers who served during the Second World War and survived to tell their story. All of the veterans featured in this book contributed in different ways. Some provided very detailed accounts of their whole wartime service, others a recollection of a particular campaign or battle.

I have been reliant on the photographs sent to me by the veterans themselves and their families, collections from veterans who do not feature in this book or other contemporary sources. Some contributed one or more photographs; others did not. Some veterans had no photos at all in their possession, having been lost, taken upon capture or destroyed during or after the war, or in some cases borrowed by researchers and never returned. To some veterans, the photos they did have in their possession were the only reminder of their military service. Whatever the contribution, these eyewitness accounts convey the horror, humanity and gallows humour of war from the perspective of those young men who served in this elite formation. In some cases these accounts were written during or shortly after the war, while others put pen to paper decades later after receiving my request for information about their wartime service.

The book is split into two parts. The first part contains the firsthand accounts of varying length, and the second features wartime diaries. The veterans featured in this book took part in the both the airborne operations and ground campaigns on many fronts during the war, from the heat of Crete and Africa to the frozen battlefields of Russia, and from the fields and hedgerows of Normandy to the mountains of Italy. Their words provide a fascinating insight into their training, combat, capture and subsequent captivity, creating an important historical record of their military service during the Second World War.

Greg Way, 2019

Bernhard Holthausen, veteran of *I/FJR12* (fourth from left) prior to a training jump at Wittstock in 1942. (Bernhard Holthausen)

Oberfeldwebel Pill's Gruppe from *8/FJR2* at the Tanagra airfield on 20 May 1941. They would soon jump over Crete as part of the second wave with *II/FJR2* west of Heraklion. Most of the men in this Gruppe are armed with an MPi. According to Richter p.83, it had been clear since Holland that it was possible to carry an MPi on the person whilst jumping from an aircraft. (Karl Jörger)

Acknowledgements

I would like to thank the following people who made this book possible:

Martin Sieden, Volker Griesser, Detlef Scheidt and Erich Craciun, who translated a great deal of written material for me in the early years, and Sean Johnstone at aretecrete.com. To Sue Doubell, Kate Eichler, Derek Kranefeld, Ronald Bauer, Lydia Jackl, Sig Schulz, Ingrid Klumpp, Sabine Reuter, Petra von Beck, Annette von Beck & Roland Foos and Reinhard Wenzel for providing me with information and photos of their fathers' wartime service.

To Professor Dr Heinz Bliss+, *Oberst* (ret) Steffen Rhode and *Major* Hendrik Krause (ret) of the *Bund Deutscher Fallschirmjäger*. Manfred Müller, volunteer archivist for the *BDF*, who has provided me with reports and images from the Müller, Jörger and Rzeha collections at the archive.

To Yannis Prekatsounakis for his support and knowledge of the battle for Heraklion and Mark Bando for his support and book-writing advice.

My old friend Volker Stutzer, veteran of *FJR27*, wordsmith, former newspaper editor and author, whom I have enjoyed corresponding with for many years and who was kind enough to write the foreword to this book and assist with some of the translation.

The biggest debt of gratitude goes to the veterans themselves who contributed to the production of this book. Without their time and willingness to contribute their memories there would be no book and we would not be able to enjoy their oral histories. Sadly, many of them have now passed away but their wartime experiences live on within the pages of this publication.

A big thank you to Charles Singleton and Duncan Rogers from Helion, and Tony Walton who copy edited the book.

Lastly, to my wife and children for their patience and understanding over the years since I began this project in 1999.

Fallschirmjäger Rank Structure

Officers (Medical ranks in brackets)

Generalmajor/Generalleutnant/General der Flieger/Generaloberst
Oberst – (*Oberstarzt*) Colonel
Oberstleutnant – (*Oberfeldarzt*) Lieutenant Colonel
Major – (*Oberstabsarzt*) Major
Hauptmann – (*Stabsarzt*) Captain
Oberleutnant – (*Oberarzt*) First Lieutenant
Leutnant – (*Assistenarzt*) Second Lieutenant

Senior NCOs (Unteroffiziere mit Portepee)

Hauptfeldwebel – Not a rank but an appointment equivalent to Company Sergeant Major and known as '*Der Spieß*'. This appointment was designated to a senior NCO and not necessarily the most senior NCO in the *Kompanie*
Stabsfeldwebel – Master Sergeant
Oberfeldwebel – Sergeant Major
Feldwebel – Sergeant 1st Class

Junior NCOs (Unteroffiziere ohne Portepee)

Unterfeldwebel – Sergeant 2nd Class
Oberjäger (also called *Unteroffizier* by some *Fallschirmtruppe* formations) – Senior Corporal

Enlisted men (Mannschaften)

Hauptgefreiter as a rank was phased out in early 1944 and replaced by the rank of *Stabsgefreiter* – Senior Lance Corporal
Obergefreiter – Lance Corporal
Gefreiter – Private 1st Class
Jäger – Private

Glossary of Terminology & Abbreviations

Formation and unit abbreviations:

Divisional level – referred to as *FJD* e.g. *FJD3* for *Fallschirmjäger Division 3*
Regiment level – referred to as *FJR* e.g. *FJR5* for *Fallschirmjäger Regiment 5*
Battalion level – referred to in Roman numerals before regiment e.g. *III/FJR5* for 3rd Battalion of *Regiment 5* or Bataillon, the German word for Battalion.
Company level – Numbered before Regiment e.g. *7/FJR1* for 7th Company of *FJR1* or referred to as *Kompanie* or *Kompanien* (plural) throughout the book
Platoon level – Referred to as *Zug* i.e. *3 Zug* for 3rd Platoon or *Züge* (plural)

Other terms and abbreviations in alphabetical order:

Abteilung – A battalion-sized unit or detachment
Amis – German term for American troops
Bataillon – Comprising a HQ, signals section, three *Jäger* Kompanien and a heavy Kompanie with appoximately 600 men all ranks (May 1941)
Bund Deutscher Fallschirmjäger (*BDF*) – The Association of German Paratroopers. Set up after the war by veterans, it began as a comrades search service and comrades, widows and orphans aid organisation. Today it supports serving paratroopers as well as veterans and their families, and promotes international understanding for the preservation of world peace (*BDF* website)
Der Spieß – A senior NCO within a *Kompanie*, responsible for discipline, personnel, supply issues and other *Kompanie* matters. Identified by two rows of NCO braid (*tresse*) on both tunic sleeves (also known as *Kolbenringe* or piston rings)
Dienstgrad – Rank
Divisions Kommandeur – Divisional Commander
DKiG (*Deutsches Kreuz* in Gold) – Instituted in September 1941 as an intermediate decoration between the EK1 and the Knight's Cross
EK1 / EK2 – Iron Cross 1st Class and 2nd Class
Erkennungsmarke – Identity disc or dog-tag
Ersatz und Ausbildungs Bataillon/Regiment – Replacement and training battalion or regiment
Fahnenjunker – Enlisted man or NCO selected to be an officer candidate
Fähnrich – Officer cadet with the equivalent rank to *Unterfeldwbel* and awaiting *Kriegschule* training
Fallschirm – The original parachute known as the RZ1 was replaced by improved versions RZ16 & RZ20 as the war progressed. The RZ36 was introduced near the war's end and saw limited use. RZ was the acronym for *Rückenfallschirm Zwangsauslösung*, or back parachute forced release
Fallschirmjäger – Parachute rifleman

Fallschirm-Lehrregiment – Parachute training & demonstration regiment

Fallschirmpioniere –Parachute combat engineer, also used as parachute infantry

Fallschirm Sanitäts Kompanie – Parachute medical company

Fallschirm Sanitäts Zug – Parachute medical platoon

Fallschirmschule – Parachute school. Four were established at different periods during the war in Germany, at Stendal, Wittstock, Braunschweig and Salzwedel. Some schools were moved to France, at Dreux and Lyon, and one to Kraljewo in Serbia. Jump training was also conducted at Chateaudun, Avignon and Troyes in France. Wittstock was the last to close in March 1945

Fallschirmschützenabzeichen – Parachute rifleman's badge produced in two versions for the *Luftwaffe* and Army

Fallschirmtruppe – Paratroops

Feldpostnummer – (Fieldpost Number) A military postal service code similar to a postal code or zip code assigned to a unit.

Flak – (*Flugabwehrkanone*) Anti-aircraft gun

Fliegerdivision 7 – The first German Airborne Division established in 1938 and initially commanded by *Generalmajor* Student. The division was re-designated as *FJD1* in May 1943 with *FJR2* used to form the nucleus for *FJD2*.

Flugtechnische Schule – Aviation technical school

Flugzeugführer – *Luftwaffe* pilot

Fremde Heer Ost – (Foreign Armies East) Military intelligence organisation focusing on Russia

Gauleiter – A regional Nazi party leader

Gebirgsjäger – German mountain troops

Gruppe – Squad

Gruppeführer – Squad Leader

He-111 – *Luftwaffe* bomber produced by Heinkel

Himmelfahrtkommando – Suicide mission

HKL – (*Hauptkampflinie*) – Main battle line or main line of resistance

Horchposten – A position used at night or in poor visibility in order to listen in on the enemy

HVPl – (*Hauptverbandplatz*) – Main first aid station

Iron Gustav – American flying artillery spotter

Jabo – (*Jagdbomber*) Allied ground attack aircraft

Jagdgeschwader – Luftwaffe fighter aircraft group

JU-52 – German transport plane used by the paratroops for airborne operations

Kampfgruppe – Battle group

Knäckebrot – Hard cracker known as German brittle bread and part of the half iron emergency rations

Knochensack – Literally bonesack, the jump-smock worn by the paratroopers

Kolchose – A Russian collective farm

Kommandeur – Commander

Kommissar – A communist political officer

Kompanie – According to The War Office, p.26, a parachute rifle company in May 1941 contained 180–190 men, but only 144 made up the combat company (Gefechtskompanie), the unit flown into action. The remaining men made up the rear party (Nachkommando), such as drivers, technicians and reserves etc. The heavy company had fewer men in its Gefechtskompanie but a higher number in the Nachkommando

Kompaniechef – An officer officially appointed as the *Kompanie* commander

Kompanieführer – A temporary *Kompanie* commander if the *Kompaniechef* is incapacitated or has been killed. The role could be fulfilled by any rank in the absence of an officer. It was not uncommon in the latter stages of the war for an NCO to become *Kompanieführer*

Krankenträger – Stretcher bearers.

Kriegsberichter – War reporter or correspondent

Kubelwagen – Military jeep-type vehicle produced by Volkswagen

Landser – Soldier

Lazarett – Hospital

Luftlande – Air-landed

Luftwaffe – (LW) Air Force of the wartime Wehrmacht

Melder – Messenger / Runner

Meldestaffelführer – NCO in charge of a messenger group

MG34/42 – *Maschinengewehr* Model 34/42, both belt or drum-fed machine guns

MPi – *Maschinenpistole* or submachine gun such as the MP40

Nachrichtenzug – Signals Platoon

Oberfähnrich – Senior officer cadet having graduated from *Kriegsschule* (war school). Equivalent in rank to an *Oberfeldwebel* and awaiting a junior officer's commission.

Oberfeuerwerker – NCO with specialist armourer training

Oberwachtmeister – *Oberfeldwebel* of the artillery

O.B Süd-West – Commander in Chief South-West

PAK – (*Panzerabwehrkanone*) – Anti-tank gun

Panzerfaust – One shot, disposable, hand-held, tube-launched anti-tank weapon

Panzerjäger – Anti-tank soldier

Panzerschreck – 88mm shoulder fired, anti tank rocket launcher, also known as 'Ofenrohre'

Panzervernichtungstruppe – Tank destruction troop

RAD – (*Reichsarbeitdienst*) – Reich Labour service, compulsory for six months prior to military service

Pionierzug – Combat engineer platoon

Pionierzugführer – Combat engineer platoon leader

Radfahrzug – Bicycle equipped platoon used for reconnaissance or as a quick reaction force. Later in the war these units were often issued with motorcycles.

Regiment – A regiment consisted of three battalions, with a *Stab*, Signals Platoon and four *Kompanien*, 1–4, 5–8, 9–12. A *Fallschirmjäger* regiment also had a *13.Kp* of mortars, *14.Kp* of Panzerjäger and *15.Kp* of Pioneers (May 1944)

Regiment 'General Göring' – Formed in October 1935 from a Berlin Police unit and became the first parachute formation. On 1 July 1938, parts of the regiment formed the nucleus of the newly raised *Fliegerdivision 7*

Reichsbahn – German railway network

Ritterkreuz des Eisernen Kreuzes – (Knight's Cross of the Iron Cross) – With 5 grades of award it was bestowed for exceptional leadership and bravery. A recipient of the award was referred to as a *Ritterkreuzträger*.

Rollbahn – A tracked road often found in Russia

Rot schient die Sonne – Red shines the sun, paratroopers marching song known as the *Fallschirmjägerlied*

SA (*Sturmabteilung*) – Paramilitary wing of the Nazi Party, effectively superseded by the *SS* with many of its members drafted into the *Wehrmacht*

SA Standarte Feldherrnhalle – An elite regiment of the *SA* that guarded important Nazi Party premises. Some of its members transferred to the *Fallschirmtruppe* before the war, and after September 1939 many other former *Feldherrnhalle* members were sent to undertake

Fallschirmjäger training. According to veteran *Sanitäter* Willi Koch, in May 1939, elements of *I/FJR1* and volunteers from *SA Standarte Feldherrnhalle* formed *III/FJR1* and *I/FJR2* in Gardelegen.

Sani – (*Sanitäter*) – Medic

Sanitäts-Zug – Medical platoon

Schweres Maschinengewehr (*sMG*) – Heavy MG. The MG34 or 42 when used in conjunction with a field mount (*Lafette*) was referred to as an *sMG*

Soldbuch – Paybook and military ID with photo and details of the recipient

Stab – Staff

Stammrolle – A nominal roll of unit personnel

Sturmgruppe 'Granit' – (Assault group Granite) One of four assault groups used in Belgium on 10 May 1940. The others were Eisen (Iron), Beton (Concrete) and Stahl (Steel)

Sturmabteilung Koch – Assault detachment that conducted glider operations in Belgium on 10 May 1940. Named after its commander, Hauptmann Walter Koch. For a time it was given the cover name Versuchsabteilung 'Freidrichshafen' (Experimental Detachment 'Friedrichshafen'

Sturmgeschütz – (*StuG*) – Self propelled tracked assault gun fitted with a 7.5cm gun

Sturmregiment – (*LL.St.Rgt.1*) Air-Landing Assault regiment, formed from *Sturmabteilung Koch* in the summer of 1940 and consisted of four battalions

T-34 – Mass-produced Russian medium tank fitted with a 76mm gun

Tante Ju – (Aunty Ju) – affectionate name given to the Junkers JU-52 transport aircraft

T-Mine – (Teller mine) – Pressure-actuated anti-tank mine

Trupp – Small tactical unit of men

TVP – (*Truppenverbandplatz*) – Field dressing station

Unteroffiziere mit Portepee – NCO with Portepee, a decorative braided knot and lanyard also worn by Officers. Made from aluminium wire or braid, it was attached to the dress uniform LW dagger or sabre. A Portepee was worn by the senior NCO ranks of Feldwebel, Oberfeldwebel and Stabsfeldwebel.

Unteroffiziere ohne Portepee – NCO without Portepee and they instead wore a different type of coloured knot on their bladed accoutrement's known as a Faustriemen. These were the junior NCO ranks of Oberjager (Unteroffizier) and Unterfeldwebel

Volksbund Deutscher Kriegsgräberfürsorge (*VDK*) – A humanitarian organisation which on behalf of the German Federal Government is tasked with preserving and maintaining the graves of German war victims in Europe and North Africa

Waffenbehälter – Weapon container, also known as *Abwurfbehälter* (airdrop container). These containers were dropped by parachute from the transport aircraft and contained weapons, ammunition, equipment, rations and medical supplies.

Wehrmacht – The German armed forces of the Second World War

Zahlmeister – Army official with a comparable rank of Leutnant and responsible for administrative matters, finance and logistics

Zug – Platoon of approximately one officer and 37 men, with a platoon HQ and three squads

Zugführer – Platoon commander

Zugtrupp – Platoon HQ section

Précis of the *Luftwaffe Fallschirmjäger* operations and campaigns 1939–1945

1939
September   Limited use in a ground role during the campaign in Poland

1940
April   First German airborne operations in Norway and Denmark
May   Parachute and air-landing operations in Holland
May   Glider and parachute assault operations in Belgium
May–June   Parachute operation in Narvik, Norway

1941
April   Parachute and glider assault on the Corinth Canal bridge
May   Airborne invasion of Crete
September   Eastern Front – Leningrad and Neva Front
November   Eastern Front – Mius Front

1942
January–February   Eastern Front – Juchnow, Schaikowka and Rshev
January–March   Libya
January–March   Eastern Front – Mius Front
April–June   Eastern Front – Volkhov Front
July–November   El-Alamein Front, Egypt
July–November   Stalingrad Front
October   Eastern Front – Smolensk
November   Tunisia

1943
January–April   Eastern Front – Smolensk
January–May   Tunisia ground campaign and glider operations
July   Airborne operation in Sicily
September   Rome, Taranto, Salerno and Foggia, Italy
September   Glider operation on the Gran Sasso to rescue Mussolini
September   Small airborne operation at Monte Rotondo in Italy
September   Small airborne operation on the island of Elba, Italy
November   Small airborne operation on the island of Leros, Greece
November   Eastern Front – Zhitomir / Kirovgrad
December   Ortona, Italy

1944

January–May	Monte Cassino, Italy
January–May	Anzio / Nettuno bridgehead, Italy
January–May	Eastern Front – Novgorodka, Novo Ukrainka, Dniester River
June–August	Normandy, France
July–August	Small glider operation in Vercors region of the French Alps
JulyNovember	Lithuania and East Prussia
September	Arnhem corridor in Holland and Belgium
September	Bologna, Florence and Rimini, Italy
June–September	Fortress city of Brest in France
December	Ardennes offensive in Belgium (airdrop and ground operations)

1945

January	Alsace region of France
January–May	Ruhr Pocket
January–May	Imola, Bologna and Po River, northern Italy
January–May	Holland and Rhine area, Germany
February–May	Glider operation in the fortress city of Breslau
February–May	Oder Front, Pomerania and the Battle for Berlin
April–May	Austria

Introduction

Part one of this book is a compilation of the memoirs of 15 volunteer and one conscripted *Fallschirmjäger* veterans. These stories cover all or part of the veterans' military experience from their personal perspective. All of these firsthand accounts are different in length and feature detailed recollections of training, combat, capture and captivity.

These men joined the *Fallschirmjäger* ranks at various stages of the war, either volunteering prior to the outbreak of war and during the early years, or after the summer of 1944 being conscripted as more and more replacements were needed to replenish the ranks. Some of these veterans were inspired to enlist by magazine articles or newsreels featuring the famed *Luftwaffe* paratroops, while others were already serving in other branches of the *Luftwaffe* and transferred to become a *Fallschirmjäger*.

Some of these veterans were regarded as 'old sweats', veterans of many campaigns and held in high esteem by the younger *Fallschirmjäger*. As the war progressed, even these young men would soon be regarded as old hands, with battlefield experience on many fronts.

The following stories feature vivid battlefield memories that reflect the brutal reality of war. On the other hand, many of the stories convey the lighter-hearted moments or gallows humour that have remained etched in their memories. The one common factor shared by almost all of these men is captivity, whether captured during bitter fighting or surrendering at the end of hostilities. These men and thousands like them would be shipped off to POW camps in the USA, Britain and France until their repatriation, which in some cases was two to three years or more after the end of the war.

Part two features the wartime diaries of three veterans which tell of survival in the face of adversity, desperation and hopelessness against all odds.

Throughout this book I have endeavoured to check the accuracy of all the accounts, as mistakes are often made when recalling names, times, dates and locations in some cases decades later. German military terms have been used throughout the book as described in the glossary. Supplementary information useful to the text has been added to the footnotes, along with references to already published books where relevant to the account.

Introduction

Part I

Part I

1

Dr Kurt Erich Schulz

The *Fallschirm-Sanitäter*

Kurt Erich Schulz was born on 16 November 1921 and was almost 82 years old when I corresponded with him in 2003. He was born and raised in Königsberg (now Kaliningrad) on the Baltic Coast in former East Prussia. Whilst a young naval cadet before the war, Kurt volunteered to become a Fallschirmjäger *and was an early member of the fledgling paratroop medical branch. Kurt took part in the limited ground operations in Poland in 1939 and the invasion of the Low Countries on 10 May 1940. Due to an injury sustained during a training jump, Kurt did not take part in the invasion of Crete, where many of his comrades were killed. He went on to serve in Russia in late 1941 and was evacuated with frostbite. After a medical role in Norway, he later he served in Normandy after the Allied invasion, where he was captured by American forces and subsequently employed as a medic near Saint-Lô. After the war, Kurt briefly worked for Walt Disney and went on to continue his medical studies, earning many honours and degrees, and finally specialised in naturopathic medicine and acupuncture, which he pioneered in the United States over the following years. Kurt and his wife Heidi eventually settled in Hawaii.*

Sanitäts-Gefreiter Kurt Schulz. Soldbuch photo from 1940 whilst serving in *Fallschirm-Sanitäts-Abteilung 7*. Kurt is wearing the cloth version of the LW paratrooper badge. (Kurt Schulz)

Kurt Erich Schulz in July 2009. (Kurt Schulz)

Studio photo taken in late 1940. It is interesting to note that Kurt is wearing the Army parachute badge, possibly borrowed in the absence of his own *Luftwaffe*-issued badge. (Kurt Schulz)

Recruitment and *Sanitäter* training

When I say I am one of the old ones (*alte Kumpels*), I don't mean to be arrogant. Far from it, since at the time when I was transferred in the summer of 1939 from the Navy to Gardelegen, some 200km west of Berlin, I was an insecure 18-year-old soldier trying to do his best. I was somewhat displeased with my transfer from the pleasant surroundings of the Baltic resort of Warnemünde, where we would lie on the beach watching the girls go by, to such a dreadful place like Gardelegen. My buddy Walter Bühler and I (he was a former youth boxing champion from Würtemberg, whose sparring partner I had been in boot camp in Schleswig) soon decided to make the best of it and take it as a new challenge, which it really did turn out to be.

Kurt Schulz (left) and his best friend Walter Bühler pose for a studio photo in Berlin in 1940. (Kurt Schulz)

Photo of Kurt Schulz's best friend, *Sanitäts Gefreiter* Walter Bühler. Note the dark blue collar tabs for *Sanitäter* personnel. (Kurt Schulz)

Kurt and Walter on weekend leave visiting the Brandenburger Tor, Berlin, in 1940. (Kurt Schulz)

In 1939, it was very tough to become a 'Springer' (parachutist). Although you belonged to a *Fallschirmjäger* unit, it did not necessarily make you one, as the majority of the men were not jumpers at all.

First of all we were drilled and drilled to our very physical limits (Walter and I were both very fit), trying to level the sandy hills of the training grounds on our belt buckles.

Sanitäts-Zug 7 was at that time being built up to *Kompanie* strength, being mostly used as an air-landing *Kompanie*, with only our drill instructors being qualified jumpers.[1] They proudly wore the golden diving eagle badge on their chest, known as the *Fallschirmschützenabzeichen*. Some of them wore the Army Paratrooper Badge, which was of a slightly different design.

In addition that meant extra money, called *Fliegerzulage* (60 Marks), which practically doubled the *Wehrsold* (monthly pay). Obviously, besides being a challenge, this made it even more tempting for Walter and I.

We were not too worried about the three-day test, which was supposed to be a tough one to pass. Out of 100 men only 20–30 usually passed, so we applied.

Remember, at that time we were only supposed to be a small special elite combat unit, trained as a single combatant, able to handle any situation, if necessary alone, dropped behind enemy lines. This called for special abilities to handle any transport vehicle on land, sea or in the air. For three days during the test they turned us upside down.

Firstly, the psychological test made you unsure whether they wanted to make you an officer or even a *General* straight away. Secondly, the physical side was obviously no problem if you came from the Navy, as one had to be in excellent shape to make it in at that time: no glasses, no flat feet and no knock-knees either. The third test was not easy; you had to be quite an athlete to pass it and had to be able to jump over a high bar with spread legs, otherwise you failed the whole test. We both passed the test and were now in line for jump school. However, Poland would come first.

Politics make strange bedfellows, and we were surprised when Stalin and Hitler became allies. All summer long there had been strained activities in the Polish Corridor (former West Prussia). We had heard about incidents where German nationals had been mistreated, discriminated and

The *Luftwaffe* Paratrooper badge was instituted on 5 November 1936 by the Commander in Chief of the *Luftwaffe* and was awarded after the recipient had qualified as a parachutist by completing six training jumps. (Nathan Hogle)

The Army Paratrooper badge was instituted on 1 September 1937 and was awarded to men of the *Fallschirm-Infanterie-Kompanie/Bataillon*, and was worn instead of the *Luftwaffe* version if they qualified between the inception date in 1937 and 1 January 1939 when the badge was discontinued. It was reinstituted in 1943 when it was awarded to men of two new *Fallschirmjäger* units introduced in that year. The *Waffen-SS* and the *Brandenburg* Regiment created their own *Fallschirm* units in the summer of 1943. (Nathan Hogle)

---

1   *Fallschirm-Sanitäts-Zug 7* was established in May 1939 and attached to *Fliegerdivision 7*. Training of stretcher bearers began with 12 men from *I/FJR1* and 12 from *II/FJR1*. See Koch & Neumann.

Hauptmann Hans Kroh (seated fourth from left) with the permanent staff of what would become *Sani Zug 7*, taken in early 1939, possibly in Gardelegen. At the time of this photo Kroh was on the staff of *Fliegerdivision 7* and most likely present to assist with the establishment and training of the unit. He later went on to command *I/FJR2* on Crete and later commanded *FJR2* & *FJD2* and became one of the most decorated *Fallschirmjäger* officers of the Second World War. Although Kroh qualified as a paratrooper in 1937, he is not wearing his paratrooper badge, possibly for reasons of secrecy. Among the medical officers present (seated left to right) are Dr Carl Langemeyer, Dr Adolf Stimpfl and Dr Heinrich Neumann. (Stephan Janzyk)

murdered against the terms of the League of Nations Agreement, which did nothing to stop the incidents as Germany had asked.

Personally, I was not interested in politics, as we three boys at home were not allowed like most other boys to join the Hitler Youth, as my father had no time for the Nazis. He was still a loyal royalist of Prussia. So everything I heard was put down to Nazi propaganda.

Unfortunately it was not the case, as I later learned in Poland. In the meantime I was selected to join a small group of 'Sanis' for specific medical training, which included surgery assistant. I had been chosen because I had been an art student with anatomy studies and had some basic knowledge of Latin.

While everybody had to go through the regular *Fallschirmjäger* training with all the weaponry, which included the most modern at that time – including the new machine-pistols and Walther pistol model 38 and the heavier 2cm guns – we *Sanis* were given twice the amount of training.

The majority of the newly formed *Fallschirm-Sanitäts-Kompanie 7* were combatants and stretcher bearers (more than half).[2] The others were *Sanis* who administered first aid in the field, and a small

---

2   After receiving more volunteers, *FSK7* was established in August 1939 with a *Parachute Kompanie* and a half *Luftlande-Kompanie*. Training and development continued after the Polish campaign. See Koch & Neumann.

special group, to which I belonged, were titled *Sanitätsdienstgrad* or medical orderlies.[3] We wore the medical sleeve patch (rod of Asclepius), while the whole *Kompanie* wore the dark blue collar tabs (para infantry wore yellow collar tabs). Our *Kompaniechef* was *Oberstabsarzt* Dr Heinrich Neumann, the first doctor to receive the *Ritterkreuz*.

In September 1939, Dr Neumann made us crawl on our bellies across the Prinkendorf-Liegnitz (Legnica) airfield to our awaiting JU-52, shouting *"auf hinlegen – auf hinlegen!"* (lie down), hitting the slower ones on the head with his helmet like a crazy man. Was this the way for a commanding officer to send his men into combat? Most of us wondered! Dr Neumann was a real tough officer. He used to tell us that if anyone had not spent some time '*im Bau*' (in the stockade), he wasn't tough enough. I made the grade.

'*Feuertaufe*' (baptism of fire) in Poland

Our planned airdrop into Poland was cancelled and we were soon transported by truck convoy across Poland. I, who had never seen a dead person up close before in my life, was chosen to practice as undertaker for the dead victims of the fighting near Wola-Gulowska.[4]

One job I will never forget was cleaning these first dead comrades and putting them into plain wooden boxes to be sent home to their relatives. One case in particular will remain with me. I knew him quite well, and when I took off his helmet his brain was inside it. That was my personal baptism of fire as a *Sani*. Nothing scared me much after that.

What I had earlier believed to be Nazi propaganda unfortunately turned out to be true according to our advanced combat troops, who found German men and women who had been killed and mutilated in the Polish Corridor.[5] They had stumbled across many civilians who had been cut in half with axes, women who had been nailed to barn doors with their breasts cut off and other horrific inhuman activities.[6]

The return to Germany and an unfortunate accident

After returning to Jävenitz / Gardelegen we were finally sent to the Wittstock jump school at the end of 1939 to undertake our parachute training. During my second training jump I watched the comrade ahead of me in the aircraft fall to his death when his parachute failed to open. The JU-52 continued to make its turn to allow me to carry on with my jump. Despite the flare from the ground, I carried on with the jump and instead of being berated on the ground for not observing the cancellation flare, the jumpmaster instead commended me for the best jump of the day.

The loss of our comrade was tragic, but I remember him standing in the line before the jump and jokingly say *"Habt ihr alle euer Testament gemacht?"* (Have you all made your will?). It became apparent later that his chute would not open due to his careless exit from the aircraft. He stepped

---

3   According to Adler, p.15, the *Kompanie* was organised as follows: *1.Zug* was to care for the sick and wounded; *2.Zug* was responsible for rescuing the wounded; and *3.Zug* had to secure the *HVPl* area in case of emergency.

4   Wola-Gulowska is located 120km SE of Warsaw on the Czarna River. *II/FJR1*, in company with *3.Zug/ FSK7*, was involved in fighting in the town on 24 September 1939. See Koch & Neumann. *II/FJR1* casualties were eight dead and 13 wounded. See Janzyk, p.55.

5   Also known as the Danzig Corridor, territory given to Poland to provide access to the Baltic but dividing Germany from East Prussia.

6   Atrocities were not confined to the Polish Corridor, but also Lodz and East Prussia after the outbreak of the Second World War.

Some of the *Springer* (parachutists) from *FSK7* at Werl prior to the airdrop in Holland on 10 May 1940.
(Sabine Reuter)

out of the plane like it was a streetcar instead of diving horizontally towards the left wing; which prevents the jumper from falling backwards as he did into his canopy as it was opening, as I of course observed firsthand.

I also remember Wittstock for its tough off-duty macho drinking sprees according to the traditional drinking song "*Wenn die wilden Fallschirmjäger saufen wieder durch die Nacht, saufen nur noch halbe liter bis der helle Tag erwacht.*" (When the wild Paratroopers drink once again throughout the night, drink just one more half litre before the break of day).

At the end of April 1940 we ended up in Werl/Westfahlen for some more merciless field training, so tough in fact, that some men were occasionally taken away by ambulance to recuperate in the hospital.[7] That also included us medics.

After a full hard day we had to carry on with our academic work, whilst the regulars went out with their *frauleins* to relax in each other's loving arms, practicing their own kind of limited female anatomy, hands on!

When finally one day the order came "all men stay in their quarters" (*Ausgangsverbot*), we knew that in the next few days we would be mobilised. It was a relief from the tension over the past few weeks and months. We were ready to jump into hell if necessary, and this was exactly what would happen.

The airborne invasion of Holland

10 May 1940 … "*Rot scheint die Sonne, fertig gemacht, wer weiß ob sie morgen für uns auch noch lacht…*" (Red shines the sun, get ready, who knows whether it will smile for us tomorrow…)

---

7   The jumpers were moved to Werl and the non-jumpers to Harsewinkel. (Willi Koch)

This sounded out of place, as it was still pitch black when we began singing whilst marching toward our waiting JU-52 aircraft (*Alte Tante*, as we affectionately called her) on that eventful morning of 10 May. It was, however, true for some of us, who sadly did not see the sun rising on the following day.

Our traditional spirited songs did not sound as strong as they usually did on our training days, partly because we were still half asleep at 0330 hours and walking in full combat gear. I can give you an idea what it felt like to be dressed like a *Fallschirmjäger*.

Over our regular uniform we wore the traditional *Knoschensack* (a bonebag), a green combination, zipped in the middle of the front and without leggings (with baggy pockets in the front). We wore special green woollen *springerhosen* (pants), with a side pocket on the right leg for your *Kappmesser* (gravity knife), which was used to cut yourself free from the parachute if necessary. Our boots were also special, high rubber-soled leather boots, laced on the side. The pants were especially baggy knickerbocker type, permitting us to carry a *Zeltplane* (tent canvas) underneath. This was carried on one side and a blanket on the other, which was wrapped around our legs. A gasmask bag hung around our neck in front on the chest, while a *Brotbeutel* (bread bag) dangled behind us on the right side. We carried a modern Walther model 38 pistol holstered on our belt and wore long-sleeved leather gloves. To top it off, our helmet was a specially designed steel helmet, cut short on the rim with double chinstraps, soon to be the most recognisable part of the *Fallschirmjäger* uniform.

Our heavier weapons and specialised equipment for our field hospital were packed into *Waffenbehälter* that were dropped from the underbelly of the aircraft.[8]

FJR5 veteran Wilfried Diehl wearing the Model 1938 helmet, the most identifiable piece of *Fallschirmjäger* equipment (Wilfried Diehl)

Fallschirm-Sanitäter Walter Bühler unloads drop containers in order to prepare them for the forthcoming operation in Holland. (Sabine Reuter)

---

8   Containers were loaded from the ground into four bomb shafts in the underbelly of the JU-52 and secured into internal frames with a release mechanism. To further ensure that the containers were not damaged upon impact, they were fitted with a corrugated shock absorber. Additional containers could be deployed from the side door of the aircraft.

Knowing how we looked on that morning gives a better impression about the pace at which we moved over the airfield to the aircraft. Despite all this, our spirits were high. Soon we were airborne, not knowing what to expect. We had not yet been informed of our impending mission, except to stay as close together as possible after landing and await further orders from our superior officers.

All we knew was that we were to be in the second wave that started half an hour later; our main mission was to establish a *Hauptverbandplatz* (aid station) and later a field hospital. Our medic unit was at that time less than half a *Kompanie* and the majority of our unit were non-jumpers. The *Krankenträger* were going to be landed somewhere at Waalhaven, independent of us.

Inside the plane the mood was sombre. As I looked around at the faces of the men I knew so well, they all appeared to stare straight ahead, lost in their inner thoughts and almost entranced by the noise of the aircraft's three BMW radial engines, which drowned all attempts to engage in conversation.

After a flight of almost one-and-a-half hours we could see the day dawning from the east. The endless tension of waiting began to ebb when we noticed a gradual altitude change. This could only mean that we were approaching our destination. Very soon life slowly returned to the men as they came alive, tugging nervously on their straps just to be sure that everything was ready, giving each other reassuring 'thumbs up' signals and smiles.

Looking down we could already see some landscape; the silver snake lines of a river with a few lights already on in some houses. As the minutes passed we could see everything clearly below us in the early dawn hours. It was a relief when we were finally ordered to get ready to jump. We calmly stood up and hooked the parachutes' static line onto a centre wire above our heads. We moved forwards in line towards the open door. Suddenly all hell broke loose as a hail of bullets struck our JU-52's corrugated metal body.

We could hear the faint cries from the wounded as we all tried to exit the aircraft at the same time, but we were to wait for the signal horn. On top of the existing confusion I heard that one of our pilots had been hit. This was supposed to be a surprise attack, yet here we were, flying dangerously close to the ground and having already suffered casualties.

When we finally heard the jump signal horn we were so low that it looked to us as though we could jump without a parachute. We later heard that it could have been as low as 60–70m.

Everything went so fast on the descent; the parachute had barely enough time to open. A quick glance to my right and I saw my *Zugführer*, *Feldwebel* Georg Ahfeld, being hit by ground fire, slumping forwards, then hanging lifeless in his harness. I then hit the ground, a fine ploughed field ready for planting. As I tried to free myself from the harness, bullets came dangerously close to me, so I could do nothing but lie still and play dead. It did not take much movement to feel for my knife, but it was not there. I had lost it. Now I could not cut myself free, even if I wanted to. If I could not move because of the bullets, how could I kneel or stand to free myself? My canopy was billowing behind me in the breeze, which I later realised probably saved my life.

Time after time the enemy bullets came too close, but as if a merciful angel was watching over me, another breeze would blow up the canopy between me and the projectiles, obscuring me from view. It was not my time yet.

So here I was, pinned down, eating the dirt and trying to dig my head a few more inches deeper into the ground, whenever the flying bullets allowed me to do so. It was not exactly what a *Fallschirmjäger* was trained to do. But what else could I do: risk my life by foolishly trying to get up? That accomplished nothing, so I stayed put to see what would happen. Nothing happened, except as the day went by it became hotter and hotter, and I was not exactly dressed to sunbathe. I thought to myself that one thing worse than being shot was suffering from sunstroke. Since my brain was not yet dried out and was still functioning, I thought of all possibilities and how I could get out of my situation. I began to get the thoughts of a man who is about to die. Why? Is this all there is to life? What about my family? Was everybody correct when they heard I had become a *Fallschirmjäger*? "*Das ist ja ein Todeskommando!*", they would assure my family, "*den sehen Sie nicht mehr wieder!*" (It's a death squad! You won't see him again!).

My guardian angel must have looked over me that day, because I was still alive in the late afternoon. As the darkness began to hide me, the gunfire became more intermittent. During the confusion of the attack on the aircraft, we were mistakenly dropped close to some machine-gun bunkers which had been shooting at me all day. I finally freed myself from the harness and began moving at a snail's pace on my belly toward the sound of our own machine guns, which I had noticed during the day. I was lucky not to be hit by friendly fire since I came from the enemy's direction, but I used our password as soon as I came within calling distance. I was finally home.

That home was a chest-deep irrigation ditch into which I half fell and was half pulled by the happy helping hands of my comrades. I did not notice the burning, tingling pain in my face from the nettles that grew all around.

I was also lucky that I had just joined a group from our own unit that had congregated from all directions. There was an officer, to whom I reported the incident involving *Feldwebel* Ahfeld. The officer assured me that there was nothing we could do right now.

I must have slept for hours, in water up to my neck. As I awoke I felt guilty, but was assured that everything had calmed down and that I had missed nothing. I could only hear the occasional single shot or the short burst of machine-gun fire now and again, which went on during the rest of the night.

As soon as daybreak approached on 11 May, the gunfire began the moment we showed our heads above the trench. Our first concern was the wounded, lying out there in the field. They may have survived the night, but under the new hail of bullets it was suicide for them to crawl to us and for us to go out for them.

One thing was for sure: we had to crack these bunkers as soon as possible to stop the machine-gun fire, but that would take more precious time and the lives of more men.

The men were asked to volunteer and retrieve the wounded. There was some hesitation from those who had not already been chosen for 'bunker busting'.

I still had *Feldwebel* Ahfeld on my mind, so I immediately volunteered to go out after him.

I did not have much time to think about it, so after looking in the direction I had come from the previous night, I saw his parachute canopy still billowing about 100m distant. This usually

One of the Dutch MG bunkers encountered by Kurt Schulz and his comrades. (Kurt Schulz)

indicated that the occupant in the harness was already dead, as those who could get away usually threw some dirt on the canopy or buried them.

I was right, it was him. How I got to him was a miracle in itself: running, falling, up and down, rolling sideways, just like training, only this time under a hail of bullets!

Feldwebel Ahfeld was unconscious, lying partly in his blood-stained canopy. It looked as though life was slowly draining out of him. His normal healthy looking face was now white, wax-like as in death, but he was still alive. After checking him I turned him over from the side he was lying on and saw the blood still oozing and pulsating from a wound in his right thigh, despite a tourniquet he had himself applied earlier before losing consciousness. This had saved him so far, but would he make it for much longer?

After reapplying the tourniquet and rolling him into his parachute canopy, I dragged him metre by metre until a pair of helping hands pulled us into the irrigation ditch (my friend and fellow medic Willi Koch, as I later found out).

It was a miracle that his life had been spared. I found out later that Ahfeld (accompanied by Koch) had been taken by *Oberjäger* Kursawe and

Sanitäts-Oberjäger Willi Koch after operations in Holland in 1940. He wears the *EK2* ribbon and paratrooper badge. Koch served with 5/ *FJR1 (Pi-Kp)* until the summer of 1939 when he transferred to *San.Zug.7*. (Stephan Janzyk)

Eugen Eichhoff to a farmhouse close by and then for proper medical care to a *Hauptverbandplatz* that finally saved his life.

I figured out later that I must have had some help from the men who were cracking the *MG* bunkers, as they drew away many of the bullets during my rescue mission.

Completely exhausted, I fell into a semi-conscious sleep.

I met Georg Ahfeld with his beautiful wife a few years later. He was at this time a commissioned medical officer. We were obviously happy to see each other again, and they both thanked me for saving his life. Looking at their happy thankful faces was enough reward for me. This action was partly why I was awarded the Iron Cross second class personally by Hermann Göring. A photograph of this ceremony was later featured in the major wartime newspaper *Das Reich.*

The situation gradually improved during those early days in Holland. We could finally spend the night under a roof, normally a barn, which at that time was comparable to a heavenly hotel room in peacetime.

After burying our dead we obtained some food (mainly Dutch cheese) for our empty stomachs in the village of Dubbeldam east of Dordrecht.

We soon found ourselves in battle at the northern bridgehead of the Moerdijk bridge, where we confronted Dutch and British troops.[9] We were to prevent them from crossing or destroying

---

9   The Moerdijk bridge spanned Holland's Diep River south of Dordrecht. During the invasion in 1940, the road and rail bridges remained intact, but were destroyed by the Germans in 1944 to slow the Allied advance.

Photograph from the *Das Reich* newspaper after being awarded the *EK2* in Holland. From left to right: Heinz Adolphs, Walter Bühler, Kurt Schulz and an unnamed *Sanitäter*. (Kurt Schulz)

Three fallen *Sanitäter* comrades are buried close to where they fell in Holland. From left to right: *Obergefreiter* Adolf Termath, aged 26; *Obergefreiter* Richard Obst, aged 20; and *Obergefreiter* Jakob Brechenser, aged 22. All three are now buried at the military cemetery in Ysselsteyn. (Kurt Schulz)

Kurt (right) and four comrades in Dubbeldam during a pause in the fighting (Kurt Schulz)

Two men from *FSK7* firing a 7.92mm *Panzerbüchse 38* (*PzB38*) anti-tank rifle. (Sabine Reuter)

the bridge. We were no longer acting as medic units, nor did we have the protection of the International Red Cross, since we now carried weapons in combat. This was necessary due to the fact that we were facing strong, determined forces, which outnumbered us many times. The exchange of fire was fierce and continued for hours. Most of us were unaware until now that the British had already landed and established a bridgehead, like in Norway. (We were told that this justified us being here, Holland was no longer neutral.)

Our small-calibre weapons were supported by several 2cm shoulder-fired anti-tank rifles, but especially effective was a captured howitzer, which we fired so fast it became as red as a hot iron stove. Some of the prisoners we took believed we had a light artillery battery supporting us. After a couple of days of hard fighting the enemy pressure became dangerously close to breaking us. We were saved by the arrival of our JU-87 *Stuka* dive-bombers, which came down out of the sky with their sirens screaming, dropping their bombs on the advancing enemy troops. Other aircraft from *Luftflotte 2* (Air Fleet 2) defeated most attempts by enemy forces to endanger us from the air. We watched with interest the many dogfights that ended in success for our aircraft. It was similar to cheering a football match. I remember one action quite vividly. A Spitfire chased a *Stuka*, which suddenly dived and came up behind the Spitfire. To our complete surprise it shot down the British aircraft.

With all of the wounded around us, we medics now put away our weapons and began to get the *Hauptverbandplatz* into action, which was our main objective in the first place.

We had been told to prepare to hold out for at least one to two weeks until tanks of the *9th Panzer Division* could reach us, but luckily our tanks showed up just as Dutch forces attempted to recapture the Moerdijk bridge. We were overcome with feelings of joy and relief as we embraced our rescuers late on the afternoon of 12 May. We would ask them jokingly "*Wo wart ihr denn so lange?*" (what took you so long?), as if they had arrived late.

The enemy forces had been broken up and we were left to clean up the

The greater part of the fighting in Holland is over and men of *FSK7* take a break at the Berkhof farm near Dordrecht, which was used as a field hospital for *FJR1*. (Sabine Reuter)

small pockets of resistance on our way to Dordrecht and later to Rotterdam, where we arrived on 14 May. The Dutch royal family and the government had been lucky and had managed to avoid capture after being evacuated by two British warships.

We arrived in Rotterdam just after the needless bombardment and destruction of the inner city by the *Luftwaffe*. This was due to lack of proper communication and misunderstandings during the surrender negotiations. We heard that our *Divisionskommandeur, Generalleutnant* Student, had been shot and killed by a Dutch sniper, but we later learned that this was incorrect and a Dutch surgeon had actually saved his life.[10]

It was sad for me to see Rotterdam again, this time in ruins, as I had really loved it there when I visited a few years before during a short summer venture trip. I was a cabin boy on a sailing ship, hoping to one day become a sea captain. At that time of my life it was my ultimate dream to be on the sea, with ships, and everything that goes with it. Throughout the war, despite the challenges of being a *Fallschirmjäger*, I longed to be transferred back to the Navy, my first love. I wanted to be a simple medical corpsman on a U-boat, but my requests were always rejected without comment.

Unfortunately, Rotterdam's fate was shared by hundreds of towns and cities in Germany by the end of the Second World War.

Although our small medic unit (*FSK7*) had suffered about 35% casualties, the overall number of dead from *Fliegerdivision.7* was considered to be quite low, in spite of the fact that the Dutch were allegedly alerted to our attack by an inside source in Berlin.

For us the sun was indeed shining bright again, after all we were heroes for Germany. Hermann Göring had arrived in Rotterdam for an inspection of his men and to see the results of his beloved *Luftwaffe*. He rewarded us with Iron Crosses before having us sent to Scheveningen for a few days' relaxation. Afterward we moved to some old First World War barracks in Münsterlager. This was contrary to Göring and the *Führer*'s orders. These new barracks looked as if soldiers from the time of Frederick the Great had just moved out. We were not there long. After complaining about the conditions, we were moved to Brandenburg/Havel into a new *Flak-Kaserne* (barracks), built like modern apartment buildings.[11] But we first had to take part in an '*Empfangsparade*' (victory parade), hosted by the town to honour their new war heroes.

We dressed in our typical *Fallschirmjäger* gear and marched past an honour guard and a military band. The march past was taken by the commanding *General*, the *Burgermeister* and many honourable guests. We marched over a carpet of flowers thrown by a jubilant crowd of townspeople who lined the street. They definitely made us welcome. Girls everywhere threw cigarette packets with their addresses written on, and soon we resembled walking flower bouquets and cigarette vendors.

There was not enough time, however, to follow up all those proposing invitations from the girls. Most of us were soon on a train, heading home for two weeks' '*Einsatz urlaub*' (mission leave), which for me meant a long overnight trip to Königsberg in East Prussia.

It is hard to describe what it was like in the early days of the war to return home to the victory-drunk public, especially for a decorated *Fallschirmjäger*. At the time it appeared that out of a population of 380,000 people, I was the only *Fallschirmjäger* in Königsberg. I knew of two more in the province; one of them was my *Feldwebel*, Franz Novack, a rough and tough man who usually treated me easier than most. Having had my face in the weekly newspaper *Das Reich* a few days before, I was now in all of the local papers. I was commended by the *Burgermeister* and was even

---

10   *General* Kurt Student hung precariously between life and death for many days, and in the following weeks lay in bed half paralysed, unable to speak or recognise anyone. It was a long, arduous path to recovery. See Kiriakopoulos, p.33.

11   The barracks at Brandenburg had previously been previously occupied by *Flak Regiment 22*.

sent an autographed book by *Gauleiter* Erich Koch, the local political governor.[12] Even the people in the street wanted to shake my hand. Wherever I went, whether it was a restaurant, bar, streetcar, bus or movie house, I never stood in a line or paid for anything. The only ones who did not benefit from all this attention were my parents. Unfortunately, I did not see them much, something I regretted later, when after the war I became the only survivor of our family of five. My two older brothers had been killed on the Eastern Front.[13] The last time we were all together was Christmas Eve in 1943, my mother's birthday. I had to leave that same evening to return to Norway, where I was stationed in Nesna below the Arctic Circle.

The euphoria of being a war hero ended abruptly when I returned to Brandenburg. The town had been a garrison town for many years, and we newcomers were looked at as intruders by the old-time soldiers who rightly defended their territory (meaning girls). After many fights, which put many men from both sides into the sickbay or hospital, we eventually came out victorious. This was to be expected from a *Fallschirmjäger*. At around this time we were renamed *Fallschirm-Sanitäts-Abteilung 7*, which consisted of a *Stab*, three *Fallschirm Kompanien* and a *Luftlande Kompanie*.

We were soon moved to the training ground at Sennelager, which put an end to all the useless confrontation. This move was even harder for us medics, with our additional training. In between our normal training we had to train as drivers in all kinds of motor vehicles. During the winter I also attended ski-school, which was more like a vacation.

In the meantime we heard about preparations for an invasion of England, which luckily never came about. We hoped that England would make peace with Hitler, but the famous 'Rudolf Hess' incident put an end to all that.[14] Training and jumping continued, and I injured my right knee whilst landing on frozen ground and ended up having surgery in a Potsdam hospital. Whilst I was still recuperating and enjoying the friendship of a nice young Japanese lady doctor, my *1.Kompanie* under the command of *Stabsarzt* Dr Robert Mallison flew from Burg/Magdeburg over Vienna to Plovdiv in Bulgaria in April 1941. They were to take part in operations on the Isthmus of Corinth on 26 April with *FJR2*, and afterward the airborne invasion of Crete.

On 20 May 1941, my *1.Kompanie* of *Fallsch-Sani-Abt.7* jumped with group centre near the prison at Aya-Chania, without me of course.[15] My buddy Walter and I were separated for the first time, something our commander Dr Mallison could never achieve. Mallison held back my promotion, as he could not stand Walter's free spirit. This eventually landed Walter in a *Strafkompanie*, where he was finally captured by Canadian troops after the battle of Monte Cassino.[16] The old spirit of *Sani Kompanie 7* was never the same after the return from Crete. They suffered high losses during that operation and we received many new replacements after their return to Brandenburg. The typical *Fallschirmjäger* training routine soon returned, and my lazy days as a convalescing switchboard operator were now over.

---

12   Koch was a *Gauleiter* in East Prussia from 1928 until the end of the war. He fled Königsberg as the Russians approached the city in 1945 and escaped to Germany via the Baltic. He was captured by British forces in May 1949, and subsequently handed over to Poland and placed on trial for war crimes. A death sentence in 1959 was commuted due to ill-health, and he served life in prison. He died in 1986 aged 90 (warhistoryonline).

13   Wilhelm (Willi) Schulz, the eldest brother and an *Oberfeldwebel*, is listed as MIA in Leningrad. Artur Schulz, the middle brother, was KIA during the retreat from Moscow. He was shot through the heart.

14   Rudolf Hess was the Deputy Führer from 1933–41. In May 1941 he flew to Scotland to negotiate peace talks without permission from Hitler. He went on to serve life a life sentence for his part in the Nazi regime, and died in Spandau prison in 1987.

15   In October 1940, *Fallschirm-Sanitäts-Abteilung* of *Fliegerdivision 7* became a *Korps* unit and was renamed *Fallschirm Sanitäts Abteilung XI Fliegerkorps*. See Koch & Neumann.

16   A *Strafkompanie* was a formation made up of men with criminal convictions.

Kurt Schulz (in black shirt) relaxing
in the sun at ski school at Mittenwald
in Bavaria, 1940. (Kurt Schulz)

April 1941. A group from
1/Fallschirm-Sanitäts-Abteilung at the
airfield in Plovdiv, Bulgaria, prior to
Operation Hannibal at Corinth. Kurt
remained in Germany due to a jump
injury. (Sabine Reuter)

May 1941. Men from *1/Fallschirm-
Sanitäts-Abteilung* in Greece prior to the
invasion of Crete. One of the men may
be holding an honour roll of comrades
killed during the Corinth operation.
(Sabine Reuter)

To the Russian Front

News soon went around that we were to be sent to Africa. By October 1941 we had been outfitted with khaki uniforms and given tropical equipment.[17] We were very shocked and disappointed when we suddenly had to exchange all our gear for winter uniforms. This meant only one thing … Russia!

For several weeks before we took off in December 1941, we were more often drunk than sober. This attitude reflected our disappointment at being sent to Russia. I already had two brothers on the Eastern Front, and everything I had heard about it was terrible. As a member of a special medical unit, we flew over Vitebsk to Smolensk, and from there we were attached to the famous *Sturmregiment Koch*. We landed on an airfield in 5ft of snow behind the Russian lines. We were supposed to take this airfield and hold it, then establish a field hospital for when our troops broke through. This never happened of course. The name of this place was unbeknownst to us; we only knew that it was not far from Moscow. We had gotten further than any other German in the central sector of the front.[18]

We were cautioned to stay behind with our field hospital equipment, which was embedded in the deep snow. The JU-52 had to get away quickly to remain safe, but it struggled to get airborne in the deep loose snow.

By late afternoon we finally made it to some of the main buildings and hangars, which had been shot to pieces by constant Russian artillery barrages. Our officers informed us that the enemy fire seemed to increase, indicating that they were possibly being reinforced. We were to once again take up the combat role.

I soon became the victim of what was to be known as action 'deepfreeze', where 'General Winter' triumphed and brought the German advance to a halt, like Napoleon's army before us. Even today I get chills when I think about it. Only the men who were there will know what it was like to sit outside all day and night in a snow hole under an open starry sky in temperatures at almost minus 50 degrees.

We sat behind machine guns or rifles fighting a relentless enemy, whose attacks were most intensive in the early morning before dawn. This was the time when we could only see their dark shadows in the snow ahead of us. We could hear the *Kommissars* driving the soldiers forward, only to be shot down by our guns. Later on we saw them, one layer of dead lying upon another, covered occasionally by snow. The smell of vodka could be found on most of them; maybe dying had been much easier for them.

I still cannot remember how many days or weeks I spent on the Russian Front. One night it was my turn to crawl into a small cellar-like hole underground where our wounded and frostbite casualties were taken care of. Here they were out of the biting wind. For several days I had no feeling from my toes. Once I took off my jump boots, I realised why. All of my toes were black. I was immediately relieved at my post and placed on the casualty list to be flown out at the next opportunity. No one knew when this would be, as the Russians were trying their best to disrupt the airlifts.

---

17 *1.Kompanie* was equipped for Africa but did not travel there until the end of September 1942 when it was in Bonjarc, France, having returned from Russia. The *Kompanie* was flown to Tunis in November 1942 and served with *FJR5* until May 1943. See Koch & Neumann.

18 Kurt's unit was attached to *I/LL.St.Rgt* under Major Walter Koch. The airfield in question is probably Anissowo-Gorodischtsche near Schaikowka. As for the proximity to Moscow, Kurt may have been referring to the town of Juchnow (Yukhnov), some 209km south-west of Moscow. A recon unit from *Panzergruppe 4* allegedly reached the town of Khimki, 20km north-west of Moscow, on 2 December 1941 and was therefore the closest German formation to the Soviet capital.

Medical evacuation

I finally earned my first night's warm sleep in that dirt hole, and by the next afternoon I had been loaded aboard an aircraft. It was almost dark and the Russians' observation had been hampered. Only six of us had been put on the aircraft, mainly frostbite victims. The plane could not take any more men, as it still had to attempt a take-off in the snow. There were a few anxious moments when we were trying to get airborne. We were unsure whether we would make it or not, or whether we would be shot down as we flew low over the Russian positions. Soon most of us were asleep amongst the many supply boxes and containers until we landed hours later at Vitebsk.

We expected everything to go smoothly after reaching Vitebsk. We imagined a warm hospital train to take us home. We had no idea whatsoever what lay ahead of us. The train was already full of men. We were loaded onto an extra freight wagon, which was fitted with an iron potbelly stove and hardly any straw to lie on. As the days passed, the train had to stop more frequently to drop off the ever-increasing number of frozen corpses. It took us 10 long days to reach the German–East Prussian border under the worst conditions imaginable with only half the men we started out with in Vitebsk. Only the toughest survived that journey.

The survivors were a sad looking bunch as we went through the delousing routine. There was not much left of the once-proud and tough German paratrooper, just leftovers in filthy rags of what had once been a uniform. Our feet were covered in rags as we limped to the showers. The most badly wounded had been carried on stretchers to be cared for at the border medical facilities, to be sent later to the proper hospitals in the Reich.

I complained when we, the '*Gefrierfleisch*' (frozen meat), were to be sent to a military hospital in Salzburg, Austria. I was currently so close to my hometown, it did not make sense. Nobody except one elderly *Reichsbahn* official, who was also from East Prussia, would listen to my protests. He took pity on me and had someone change the name of my destination to a hospital in Königsberg. He took me aside and told me that I would ride in style. A train loaded with men of the Spanish *Blaue* Division were ready to leave for Königsberg.[19] He took me to the train, but this time it was second-class and upholstered. It was not long before officers of the *Blaue* Division joined me on my journey home.

I finally arrived at the *Luftwaffe* hospital in Maraunenhof / Königsberg. I thought I was in heaven when I awoke the next morning in a crisp, clean white bed, which was bathed in bright sunlight. A young blonde nurse stood beside my bed with a thermometer in her hand. I was still alive!

My recovery from frostbite was a miracle. Due to my stubbornness, I refused to go through with the radical surgery of having my toes amputated to avoid gangrene. I do not know why, but I chose the all-or-nothing approach. What would I do without toes? The doctors listened intently at my suggestion to smear them thickly with Ichtyol-salve (fish salve) and dress them in thick cotton. I assured them that I would take full responsibility.

What is important to note is that this old house remedy actually worked, and after a couple of months my toes were back to normal, as they still are today [in 2003].

It also goes without saying that my parents enjoyed having me close by at this time and they regularly visited me for the first month in hospital. I recuperated at home after my time in hospital for another month.

---

19   A Spanish infantry division that served in the German Army on the Russian Front.

In a quiet backwater

What followed until D-Day in June 1944 is not really important to describe in detail. I was used like many other of our '*Alte Adler*' (old eagles) and loaned out to train new units in different training areas all over Germany, and also France and Norway. As I mentioned earlier, I spent some time in Norway with *14.Luftwaffen-Feld-Division*, where I relieved a Navy doctor and took over a dispensary which took care of several thousand German soldiers and the local Norwegian civilians. It was here that I finally received my commission, being promoted in 1944 from *Sani-Feldwebel* to *Sanitäts-Oberleutnant*, retroactive from 1941. The back pay would have been very nice if the Allied invasion had not come along.

Whilst in Nesna, Norway, I built up some very good relationships with the local people. I used to treat the locals as well the soldiers. They trusted me so much that they would even tell me when the British had landed some men at night from their submarines. I told them it was not my job to guard the coast, only to take care of their health, which I did like any other country doctor. The next doctor was half a day away by boat. I was treated as one of them. "You are no *Tysk*," they used to say. "You are *Norske*!"[20]

Two friends in Nesna, Norway. Both men are recipients of the *EK2* and *EK1*. These men may have been transferred to Norway after recuperating from wounds sustained on the Eastern Front in order to train members of *14. LW Feld Division* mentioned by Kurt. The man on the left appears to be an NCO candidate and the man on the right a *Fahnenjunker-Feldwebel* officer candidate, as denoted by the double braid loops and single pip on the shoulder boards. Neither men are wearing collar tabs. (Kurt Schulz)

Normandy 1944

I have already mentioned that I belonged to select group of medics who received additional medical training in order to be used as doctor's assistants in the field hospitals. In my case I specialised in surgery. Later, after the Allied invasion in Normandy, I found myself carrying out the work of a doctor, standing for many hours in an operating theatre tent with no end in sight, patching up friend and foe alike as they were brought in from the Normandy battlefields, all the while being kept awake with Pervitin pills.[21]

I later experienced something that was to change my entire professional life as a medical doctor. One day, we had just placed two supposed helpless and considered dead soldiers out into the 'dead' area, when I saw something that made me realise that there is much more to be learned than from the standard medical books.

---

20   *Tysk* is a native of Germany and *Norske* is a native of Norway.
21   A Methamphetamine stimulant, which came to be known as *Stuka* tablets and were later withdrawn due to their side effects.

Two of our best surgeons (and we had the best) were sticking needles into the lifeless bodies, reminiscent of voodoo. In both cases life gradually returned. That day I saw miracles being performed. This experience made a lasting impression and eventually made me the enemy of the American medical establishment.

Anyway, it was from the small group of special *Sanis* that a military medical pool was formed from which they would replace their much-needed doctors.

After the initial few days of hard fighting and the loss of so many young lives on both sides, the German soldier finally had to make the decision on who was the real enemy. There had never been any animosity against the soldiers whom they were fighting in Normandy, but the cruelties and atrocities committed by the Soviets as they moved through Eastern Prussia towards Berlin was a different matter. There was no other choice: give up here and try to stop 'Ivan'. The Germans in general had the idea, or at least hoped that if they ceased fighting in the west, the Allies would join them in stopping the Soviets from spreading communism throughout Europe.

We slowly moved our field hospital between endless columns of weaponless soldiers who carried just their *Kochgeschirr* (mess tins) and a few other personal belongings on their backs.

One day I sat in the passenger seat of an ambulance when suddenly we heard the tack-tack-tack of approaching low-flying P38 Lightning aircraft.[22] Fearing that we would be fired upon, we froze with terror, but nothing happened. There came a few moments of quiet, then we saw in front of us those weaponless columns of soldiers who had been mowed down like ripe grain in a field. There was nothing we could do as we were already overloaded with wounded. We could see no signs of life; the aircraft had done their job well, and were probably flown by new pilots looking for some action. So much for our liberators from America, the land of my dreams!

When I was a young boy of 9 in 1930, my family, with immigration papers in hand, prepared to board a ship to America but were halted by my father's offer of a good secure position within the city of Königsberg. I had always wanted to go to America; now I was ashamed and deeply saddened of what I had just witnessed in front of me. It was nothing but a cold-blooded massacre by the Americans.

Heinz Adolphs (left) with two comrades. The *Sanitäts-Oberjäger* on the right wears the Army paratrooper badge and the Iron Cross 1st Class. (Kurt Schulz)

---

22   Lockheed P-38 Lightning, known in German as *Der Gabelschwanzteufel* (fork-tailed devil).

Unfortunately there was not much time to think about it; we just had to keep going. Most of the troops headed towards Paris, but we headed south towards Rennes and from there to Le Mans.

Before we arrived, my commanding officer gave me the order to take one man and get back to Rennes to see if we could salvage any of the medical supplies that we had left behind there. The area was supposed to be quiet and free of the enemy. We were given a motorcycle so we could easily manoeuvre in case of enemy contact.

I took along an old reliable friend from the original *Sani Kompanie 7, Gefreiter* Heinz Adolphs, whom I had recently met again in Nancy, where I had joined this new ad-hoc unit before going into combat in Normandy. I had been en-route to Mourmelon to attend an officer's school, which was suddenly cancelled due to the Allied invasion. As I was not yet a doctor, they made me a *Sanitätsoffizier* (non-physician) as we had very few within the medical units.

Kurt outside a medical tent at a POW camp in Varennes near Paris in 1944. (Kurt Schulz)

We drove to Rennes as ordered (I drove the English Triumph motorcycle myself), mile after mile along an empty highway, when suddenly we heard the rattling clinking sound of tank tracks, muffled somewhat by the sandy ground of the pinewoods on both sides of the road.

"*Uh-oh!*" said Heinz, "*das kann nur der Ami sein!*" (that can only be the Americans). Our *Panzers* would normally drive in sight of the road or on it, conditions permitting of course. "What shall we do?" We both had our official Red Cross identification. I had my armband and Heinz had a flag on his back. We were not carrying any weapons. Should we turn around or should we risk becoming prisoners? Our orders were to go to Rennes, so we could not turn around. As a precaution against being captured and separated, I removed my temporary officer silver sleeves from my sergeant's shoulder straps.

Heinz Adolphs and Kurt Schulz as POWs, Christmas 1945. (Kurt Schulz)

We then carried on toward our destiny. We covered close to 80km when we drove through a village with wilted flowers on the pavement. We did not speak, just turned the bike around and took off. As we turned the last corner, we suddenly faced an American Sherman tank, its big gun barrel and *MGs* pointing at us. That was it, the beginning of two years as a PP (Protected Prisoner).

PRISONER OF WAR

Date of capture

Place (or sector) of capture

Unit making capture

Kurt's POW tag after being captured near Rennes in France on 10 August 1944. (Kurt Schulz)

Epilogue

After the war had ended, I found myself unable to return home. Königsberg had become Kaliningrad after 700 years of being the heart and birthplace of Prussia and the coronation city of their kings. When my parents came out on the last train, 15 million people had been driven from their homes and land in the Eastern Provinces. They lost everything, including my two brothers who were killed on the Eastern Front. When they left Königsberg, they were only allowed to take along a backpack. My own grandparents, who were in their 80s, were killed like so many old timers because they could not run fast enough when driven out of the city by the Russians.

In order to return to America after my release, I had to detour through Canada. America had rejected me for not having a sponsor. It was none other than Walt Disney who finally sponsored me and gave me a chance to go to Hollywood. When we finished the motion picture *Fantasia*, he helped me get a steady job as an assistant animator at Warner Brothers for six years. This enabled me to finish all of my graduate and postgraduate studies at different universities in Los Angeles.

In conclusion, I must add a personal note about my whole experience from that war. We all have or should have learned that people are the same all over, as I have seen again and again in every country. I have made many friends among our so-called enemies. Whilst I was a POW in the Saint-Lô area in August 1944, I was called to attend a British field hospital and treat the wounded from a truck that had rolled over on a road. I was treated with such friendliness, being offered cigarettes, chocolate, tea with milk and biscuits, and it was mentioned that I did not look like a German, so I must have been English. It must have been due to the lack of a square head, I suppose!

I always found it impossible to hate someone because I am told to. Political squabbles do not influence me at all. Take America's great friendship with Russia during the Second World War, and then it later becomes known as the evil empire by the US. Every generation has to go through their own destiny; they never learn.

(Kurt Schulz passed away on 8 May 2012, aged 90.)

2

Wolfram von Beck

Fighting in the East

Wolf von Beck was born in Karlsruhe on 25 July 1925 and volunteered for the Fallschirmtruppe *directly from school in 1943 at the age of 17, celebrating his 18th birthday at the close combat school in Le Vast, France. After serving briefly in Italy, he was sent to Russia as a* Kompanie-Melder *(messenger/runner) with 1/Bataillon Schirmer, where he witnessed the brutality of war. After recovering from wounds sustained in Russia, he volunteered to follow his former commander and joined FJR16 Ost, which later became* Panzer Grenadier Rgt.3 HG, *subordinated to* 2.Panzer-Grenadier-Division (Hermann Göring). *These formations saw service in Lithuania and Eastern Prussia in late 1944 and early 1945. In the final days of the war, Wolf came into British captivity in Schleswig Holstein as a member of the* Großdeutschland Division, *spending three months in a prison camp before his release. In the postwar years, Wolf was the leader of* Fallschirmjäger Kameradschaft 'Schirmer' *in Karlsruhe for 40 years. Wolf made friends with his former opponents, finally realising that we all want the same thing on this earth – peace and understanding. As a result, he cultivated friendships far beyond Germany's borders: in France, Greece, Canada, Italy and England. His daughter Annette described her father as a very cheerful person with a great sense of humour, a philanthropist and someone who showed a lot of empathy for his fellow human beings.*

Left: Wolf at the *Luftlandebrigade 25* Ball on 9 June 1989. (Annette von Beck) Right: Wolfram von Beck as a *Gefreiter* at the beginning of 1944. (Annette von Beck)

The volunteer

After volunteering for the *Luftwaffe*, I was finally called up for service in early 1943. Along with a comrade of mine, we were sent to Eindhoven in Holland for *Luftwaffe* basic training. Of course, we wanted to become fighter pilots like everyone else, but at the end of our training we were told by our *Kommandeur* that only 10 men would get to fly because fuel was in such short supply. So my friend Gert Kull and I volunteered to become paratroopers. The very next day we were sent by train to the garrison town of Gardelegen to begin paratrooper examinations. We were found suitable and sent immediately to the Wittstock jump school. In order to become a paratrooper we had to make six jumps. We were given the cloth version of the paratrooper badge after the completion of our jump training; the metal badge was given to us later.[1]

Wolfram von Beck (right) with his friend *Gefreiter* Erich Kasper at the Halberstadt training ground. Kasper was later killed in action. (Wolfram von Beck)

Fallschirmjäger preparing for a training jump at Wittstock in 1942. (Franz Wolf)

---

1   Wolfram von Beck was awarded the *Fallschirmschützenabzeichen* on 1 October 1943.

Recruitment into Battalion Schirmer

On completion of the jump course a *Hauptmann* and a *Feldwebel* came to pick 20 men as replacements to join *Bataillon* 'Schirmer'.[2]

Gert Kull and I were among those who were picked and found ourselves travelling to Orange in southern France, where the *Bataillon* was quartered in an old French Army barracks. Before reaching Orange, we were sent to Le Vast near Cherbourg for three weeks at the close combat school.

Major Gerhart Schirmer. His men showed amazing loyalty to him. Von Beck and Schirmer maintained a lifelong friendship. Wolf saved him from certain death by carrying a wounded Schirmer on his shoulders from a minefield under fire. Schirmer was awarded the *Ritterkreuz* on 14 June 1941 for his part in the Corinth operation. He was later awarded Oakleaves to his *KC* on 18 November 1944. When Schirmer surrendered to British troops in Hamburg on 5 May 1945, his *Ritterkreuz*, *DKiG* and wristwatch (from Walter Koch) were taken as war booty. He traced his *RK* to a museum in southern California and it was eventually returned to him. (Gerhart Schirmer)

Hauptmann Gerhart Schirmer in 1942. (Annette von Beck)

---

2   *Oberstleutnant* Koch set up a detachment led by First World War veteran *Oberfeldwebel* Berg, consisting of soldiers of *FJR5* who had escaped from Tunisia (some in adventurous ways), the wounded who had been evacuated or men on home leave. From this cadre of experienced *Fallschirmjäger* a *Bataillon* was set up in Halberstadt on 1.6.1943. It initially recieved no unit number and was thus called *Fallschirm-Bataillon Schirmer* after its commander, *Major* Gerhart Schirmer. See Schirmer, p.3.

To Italy

At the beginning of July 1943, we were finally transferred to Orange in southern France. Two days after Mussolini was deposed on 25 July, we took off in gliders, JU-52s and He-111s from Orange to the Practica de Mare airfield near Rome. Upon our arrival, we were greeted by enemy bombers and fighters. All hell broke loose. We suffered many casualties during this attack, but the war went on.

Our first task in Italy was to secure the borders of the Vatican, followed by coastal defence between Civitavecchia and Ostia, and from September 1943 we had to guard the important supply lines from Orvieto to Cassino. I found myself in the last railway pointer hut in Cassino.

We were also used to combat partisans in Rome. One day I had to watch over 10 men who were to be delivered to a jail in an ancient small fort. Apparently one of the men was an English spy. In one of the prison corridors the men's details were all registered by an official. As I stood there, I noticed that the observation flap in one of the nearby heavy wooden doors was open. I went over and looked into the cell. Standing near the flap was a *Luftwaffe Gefreiter* and five or six other soldiers. I asked the *Gefreiter* what he had done wrong and why he was imprisoned. He told me that a *Wehrmacht* patrol had caught him in Rome without a special leave pass for the city. Apparently he was going to be collected the following day. Then he went and sat in the corner of the cell and opened up to me, and told me he was going to be shot tomorrow because he raped a woman in the city. He could tell me nothing further because one of the officers came over and forbid me to speak with the prisoners.

Russia is hell

On 9 November 1943, *General* Kurt Student came to see us on a sports field near Rome and issued orders for us to move to Russia. The next day we boarded a freight train from Rome to Berdichev (Berdychiv) in the Ukraine.[3]

After a few days travelling in a goods train we arrived at Zhitomir (Zhytomyr) in Russia. We stopped in a wide-open space with nothing in sight except a German ambulance. As we moved closer, we saw that the Russians had killed all the wounded men who had been inside, including the driver and the medic.

The bodies were all beside the vehicle and had all been butchered. We immediately informed our commander and shortly after a signal came down from *Division*:

"No more prisoners are to be taken." Surely, not even animals could be so cruel.

On that same day I would not have taken any prisoners, but a few days later I took two.

It was one day after relieving *Gefreiter* Fritz at the *MG* position. It was night-time and I was digging out the bottom of the trench. Suddenly, I heard a noise in front of the position. I readied the *MG*. A voice came out of the dark in broken German, "Don't shoot!" At first I thought it was a trick. I called for them to come closer, one at a time. I also told them I would not shoot.

With my pistol in my hand, I clambered out of my ditch and approached the prisoner. First I checked for weapons, but he promised me that he had thrown them away.

I asked him how he spoke such good German.

---

3   *Bataillon Schirmer* was sent to Russia with elements of *FJD2*, which was now under the command of *Oberstleutnant* Hans Kroh. These forces were relocated by rail within 56 hours to Berdichev and participated in the recapture of Zhitomir (40km to the north), which had been taken by the Russians on 14 November. See Schirmer, p.3.

"Before the war I worked for Blohm *und* Voss in Hamburg," came the reply.[4] "I have many friends there and I hope to return some day."

I told the Russian to call his comrade forward and then I took them to my trench.

Later that day I delivered the prisoners to the *Bataillon HQ*. I told them everything would be Ok! I hoped he made it back to Hamburg.

Every night at the front I would accompany the *Kompaniechef, Leutnant* Bickel, to inspect our positions and check that no-one was asleep. One night, Ivan began to fire tracer at us and we were forced to take cover. I dived into a small ditch and found myself beside the body of a dead Russian *Kommissar*. He had been shot in the back of the head. I removed his map case and later delivered the contents (maps and notes) back to *HQ*. The *Kommissar* had some medals on his chest and also a large red badge, which sparkled in the night. It looked so nice that I took it, but then put it back on his chest. The dead should rest in peace.

Our unit received orders to relieve a *Waffen-SS* unit, which had almost been destroyed during the fighting.[5] I was the staff runner for *Leutnant* Bickel's *1.Kompanie*. He told me to go and obtain a situation report from the *Waffen-SS Kommandeur*. In order to reach the *SS* command post quickly, I decided not to use the road but to follow the sound of guns through a wooded area. When I finally reached the *Kommandeur*, he reprimanded me about the absence of my unit. He then showed me which part of the front line we were supposed to occupy.

In front of his command post sat a *Kubelwagen*. It was full of men just about ready to leave. I asked the driver if I too could jump on to his vehicle and hitch a ride. He replied that it would not be a problem, but asked if I could lift the *SS-Sturmmann* (Corporal) so he would not fall off the rear of the vehicle. I was under the impression that these men were wounded. They were not; they were all dead. The *Waffen-SS* never left their dead on the battlefield. Even their wounded men had to march.

I was glad to finally leave this hearse behind me, and after reporting back to *Leutnant* Bickel the *Kompanie* moved forward into the line. Our position was near a so-called runway, a clearing in the middle of a large forest. On the other side of the runway, Ivan was waiting.

After a day or so we made a dawn attack and drove the Russians from in front of our positions. Suddenly, we received well-aimed fire from a thicket of trees. I quickly noticed the source of fire: the Russians had removed the lowest branches from the trees, so they not only had a good field of fire but also a good view of any attacker.

A comrade and I turned their flank and finished them off from behind. My comrade, a machine gunner, was hit. While he was dying he passed me his wallet. All he could say was "Mama, Mama". I took the wallet and handed it in to *Bataillon HQ*. I do not know if it ever reached Mama.

We were rolling up the whole Russian trench line, but we stopped in front of a soil-covered bunker which had not been inspected yet. For good measure we threw in two grenades and after the detonation, three smiling, uninjured Russians came out.

We were surprised that anyone could survive such an attack, but we naturally took them prisoner.

Our unit continued our offensive toward the direction of Kirovgrad (Kropyvnytskti).[6] Before Novgorodka (38km SE of Kirovgrad) we found ourselves alone, without friendly units on our flanks. *Leutnant* Bickel ordered us to build a defensive perimeter on a nearby hilltop for the night. I was now a number two machine gunner and the number one was my good friend *Gefreiter* Fritz. We dug an emplacement for our machine gun at the front of the hill.

---

4   German shipbuilding and engineering company which built U-boats, battleships and flying boats.
5   *1.SS-Panzerdivision "Leibstandarte SS Adolf Hitler"*.
6   *FJD2* was airlifted from Zhitomir to Kirovgrad on 15.12.43 to counter a Russian breakthrough near Novgorodka.

The Russians suddenly fired several shells from an anti-tank gun.[7] We were joking that the Russians certainly needed some target practice, then after one detonation I found an arm and half of my comrade's chest in my lap. I lifted *Gefreiter* Fritz to see if I could help him, but he was already dead. I now dug faster and deeper in order to get my machine gun in place.

During this same night, *Obergefreiter* Zischka (who spoke fluent Russian) and I crept up on the enemy positions so he could overhear the Russians talking. We noted the position of the enemy *MG* nests and the next morning we attacked, driving the Russians out of Novgorodka.

I was made machine gunner one and found myself having to hump the *MG* during the assault. When *Leutnant* Bickel needed me again to be staff runner, I was only glad to give the 'Adolf-Hitler-saw' (nickname of the MG42) to someone else.

On 23 December 1943, whilst storming Kirovgrad, I was wounded by a round from a Russian anti-tank gun. I was sent to the field dressing station, and on 25 December I was sent to the *Reserve-Lazarett* at Meinigen. I was also awarded the Iron Cross 2nd Class and promoted to *Gefreiter*.

Halberstadt and the move to France

After my convalescence, I was granted six days of home leave and then posted back to Halberstadt, our home garrison. It wasn't long before a rumour had spread that *Oberstleutnant* Gerhart Schirmer was rebuilding his command at Halberstadt and we, his old hands, were going to join him.[8] I became an instructor in *1.Kompanie* under *Oberleutnant* Wilhelm Kuhlwilm.[9] We trained three classes, during which we made paratroopers out of young soldiers. Most of these men joined *FJD2* in Italy.[10] We kept the third class for ourselves. Our *Bataillon* was later formed into a *Regiment, FJR16 Ost*.[11]

I was transferred as a staff runner to the *I.Bataillon* under *Hauptmann* Hans Teusen. We were about to embark on a new mission and were subjected to a strict curfew. Nobody knew where and when the mission would be at that time.

In mid-May 1944, our *Bataillon* was sent by train to Abbeville in northern France.[12] We waited for two days at the train station whilst *Hauptmann* Teusen received his orders in Paris.

Wolf in May 1944, having been awarded the *Luftwaffe Erdkampfabzeichen*.
(Annette von Beck)

---

7   Known as a *Ratsch-Bumm* by German soldiers because the sound of the shot and the impact were almost one.
8   *Bataillon Schirmer* was dissolved in mid-December 1943 and set up again in Halberstadt with a permanent cadre of five *Kompanien*. See Schirmer, p.3.
9   Kuhlwilm was awarded the Knight's Cross on 30.11.44 as a *Kompaniefuhrer* in *Fallsch-Pz.Gren.Rgt.3*.
10   In Jan / Feb / March 1944, *Bataillon Schirmer* received 500 *Luftwaffe* soldiers for infantry training each month. After each four-week period these 1,500 men were sent as replacements to *I.Fallsch.Korps* in Italy. See Schirmer, p.1.
11   *FJR16 Ost* was officially established on 1.4.1944. Two thousand *Luftwaffe* soldiers were sent to Halberstadt via the training and replacement formations of the *Fallschirm-Armee*. See Schirmer, p.4.
12   The *Regiment* was sent to *FJD6* which was being established in northern France under the command of *Generalmajor* von Heyking. Their mission was to stand by to ward off the expected invasion. See Schirmer, p.6.

We were told not to leave the train as we could depart at any minute. I knew that the trains would not go anywhere until *Hauptmann* Teusen returned from Paris. We became very bored, so I and a comrade left the train for the nearby village. We were very thirsty and on the lookout for a friendly bar. We soon found a café, from which we could hear German voices. Upon entering the café, we saw our *Hauptfeldwebel*, *Oberfeuerwerker* and *Meldestaffelführer*. The red wine was pouring down their throats by the litre.

Technically, they were under the same rules as us and were not permitted to leave the train, so we realised that we were on safe ground. When they saw us they passed some bottles of red wine. The return journey to the train was long and difficult to negotiate, and I cannot remember anything about it whatsoever.

I woke up the next morning about 0600 hours on an open wagon next to our anti-aircraft gun. Others were also lying there, all under guard.

I saw our *Spieß*, *Hauptfeldwebel* Rüder, walk by and I asked him if I could be released. He ordered the guard to let me go and I followed him back to our wagon. On the way he told me what had happened the previous night and that I should keep quiet about his involvement in the matter.

He and our *Meldestaffelführer* had more or less carried me back to the train, and there we ran into *Oberfähnrich* Klämbt. He and some other men had been posted around the train to catch all those who had tried to sneak away from it. Apparently I had hit him and told him to take off. He had threatened to shoot me for assaulting a superior. Thanks to my two comrades I am still alive today. Actually, I do not remember this part of the evening; my comrades had to fill me in with the details.

In the afternoon, the whole *Bataillon* had to form up before *Hauptmann* Teusen's second in command. *Oberleutnant* Franz Veitenhansel punished several men for being absent with three days of house arrest, and I received five days for insubordination.

When Teusen returned from Paris in the evening, I was called in to explain the whole episode to him. *Hauptmann* Teusen ordered *Hauptfeldwebel* Rüder to cross out the punishment from the order book. I was due for promotion to *Oberjäger*, and with the punishment on my file I would have to wait at least another year for promotion.

Training for a special mission

Our *Bataillon* returned to the Wittstock jump school in early June 1944, where we carried out night jump training.[13] We made one warm-up jump, one jump at dawn and another during the night. During the second night jump an accident occurred when one plane flew lower than the dispatching aircraft. The first two or three jumpers crashed into the aircraft's wings. The other jumps were immediately cancelled.[14]

---

13   Shortly after arriving in Abbeville, Schirmer met *General* Student in Nancy and was given the order to immediately relocate the *Regiment* by rail in order to train in night jumps and close combat. *I/FJR16* with *13/14 Kompanie* were sent to Wittstock, *II/FJR16* to Stendal and *III/FJR16* to Salzwedel. See Schirmer, p.3.

14   On 2–3 June 1944, the *Regiment* took part in a night training assault near Wittstock in the presence of *General* Student. This was the only time in the history of the *Fallschirmtruppe* that a parachute *Regiment* jumped from over 200 JU-52 aircraft to perform a night-time combat exercise. See Schirmer, p.6.

We were later told that this training was in preparation for a raid on General Eisenhower's headquarters behind the lines in France. The plans were rumoured to have fallen into enemy hands so the operation was called off by Hitler himself.[15]

Move to the Baltic

At 2000 hours on 6 July 1944, the *Regiment* was ordered to move to Lithuania in the Baltic at first light on the following day. *I.Bataillon* travelled by train to Vilna in Lithuania, and *II.* and *III. Bataillon* were air-landed into Vilna airport. Shortly before we reached the city, I was relaxing in the bright sun on top of the ammo crates in the ammunition wagon. Suddenly I heard a bang from underneath me. I immediately thought we had come under fire, but soon realised that a wheel had run hot on the wagon as it rolled along. I quickly left my sunny spot because I could hear other bangs from elsewhere on the train. Nothing can shake a true paratrooper!

We went into position along the River Vilna to secure the crossing of our comrades who had managed to be withdrawn by *General* Reiner Stahel from the Vilna cauldron. *Hauptmann* Teusen and I greeted Stahel on the last intact bridge.

26 July 1944 near Kauen in Lithuania, and a birthday table has been prepared for *Hauptmann* Hans Teusen of *I/FJR16 Ost*. The cakes were made by a baker in the unit and Wolf carved the cork men on the bottles. The officer in the photo was killed the following day. (Wolfram von Beck)

---

15   *General* Student wanted to deploy the *Regiment* during the first night of the invasion in one of the enemy beachheads. Hitler rejected this plan. Hitler had trusted Rommel when he said the Allies may also land elsewhere in France. Hitler approved the mission on 10 June, but Göring and Rommel advised against it. They were concerned about Allied air superiority and the size of the ever-increasing beachheads. See Schirmer, p.7.

I soon received bad news. My good friend Gert Kull had been killed by a sniper's bullet during the withdrawal, but my comrade Dr Pohlschmitt killed the sniper in return. An eye for an eye! It was Pohlschmitt who told me about the death of Gert Kull two days after the incident. We now conducted a fighting retreat to the old First World War positions at Kauen. We only stayed here for two or three days because the Russians were using balloons to observe the area. Whenever we called in fighter planes, the Russians had long landed their balloons.

We also received some tanks to support our positions, but they could not do much to help. The Russians had many T-34s positioned on a nearby hilltop, and I mentioned to a *Panzer* commander that he should fire at them. He told me that he would not leave his cover behind a house because as soon as he fired one round they would have finished him off.

When we withdrew from Vilna to Kauen we were ordered to shoot all of the horses at the edge of the road, so the Russians could not use them.

I had mounted a *Panzer*, which was driving on the road. We passed a beautiful brown horse. I fired a burst from my *MPi* into its chest. The horse looked at me, then a jet of blood came from the wounds, the animal ran, began to tremble, fell on its knees and then collapsed to the ground. I will never forget this picture in my mind, and I would rather shoot myself than have to shoot another horse.

Russians on German soil

There are still many unusual things in my memory, which should not be forgotten.

In October 1944, we moved in the direction of Gumbinnen, fighting constantly and taking many casualties. Here we built up a defence line with the remnants of our *Regiment*, and were even given a *Flak* battery who had been sent from Hamburg for their first ground operation. Their accuracy was excellent. It was impossible to count the number of enemy tanks that they knocked out, but their own casualties were so high that they were destroyed within a short time.[16]

From Gumbinnen we withdrew to Nemmersdorf, which had just been retaken by another unit the day before on 22 October. *Hauptmann* Hans Teusen and I went into the village in a sidecar combination, and what I witnessed I will never be able to forget. A complete wagon train of civilians, which was about to leave the town, had been rolled over by Russian armour. Household goods and human remains had been pushed into the drainage ditches alongside the road. On the outskirts of the town there was a large farm, where we found a huge pile of dead bodies. They had been badly mutilated in a barn: old men, women and children.[17]

Oberjäger Heinz Halmes in Tunisia in 1942 whilst serving with *FJR5*. He went on to serve as a *Fähnrich* and *Zugführer* with *11/FJR16 Ost*. Like Wolf von Beck, Heinz Halmes was well decorated and he was awarded the *DKiG* on 19 October 1944 when the *Regiment* was in Gumbinnen. (Heinz Halmes)

16 This may have been one of the *Abteilung* from *Flak Regiment HG*.

17 Known as the Nemmersdorf massacre and allegedly committed by Russian soldiers on 21 October 1944. An international commission was set up to investigate the shootings. The actual number of deaths may have been embellished by German authorities as a propaganda tool.

Oberjäger Georg-Marcus Stiehl, a well-decorated comrade from *Fallschirm-Panzergrenadier Regiment 3 HG*. His baptism of fire came in Tunisia, where he became the youngest *Fallschirmjäger* to ever win the *EK2*. Later, as an *Obergfreiter*, he led a *Zug* in holding an advanced observation post against the advancing Soviets, covering the withdrawal of the remainder of the *Kompanie*. A single earthen embankment separated this group from the enemy's front line. A precarious situation in the opinion of the young *Zugführer*. Alone and without orders, he stormed over the embankment, firing from the hip. Immediately in front of him was a group of 20 Russians, but his battle cry and the salvos from his *MPi* were so effective that the Soviets fled in panic. His comrades followed, and heeding his example, they rolled up the entire section of the front line. The danger was eliminated and the *Kompanie* could disengage in safety. For this action he was awarded the *EK1*. In later life he became the *Kameradschaftsleiter* of the *Luftlande Sturmregiment*. (Georg-Marcus Stiehl)

When we left, *Hauptmann* Teusen said to me: "Boy, do not go into another house."

Hans Teusen is still alive (at the time of writing) and retired as a *General* of the *Bundeswehr*, and he can confirm my story.

On or about 24 October 1944, *FJR16 Ost* was redesignated as *Fallschirm Panzer Grenadier Regiment 3*, subordinated to *Fallschirm Panzer Grenadier Division 2 Hermann Göring*, despite protests from *Oberstleutnant* Schirmer.

It was soon rumoured that Schirmer was once again rebuilding *FJR16 Ost* in Halberstadt. There was no stopping the old Schirmer men![18] [There is no indication exactly when this occurred – probably between 8 November 1944 and 20 January 1945 – or for what reason Wolf was absent from the front.]

With *Feldwebel* Melzenbach, *Feldwebel* Ostermeier (our cook) and an *Oberjäger*, whose name I don't remember, we drove off in a truck in the direction of Halberstadt.

It was an adventurous trip through Berlin, where we stopped for one night. On the way we were stopped several times by the Chain Dogs and asked where we were going.[19] Melzenbach had had enough of the marching orders, which were issued again and again because you could only drive so far with the truck before having to get it loaded on to a train. This

---

18   Schirmer was arrested on 7.11.44, believing it was about his leadership of the *Regiment*. Roth, p.20, stated that Göring instructed the *Fallschirm-Panzerkorps HG* that *FJR16* was to recapture the Reichsjägerhof and hunting grounds on the Rominte Heath, but this absurd order was not carried out. Wolf Schirmer informed me that his father had written to the Von Stauffenberg family informing them that *Leutnant* Alfred Graf von Stauffenberg (a *Fallschirmjäger* officer and nephew to Claus von Stauffenberg, one the main 20 July conspirators) had been captured by the Americans in Tunisia on 13 April 1943. This letter later led to his arrest and he was questioned by the infamous judge, Roland Freisler. Schirmer was taken to Berlin and never saw his *Regiment* again, but was awarded the oak leaves to the Knight's Cross on 18 November 1944.

19   The *Kettenhunde*, or Chain Dogs, was a nickname given to the *Feldgendarmerie* (Military Police), who were recognisable by the metal crescent-shaped gorget worn around the neck.

Kreuzburg, East Prussia, 4 February 1945. Von Beck and *Oberleutnant* Herbert Hagemeyer are sat in the *Kompanie* horse-drawn coach, having arrived at the *Kompanie* command post where Wolf recieved the *EK1* and was promoted to *Fahnenjunker-Oberjäger*. Just after they entered the HQ in the basement of a house, the Russians shot up the horse and carriage with an AT gun. (Wolfram von Beck)

was no good for us; up to now we had rewritten the marching orders ourselves. Melzenbach managed to dupe the Chain Dogs on at least four occasions. He would immediately handover the requested paperwork when we were stopped, and at the same time ask for the nearest refreshment centre as we were hungry. He would politely address the policemen as his comrade, and since we all had some medals on our chest they were visibly impressed that we had referred to them as comrades. They gave us precise information about the next refreshment stop and seemed to forget about inspecting our paperwork. After two days we arrived in Benzingerode, near the Harz Mountains. This was the location where a collection point had been set up for Schirmer's people. Here we found a *Feldwebel* with a typewriter and he presented me with a special leave pass for eight days, so off I went to Karlsruhe. When I returned from leave the collection centre office was closed. The dream of being part of the reorganisation and rebuilding of my old *Regiment* had been burst, so I took the train back to *Panzer Grenadier Regiment 3*, which if I remember correctly was located in Tilsit in East Prussia (now Sovetsk, which fell to the Russians on 20 January 1945).

Oberleutnant Wilhelm Kuhlwilm (17.8.19–19.9.68) from *Panzergrenadier-Regiment.3 HG*, veteran of Crete, recipient of the *DKiG*, *Ritterkreuz* and two tank destruction badges. (Birger Kuhlwilm)

We continued to fight for the Fatherland in the newly formed *Kampfgruppe Kuhlwilm*, under the command of my old *Kompaniechef*. I went to *Oberleutnant* Herbert Hagemeyer as *Kompanietruppführer* and his deputy. He was a good officer but came to us from the flying personnel. Kuhli told me I would have to show him the ropes.

On 4 February I was awarded the Iron Cross 1st Class and promoted to *Fahnenjunker-Oberjäger*.

In the next few days of February 1945, during a large-scale Russian attack with tanks and Stalin organs (rocket launchers), our entire *Kampfgruppe* was wiped out.[20] This happened in the area between Heiligenbeil (Mamonovo) and Danzig (Gdańsk).[21] Our *Kompanie* of about 30 men were in an advanced position in a small shrubbery forest. We were surrounded. Russian tanks were behind us and Russian troops marched towards us in rows of six. To our right was a small meadow about 100m wide bordering a dense forest, so we decided to race across the meadow and form a new defensive position at the edge of the forest. Unbeknownst to us, the whole edge of the forest was already occupied by Ivan. Hagemeyer ran right in front of a Russian *MG* and was shot in the thigh and upper arm. He screamed at me: "Bubi, I am wounded." I had just taken my last men from their holes to occupy the edge of the forest when I ran over to Hagemeyer. He was about 10–20m right in front of the *MG* barrels. The whole edge of the forest was full of young Russian heads. Only the man behind the *MG* was about 30–40 years old. Hagemeyer and I looked at each other and I just shrugged my shoulders. I put my *MG* on the floor and picked up my *Kompanie* boss. He greeted me and shouted something derogatory to Stalin's disciples. Without further ado I put Hagemeyer over my shoulder and ran away in the opposite direction. I figured I would receive a helping of lead at any moment, but it did not happen. After a few hundred metres I saw one of our *Flak* positions that I did not know about. Out of the whole *Kompanie* I still had one man near me. That was my messenger, *Gefreiter* Mahlherbe. There were only a few wounded. The boss of the *Flak* battery said I should go with my men in front of their position. I said with whom, there were not many of us, and besides, I had to take my wounded boss to the field hospital.

These *Flak* soldiers had no idea that the Russians were practically lying in front of them. This was the sad end of our *Kampfgruppe*. *Oberleutnant* Kuhlwilm was in Germany at the time, and his deputy, *Leutnant* Heinz Beck, was lying in Danzig having been shot in the legs.

At the *TVP* (*Truppenverbandplatz* – field dressing station) was *Oberstarzt* Dr Neumann, my old regimental doctor who patched me up at Kirovgrad.[22] This was a stroke of luck because he presented us with maps of the *Heimat Lazaretten* (home hospitals). He said: "How you get there is up to you!" After Hagemeyer was properly treated we made our way to Pillau. Here we boarded a boat, which took us and several other wounded men to the harbour in Danzig.[23] We then boarded a large hospital ship bound for Stettin;[24] unfortunately I do not remember the name, but thankfully it was not the *Wilhelm Gustloff*![25] First I visited the lower deck, which was crowded with the wounded and already deceased, and I told Hagemeyer that I felt uncomfortable travelling on this corpse ship. I preferred to walk. In the meantime we had taken a *Panzer Hauptmann* into our club. He was totally burned, and only his eyes and mouth were visible through his bandages and dressings. When we disembarked the steamer in Stettin, I walked through the big packing halls which were crowded with the wounded. I was looking for any of our men and chanced upon *Leutnant* Heinz Berg. Both of his legs had been amputated above the knee. I gave him my farewell

---

20 Wolf's awards are testament to the heavy fighting during this period. He was awarded the *Panzerkampfabzeichen* in black on 18 February and the *Luftwaffe* close combat clasp in silver on 20 February 1945, having accumulated the required 30 *Nahkampftage* (close combat days) in locations on German soil such as Neustadt, Girnen, Angerapp, Kreuzburg, Tiefenthal, Wilmsdorf, Forst Waldburg, Domlitten and Holstädt.

21 An area in the so-called Heiligenbeil pocket, where German forces found themselves surrounded with their backs to the *Frisches Haff*, or Vistula Lagoon, on the Baltic Sea. *Fallschirm-Panzerkorps HG* was evacuated from the encirclement on 25 March 1945. See Bender & Petersen, p.55.

22 Dr Heinrich Neumann was the *Bataillon Arzt* in *Fallschirm-Panzerfüsilier-Bataillon 2 HG*.

23 Located north of Mamonovo across the Vistula Lagoon, now called Baltiysk, which fell to the Russians on 28 March 1945.

24 Former German seaport on the Oder River, 30 miles from the Baltic Sea and now called Szczecin.

25 German military transport ship torpedoed by a Russian submarine in the Baltic in late January 1945, with the loss of over 9,000 lives.

hand and had to move on quickly, otherwise I would have just cried. I later heard by chance that he died the same day, 28 February 1945.[26] At the harbour, the last hospital train was about to leave. In front of the train carriage stood a *Feldwebel* of the *Kettenhund*. He stood in front of the train door and sternly informed me that the train was crowded and there was no more space. I pulled out my pistol, placed my hand on the door and told him I would shoot him if he did not move aside. *Oberleutnant* Hagemeyer, the *Panzer Hauptmann*, *Gefreiter* Mahlherbe and I climbed aboard the train as it was about to leave the station. Shortly after we left the Russians were already upon the railway line, but on the last car was a mounted four-barrel *Flak* gun. Those barrels fired all round and we came through without any losses, and it was homeward to the Reich!

I left the train in Bad Nenndorf near Hannover (Reserve Hospital *Bahnhofgaststätte*), and my comrades stayed on the train for a few more stops. After two weeks Hagemeyer wrote to me and told me that the British stood at the gates of Bad Nenndorf, and it had been declared as a hospital town. Hagemeyer would not be returning to the war. Since I did not want to go into captivity in a bed, I noticed a marching order to Halberstadt in

On the boat from Pillau to Danzig.
(Wolfram von Beck)

my garrison. A guard at the barracks informed me that *Oberstleutnant* Schirmer's unit might be in Groß Schönebeck, north of Berlin, but if I got to the barracks I might not get out again.[27] I thanked him for the information and turned on my heels to begin an adventurous journey in the direction of Berlin. From my short time in Halberstadt I had a girlfriend in Benzingerode. She was the daughter of the Mayor, Bollmann. I planned a short break, but she had been drafted as a *Flak* helper at a searchlight position in Gommern near Magdeburg. This was in the direction of Berlin, so I decided to take a look.

The next day I was there. The position consisted of a searchlight, a wooden hut and four girls. It was of course a big "hello" visit from an old warrior. In front of the hut was a wooden table, and we were just sitting comfortably drinking coffee. The *Bataillon* boss called on the phone and said that a bomber group would soon fly over the position, but they had already dumped their load on the Reich.

Soon there was a buzzing sound in the air and the bomber group with their fighter escorts flew over us. I looked up when I heard an unusual noise, and saw a turbine fighter flying into the middle of the pack, shooting down an escort, and then it was gone before the Americans knew what was going on. The pilot was able to jump, his parachute opened and he landed about 200–300m away from us. I took out my pistol and ran to meet him. First I had to cross a 100m-wide freshly

---

26 Heinz Berg was born on 26 October 1919 in Steinkirch and died in the reserve hospital in Stettin.

27 In February 1945, after the intervention of Hermann Göring, Schirmer was reprieved and became the 1a (Chief of Operations) of *Fallschirm-Ausbildungs-Division.1* being built north of Berlin under the command of *Generalmajor* Paul Conrath. This formation was filled with young men from the *Luftwaffe* schools. Schirmer ordered 8,000 of these green troops westwards to prevent them from becoming cannon fodder. (private correspondence)

ploughed field with the girls running after me. Suddenly the comrades of the downed pilot roared over us, firing their guns. I shouted at the girls to lie down in the furrows. The bullets whistled over our heads and thank God we were unharmed. On the other side of the field were about 15 farm labourers working with scythes and hoes. A farm wagon and two horses were shot up during the attack. The pilots must have thought they could help their comrade escape, but they were wrong.

When the planes had flown by, all the farm labourers went over to the parachutist with their tools in hand with the intention of killing him. He could not be held responsible for the actions of his comrades, and since I was already closer I said to him: "Give me your pistol and stand behind me." He reached out and handed me his Colt pistol. Now I had to defend myself from the angry crowd, because they saw him as responsible for the incident. I raised my pistol and warned them that if they took one more step I would shoot. I declared to them that the pilot was my prisoner and now I was responsible for him. We took him back to the searchlight position and I searched his pockets. He had a silk scarf with a map of Germany on it, some fine saws, cigarettes, lighter and his aviators ID card. He was a *First Lieutenant* in the Canadian fighter escort wing.

My girlfriend Irmgard Bollmann now called her boss and asked what we should do with the prisoner. He said we should take him to the Mayor in Gommern. I sent one of the girls on a bicycle to Gommern, and she soon returned with the village teacher. By order we should bring the prisoner to the Mayor. The teacher spoke perfect English and asked me if I would go as well, so we went on our way.

Thereafter we sat in the Mayor's living room and had to wait for him to be fetched. The pilot asked me if he could smoke a cigarette and I allowed him. The Mayor arrived soon after and swept in with a bright crimson head. He was a little fat man in uniform. First he knocked the pilot's cigarette out of his mouth before a word had passed his lips. Then I yelled at him that it was me who allowed him to smoke. At first I did not understand why he was so angry, but I soon learned that the team of horses, the cart and the farm labourers belonged to the Mayor.

The teacher translated everything to the pilot, who tried to excuse his comrades. The pilot thanked me because the teacher told him that if I had not been there when he landed he would not be alive now. Then a policeman arrived with a SAX motorcycle and took the prisoner to the closest POW camp.

The next day I continued my journey to Groß Schönebeck. The war was slowly coming to an end, and to continue my tour I had to borrow a bicycle. On the way I met two *RAD* (*Reichsarbeitsdienst* – Reich Labour Service) girls, who were also on their way to Berlin as their unit had already been disbanded. Since one of their tyres was flat I had to help them rent a new bike in the next town. In the evening we arrived in Berlin and looked for some lodgings. We passed an empty barracks, which seemed like a good place to stay. The caretaker of the barracks, an old *Oberfeldwebel*, would not let us inside, but thanks to my uniform and medals he relented and let us in. So we found ourselves in a big room with a cannon potbelly stove, and since it was very cold I chopped some wood between our building and the adjacent barracks. Unfortunately the *Kommandeur* saw me from his office window. He was an old *Oberst*, a veteran of the First World War. He kept asking me where I had come from and where I was going. I explained everything to him, but he would not listen. Then he asked if I was related to *Oberst* Wolfgang von Beck, and I could answer him truthfully: "Yes, I am!"

Now he became talkative and told me that he was once with my uncle at the Cadet School in Karlsruhe, and I should send his regards when I see him. Then everything was fine! He then told me something he was not permitted to share. The next day Berlin would be declared a Fortress, with no soldier able to leave the city.[28] If I did not want to die for the Fatherland in Berlin tomorrow I should leave as soon as possible.

---

28   Operation Clausewitz, the defence of Berlin, initiated on 20 April 1945.

I thanked him for the information, but unfortunately I forgot his name when I met my uncle again after the war.

At dawn we started cycling and put Berlin behind us. Then it was time to say goodbye to the *RAD* girls as I branched off and cycled towards Groß Schönebeck.

As I was cycling around a corner in a village, I came across another cyclist coming towards me who happened to be an old comrade, *Oberjäger* Heinz Schmizak. I was glad to be back at my old unit, but the story about Schirmer being here was just a rumour. Heinz was a courier for *General* Conrath and he was here with his staff. He took me with him and I was employed as a second courier by *Oberleutnant* Hamer (another old paratrooper). Shortly afterward, *Kampfgruppe Conrath* was disbanded because the war was over. Nearby was *Pionier-Bataillon Schacht* under the command of *Ritterkreuzträger* Major Gerhard Schacht. Heinz and I went over to join him.

We moved in the direction of Flensburg and experienced many crazy things before we came to the prison camp at Wisch in Schleswig-Holstein. We were not technically captured, but had to drive to the camp to obtain certain paperwork for that particular German state. In Flensburg-Mürwig we met up with the remains of the famous *Panzer Grenadier Division 'Großdeutschland'*. The *GD* commander and Schacht were former classmates. We heard that *Fallschirmjäger* and *Waffen-SS* men could not get release documentation, so the *GD* commander decided to take 30 men of sergeant rank into his ranks and we went into captivity as members of the *Großdeutschland*. The English had limited manpower to guard the camp and provided only a few men to monitor the perimeter, so they let us take over surveillance of the camp as we were the largest and most intact unit to enter captivity there. We now had to make sure that nobody escaped.

Epilogue

I was released from captivity on 23 August 1945. When I finally returned home, our apartment had been burned out and my mother was living with acquaintances nearby. My father and brother were still in captivity and my sisters were in Freiburg, so although my war was over for me it was not yet over for my family.

(Wolfram von Beck passed away on 7 April 2012, aged 86.)

Wolfram von Beck's wartime awards and decorations.
(Roland Foos)

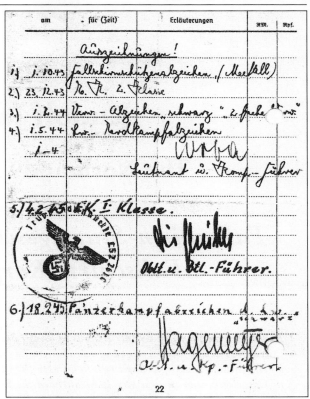

Page one of the awards section in Wolf von Beck's *Soldbuch*. He was awarded the following awards and decorations, which he retained after the war:
Luftwaffe Parachutist's badge on 1 October 1943
EK2 on 23 December 1943
Wound badge in black on 1 February 1944
Luftwaffe ground battle badge on 1 May 1944
EK1 on 4 February 1945
Luftwaffe Panzer battle badge in black on 18 February 1945
Luftwaffe close combat clasp in silver on 20 February 1945 (not shown)
This page also bears the signatures of *Oberleutnant* Kuhlwilm and *Leutnant* Hagemeyer. (Wolfram von Beck)

Wolfram von Beck (second from right) with former comrades at the third annual meeting of *Fallschirmjäger* veterans in Kassel in 1953. (Petra von Beck)

3

Rudolf Jackl

The Normandy Missions
&
Fallschirm-Sturmgeschütz Brigade of
I.Fallschirm Korps in Italy

Rudolf Jackl was born on 29 July 1923 at Mühldorf am Inn in Bavaria. He volunteered for the Luftwaffe *in 1942. After several drafts as a* Luftwaffe *ground crewman he volunteered to become a* Fallschirmjäger *in September 1943. In October 1943 he joined a* Fallschirm.Ersatz.Abteilung *in Gardelegen, and in February 1944 attended the* Fallschirmschule *at Wittstock. After the completion of his training, Rudolf was assigned to the* Pionierzug III/FJR8 *in Brittany. He saw extensive combat near Saint-Lô in Normandy in the first days after D-Day, and was evacuated after sustaining an injury in July 1944. He went on to serve in* Fallschirm-Sturmgeschütz Brigade Schmitz *in Italy and was subsequently sent to the officer school of the* 1. Fallschirm Korps *in northern Italy as the war drew to a close. After the war he became an engineer and regularly wrote articles for the* Fallschirmjäger Pionier *veterans' yearbook.*

Portrait photo of *Flieger* Rudolf Jackl in 1942, with *Luftwaffe Ausbildungs Regiment.63*. (Rudolf Jackl)

Portrait in tropical uniform whilst serving with the *Luftwaffe* in Crete. (Rudolf Jackl)

Passport photo taken in November 2006. (Lydia Jackl)

In April and May of 1944, *FJR8*, under the command of *Oberst* Egon Liebach, was stationed in Brittany. Training of the *Regiment* took place east of the important U-boat port at Brest. The *Pionierzug* from *III/FJR8* of *Fallschirmjäger Division 3* was located at Bodenna near Mont de Saint-Michel north of Brasparts. This position was one of the highest peaks in Brittany. We spent our time practising mine laying, constructing and destroying bunkers, tank destruction and using the flamethrower.

III/FJR8 Assault *Pionier* training, building a bunker in the autumn of 1943 in Sizun, Brittany.

In the early hours of 6 June 1944, the alarm was sounded. The Allies had landed in Normandy. The long-feared invasion had begun. Everything started to move fast. We exchanged drill uniforms for combat uniforms, and the *Pionierzug* was equipped for war. On the same day, trucks from *FJR8* appeared for loading. Our *Pionierzugführer*, *Oberfeldwebel* Fritz Heinemann, a veteran paratrooper, briefed us on our mission.[1] *FJD3* was to be used in Normandy, where the enemy had already obtained considerable successes during the first day.

The *Division* as a whole was only equipped with a handful of trucks. Most had been taken away for service on the Eastern Front. Only *I/FJR8* could be motorised, the rest had to follow on foot.

Hauptmann Josef Krammling addresses men of his *Bataillon*. (Rudolf Jackl)

---

1   Fritz Heinemann had been a squad leader in *Sturmgruppe Granit* that attacked the Fort at Eben Emael in Belgium on 10 May 1940.

III/FJR8 commanded by *Hauptmann* Josef Krammling[2] was assigned to a *Kampfgruppe* under the command of *Major* Friedrich Alpers, the *Ritterkreuzträger* who was later killed near Quevy Le Grand in Belgium.[3] The 40 men of the *Pionierzug* were attached to this *Kampfgruppe*.

Mission near Bérigny, 8–10 June 1944

After two days travel we reached Normandy. The columns moved only at night. There were also many different *Wehrmacht* troops, tanks and vehicles heading for the front.

The Allies had complete air superiority in the skies over Normandy, and near the town of Torigni-sur-Vire (14km south-east of Saint-Lô) we encountered this superiority. Eight to 10 P-51 Mustangs strafed the area.[4] Luckily, French roads have many trees, nevertheless our part of the column was discovered and we experienced the first *Jabo* attack. They swept the road, firing all the way, vehicles were hit and the first casualties were taken. We threw ourselves into a nearby orchard and hid behind the apple trees. Everyone fired wildly at the *Jabos*, without hitting them. I fired half of my ammunition at them, but to no avail. When we thought it was all over they made another pass, this time next to each other in line. The middle of the road again came under fire, and also the positions occupied by the sheltering soldiers at the sides of the road. I heard cries; a salvo of bullets passed over me and hit the crown of one of the trees I was sheltering under.

I was covered in leaves and branches, but fortunately the thick trunk of the tree had protected me. We young soldiers, 18–20 years old, were shocked at the carnage. The cruelty of war had finally reached us.

Oberfeldwebel Heinemann, the old veteran, tried to reassure us. The *Pionierzug* had suffered its first casualties: a bullet from one of the *Jabos* had injured a young comrade beside me in the shoulder. A *Wehrmacht* car took him to a *Hauptverbandplatz*. The walking wounded remained behind to carry on.

After the *Jabo* attack near Torigni, we were issued with the following instructions:

1.   Shooting at enemy aircraft was prohibited.
2.   Great attention was to be paid to camouflage in case of *Jabo* attack.

The chaos was soon sorted out. The shot-up vehicles were pushed to the side of the road. The dead were removed from the road and the wounded were taken to a military hospital in the rear. Our column then proceeded in the direction of the front by foot, occasionally taking side roads.

On the evening of 8 June 1944, we reached our position. It was at a road junction near Bérigny, 11km east of Saint-Lô on the road to Bayeux. The road formed a triangle made up of the main road and other subsidiary roads.

---

2   Krammling was involved in the biggest POW escape attempt in Great Britain during the Second World War. On 11 March 1945, 70 *Wehrmacht* officers tunnelled out of POW Camp 198 in Bridgend, Wales. Krammling, prisoner number A-428903, was captured by a farmer on 12 March, hiding in the corner of a field. (courtesy of Brett Exton)

3   Friedrich Alpers was a Nazi party member, *SS-Obergruüppenfuhrer* and member of the Brunswick State Parliament. In 1933 he was directly involved in the murder of several communists. He was a reserve *Luftwaffe* officer and volunteered for front-line duties, and transferred to *FJR9*. Rudolf Jackl believed he had been KIA on 3.9.44, but other sources state he committed suicide after capture by American forces. *Kampfgruppe Alpers* was made up of *III/FJR8*, *I/FJR9*, the *Pionierzug* and a *Sani* unit. See Frühbeißer, p.28.

4   American long-range single-seat fighter and ground-attack aircraft.

An 88mm *Flak* gun was in place at the road junction. It was well positioned and camouflaged at the side of the road, and had a direct line of sight up the Bayeux road. Our *Zug*, along with the 88mm, formed a blocking position between Bérigny and Saint-Quentin to the north-east. Overnight on 8/9 June, we dug in.

By daybreak, everything had to be camouflaged. This was because of American 'Iron Gustavs', the flying artillery spotters. They constantly circled in the sky unhindered. The absence of the *Luftwaffe* was very depressing to us.

With the coming of daybreak on 9 June, *Oberfeldwebel* Heinemann made a bad discovery. The *Gruppe* on the left flank, under the leadership of an *Oberjäger*, had disappeared. It should have been in a position protecting Saint-Quentin.

They had probably wondered too far and fallen foul to an American ambush. That was a bitter blow for the *Pionierzug*, which now counted 25 men.

Oberfeldwebel Heinemann organised a three-man *Panzervernichtungstruppe* under my leadership. We were entrenched at the southern mouth of the main road. We were to lie in wait until the enemy *Panzers* rolled past. We were armed with 3kg and 5kg charges, and we were to jump out from behind cover, attach the charges and then rush back under cover without being seen. This was the only way to destroy the enemy *Panzers*, as we had not yet been equipped with the *Panzerfaust*.

On the hard shoulder of the road we arranged camouflaged T-Mines, which were all attached to each other with bitumen tape. They could be quickly pulled across the road, but the road had to be left open. This was because 700m ahead of us was *Kampfgruppe Alpers*, positioned on either side of the road. The route had to remain open until the last minute for our own vehicles to pass.

The Americans had already occupied the Forest at Balleroy (Forét de Cerissy). Approximately 1,200m away, we recognised American troops and tanks forming up in great numbers. Soon after, the enemy moved forwards on a broad front toward Saint-Lô, completely unaware of the new German *HKL* (main battle line).

The American advance took them into the defence positions of our *Jäger Kompanien*. The assault broke down with heavy losses, and the *Amis* withdrew into the protection of the forest. The defence of Bérigny had halted the US advance toward Saint-Lô.

Up until the afternoon the fighting dragged on before Bérigny. The *HKL*, particularly the left flank, was under constant bombardment. Suddenly we observed detonation clouds in the air. The Americans were firing shrapnel shells, which were detonating 20–30m in the air. It began to rain fragments on our open positions at the road junction. *Kampfgruppe Alpers* fared much worse and they suffered heavy casualties, mainly head and back injuries in their positions 700m from our own.

The *HKL* was vacated as soon as possible. Only when evening fell did the bombardment cease. At night we began to recover the dead and wounded.

By the morning of 10 June, the Americans were only aiming defensive fire at our positions. With my two comrades we went forwards to our old positions. On our left was a machine-gun position, and in between lay destroyed weapons and abandoned equipment. We crossed to the right side of the road, where a farm was situated.

We knew there was a mortar position in the farm whose crew was missing. We found our three comrades in the yard of the building. All were dead. We returned to our position. We were instructed to retrieve the bodies of our comrades, so equipped with a Red Cross flag we returned to the farmstead. In the shot-up barn we found a farmer's truck with a broken axle. After loading the dead, we risked driving out toward the road. The vehicle was very difficult to steer and swivelled all over the road. We hung the Red Cross flag from the window. Nothing happened and we were not fired upon. The *Amis* allowed us safe passage. We could clearly see them in the distance. This was the first instance of humanity I had encountered since the beginning of the invasion.

Many graves were dug in those first few days, but as the bodies began to pile up they were just left at collection points.

During the afternoon of 10 June, I spent some time at the 88mm gun position. It was situated beside the hedge embankment, or *bocage*, at the side of the road. It was very imposing. Its powerful barrel was directed toward the Sherman column; the range of the targets was approximately 1,200m. The camouflage had been removed and it was shaded from above by the branches of the trees.

It would have been so easy to take a shot at the Americans, but the gun commander, an *Oberwachtmeister*, forbid any shooting with the 88mm. He was only to fire freely during a *Panzer* breakthrough, which had not yet happened.

It was not long before the 'Iron Gustavs' made another appearance over our positions, (in front jargon, 'Crows'). In pairs they circled around, waiting for movement below.

Then they would call in accurate artillery fire from positions behind the American front line. They were searching for the German front line so they could smash our machine-gun, mortar and anti-tank positions.

One 'Crow', appeared to take interest in the road junction, although no movement could possibly been seen from above. All of the men were under cover; the positions were well camouflaged. He circled and circled right above our positions, and then he disappeared. Had he discovered us?

I had borrowed the binoculars from the *Oberwachtmeister* and observed for myself the well-camouflaged American positions on the edge of the Forét de Cerisy. We knew what was hidden beneath the camouflage netting and that we could not oppose anything they had in that forest.

Suddenly, we heard the dull sound of artillery fire. Before we had a chance to react, we could hear the howling of the artillery shells as salvo after salvo began to rain down on our positions. The air was full of dirt and dust as the barrage closed in. Branches in the trees started to shake. We scattered to escape this zone of fire. I heard the *Oberwachtmeister* shout "*Zugmaschine Weg*" ("Tractor away"). The 88mm towing vehicle was literally behind us, camouflaged under the trees. We had not even seen it before. One of the gun crew ran over to the vehicle and started the engine. The gun crew, several of my *Pionier* comrades and I jumped on to the fenders and held on to the headlights and anything else we could grab. The vehicle turned and headed away from the artillery fire zone.

With luck the first salvos fell too short; if they had been on target then our positions would have been completely destroyed. The men had a chance to evacuate their foxholes, but we still suffered several lightly wounded during the bombardment.

When we were clear the driver throttled back and we *Pioniers* jumped from the vehicle. The tractor and the *Flak* crew then returned to our former positions to retrieve the 88mm. We did not know whether it could be saved or whether it had been hit by artillery shells. I had my souvenir, the *Oberwachtmeister*'s binoculars, still hung from my neck. Whilst observing distant aircraft, an officer approached me and seized the binoculars from around my neck: "Do you know that these are *Wehrmacht* property?" I could have howled. My souvenir was gone.

We *Pioniers* returned to the front, just a few hundred yards from our previous positions. There we came across an *MG Kompanie* who had set up a third *HKL*. They were broadly stretched and had a good field of fire over the road junction near Bérigny. We were met by the *Kompaniechef*, an elderly *Hauptmann*. Our *Gruppe* of eight men reported to him and he told us to dig in as this was the new defence line. The *Kompaniechef* then gave orders to stay put, regardless of what happened.

In 1984, on the 40th anniversary of the invasion, I returned to this road junction near Bérigny. The landscape had changed slightly with the building of a new freeway and asphalt-covered roads, but our foxholes were still visible.

Later that evening we were ordered to pull back from our positions. Whilst withdrawing from our positions we were filmed by a *Kriegsberichter* (war correspondent) who was making a film for the *Deutsche Wochenschau*, a weekly news programme for the people at home.[5] What a sight we must have made.

The men of the *Pionierzug* were gathered at the *Regiment* command post and numbered 20–30 men. *Oberfeldwebel* Heinemann carried out a stock-take. During the defence of the road junction at Bérigny we had suffered only a few casualties, but had lost a lot of materiel and weapons. We could not return to the former positions as the *Amis* had advanced on the road junction.

In the following weeks, work was found for the *Pioniers* within the *Regiment*, mainly mine-laying. For my part in the mission, I was awarded the Iron Cross 2nd Class.

Epilogue

The collision of *FJD3* with US troops near Bérigny was a bad experience. Their materiel superiority and complete control of the skies over Normandy required special tactics. We became masters of camouflage. Everything along our *HKLs* had to be under cover and nothing could afford to be out in the open. As soon as something moved on the ground, the 'Crows' would call in artillery. We were to wait for the attack and then give full defensive fire. The impenetrable Norman hedgerows worked both for us and against us, but did provide us with excellent defensive positions.

Saint-Pierre-de-Semilly 25–26 July1944

After the fighting at Bérigny, the Americans did not carry out any more large-scale attacks, just some local engagements. The greater part of *Fallschirmjäger Division 3* arrived and took up position. Among the American troops were the so-called Indian Division (2nd Infantry Division), recognisable by the Red Indian's head badge on the upper arm of their uniform tunics.

The *Amis* brought up more units to the front during June and July. Above all they were bringing up armoured formations from the beachheads.

Our *Pionierzug* was constantly in use. Our area was south-east of Bérigny. Places such as Saint-Germain-d'Elle, Vidouville, Biéville, La Vacquerie and down to Sept-Vents will always be in my memory.

We were very versatile and built command posts, repaired supply roads, laid mines, carried out demolition work and conducted reconnaissance patrols. These were everyday tasks for us *Pioniers*.

I took part in one reconnaissance patrol to the enemy-held town of Caumont-l'Éventé, 15km south-east of Bérigny. *Oberfeldwebel* Heinemann led us in a calm and collected manner under adverse conditions. The 'Iron Gustavs' circled over us constantly, and *Jabos* controlled the airspace. Camouflage was the most important factor for us, and most of our movements could only be carried out at night. American artillery fired endless amounts of ammunition. This and the bad weather played on our already stretched nerves. We did not go without losses, usually wounds caused by mortar fragments. By mid-July, the *Pionierzug* only had approximately 20–23 men, and we received no replacements.

We were then taken out of the line and sent to a resting position near Torigni. We were billeted on a farm, which we had to share with a *Jäger Kompanie*.[6] Supplies were low and it was difficult to maintain hygiene and weapon maintenance. However, in July we were equipped with a new anti-tank weapon, the *Panzerfaust*. It was much better than the hollow charges we had been issued

---

5   Newsreel series that ran from 1940–1945 using film provided by war reporters.
6   Parachute infantrymen – the non-*Fallschirm-Pioniers*.

with. The Sherman could now be fired on from 30m. We received a handful of these weapons, but we could not carry out any practical training as they were so valuable. We were given some theoretical training, but this did not make up for firing the *Panzerfaust*. We could not get a proper feeling for this weapon or an appreciation of the charge's flight path, which later cost me two misses.

At the end of July we had a few days peace before the *Amis* began to press on toward Saint-Lô. This time they advanced from the north, near Saint-Georges-d'Elle and Hill 192, which had been defended by *Fallschirmjäger Regiment 9*.[7]

There was a general alarm: the enemy was on the Bayeux to Saint-Lô road.

We hastily loaded our truck and by that night we were driving to Saint-Pierre-de-Semilly. This was the sector of *III./FJR8* east of Saint-Pierre-de-Semilly, a marsh-filled valley and also the source of several brooks. Some 200m south, running parallel to the main Saint-Lô to Bayeux road, is a second road, and it was here that we built the new *HKL* under the cover of trees. South of this road was some high ground leading to the valley that provided excellent observation of the Saint-Lô road and was the ideal position for a platoon of heavy *MGs*. The range of fire from this position was around 1,200–1,300m.

Our *Zug* received its orders: act as operational reserve for the *Jäger Kompanien* positioned in front of us and use the *Panzerfaust* to attack any Sherman tanks that break through the lines.

We prepared an earth bunker for *Oberfeldwebel* Heinemann, and at the same time prepared a safe zone in a north–south running country lane, so we could quickly come to the aid of the *Jäger Kompanien* during an engagement.

Our *Zug* took up positions halfway up the slope of the high ground. With our ranks spread apart, we formed a second security line immediately behind the *Jäger* positions. We dug new foxholes, but this time we built them under cover to protect ourselves from shrapnel shells that detonated in the air, a lesson we learned from 'shrapnel corner' near Bérigny in June. I was the right-wing man in our security line. *Oberfeldwebel* Heinemann remained in the country lane and kept hold of the precious *Panzerfausts*, which were only to be distributed when necessary.

It rained continuously on 24 July 1944.

I will now add something, which concerned me personally at the time. I was in great pain from the right side of my groin area. At first I hardly considered it, but it became worse. My groin began to swell and turned bluish in colour. I could only move around by hobbling.

Oberfeldwebel Heinemann sent me to see the medic. The dressing station was just east of our positions, by a stone house, which is still there today [at the time of writing]. The wounded men were tended here until they could be evacuated.

A young doctor checked my groin and told me that I would need an operation immediately. I had a septic lymph gland in my groin. Evacuation would not be possible until the morning of 25 July, as there was no ambulance until then. I received instructions on how to make a cold compress from linen and apply it to the groin. I had to report back at 0800 hours the next morning so as not to miss the ambulance.

I limped back to my wet foxhole. It was a very long night as I anxiously waited for the morning to come. It came, but not as I expected.

At 0700 hours on 25 July, the earth around Saint-Pierre-de-Semilly began to tremble as a deafening drumfire began. Our *Bataillon* sector was under heavy bombardment. Salvo after salvo

---

7   Hill 192 is located between Cloville and the Saint-Lô to Bayeux road and provided excellent long-range observation of the surrounding terrain. US forces had failed to take the height on 16 June. The 2nd US Infantry Division attacked the hill on 11–12 July, retaking the height from *III/FJR9*. See Mueller, pp.253–54. *FJR9* suffered its highest losses of the Normandy campaign on 11 July 1944, with 104 dead, 250 wounded, 197 missing and 24 men taken prisoner. See Frühbeißer, p.101.

sizzled around us in the wet earth. This was a large-scale attack. Already there were dead and wounded. Nobody could help us now.

Finally the artillery stopped. Beyond the main road to Saint-Lô, tank engines howled into life. Our nerves became strained as it penetrated the quiet. I pushed myself out of my foxhole to take a look.

Then they came. Sherman tanks. They were the older type with the short barrel. They rattled over the roads and broke through the front line, moving southwards. Our *Panzerschreck* rocket crew were killed after a Sherman opened fire on them. The American infantry followed on a broad front; the plain was full of *Amis*.

Suddenly, machine-gun fire came from behind me: an *MG42*. Light tracer fire hissed over me toward the advancing enemy. The *sMG*-platoon also opened up with sustained fire. I could only see a small part of the battlefield, but the effect of this fire was devastating on the enemy ranks. They fell on the open ground in their dozens, while many more ran for cover. The *Ami* attack began to falter as they started to receive flanking fire from the

Kopfschoss (head shot) Para helmet and bullets found by Rudolf Jackl in former defensive positions at St. Pierre de Semilly in June 1981. (Rudolf Jackl)

Jäger Kompanien. The Shermans in front of me held back and turned off laterally toward the marshy valley. There the road led to the south. The *Amis* halted the attack and there was the usual pause before the artillery would begin. The *sMG Zug* was also silent; the noise of combat died down.

Then a comrade approached me, his face unknown to me. He had a *Panzerfaust* in his hands. He said he had no training in the use of the weapon but he wanted to crack a Sherman. I hastily explained the function, examined the warhead and ignitor, and showed him the more favourable firing position.

Suddenly there was a loud crack, and the air was full of fragments. A tank shell detonated on the earthen wall in front of us. The air pressure threw us to the side. While I remained intact, the comrade was mortally wounded. I leaned against the embankment; that was all one could do for the moment. After recovering from the shock of the blast, I left my rifle and with *Panzerfaust* in hand I proceeded toward the Sherman, which had broken through to my right. Behind the next earthen wall I could see them distributed on the plain. In the background were jeeps. *Ami* infantry were on the embankments. The whole attack was still in a southerly direction. It seemed as though they were waiting for orders.

The right-wing tank was my target. Caution! If I was discovered now it would be the end. Under cover, I made short work of preparing the *Panzerfaust*. I had been taught that the range should be 30m, so I did not move closer. I estimated the range to be more like 40m.

The Sherman would be attacked diagonally from behind. I thought it more advisable to aim for the turret. I pushed the arming lever forward, safety off, the firing lever was visible and the weapon was ready. Then I jumped out from cover, aimed and fired.

A jet of fire and smoke drove out of the back, and the warhead, with extended fins, rushed in the direction of the Sherman.

The warhead shot over the turret; I had aimed too high. It was too late. Then I heard shouting, the tank engine started and the turret began to turn in my direction. The Sherman fired several high explosive shells in a fan pattern, but I was already away and reached the relative safety of my foxhole.

I was now in agony from my groin injury. When I looked at my trousers, I noticed that they had been burned by the jet of fire from the *Panzerfäuste*.

It was noon. Bread crusts and the contents of our water bottles satisfied the roughest hunger. *Oberfeldwebel* Heinemann collected his men. Once again our numbers were reduced. We also had some stragglers from the breakthrough positions, who had managed to escape.

In the protection of the valley we were told of the situation. It began to rain again. The last ammunition was passed out and the few remaining *Panzerfäuste* were distributed. I inherited a replacement *Panzerfaust*.

The *Ami* tanks once again regrouped. The direction of attack changed from the south to the west and Saint-Lô. This meant more danger. The German front line was at risk of being rolled up from the flank.

The next command post had to be alerted. *Oberfeldwebel* Heinemann took over this task. He handed me his *Panzerfaust* for safekeeping and went on his way. As an immediate measure he ordered a blocking position in the country lane running to the south.

Only 150m of cattle pasture now separated us from the Americans. On the right wing stood our last *MG42*, which could sweep the plain from its position. We others divided ourselves up in the country lane, which was completely covered by bushes.

We saw the Shermans over the embankment, turret next to turret, as though they were on parade. At least 12 could be seen from my position. They could take this liberty because of the lack of German anti-tank guns. We could see the turret machine guns swivelling, looking for targets. Time dragged on, and soon it was evening. We observed enemy infantry advancing through the drizzle. Then all hell broke loose.

MG fire swept the hedge barrier of the lane that we had been sheltering behind. Tracer fire hissed in the hedge only a metre away from me. We were covered in dirt, branches and leaves as the fire continued.

Then the fire grew silent and the first Sherman pushed itself over the embankment. Groups of infantry sheltered behind it. We took the tank under bombardment, our *MG42* constantly firing short bursts.

The *Amis* suffered losses; they threw themselves down in the wet grass, which held back the rest of the tanks.

Still their *MG* fire continued, with high explosive rounds detonating around our positions. Our *MG42* fell silent. Then the Shermans advanced again, this time alone, without the infantry. Spaced broadly apart, they came in at full speed. If we did not want to be rolled over we had to vacate our position in the lane and escape. With my rifle and two *Panzerfäuste*, I ran back in the direction of the valley. I went through the gate into the cattle pasture. I left the second *Panzerfaust* and with some leaps and bounds was on the plain, and in my haste did not notice a moving Sherman tank, only 20m from me. He was on the right wing of their attack.

There was nothing else for me to do but attack it with the remaining *Panzerfaust*. The weapon was already prepared, and I fired it almost immediately. The warhead rushed toward the tank, but the Sherman as I said was moving. I should have fired with more of an angle. The warhead flew past the turret. It did not even detonate when it hit the ground. Disappointed, I remained in my firing position for several seconds. Then balls whistled past. I was fired upon. With giant steps, I disappeared back into the shelter of a lane leading to the valley.

It was then that I remembered the second *Panzerfaust*. I wanted to get it back but it was too late, the Sherman was already there. The *Panzerfaust* was lost.

After hearing the noise of battle, *Oberfeldwebel* Heinemann returned to us. The *Ami* tanks rolled themselves over our blocking position. The infantry advanced. We heard calls and commands; the *Amis* were almost beside us. We squatted in a lane at the edge of a brook, huddled together.

We were completely exhausted. My groin hurt and burned like a fire. The noise of battle died down, the *Amis* had finished firing for today. Finally night came.

One courageous *Oberjäger* carefully explored the surrounding area. There was no doubt that we were surrounded. We would have to be away by morning or it would be captivity or worse. Stragglers trickled in overnight, mostly lightly wounded without weapons. Thus our numbers increased to some dozen men. There was still the chance of a breakout towards Saint-Pierre-de-Semilly, so in single file we waded through the brook, making no noise whatsoever.

I hobbled in agony, supported by my rifle. We reached Saint-Pierre-de-Semilly unnoticed, but turned off south on a side road. This area was free of the enemy. The road ahead was clear. We were south of the valley and *Oberfeldwebel* Heinemann had saved us from the American encirclement.

Epilogue

My personal problem was also solved after the breakout. *Oberfeldwebel* Heinemann secured my evacuation to the dressing station on 26 July. With that I made my departure from the *Pionierzug* of *III/FJR8* and *Oberfeldwebel* Heinemann. I could count only a handful of comrades before I left. My good friend Wilhelm Jäger was killed that same day.

Gedenket im Gebete
an unseren lieben Sohn,
Bruder und Neffen

Wilhelm Jäger

Gefr. in einem Fallschirmjäger-Regiment.

geb. 3. Juni 1924

gef. im Juli 1944 bei St. Lô (Frkr.)

„Wer im Gedächtnis seiner Lieben lebt,
der ist nicht tot, nur fern . . . Tot ist
nur, wer vergessen wird."

J. Pfeiffer's Kunstverlag München 2

O Herr, gib ihm die ewige Ruhe! Und
das ewige Licht leuchte ihm! Herr, laß
ihn ruhen in Frieden! Amen.

Rudolf Jackl's friend Wilhelm Jäger, killed near St. Pierre de Semilly on 26 July 1944, aged 20.
He is buried at the German cemetery at La Cambe in Normandy. (Rudolf Jackl)

Wilhelm Jäger's gravestone. (Rudolf Jackl)

Fritz Heinemann was himself captured on 28 July near Saint-Lô. We met again after the war and remained good friends until his death in Braunschweig on 23 December 1999, aged 82.

After my operation and recuperation in both Paris and Metz, I joined an *Ersatz Bataillon* in Nürnberg, followed by a *Pionier-Ersatz-Bataillon* in Güstrow.

Old comrades Fritz Heinemann (left) and Rudolf Jackl in Frechen near Köln, January 1989. (Rudolf Jackl)

The *Fallschirm-Sturmgeschütz-Brigade* of the *I. Fallschirm-Korps* in Italy
Ferry construction on the Po River

At the end of July 1944, as a *Fallschirm-Pionier Gefreiter*, I had survived the invasion battles in France.

My way did not lead back to my old unit, *FJR8* (under *Oberst* Liebach). After military hospital and various intermediate stations, I ended up in *Fallschirmjäger Ersatz Bataillon 2* in Güstrow-Mecklenburg. It was here that I was collected, re-equipped and returned to the front lines. There were also recruits who received a front education before they were mixed in with the replacements.

For some time I was used as an assistant trainer to teach the newcomers the bare essentials in weaponry and proper behaviour on the battlefield. We old hands had enough practical experience. One morning, *Der Spieß* read out a notice. He was looking for 30–40 front-line experienced *Pioniers* for a *Panzer* unit in Italy. That did not sound bad to invasion-tested ears. It was no wonder that I was among those assigned to this unit.

The railway wagon first went to Nuremburg-Buchenbühl to pick up more replacements. Once attached to the transport train, we crossed the already autumnal Brenner Pass (through the mountains between Austria and Italy). The camaraderie of the men grew quickly. The final destination was the village of Borgoforte, south of Mantua on the River Po. Here we were to learn more about our future use.

The new unit turned out to be *Fallschirm-Sturmgeschutz-Brigade* 'Schmitz' of the *I. Fallschirm-Korps*. Our contact point was the workshop *Kompanie* in Borgoforte. There were no tanks as stated to us in Güstrow, but it was apparently to be armed with the Italian made *Semovente*, 10.5cm calibre *Sturmgeschützen*. The *Brigade*, with its estimated 50 guns, required *Pioniers* for a variety of tasks. Initially we were to be a 40-man *Zug*, which might be expanded into a powerful *Pionier Kompanie*.

The *Pionierzug* formed the squad from which the *Zug* and *Gruppe* leaders were to be selected. At first, however, the *Fallschirm-Korps* dropped off some experienced NCOs as our transport consisted only of enlisted men.

At the end of 1944 we had the following NCOs, some of whom met tragic fates:

- *Oberfeldwebel* Georg Schmitz (*Pionier Zugführer* and well-known Cassino veteran. Promoted to *Leutnant* in 1945, intended to be *Kompaniechef* of the *Pionier Kompanie*);
- *Oberjäger* Wolf (*Gruppeführer*. In May 1945 he was a *Fahnenjunker-Oberjäger* at the *Führerschule* of *I.Fallschirm.Korps*. Officer Cadet intended to be *Zugführer*);
- *Oberjäger* Kurt Wischmann (*Gruppeführer* who was killed on 8 April 1945 in an *fatal* accident caused by a detonating hand grenade. Buried in the Futa Pass cemetery);
- *Oberjäger* Heinz Bruhn (*Gruppeführer*. He committed suicide on 2 May 1945 with a pistol as the result of bad news from home. Buried in the Futa Pass cemetery);
- *Obergefreiter* Rudolf Jackl (*Gruppeführer*. May 1945 promoted to *Fahnenjunker-Oberjäger* at the *Führerschule* of *I.Fallschirm.Korps*. Officer Cadet intended to be *Zugführer*);
- *Obergefreiter* Karl Wilhelm (killed in April 1945 by a tank round. He was intended to be *Oberjäger* and *Gruppeführer*. Buried at the Futa Pass cemetery);
- *Obergefreiter* Günter Prinke (due to attend an NCO course in early 1945 and intended to be *Oberjäger* and *Gruppeführer*).

The new *Pionierzugführer* was slow in coming. In the meantime, a *Pionier Feldwebel* on loan from the Army took command. He was a good man from whom we learned a lot. He immediately provided the necessary equipment so that we became fit for action.

The workshop *Kompanie* possessed a cable-operated ferry, which was camouflaged during the day and then used to bring *Sturmgeschützen* over the River Po at night. It consisted of pontoons with a stable wooden platform. The ramps were in need of repair; they were sagged and damaged. We repaired them with tree trunks, iron braces and countless wheelbarrows full of gravel. This was a bone-shattering job. Next to the ferry were smaller rafts made from planks fixed to empty wine barrels, which were confiscated from the local farms despite the protest *"Mama Mia"*. They were moored to the south bank of the river and were to be used to transfer soldiers during a retreat. Thanks to our Army *Feldwebel*, we completed an apprenticeship in water engineering.

A command came in from above, stating that every town and village had to be prepared for defence, so my group formed a solid wood and earthen bunker with two *MG* gun ports at the entrance of the village. This was enough to fulfil the order.

At the river bank we worked under the constant danger from *Jabos*. American twin-boomed hunters of the Lightning P38 type patrolled the River Po in groups consisting of several aircraft. Since all the bridges had been bombed, they were looking for command posts, ferries and pontoon

Georg Schmitz, the Cassino veteran and *Zugführer* of the *Pionierzug*. (Rudolf Jackl)

bridges. Camouflage was therefore a priority. All structures were immediately covered with branches and twigs. On the dyke stood a *Jabo* guard, on whose warning call everyone would disappear into dugouts. The *Amis* often used to scatter land mines over the river banks. They were larger than hand grenades, similar to our own S-mine. Once activated by foot pressure, the explosive would detonate in the air, causing devastating effects (M16 bounding AP mines). These mines formed a constant threat in the overgrown bushes and sand. In one incident we retrieved an Army *Zahlmeister* with a torn-off foot. How many men must have been harmed by this homicidal weapon?

It was November when the new *Pionierzugführer* arrived. The commander of the workshop *Kompanie*, *Hauptmann* Eckert, inspected the construction sites with him in his Citroen car. A decorated *Oberfeldwebel* climbed out of the car and we set our eyes on him for the first time. His name was Georg Schmitz from *Fallschirmjäger Division 1*, a well-known Cassino veteran.[8] A friendship developed from this meeting that would last until his death in 1994.

The *Pionierzug*, with about 40 men, was now complete. In the evening, command was handed over from our proven Army *Feldwebel*.

---

8   Georg Schmitz destroyed an enemy tank in Cassino and was awarded the Tank Destruction Badge in silver whilst serving with *4/Fallschirm-Pionier-Bataillon* of *FJR3*.

Operation in the Apennines, Italy

A new marching order was imminent. The equipment and supplies were to be brought by truck to the front area in the Appennines. The *Sturmgeschütz-Brigade* along with some Army units had blocked the wide Reno Valley at Sasso Marconi. It was feared that there might be an Allied break-through towards Bologna through the Futa Pass.

Our trucks climbed a narrow road to the high-altitude village of Mongardino, with its old-fash-ioned pilgrimage church. According to command, the *Brigade* command post should be moved from the valley to the heights. Near the church was a suitable farm; however, it lacked a protective bunker. The homestead was located within firing range of the enemy artillery. The *Pionierzug* came to the deserted church rectory, whose thick walls offered some protection. At the new command post, previous generations had cut into the slope in order to gain space. Only here could the bunker be driven into the mountain, and it was back-breaking work. Someone said that Schmitz himself designed the plan for the bunker. His actions showed the experienced engineer and super-visor he was. Two 10m-long tunnels were to be dug into the mountain. The tunnel dimensions were 1m wide and 2m high, roughly lined with wood. At a depth of 8m into the mountain, both tunnels would meet and end in a 3m x 3m cavern. These were clear guidelines and we began two construction sites. In each tunnel, eight *Pioniers* worked in double shifts because of the limited space available.

The material, a brittle rock and marl mixture, could not be removed by pickaxe alone. It had to be blasted with small explosives and removed by wheelbarrow, and we worked under the constant risk of collapse. *Oberfeldwebel* Schmitz designed the log frame that was fitted to the sides and roof of the tunnels and covered with boards. The wall cavities were filled with boulders. The boards were taken from a barn in the village. There was a competition amongst the young lads as to which side would finish their tunnel first, very much to the delight of the *Zugführer*, who was under considerable pressure from above. *Oberfeldwebel* Schmitz was always very supportive of the *Pionierzug*. He procured more food, provided warm blankets and plenty of dynamite cartridges. He had a *Zündapp* sidecar combination at his disposal. Trucks were scarce, and had to be requested from *Brigade*.

Even high up in the Apennines, we were not spared visits from enemy planes. A clumsy high-winged aircraft rumbled around, similar to our Fieseler Storch spotter plane. Nothing escaped the attention of this artillery observer. Anything suspicious was targeted with artillery salvos. We called him 'Iron Gustav'. Shooting at him was pointless because of his armour. Back in Normandy we were prohibited from shooting at these aircraft. Only good camouflage was recommended.

At the end of the year, the onset of winter hit us. It was snowing for days and we trudged through knee-deep snow. Our mountain road was impassable and we were cut off for several days. Food supplies could not get through; we suffered from ravenous hunger and were freezing cold. The work on the bunker continued and we did our best to complete it. The winter also had nice days, with a warming sun that bathed the mountains of the Apennines in dazzling white. If it weren't for the rumbling sounds of the front and the artillery impact craters, you could imagine yourself in deepest peace.

A word now about a courageous woman! On many an occasion, the old parish housekeeper visited us. She wanted to look around the church and house next to it. We reassured this devout lady that the church remained untouched by us. Nevertheless, she was not very happy that we had filled the pastor's rooms with a thick layer of straw. "C'est la Guerre," as the French would say! Who wants to sleep on bare floors during the winter?

In the bunker, both of the tunnels had been completed and the excavation of the cavern was in progress. In January 1945, an order came in which took our breath away; stop work immediately, prepare everything for loading and during the following night transfer of the *Pionierzug* is to

Italy, 1944. *PAK* and towing vehicle from *Fallschirm-Panzerjäger-Abteilung* near Roccaraso in central Italy. Natural camouflage has been applied to avoid detection by Allied aircraft. (Kate Eichler)

commence. We were to proceed to the Po plain area near Imola. So for weeks we had worked in vain, and our *Kommandeur* had not even seen the bunker.

The German leadership had logically recognised that the main Allied thrust was not to be expected from the Apennines but from the Adriatic area of Faenza. The main artery, the *Via Emilia*, was in great danger. Strong German forces, including the *Sturmgeschütz-Brigade*, were ordered to that location.

In 1955, I returned to the Apennines with my wife, Volkswagen car and camping equipment. We noted with satisfaction that Mongardino and its beautiful sanctuary had remained undamaged. The farmer, who had returned and used our bunker as a storeroom, was unaware that one of the builders of this useful place was standing before him.

At the front near Imola in February 1945

We were half asleep aboard overloaded trucks, rumbling through the night. At dawn, the column arrived in the new mission area north-east of Imola. We were happy to see that the Po Valley was already frost-free. The flat land was fertile, with wine, fruit and vegetable cultivation, and was therefore densely populated with farms. One advantage for us was that the *Brigade* command post, *Kompaniestab* and *Pionierzug* were close together.

The landowners did not want to leave their property, despite the risk of staying. *Oberfeldwebel* Schmitz let them stay, and we lived together peacefully in the big kitchen. A spacious cowshed full of warming animals offered a thick layer of straw, albeit perfumed, and it was the right temperature at night.

The new *HKL* ran along the *Via Emilia* near the Senio River. In the flood dykes, *Fallschirmjäger Division 1* & *4* had dug in. This well-developed front line was known as the Senio Position. The front-line town was Castel Bolognese, with a large German military presence there.

Opposite this position was an Indian Division of the English [*sic*] Eighth Army. Instead of steel helmets they wore their traditional turbans. These elite soldiers were feared for conducting silent nocturnal raiding parties with long knives. The British did not fail to notice the massive concentration of German troops on the *Via Emilia*. Because of the potential for high Allied losses, this defensive barrier was not attacked.[9] After our constant employment, the *Zugführer* wanted to give his men some days of rest. We bitterly needed to take care of our personal hygiene, weapon cleaning and equipment maintenance. Nothing came of it; we were required to construct an artillery resistant bunker for the *Brigade* command post, which was a priority.

We were now faced with completely different conditions than the rocky Apennines, with soft soil and high groundwater level which prohibited a deep earth bunker. *Oberfeldwebel* Schmitz, the experienced engineer, found the optimal solution here as well. In the house of the command post, a suitable room was cleared out. There we built a kind of log house with railway sleepers taken from the Imola train station. The floor was removed from the room, and then we dug a pit about 2.5m square and 1m deep. The pit was fitted with floorboard cladding. On the edge of the pit we stacked the sleepers in a lattice until head height was reached. They had to be laboriously sawed to the correct length, and were back-filled with earth. Iron braces were used to connect them together. Sleepers were inserted crosswise as a cover layer, which resulted in a room height of over 1m. The shelter door was accessed via some wooden steps, and we even found a few chairs and a table. It was a very stable bunker and only a direct hit by an artillery shell would have damaged it. Somehow we were very proud of our work, which took a good week to complete with two shifts a day. We eagerly awaited an inspection by the *Kommandeur*.

It was *Oberstleutnant* August Schmitz who got out of the car, and although he had been with the *Brigade* for several months, this was the first time we had seen him.

Oberstleutnant August Ludwig Schmitz, *Kommandeur* of the *Sturmgeschütze* Brigade of *I.Fallschirm.Korps*. He was the former commander of *Fallsch-Panzer-Jäger-Abteilung* of the *7.Fliegerdivision* on Crete and in Russia. Born on 22 October 1907, he was killed on 26 April 1945 near Verona. (Rudolf Jackl)

Our *Zugführer* reported the completion of the bunker. The officer greeted him briefly, went into the house, looked into the shelter and asked for the coating thickness. The 1m seemed sufficient to him. He nodded again, got back into his car and was gone. The whole inspection had only taken a few minutes. We *Pioniers*, who expected a word of appreciation or a pat on the back, were very disappointed. He never even used the bunker for its intended purpose.

The house bunker was the last work carried out by the *Pionierzug* in its entirety. For further missions in the *Brigade* area, only individual groups were used as required. Our positions stretched both sides of the *Via Emilia* between Senio and Santerno. The small rivers are comparable to the

---

9   In April 1945, the Allies would launch their major offensive north to Ravenna and Lake Commachio, thereby threatening to encircle the Senio Position.

German Ahr River, and only a few meters deep.[10] Over the Santerno we built some hidden planks, helped the *Sturmgeschützen* in the emplacements, managed to de-obstruct lines of fire, repaired field fortifications and damaged paths and were brought in to conduct blasting operations.

Pioniers were in demand for everything. We had fun while building dummy positions. With boards, we quickly made a dummy tank and used a round length of wood for a barrel. Under the cover of darkness, a *Sturmgeschütz* drove up to the dummy tank and then returned over the same tracks to add some realism. This fooled the *Jabos*, and we observed them swooping down and firing off their ammunition. Here too the 'Iron Gustav' turned around searching for targets. In the absence of the *Luftwaffe*, enemy aviation was a constant danger for all soldiers who were on foot.

I soon built up a good relationship with our *Zugführer*. It did not take long for the informal conversational use of 'you'. Only when we were alone of course! He would often pull me out of *Gruppe* service to be at his disposal. Two of my talents caught his eye: the ability to sketch quickly and note down details. This was probably why I became an engineer after the war.

I do not know if the possibility of retreat had been considered, but in any case the *Kommandeur* decided to determine the most favourable departure route for each assault gun. This required adequate maps. Only *Oberstleutnant* Schmitz had a good general staff map with a scale of 1:50 000. This was a most secret document, as all the command posts, positions and even Army artillery batteries were registered on it. Appropriate sections of this map had to be copied, particularly locations, watercourses and roads. The *Zugführer* commissioned me to carry out this delicate task. I sat in the commander's room with a staff room *Feldwebel*. Tracing paper was used to copy the original map and I worked diligently, even adding descriptions and labels, creating acceptable copies of the original. Each *Kompanie* received a copy of their relevant section.

The English [sic] artillery fired daily harassing fire, normally consisting of salvos of four rounds. We could only dream of such ammunition consumption. Our guns were under orders not to fire unless we were attacked. I remember a funny event when we were at the farmstead. There was sudden firing and we heard the salvos howling. With a leap we jumped behind the house and into cover. The shells detonated in the nearby vineyard without causing any damage, only one man was unlucky because he jumped too far and ended up knee-deep in a septic tank. I cannot repeat the words that came out of his mouth. On one occasion the firing came close to being fatal. The Santerno road bridge in Imola was a very important location for our *Brigade* and suffered shell damage. I stood with *Oberfeldwebel* Schmitz and a motorcycle rider discussing the levelling of the shell craters. The Tommies suddenly opened fire on this bottleneck. After the dull firing noise came the howling salvo. We just managed to throw ourselves into a ditch before they struck the ground. We scrambled away covered in dirt and dust, but luckily nobody had been injured. Again, I cannot repeat the words that came out of our mouths!

Our capable rider and his *Zündapp* motorcycle had discovered a wine cellar containing delicious red wine, but obtaining the wine required certain paperwork to be submitted to a certain Army *Zahlmeister*. The boss of the *Stabskompanie*, *Leutnant* Tonko, was grateful for the tip-off and hastily prepared the required paperwork. The *Zündapp* set off with me as a passenger and a 50-litre glass demi-john in the sidecar to pick up the wine. Everything went well despite the bumpy journey. When we returned we unloaded the wine under expectant eyes. Did we not handle the heavy glass balloon delicately enough, or was there a pebble on the ground? Anyway, there was a crack, the glass broke and 50 litres of wine suddenly created a large puddle around us. We barely escaped a lynching, and again I will not say the words that fell on our ears. *Oberfeldwebel* Schmitz provided new paperwork so we could receive a replacement supply the next day, but I declined the offer to collect it again.

---

10   The Ahr is a tributary of the River Rhine.

Our *Zugführer* liked to sit with his people in the evenings, especially since we had a supply of wine. One evening we consumed Marsala wine, and in the morning we all suffered from severe hangovers. I like to think back to those evenings.

At the end of February 1945, one could already feel a spring awakening in the Po Valley, and from a distance we even had subtle lighting. The British had aimed their *Flak* searchlights vertically to mark the front line for their returning bombers.

Our commander, *Oberstleutnant* August Schmitz, was already an old man to us youngsters. To me he was not an accessible person and was bad mannered. He had lost an eye at Dunkirk in 1940. His hobby was conducting war games for the *Stabskompanie* on a large sand table, where *Brigade* sections were modelled and attack scenarios considered. Every week he would give tactical lessons to about 20 men from the *Sturmgeschütz* crews. He would invent an attack situation and then delegate someone to suggest countermeasures for that attack. This moment was always feared and always followed by harsh criticism. *Leutnant* Tonko was often one of his victims. *Oberstleutnant* Schmitz did not survive the war. He was killed at the end of April 1945 near Verona. His final resting place was a collective grave in the German cemetery at Costermano.[11]

On 3 March 1945, the day ended with a tragic event. At dusk we sat in front of the house and drank *vino* together. The hour was popular as the *Zug* was scattered during the day and we did not meet up until the evening. Concerns were raised and problems were discussed. *Oberfeldwebel* Schmitz had an open ear for anything. Nobody noticed that *Oberjäger* Heinz Bruhn was missing. He was sitting with the farmer in the kitchen, having been given some mail from home.

Suddenly a shot rang out! We all got up and rushed into the house. Heinz was bent over the table in a pool of blood. He had shot himself in the head with his P08 pistol. The bloodstained paper revealed that his fiancée had left him. The *Zugführer* rushed over to the command post and soon the *Kommandeur* turned up with the Staff doctor. He officially stated suicide by gunshot wound to the head. Everyone had to leave the room, and only the officers and the *Zugführer* were allowed to stay and discuss the necessary actions.

Having left instructions not to move or touch anything, they drove back to the command post. The farmers who had been sat by the hearth were outraged. We tried to calm them down, as they had nothing to do with it. Around midnight, the *Zugführer* returned. The suicide had been reported by telephone to the military court. Its verdict was a shocking example of heartless military justice:

- The suicide victim is hereby expelled from the German *Wehrmacht*.
- The dead person may not be buried in a public cemetery.
- The body is to be buried naked in an open field.
- The gravesite is to be levelled and unrecognisable.
- The erection of a memorial cross is prohibited.
- Execution of these orders are to be reported to the military court.

---

11   In a letter from December 1997, former *Hauptmann* Günter Hartmann Kompaniechef of *1 KP* wrote to Rudolf Jackl regarding their former *Kommandeur*: Schmitz spent only a few days at Bosco Chiesanuova because he had to go to Abano for medical treatment. He then fell on the way back to Bosco. In the car with him were his driver Heinrich Peters and his secretary, office *Feldwebel* Willi Demmer. Willi Demmer wrote in 1946: "It was on 26th April 1945 at 8 o'clock in the evening. It was cloudy and already quite dark. I cannot say with certainty whether the shooters were partisans or enemy troops. We were at the entrance of San Martino and were shot at with a machine gun. The car stopped after about 80m. Peters told me 'the *Kommandeur* is dead'. The *Oberstleutnant* had a wound on the back of his head and one on his left eye, probably an exit wound." Peters and Demmer were able to flee but had to leave the commander in the car.

By lamplight, the bitter work began. In front of a gnarled willow tree at the homestead enclosure, we dug a grave. The undressed corpse was placed on a board and covered with a tarpaulin. Then the levelling of the grave took place, according to the judgement of the military court. So we silently buried *Oberjäger* Heinz Bruhn. We had lost an experienced *Pionier* and a good friend.

In the morning, *Oberfeldwebel* Schmitz took the man's equipment and personal belongings to the *Stabskompanie* and reported the burial completion. I do not know what was told to the relatives of the dead man. We could not understand the dishonour placed upon this proven and decorated *Oberjäger*. One could have declared what happened as an accident as a result of cleaning his weapon. Three days later, a wooden cross appeared on the grave overnight with the inscription: Heinz Bruhn 3.3.45. Nobody removed it, regardless of the military court ruling!

Many years later, I stood in the Futa Pass cemetery, searched for and found graves of my comrades from the *Pionierzug* of *Fallschirm-Sturmgeschütz-Brigade* 'Schmitz'. One plate moved me dearly: Heinz Bruhn 3.3.45. The brave farmers had reported the grave at the end of the war, so my friend found a worthy resting place amongst 30,000 others who lost their lives.

A little later we finally received some good news. Our popular *Zugführer* was promoted to *Leutnant*. This was another award for him. During the war, this field-tested and decorated *Oberfeldwebel* could be part of the officer corps without attending war school. Georg Schmitz certainly met these conditions as a fêted Cassino veteran. He wore both Iron Crosses and a tank destruction badge on his upper arm. It goes without saying that this promotion was thoroughly celebrated.

September 1945. POW internment camp at Grottaglie in Taranto. *Fahnenjunker-Oberjäger* Rudolf Jackl (third from right) and *Leutnant* Georg Schmitz (fourth from right). Note the weight loss experienced in captivity. (Rudolf Jackl)

Epilogue

In the middle of March 1945, our front area became a so-called quiet section and the enemy did not attack. The expansion to a *Pionier Kompanie* was further pursued and the appropriate men were sent to NCO schools. *Oberjäger* Wolf and I were commandeered to an officer selection course at the leadership school of the *I. Fallschirm-Korps* in Bosco Chiesanuova, north of Verona. The men of this final course were utilised during the great collapse as *Kampfgruppe Bosco*, which was wiped out in the Bondeno / Po bridgehead.

I met some of my comrades in the Etschtal (in the Adige Valley) after the capitulation on 6 May 1945, where we stayed together. Later, in September 1945, there was a joyful reunion with *Leutnant* Georg Schmitz at the internment camp at Grottaglie near Taranto in southern Italy.

(Rudolf Jackl passed away in March 2017, aged 93.)

4

Sebastian Krug

A veteran of many fronts

Sebastian Krug was born in the Allgäu region of Bavaria on 14 January 1920 and volunteered to become a Fallschirmjäger *in January 1939. He joined the ranks of FJR2, and on completion of his training took part in the Polish ground campaign. Whilst in Poland, Krug threatened to shoot an SS soldier and was later reported. Only the intervention of his commanding officers saved him from the clutches of the Gestapo. He took part in the invasion of the Holland in May 1940, the capture of the Corinth Canal bridge in April 1941, the invasion of Crete in May 1941 and completed three tours of duty on the Eastern Front. Towards the end of the war he took part in the chaotic withdrawal from the eastern provinces back to Germany, where he surrendered to US forces at the end of April 1945. After the war, Krug became a border guard until his retirement. In 1992 he conducted three parachute jumps in Russia, and in 1993, at the age of 73, he took part in a parachute jump in Crete, 52 years after his combat jump over the island on 20 May 1941.*

Feldwebel Sebastian Krug in 1943 with Iron Cross 1st Class, parachute qualification badge, silver wound badge, *Luftwaffe* ground assault badge and the Crete campaign cuff title on his left sleeve. (Sebastian Krug)

Sebastian Krug aboard a Hercules aircraft prior to his jump over Crete on 23 May 1993. He was 73 years old. (Sebastian Krug)

Recruitment & training

I attended school from April 1926 until April 1933, and after that I attended a continuation school for two winters. From February 1935 until October 1938 I was employed as a farmer, working six-and-a-half days a week and sleeping under bare roof tiles on straw sacks at home. I could no longer put up with these primitive conditions, so I volunteered for the *Wehrmacht* and was recruited on 15 October 1938 to join *11. Kompanie* of the *SA Regiment Feldherrnhalle* in Stuttgart.[1] In December I was ordered to Hattingen in the Ruhr, and in January 1939 I volunteered to become a *Fallschirmjäger* – the medical and fitness examinations were conducted in Cologne in April 1939.

On 20 April 1939, I participated in the parade for Hitler's 50th birthday in Berlin and at the beginning of June 1939, I was officially accepted into the *Fallschirmtruppe* and joined *3. Kompanie* of *FJR2*, a newly created unit based at Gardelegen. The *Zugführer* was *Oberleutnant* Arnold von Roon and the *Bataillonskommandeur* was *Hauptmann* Herbert Noster.[2] From 20 June until 30 July 1939, I carried out jump training at Stendal. This consisted of six jumps from 400–120 metres. Afterward I was sent on an infantry and a medics course and I also gained my driving licence 3rd class.

In the summer of 1939, *3. Kompanie* was disbanded and divided in to the other three *Kompanien* and I was ordered to *4. Kompanie* under the command of *Hauptmann* Günter Morawetz.

4.Kompanie, Fallschirmjäger Regiment 2, under the command of *Hauptmann* Günter Morawetz, pose for a *Kompanie* photo at the Sansoucci Palace in Potsdam in October 1940. Morawetz and one of his Zugfuhrers, *Oberleutnant* Simon, are missing as they were elsewhere on *Kompanie* business. The two officers are possibly *Oberleutnant* Heinz Klopges and *Leutnant* Franz Hüttner. (Sebastian Krug)

---

1   Many men from the *SA Regiment Feldherrnhalle* volunteered to become *Fallschirmjäger* and joined *FJR2*. (Private correspondence with Sebastian Krug)
2   On 10 May, Herbert Noster was wounded and became a prisoner of the Dutch and then the British. In November 1943 he was exchanged for a British officer and he had to give his word as an officer that he would only return to homeland service. He went on to serve on the front line in Normandy in 1944 and later killed himself during the battle for Berlin in April 1945. Many of his former comrades believe he committed suicide because he could not live with himself having broken his word of honour as an officer. (Jackl)

On 12 September we were sent by truck from Gardelegen to Breslau-Liegnitz (Legnica) in Lower Silesia, the staging area for the invasion of Poland, and placed on standby for a parachute mission.

End of August 1939 at Lüben near the Polish border during the build-up to the campaign in Poland. (Sebastian Krug)

Fall Weiss (Case White) – The Invasion of Poland

Whilst in Liegnitz, we sat with parachutes on our backs in the Ju-52s, the engines were running. Then we were told unexpectedly "everyone out of the airplanes, the airborne mission has been cancelled!"

On 25 September, *I/FJR2* was airlifted to the Deblin airfield to support *I/FJR1*. The nearby River Weichsel (River Vistula) was the demarcation line between the German and Russian zones. On the other side of the Weichsel were tonnes of copper, zinc, lead, mercury, weapons and other war materiel stored at the Deblin airfield. On 25 September, we assisted *I/FJR1* in transporting these precious raw materials across the Weichsel demarcation line in trucks before the Russians arrived to prevent it falling into their hands.

Return to Germany

At the end of September, before the capitulation of Poland, we left the operational area and were transported back to our barracks in Gardelegen. During our return through Poland our convoy was halted. Jewish men were being forced to clear the rubble on the street, and I suddenly recognised a Jewish man from my hometown. I talked to him but he did not answer. Immediately an *SS* soldier came running over to us with his rifle at the ready and ordered us to move. My comrades and I told him to piss off or there would be 'blue beans' for him [blue beans is a word for bullets]. He quickly took his rifle and walked off.

When I returned to my hometown after the war, I was told that the Jewish man and his whole family did not live there anymore.

During our time in Poland, the barracks in Gardelegen had been occupied by *Luftwaffe* pilots. We were sent to Klosterneuendorf (4km east of Gardelegen) to occupy private rooms on farms. Until we could return to our barracks, we helped the farmers with the beetharvest.

In January 1940, I was sent on a locomotive engine driver course in Berlin-Pankow and at the beginning of May, we were sent to Münster, where we slept on the ground in aircraft hangars.

On 9 May 1940, the day before the invasion of the Low Countries, we attended a mission briefing where every soldier was informed of his assault target and mission. In case we

During the return journey to Germany from Poland in September 1939, Sebastian witnessed forced labourers preparing roads under guard by SS soldiers. He threatened to shoot an SS guard after speaking to a Jewish man he knew from his hometown. (Sebastian Krug)

should lose our leaders during the assaults, everyone had to be able to take over the leadership himself in order to accomplish the mission.

I was sent with a heavy machine gun to *3. Kompanie*, under the command of *Oberleutnant* Arnold von Roon. *3. Kompanie* had to take the auxilliary airfield at Ockenburg in Holland.[3] Once the airfield had been captured it would be used to land elements of *Infantry Regiment 65* of the *22. Luftlande-Division*.[4]

Fall Gelb (Case Yellow) – The Invasion of the Low Countries

On 10 May 1940, we were woken up at 0300 hours to get ready for battle and to board the JU-52s. We took off at 0500 hours. After a two-hour flight to Holland, we were dropped with 70 men, 10km south-west from the target. During the flight we had met hardly any anti-aircraft fire. As we reached the target area, we saw explosion clouds very close to our aircraft. *Flak* ripped 1 metre off the left wing of our JU-52, which gave us all a bad feeling about the mission.

A short distance away from us was a JU-52 that had been hit and started to burn. The aircraft was going down, and the *Fallschirmjäger* that jumped from this low altitude were killed immediately.

After our successful jump onto an open field, we all met at the collection point in a forest. There was a road through the forest that the Dutch used to travel to work, so we requisitioned all the vehicles that passed us. Our *Kompanieführer* estimated the cars' value and gave their owner a piece

---

3   Ockenburg, along with the airfields at Valkenburg and Ypenburg, were to be captured in order to land elements of the *22. Luftlande-Division* and advance on The Hague.

4   Formerly the *22nd Infantry Division* and it was trained in air-landing operations in 1939. These air-transportable troops could be landed on the ground once paratroops had secured the landing areas.

of paper, so these people could later claim money for their cars from the German government. We took the car owners some of the way with us so they could not tell enemy troops that we had landed.

I was posted with my machine gun on the cabin of a truck and we drove into Grafensande on the Hook of Holland, the nearest town to us. As we entered the town, we met heavy resistance from Dutch soldiers. There was gunfire from all of the houses. I was shot through the ear and also received a flesh wound to the left side of my head. As fast as I could, I took cover with my machine gun in a water trench next to the street.

Some minutes later there were Dutch troops coming from our rear on motorcycles. Some of them took cover behind a small wall in front of a cafe and fired at us.

Our *Kompanieführer* stood on a balcony and ordered everyone to go back and make an assault on the cafe. One of our *Feldwebels* rushed from the other side of the street to the cafe and shot all of the Dutch soldiers lying behind the wall with his *MPi*. I gave my machine gun to a comrade, ran with my pistol into the cafe and checked all the rooms. On the upper floor I found a Dutch medic. I took him prisoner and afterward let him bandage my wounds.

Our *Kompanieführer* ordered me and another lightly injured comrade, who had been shot through the upper arm, to take the Dutch prisoners out of the town. We were only armed with pistols, and the Dutch soldiers still carried their own weapons and ammo. We made sure that we took out the receivers beforehand.

In an open field we received fire from Dutch heavy howitzers. We immediately took cover. The prisoners did not want to make a move with all the shells flying around, so we let them lie down, while we left and tried to rejoin our *Kompanie*, which in the meantime had disappeared into the forest.

After more than an hour of walking around we eventually found our *Kompanie* in the forest. We came across many dead and wounded on the way. We were very lucky that we did not become prisoners.

In the meantime, elements of our *22. Luftlande-Division* landed in the streets and other open spaces because the airport at Ockenburg was still in Dutch hands. Once on the ground, the JU-52s could not take-off again. We had to form a hedgehog defensive position in the forest. One *Zug* from *3. Kompanie* jumped onto the airport at Ypenburg to the east of The Hague. All of them were either killed, wounded or taken prisoner. Because we were running out of ammo, we took out all the guns and ammunition from the JU-52s.

The Dutch had surrounded us in the forest. Some JU-52s dropped ammunition for us, but unfortunately everything landed in a open field. Neither us or the Dutch would dare recover the containers. During the night we tried out our luck and we managed to recover one of them.

During the night of 11–12 May, we were ordered to break out of the encirclement. I was ordered to make some fireworks as a feint attack at the rear of the breakout area. The breakout was a complete success. I had to stop the fireworks display and follow the *Kompanie*, who fired flares from the direction that they were marching. Near daybreak we reached the village of Wateringen on the outskirts of The Hague.

To fool the Dutch we marched in line formation. When they finally recognised us they opened fire. I rushed into the nearest house. All the residents were sleeping peacefully in their beds, and were very shocked when I switched on the lights.

I quickly left the house and tried to find my comrades. I soon came across a *Feldwebel*, who had been ordered to occupy a nearby schoolhouse. The *Feldwebel* and I jumped over the schoolyard wall and took position by the wall of the building. Minutes later, bullets penetrated the wall just centimetres next to us. The *Feldwebel* was shot through the chest and he collapsed onto me. I was covered in his blood. I ran as fast as I could back to the schoolyard wall and jumped over it. Once again I had to try to find my comrades, which was not so easy because the enemy was all around us.

Finally I came across *Oberleutnant* von Roon and reported the death of the *Feldwebel*. He told me that the schoolhouse was the Dutch headquarters.

General Graf von Sponeck (*Kommandeur* of the *22. Luftlande-Division*) received the order to go to Overschie via Wateringen and Delft. *3. Kompanie* had to provide the rearguard. Overschie is between Rotterdam and Schiedam, and in Overschie the Dutch welcomed us with a hail of fire. We just managed to escape into a lacquer factory. In this factory and the nearby houses, we built up our defensive positions.

Myself and a comrade took up a position with our *MG* on a boat in the canal beside the street. We were instructed to shut off the street, which we managed for some time.

When the Dutch noticed us on the boat they opened fire, so we had to leave very quickly. In the lacquer factory we marked the ground with swastikas so our airplanes could easily find us.

Rotterdam was bombed. The bombs came down not far from us. On 15 May, we saw the white flag flying over Rotterdam and in the afternoon our *Panzers* rolled in and liberated us. Finally we came to a hotel in Bad Scheveningen, and after that to the Hotel Central in Den Haag.

We were taken back in confiscicated buses to Gardelegen in Germany. When we arrived there we were welcomed with ringing bells and open arms, but we were more concerned with our many dead and wounded comrades. Some weeks later we were transfered to Magdeburg and raised back to full strength.

Preparations for the invasion of England

At the beginning of July 1940, we were sent to a barracks in Paris. There was to be a regimental parade, put together under the authority of *Oberst* Bruno Bräuer and called the 'World Peace Parade', but because England did not want to make peace the big parade was cancelled and we took part in a smaller parade instead.

At first, we had a good time in Paris. After the many evenings in the city there were several alcohol-related deaths. French civilians brought some soldiers back to the barracks very much worse for wear. There were many arrests during the next day because these men had alledgedly damaged the repuation of the German *Wehrmacht*.

From Paris we were transfered to Döberitz near Berlin to prepare for the invasion of England. The invasion was cancelled, and instead we were sent on winter training in the Alps. From there we went back to the barracks at Döberitz.

Assault on the Isthmus of Corinth

On 27 March 1941, we were transported south by train across Bad Vöslau to Wiener Neustadt, Budapest, Bucharest, Sofia, through the Schipka Pass in the Balkan Mountains to Malokonare in Bulgaria. The whole *Bataillon* was transported on one long train. In spite of two locomotives, the Bulgarian engine drivers were not able to bring the train across the Schipka Pass. The *Bataillonskommandeur*, *Hauptmann* Hans Kroh, called together all of the trained engine drivers, and with united manpower we managed to bring the train across the pass.

The whole *Bataillon* stayed in tents near Malokonare. In the morning, Bulgarian women came over to us with baskets full of eggs at 0.5 pfennings each. We said goodbye to the field-kitchen and filled our stomachs with eggs.

Not only was 20 April Hitler's birthday, it was also the Bulgarian Easter celebrations. We were invited to celebrate with the Bulgarian families. There was everything you could imagine, including mutton. We celebrated well into the night, and some of the men could not find their tents in the morning. From Malokonare we went to Sofia to watch an entertaining event hosted by some German actors.

On 24 April, we were transferred to the airport near Plovdiv. I drove in advance with an *Oberjäger* in a truck loaded with parachutes. All the other men followed in the Tante JUs. When we arrived at the airfield near Plovdiv, we saw female underwear hanging in front of two barrack houses, so we went over to take a look.

On the door was a piece of paper that said, 'Visiting the ladies after X hours only', so we were not allowed to go in. Being soldiers, we went in anyway and found ourselves in an anteroom.

The *Oberjäger* sat on a chair and I stood by the door. Just minutes later a young lady came in and took a seat on the *Oberjäger*'s lap.

No sooner had she sat down than a *Stabsgefreiter* showed up with a rifle hanging around his neck. He was from the *Jagdgeschwader* unit that was stationed at the airfield and he ordered us to leave the room immediately. The girl quickly hurried away. The *Stabsgefreiter* unlocked the safety catch of his rifle and told us that he would count to three, and if we hadn't left then he would open fire. We did not believe that he was serious, so we stayed where we were. However, the *Stabsgefreiter* was not in the mood for games; he counted to three and then shot the *Oberjäger* through the chest.

This caused a lot of trouble. The man was arrested and we *Fallschirmjäger* were grounded.

On 25 April, we were transferred with the JU-52s to Larissa. That night we slept under the aircraft. On 26 April, we received the order to put on the parachutes and prepare ourselves for an assault on the Corinth Canal in the Peloponnese of Greece.

When we crossed the mountains at an altitude of 1,500m, we flew into a hailstorm. Visibility was terrible. The JU-52 flying on our right had been lost by the time the storm was over. Later, it was revealed that it had smashed into a mountain and only the two men standing in the door were able to jump out, without chutes, into the deep snow. All the others were killed. The two survivors had to walk through the snow to a low-lying village, where they were well looked after. They came down to the valley on a donkey, where they met German soldiers.

As we approached the canal we were met by strong anti-aircraft fire. We suffered many jump casualties on the stony and hilly ground. Our *Bataillon* jumped on the northern side of the canal. Our mission was to stop the English [*sic*] troops that had rushed southward and take them prisoner. We had no idea what we were going to do with so many prisoners.

A short time after our jump I heard a fearsome explosion and I saw the canal bridge crumple and fall into the 80m-deep gorge. Several *Fallschirmjäger* and a war correspondent were lost when the bridge blew up. Our *Kompanie* then built a temporary bridge at the mouth of the canal.

A German *Panzer* unit arrived on 29 April. For us the battle was over. Now we had to recover the dead, bury them and take the wounded to the field hospitals.

After the battle we stayed for some time at the canal near Loutraki. We had to capture small ships along with their crews in the Peloponnese, so that they could later carry our heavy guns and the *Gebirgsjäger* on to Crete. On 15 May, we were transferred to the airfield at Megara in Greece.

Operation Mercury

On 20 May, our whole *Bataillon, I/FJR2*, was supposed to jump in the second wave at Rethymnon in order to take the airport and town.[5]

---

5   Rethymnon (*Gruppe Mitte*) and Heraklion (*Gruppe Ost*) were objectives of the second wave in the afternoon of 20 May.

Not all of the JU-52s returned from the first wave that dropped paratroops in the morning at Chania and Maleme. Some that did return were badly damaged. We were supposed to start at 1300 hours, but not all of the men could go due to the lack of aircraft.

I was very sorry that I wasn't going with them. Maybe it was luck that I did not jump with my *Kompanie*, because none of the officers and very few NCOs survived the jump; most of them were killed in the air by heavy ground fire. Out of 156 men who jumped, 140 of them now lie in the cemetry at Maleme, including *Hauptmann* Morawetz.[6]

I was dropped late in the afternoon with my *Gruppe* from *4./FJR2* in front of the west gate at Heraklion.[7]

When we were approaching the drop zone, the *Jäger* standing in the door was shot through the foot and had to fly back with the aircraft. Once on the ground, many men could not reach their weapon containers so they had to defend themselves with only pistols and hand grenades. After the jump we encountered heavy fighting against British and Greek troops, as well as civilians. During the night we did not know who was friend or foe, so we tried to group ourselves as best as we could.

As a password we used the name Hermann Göring. The approaching man had to say 'Hermann' and the sentry had to reply 'Göring'. Unfortunately, some of the British troops spoke excellent German and they baited our *Jäger* out from their cover, which meant either death or captivity.

The grave of *Major* Günter Morawetz at the Maleme cemetery. (aretecrete.com)

Outside the Chanioporto in Heraklion, where several *Fallschirmjäger* from *III/FJR1* were killed when they landed close to the gate. It was also attacked on 21 May in an unsuccessful attempt to capture the town and harbour. (Jose Ramon Artaza Ibañez)

---

6   Listed as a major on the Volksbund website. According to Richter, p.131, *4 & 1/FJR2* were dropped correctly to the east of the Rethymnon airfield, but were engulfed by the Australian defenders who were occupying the vine-covered Hill A, east of the airfield, in well-camouflaged positions. All of the officers from *4/FJR2* fell and both *Kompanien* suffered heavy losses.

7   The town of Heraklion and the airfield east of the town were objectives of *FJR1*, assisted by *II/FJR2* under the command of *Hauptmann* Gerhart Schirmer. Schirmer's *Bataillon* jumped west of the town to cover the western approaches. The west gate was known as Chanioporto. See Prekatsounakis, p.161. It would appear that Krug's *Gruppe* were dropped further east than planned, near Chanioporto, in the area of *III/FJR1*.

sMG from *8/FJR2* on a hill near Gazi, west of Heraklion, on 25 May 1941. (Karl Jörger)

A high wall surrounded the town of Heraklion, with only a few gates for access. The wall was so big that it made an excellent observation point for the enemy. They could cover the whole area in front of the wall with their guns.

On 21 May, we attacked the west gate, which had been barricaded with rocks and stones.[8] We successfully breached the gate and almost made it to the town centre and the harbour mole, but the British chased us back out of the town. We attempted another attack, but it was unsuccessful. After that, the British attacked our positions, but they could not dislodge us. We carried out smaller attacks to win some ground, but that ground would only be held for a few hours.

During one such attack we witnessed a cruel incident. A heavily wounded *Fallschirmjäger* had been nailed naked, upside down, on to a wooden gate. His genitals had been cut off and were stuck in his mouth. This *Jäger* must have been wounded during one of our assaults and then butchered by the locals. At other times, dum-dum bullets were used against us, which caused dreadful wounds.[9] Another incident happened when I was ordered to carry a wounded *Jäger* to the field dressing station. On passing a vineyard, I heard moaning and saw a civilian with a machine-pistol in his hands firing single rounds. I dropped my wounded comrade, crouched and moved into cover near the civilian. He suddenly saw me and tried to shoot me, but my *MPi* was faster!

Shortly after, I noticed the victim, who was one of my comrades. He was lying on the ground seriously wounded. The civilian had taken the *MPi* from him and then slowly fired single rounds from the feet upwards into the defenceless *Jäger*. I carried the wounded man to the field dressing station and then returned to collect my other wounded comrade from where I had dropped him. When I returned to the dressing station a few days later, I learned that both men had died.

8   Chanioporto was attacked by *10/FJR1* under the command of *Oberleutnant* Egger and joined by an attack group from *FJR2*.

9   Dum dum rounds expand on impact, causing more damage than conventional rounds, and use of these bullets contravenes the 1899 Hague Convention. These wounds were more likely to have been caused by the large 11mm rounds fired by the Fusil Gras Model 1874 rifle, which was still used by Greek forces and Cretan civilians.

The doctors and medical staff at the dressing station were running dangerously short on medical supplies. Even lightly wounded men were dying like flies.

The list of atrocities by Cretan civilians was endless. The British disapproved of this but were powerless to stop them. During the evening of 25 May, *Oberst* Bräuer gave the order to evacuate the positions near the west gate and to march south-east by night, without any noise, to Hill 296 (Apex Hill), located south of the airfield at Heraklion. It was almost morning when we reached our new positions.

When we attempted an assault on the hill, the British welcomed us with a fearful firestorm. We eventually managed to occupy the hill, but we suffered heavy casualties in the process.

We laid down in our new positions on the hill, with no shade to protect us from the baking sun, and we were exhausted through lack of sleep and dehydrated from lack of water. All this was under constant British bombardment. After six days we felt that even death did not matter any more. The water source was under direct fire. It was only possible to obtain water at night, and only then with helmets and parachute cord. The well was surrounded by dead and wounded, men who had tried before in desparation to get some water. The British heavy weapons were zeroed in on the well and they only had to pull the trigger if someone came in sight.

Late on the afternoon of 27 May, a JU-52 landed on the reverse side of Hill 296. The aircraft brought in ammunition, food and medical supplies.[10] The landing strip was covered in rocks and bushes, and was far from flat. The aircraft was filled with wounded men and began its return trip. We felt goose bumps on our necks as it reached the slope of the hill during its short take-off. It took off, dropped, and then headed upwards into the sky. A great perfomance, and all under artillery fire.

Some of my comrades took some ammo for our mortar. One of my comrades dropped two boxes of ammo behind our position. As he dropped it, the boxes exploded, killing several men.

Later, we fired some mortar rounds toward one of the roads near the hill. Unknown to us, however, there was a British field hospital near the road. Several rounds hit the hospital because of this misunderstanding. *Oberst* Bruno Bräuer gave the order that some men should take a white flag, go to the hospital and apologise for the incident. I marched along with some comrades down the hill to the hopsital.

We dropped our weapons outside and went in. The British did not differentiate between friend or foe; they saved the lives of both sides. After our visit we got something to eat and drink, picked up our weapons and walked back towards the hill. After our return the shooting began once again.

Oberst Bräuer had an agreement with the British that our wounded would be picked up at a certain time and taken to hospital, and vice-versa.

During the night of 29 May, the British evacuated Heraklion and the surrounding areas. We had been ordered to attack on that day, but it was cancelled. We could now occupy the town and airfield without a battle. On that same day, *Fallschirmjäger* and *Gebirgsjäger* reached us from Rethymnon.

After the fighting we spent some time relaxing on the beach, where a tragic accident was about to take place. We laid in a circle on the beach, playing cards. One comrade loaded his pistol and a shot suddenly rang out, hitting another young *Jäger*, killing him instantly.

---

10   *Oberleutnant* Franz Lankenau from *7/KG z.b.V.1*, flew in supplies and embarked 20 seriously wounded men late in the afternoon of 27 May. See Prekatsounakis, p.242.

The return home and a lucky escape

We were eventually loaded onto trucks and taken to Maleme, and from there flew back to Magara in Greece. We then drove up through Europe via Skopje in Yugoslavia to Berlin. During this journey I was a *Bataillon* despatch rider with a motorbike and sidecar, and on the way I had to tell the vehicles the location of the next meeting point.

On 15 July 1941, there was a big regimental parade on the Seestrasse in Berlin. There was a huge welcome from the public. After this we received a few days' leave. During my leave, the committee of the *Kyffhäuserbund* asked me to make a report, to tell the story of my experiences up until then.[11] During my report ,which was two hours long, some of the committee wrote my words down. I did not know if they were reporters or whether they were from the *Gestapo*. A short time later I found out more about this episode. I received a telegram which said that I had to return immediately to my *Bataillon* in Berlin.

I was told the reason from our *Kreisleiter*.[12] I had been reported to the police because during my report/story I mentioned the episode with the Jewish man, when my comrades and I ridiculed the *SS* soldier. With telegram in hand, I arrived at our barracks. I immediately had to meet with my new *Kompanieführer, Oberleutnant* Raimund Nagele, who had a copy of the telegram. I also had to report to the *Bataillonskommandeur, Hauptmann* Hans Kroh, who also had a copy. Kroh also had a copy of the *Gestapo* report, but he declared it as nonsense. I have to thank these two officers that the incident did not go to a military court.

After my leave, our unit was rebuilt and we were moved to the military manoeuvring ground at Grafenwöhr. Afterward, we returned to our old barracks at Gardelegen.

Orders to move east

On 1 December 1941, a new operational order came in: 'Move to Russia'!

On 6 December, our reinforced *Regiment* under the command of *Oberst* Alfred Sturm was moved by railway transport (30 men in a goods wagon) to Dnepropetrovsk (Dnipro) on the west bank of the Dnieper River in the Ukraine.[13]

After a few days' break, we travelled even further south-east, across Stalino (Donetsk) to Charzyk near the River Mius. The temperature was around minus 30 degrees centigrade with snowstorms, and we had to march 40km to our mission area in this weather. On 27 December, we reached the ordered area, where we were subordinated to an Italian *Division*.[14]

The Russians had pushed the Italians out of their positions again and again, so we had to push the Russians back with a counterattack. As a *Gruppeführer*, I had orders to to take position beside the train tracks near a signalman's house. Digging a hole was impossible; the ground was frozen. Digging with the spade was hopeless. Again and again the Russians attacked, but not before they delivered a shellstorm from all barrels of their artillery.

During one attack with the dreaded Stalin Organ, I lost my whole *Gruppe*.[15] All were dead, some were terribly mutilated, legs ripped off, destroyed limbs or just ripped into pieces, so that sometimes an

---

11 *Kyffhäuserbund* was a war veterans and reservists association.

12 The local *NSDAP* leader.

13 This reinforced regiment consisted of *I* & *II/FJR2, IV/LL.St.Rgt, Fallsch.Pz.Jager.Abt*, MG.Btl.7 and *2/ Fallschirm-Sanitäts-Abteilung XI Fliegerkorps*.

14 3rd *Celere* (Cavalry) *Division* under the command of General Mazarani, part of the Italian Expeditionary Corps in Russia.

15 The dreaded truck-mounted Katyusha-rocket launcher.

Werner Eichler (right) and his comrades, having arrived in the Ukraine. Although the temperature was below freezing, the men had their regular *Fallschirmjäger* clothing and no winter clothes except greatcoats. (Kate Eichler)

Men of the *Fallschirm-Panzerjäger-Abteilung* prepare to move east to Russia with *Regiment Sturm*. Werner Eichler is on the far right. (Kate Eichler)

identification of the body was impossible. I received new men by order. The Russians always attacked again and again with an endless amount of men. We began to run low on ammunition because of this.

During our counterattacks we came across many Russians. Some were dead, but others pretended that they were dead and shot our men in the back. That was a warning to us for the future. The men who were seriously wounded and had not been evacuated, died from the cold. At the beginning of April 1942, we should have been relieved and transported back to Germany. At Stalino we were deloused, then put on to trains heading west. Then we went north, across Tosno (Tocho) to the Volkhov River.

When we at last arrived east of Leningrad, the muddy period began. All vehicles, even tanks, became stuck in the mud and had to be pulled or pushed out. Corduroy roads had to be built using logs in order to move vehicles over the impassable terrain.

We were attacked by Russian troops again and again. In the forest area where we were located, you would get lost without a compass. It was either cold, approximately minus 10 degrees, or it was raining continuously; and once wet, you stayed wet.

The ones who had to walk through the mud took off their boots and socks, otherwise they got stuck in the mud. Some weeks before our *Bataillon* was replaced, I was wounded and transported to a military hospital at Haldensleben. There I contracted malaria and was transported to Stendal.

After the replacement of my *Bataillon* in Russia at the end of June 1942, they were sent for a short time to Mourmelon in France and then to Africa.[16] After I was released from hospital, I was sent to a replacement unit at Stendal, and from there back to the Eastern Front in early December 1943.

---

16   *Kampfgruppe Sturm* was sent west to recuperate after suffering heavy losses in Russia. *I/FJR2* became part of *Fallschirm-Brigade Ramcke* and was flown to Tobruk on 4 August 1942. See Quarrie, pp.25–27.

The spring of 1942 on the Wolchow (Volkhov) Front in Russia during the muddy period, or *Rasputitsa*. The only vehicles capable of traversing the territory were those puled by horses. Log bridges allowed lighter vehicles and men to cross the worst-affected areas. (Sebastian Krug)

Fallschirmjäger cemetery for those who fell on the Volkov Front in Russia. (Franz Wolf)

The Volkov Front, April 1942. Men of *II/FJR2* before an attack on Lipovik. (Karl Jörger)

Second deployment to Russia

I was now a member of *FJD2* in the area of Shitomir (Zhitomyr) in south central Ukraine.[17] Rain and mud stopped all movement. Our orders were to push back the Russians who had broken through our lines, which was only possible in some places. There followed heavy fighting with heavy casualties on both sides.

Some days later we were surprisingly pulled back, and on 15 December the *Division* was ordered to airlift to Kirovgrad some 400km to the south-east. There the Russians went through our lines. Still in December 1943, the Russians were able to attack with masses of men and materiel.

The Russian *Panzers* drove over our foxholes and turned around so that our comrades were crushed to death. Only when our *PAK* arrived from the rear could we stop the attack. Immediately there were new orders to push the Russians back, which meant an attack with all reserves. Then it started to snow. We sat, soaking wet in our holes; there were no thoughts about eating, drinking or sleeping, there was no time for that. Most of our *Panzers* were either destroyed or under repair, but nevertheless we dared a counterattack, where we took a lot of prisoners and captured or destroyed a lot of materiel.

Then Christmas 1943 arrived.

One day we were pulled out of the line to attend a small Christmas party. During this celebration the Russians began firing from all barrels and we had to return to our positions. There was to be no rest at Christmas or on New Year's Eve of 1943.

On 5 January 1944, the Plavny offensive began and the Russians attacked along the Novgorodka to Kirovgrad highway with a fearful firestorm of Stalin organs, mortars, artillery and other weapons. There were hundreds of tanks! After that, unknown numbers of Russian infantry followed, who managed to surround us and split us into small groups. We managed to destroy some of the tanks with anti-tank weapons. I still ask myself today how several comrades managed to crawl out of their foxholes during the night and live to tell the tale.

We were surrounded by the Russians. There was a severe lack of ammunition and the area was devoid of cover so we could not use messengers. The field telephone had been destroyed by gunfire. We were cut off from the whole world, and we lay in our foxholes not knowing which minute would be our last.

At night we had to pass through the Russian lines to reach our own new front line. Sometimes the few Russian words that we knew helped us, and probably saved our lives. At dawn, the Russians attacked again and our positions were again overrun in many places. Once again we stayed in our foxholes until it was dark. I had a pair of night binoculars and a compass.[18] It was due to these vital items that I managed to travel through the enemy lines at night to reach our own. When I reached the relative safety of our lines, I looked for my men, but only found a few of them.

Weapons and ammunition were a scarce commodity. After several attacks, the front line was quiet for a short time. After four weeks we were sent to Novo-Archangelsk, by foot: 80 km on foot, with regular snowstorms and huge snowdrifts. Sometimes we had to tie ourselves to the comrades next to us to prevent disorientation. Those who got lost died from the cold. Even *Panzers* had to surrender sometimes, when they found themselves lost.

At a river near Jerki we took up new positions. At the beginning of March 1944, a major Russian offensive began with masses of men and materiel. Again we were overrun by unknown numbers of tanks and Russian soldiers. Returning to our lines was only possible at night. We went without a re-supply of ammunition and food for several days as they were not reaching the frontline.

---

17 FJR2 was used as the nucleus for the formation of FJD2 in February 1943.
18 Possibly an early hand-held device manufactured by AEG in the mid-1930s.

Sleeping was impossible. We had to destroy many of our large-calibre weapons when they became stuck in the mud.

After this big Russian offensive, most of the *Kompanien* were shattered, with only enough men to fill the ranks of a small *Zug* or *Gruppe*. During these battles I was wounded for the third time. Luckily, I managed to get onto a hospital train that took me back to a military hospital in Germany.[19]

After leaving the hospital I was sent to a reinforcement *Bataillon* at Stendal, and from there I was sent to a *Fallschirmjäger* recuperation centre at Mariazell in the Steiermark (Austria).

After two weeks I was sent to the *Luftwaffe* hospital in Vienna, where I received three operations, and was then sent to Baden near Vienna. After my recovery I was sent to Stendal, and from there they sent me home for a well-deserved leave.

After my leave I was ordered to report to Parachute School IV at Salzwedel as an instructor. As a *Feldwebel* I received officer education, first in Freiburg and later in Salzwedel. In the late summer of 1944, the school was to be disbanded and sent to the Eastern front.

On 20 July 1944, an attempt was made on Hitler's life. *3. Kompanie* from the school were made ready for action in a forest near the school. I was with two message runners from the school, and we had to immediately forward the orders that came from Berlin to the *Bataillonskommandeur*. These orders came from the Military High Command in the Bendlerstrasse, Berlin. After the failure of the assasination attempt, we had to return to the school to continue with our education.

The jump training was carried out in JU-52, Savoje and Capronie aircraft. One of these aircraft had two doors and the jumping was carried out from both sides. During one training jump with three aircraft, the lead one was too high. Some jumpers from that machine flew directly into the propellers of the right-wing aircraft, causing several fatalities.

Third deployment to the Eastern Front

In late summer 1944, the time had come for the school to be sent east. We took a ride with 30 men in the cattle wagon of a train. Whilst on the train we were shot at by Russians, and we had to disembark immediately and defend ourselves.

In Graudenz I came across a German hospital train that was being guarded by soldiers in Russian uniforms.[20] Whilst taking cover, I heard that some of the soldiers were speaking German. I screamed over to them that they should let the train cross the Vistula River in the direction of Germany. After a long discussion amongst themselves, they let the train go. This train was the last one to cross the Vistula River to the west.

The Russians had layed railroad sleepers on the ice of the Weichsel so they could march across it, south of Graudenz. Some of our troops were still in or around Graudenz to defend the city. Many of our artillery pieces had to be destroyed because of the lack of ammunition. The last bridge on the Weischel was so jammed with men and materiel that it almost seemed at a constant standstill.

The Russian artillery fired without pause at the bridge. Only one of our artillery pieces had ammunition: it fired only one round every 15 minutes. We could see the shell flying and the big detonation when it hit the target.

When I was two-thirds of the way across the bridge, an artillery shell hit the end of the structure. Soldiers, horses and weapons of all kind were ripped into pieces and thrown through the air. It was a terrible sight. Some seriously wounded, half-mutilated soldiers begged us to take them

---

19   The remnants of *FJD2* returned to Germany at the end of May 1944.
20   Graudenz, now Grudziądz in Poland, situated on the east bank of the River Vistula, or Weichsel as it was known in German.

with us. The pressure from behind and the panic was so big that you found yourself being pushed forward whether you wanted to or not.

You marched on like a robot, even over the seriously wounded, who were often crushed underfoot. You just fought for your own survival.

At the end of the bridge we scurried away to find cover. I rushed to a nearby cemetery. There was a hay barn very close by that was filled with wounded soldiers. Then came a surprise enemy tank attack. One tank drove directly through the barn and crushed the soldiers lying inside. Only the medic managed to escape to the cemetery. He was in shock: he hugged me tightly and cried like a child.

Now the tanks began to fire into the cemetery. Gravestones flew through the air, causing many casualties amongst those who had sought shelter there. Every man who was able to, ran away and took cover. The wounded had to remain behind and suffer the onslaught.

Together with five other men I walked across an open field in the direction of a nearby village. Just a short distance away in front of the village, some Russian soldiers came out of the forest. Like us they had their weapons slung over their shoulders; neither German nor Russian dared to draw these shouldered weapons. With only around 10–15 metres separating us from the Russians, we marched parallel towards the village.

When we reached the first house, we immediately took cover and thought about the situation. Unfortunately for us, the village was already occupied by the Russians. Russian infantry, tanks and all kinds of military vehicles drove through the village in a westerly direction. Sometimes we camouflaged ourselves with Russian army caps.

Now we had to try and break through the Russian lines. We could not move on the roads, so we decided to take a chance and move across the open fields. We fooled the Russians by marching in line through the open field, then after a few metres we began to run as fast as our legs could carry us. When the Russians noticed us, they began shooting at us, luckily without success. As we carried on running, we noticed three *Jabos* in the sky. One after the other they swooped down at low level and opened fire on us. This attack lasted 30 minutes. The bullets flew around our ears, but luckily we only received a few grazing shots and no serious wounds.

Later during our escape we came across some destroyed German vehicles, which we searched for food. That evening we made contact with some German soldiers. We were immediately approached by an artillery *Leutnant*. I asked him about my unit, but he knew nothing abouth them; they could not be found. I walked with him, accompanied by a message runner, to reconnoitre new positions. The artillery pieces were pulled by horses as there were no more vehicles.

When it got dark we stopped in a forest. The *Leutnant* and I walked ahead and we soon arrived at a train track. Behind the tracks we heard noises and saw covered lights from tanks and other military vehicles. They were Russian. The *Leutnant* and I watched them for some time. As quietly as possible, we tried to pull back with our men. Unfortunately we did not go un-noticed by the Russians, who opened fire on us but missed.

After several days we finally met up with our unit again. On the western side of the Vistula River, our forces were withdrawing in the direction of Danzig (Gdańsk). In front of Danzig we had to give up a village, but on the next day we took it back.

During the fighting I checked a house and its nearby barn, where I thought I heard a moan. What I found was undescribably cruel: a woman was lying naked on the floor of the barn: she had been nailed by her hands and feet onto the wooden floor. She had also been raped and badly maltreated. I freed her but after a short while she died. Her last words were "many Russians".

When we reached Danzig, our mission was to defend the city. One day Russian bombs fell, creating a raging inferno.[21] Everything was destroyed. The people who were not burned alive or

---

21   Possibly the intense artillery barrage of 19 March 1945. See Taylor, pp.295–300.

torn apart by the blasts, suffocated in the bomb shelters below ground. We later had to capitulate the city and evacuate, proceeding to the town of Langfur. Between Danzig and Langfur, large trees lined the road. On every tree hung several German soldiers with a sign around their neck, on which was written 'I was too cowardly to fight'.

Under the trees lay dead children, women and old men. Russian airplanes took aerial photographs of the trees and dropped these pictures with pass permits attached to them. On the pass permits was written 'come to us and you will get food, something to drink and fresh clothes every week'.

From Langfur we went toward the Frische Nehrung (Vistula Spit), a coastal area in East Prussia in the direction of Pillau (Baltisk). We were surrounded, along with a million refugees.[22]

Final return to Germany

On the morning of 25 April 1945, I developed the shivers, so I went to see the doctor. He diagnosed a malaria relapse, and because he had no medical supplies he gave me a ship ticket to the military hospital at Usedom. The bad news was that I would have to make my own way to the ship, which was already on the open sea.

On 26 April, I and several comrades sailed in a small boat to the ship. The ship was overloaded with sick and wounded soldiers and refugees. Nevertheless, we made it to the military hospital at Usedom the next morning. There I received a few tablets and was sent to a hospital at Stralsund. On my arrival, I received some more medicine and was then sent by foot to Rostock and later to Wismar.

On the way I saw endless columns of refugees heading towards the west. The wells in the villages were almost dry. The Russian *Jabos* attacked the refugee columns again and again. Hundreds of dead and wounded lay in the trenches at the side of the road, but nobody cared about them; the refugees were only interested in escaping from the Russians.

At the end of April we reached Wismar. Between Wismar and Grevesmühlen in northern Germany we found something to eat in a local house. After that we went to the village pond and threw our weapons into it. After a short farewell we went further. The Americans rolled over us and they ordered us to surrender. Together with a comrade, I wanted to try to go south, but we were stopped by the Americans and made to go to a camp at Grevesmühlen. All around us were foreign soldiers and civilians who had just been liberated. They were not very friendly toward us.

In front of the camp we had to line up until 100 men were gathered together. Then we had to camp in an open field and laid there for weeks without a tent in occasional torrential rain. We received a quarter-litre of watery cabbage soup, and in the evening one herring and one sliced crispbread between 10 men.

Because we were unprotected from the bad weather, I dug a hole and covered it with branches. Later I caught a cold and my teeth began to ache like hell. The dentist had no medicine, so he had to pull out my molars without drugs. For weeks after I had swollen cheeks and painful gums. The rain went through the cover of my new home and made the ground wet, turning my camp bed into mud.

After some time we were moved to the Schönberger beach near Kiel, which was guarded by English [sic] soldiers. There was a tent for every four men. We were released from captivity according to our civilian occupations: first the miners, then the farmers etc. I was supposed to

---

22   This pocket was bypassed by Russian forces and cut off, finally surrendering on 13 May 1945. See Taylor, p.326.

go to the French zone with the first transport. The leader of our 100-man group begged me to exchange my place with a father who had several children.

I gave up my place. I later found out that the transport had reached France, but the men were sent back into captivity. Many men died or were sent to the French Foreign Legion.

Epilogue

On 27 August 1945, I was released into the American zone of occupation and went by train to Ulm on the Donau River. The next day I travelled from Ulm to Memmingen.

Just a few minutes before the beginning of curfew at 2200 hours, I stood outside the front door of my parents' house. I was home again. My parents were surprised and happy to have me back alive. They had heard nothing from me for more than a year because none of my letters had reached them.

The war in medals and awards:
1940 as a *Gefreiter* – Iron Cross 2nd Class
1941 as an *Oberjäger* – Iron Cross 1st Class
1941 Kreta cuff title
1942 Medal for the Winter Battle in the East
1942 *Luftwaffe* Ground Combat Badge
1942 Italian Bravery Medal
1942 Wound Badge in Black
1943 Wound Badge in Silver
1944 War Merit Cross with Swords

Military Ranks:
1939 *Gefreiter*
1940 *Obergefreiter*
1941 *Unteroffizier*
1942 *Feldwebel*

From December 1944 to April 1945, I was a *Feldwebel* and *Kompanieführer* of 6./Pz.Gren.Rgt.'HG'.

Near the end of war, there were not many officers left at the front. They wanted to promote me to *Leutnant*, but I said no because I did not want to fall into Russian hands as an officer POW. Because of my malaria relapse in April 1945, I came out of the Russian encirclement just 13 days before the end of the war.

Special Training:
1939 Medics Course
1940 Engine Driver Course, Assault Engineer Course, Sniper Course.

My Wounds:
In Holland – shot through the ear and suffered a bullet graze to the left side of head.
On Crete – several bullet grazes on body and to my steel helmet.
In Russia – shot through the upper arm, broken ribs, many bullet grazes to my equipment, grenade fragments to the right wrist and right side. Malaria.

Bad experiences of the war

Some bad experiences from the war are forever in my memory.

In December 1941, we travelled in train wagons towards southern Russia. Near to our destination, the train stopped to take on food supplies. We looked around the nearby village and witnessed how two Russian volunteer policemen had driven some of their own people into a house.

We walked behind them and waited to see what was about to unfold. The house was the only one with a balcony, and on it were tied five ropes. Suddenly two *SS* men and a civilian came out onto the balcony. They put the rope around the civilian's neck and just threw him over the balcony railing. This carried on until the third man came out. The rope broke rope and the man fell to the ground. Two *SS* men took him back up to the balcony, attached a new rope and threw him back over the railing again. Then followed the fourth and fifth men. After this terrible incident was over, a big sign was erected, which said in German and Russian 'These gangsters blew up a German ammunition train. As a punishment they have been hung.' These unfortunate men were to be left hanging for a few days to deter others. Some of the men who had been hung had their eyes turned inside their skulls and moved convulsively; not a nice sight. These men had blown up the train ahead of us, which was the reason that our train could not move any further.

Another time we had to participate as witnesses when a German deserter was shot in a gravel pit. The execution squad consisted only of volunteers. The *Kompanie* had to provide 10 men. Everybody was asked if they would volunteer; nobody wanted too, but somehow 10 men had to be found. The men who finally came forward received a loaded rifle and on the order 'fire', had to shoot. Missing the prisoner would have been useless, so the men aimed at the heart so that death would be instant. There were no good feelings about this from the shooters or the witnesses.

In the parachute school at Salzwedel, I was an associate judge at a court. There was a case of theft amongst some of the men. The defendant was punished with a long term in prison. After his judgement I had to escort him to the Spandau prison in Berlin. This was the same prison which was later used for the Nazi war criminals.

The post-war years

After the war I worked with my parents as a farmer. In 1947, I moved to Karlsruhe and worked there as a construction worker. I met my wife, married her on 20 May 1948, and we had two daughters.

In May 1951, I went into the *Bundesgrenzschutz* (Federal German border guards). My operational areas were Lübeck, Aachen, Deggendorf and Neubruecke on the Nahe River, Saarbruecken, Helmstedt, Frankfurt and Kehl. I retired on 31 January 1980.

As a former paratrooper, the thought of parachuting never left my head. One day whilst reading the paratrooper journal I read a letter entitled 'Operation Red Star in Ryasan/Russia'. I registered myself, and on 21 May 1992 I went by train to Berlin. Participants from seven countries (America, France, Italy, Switzerland, Austria, Greece and Germany) had gathered in a hotel there. After a short sightseeing tour, we flew to Moscow. We were welcomed there by Russian paratroops. Loaded aboard three buses, we travelled 200km to a hotel in Ryasan.

The next morning we went to a manoeuvring ground for weapons training. Everyone was able to shoot all kinds of infantry weapons, exept mortars.

Later we visited the town of Ryasan and the paratrooper museum there. On 24 May, we went into the paratrooper barracks. There we received instructions on the weapons and equipment of the paratroops and their training. We were able to participate in all lessons. In the evening we were shown traditional Russian folklore.

The next day we went to the dropzone, and after receiving some lessons on the parachute and some jump training, we made two jumps. These jumps were made out of the Mi8 helicopter, each carrying 16 men, at an altitude of 600 metres. The jumps were successful except for a few minor injuries, and afterward a Russian general made a speech. Looking at the Germans before him, he said that the Russians fought against the Nazis and not the German people. He hoped and wished that there would always be peace between our two nations.

The following day we made a jump on another dropzone from 1,000 metres. During and after these jumps, Russian paratroops carried out demonstration jumps for us.

In the evening a big banquet was held, and we were awarded jump wings and a diploma from General Schukov. He showed me his deepest respect as a veteran with three combat jumps behind me, and he asked for a photograph, as the only German soldier, for the paratroops museum at Ryasan.

This stay in Russia was a great experience for me, and I think we made many friends.

My next and last engagement was in Crete in May 1993. After an invitation from the organizer, Mr Liolios, I flew to Athens on 20 May and attended the paratrooper school of the Greek Army. I had no jump permit from the Greek Defence Ministry or the Consulate. I was 73 years old at the time and not sure that I was even allowed to jump. I could, however, participate in the jump training. I spent several days carrying out tower jumping, hang training, ground and falling training until I received permission to jump. We flew in a Hercules transport aircraft with parachutes on our back to the dropzone at Tiubaki on Crete. There we jumped out at an altitude of 400 metres.

As the only German soldier who jumped there 52 years before, I was allowed to jump as the personal guest of the organiser. Later I gave an interview for Greek television that was aired during the same evening.

In the evening of the following day, we received our diplomas in the presence of an honour guard of the Greek Army. This operation was an unforgetable experience for me.

Now I must say something that has made me angry for a long time. About 20 years after the war, I saw films on TV that I had never seen before or heard about during the war. I only knew the front and the hospital. I am ashamed as a German that so many people were murdered in camps and elsewhere, and it was kept so secret that many Germans did not even know about it.

(Sebastian Krug passed away on 26 February 2010, aged 90.)

5

Wilhelm 'Willi' Schulte

My experience as a POW in American and British captivity

At the end of 1939, Willi Schulte was a Luftwaffe *radio operator. He saw active service in Norway and France in 1940. At 20 years old he answered* Reichsmarschall *Göring's call for* Fallschirmjäger *volunteers, and on completion of his initial training at Hildesheim and parachute training in Stendal, he returned to Hildesheim to carry out further training in ground combat and glider assault training in preparation for Operation Mercury, the invasion of Crete. After Crete, Willi served with the* Sturmregiment *in the northern sector of the Russian Front in the winter of 1941/42. It was in the fortress city of Brest in 1944 that Willi would see the end of his war and the beginning of captivity, in both America and Britain.*

Soldbuch photograph of *Feldwebel* Wilhelm Schulte. (Wilhelm Schulte)

Prelude

On 20 May 1941, my Radio *Truppe* started out in a glider with the first wave for the invasion operation on Crete. As we came in to land we came under heavy fire and crash landed in an olive grove, but luckily none of my comrades were injured.

We had an 80-watt radio, which had originated from the Polish air force, and it was our job to make radio contact with *Fliegerdivision 7* on the mainland.

After the successful mission on Crete, I served with the *Sturmregiment* in the northern sector of the Russian Front in the area of Lake Ilmen.

The *Regiment* was later almost destroyed on the Eastern Front and I was sent to the *Stabskompanie Nachrichtenzug* of *FJR7*. With this *Regiment* I saw service in Rome, Kiev/Shitomir and Kirovgrad in Russia and finally Brittany in France.

Brest, France

On 18 September 1944, in the fortress city of Brest, I was in an air raid bunker in Wilson Square where we had retreated 10 days previously from the city's main defensive line under pressure from the Americans. After nearly six weeks of fighting for the city and harbour, it had become much quieter that morning. Sentries announced that the Americans were not far from our bunker. The *Regiment Nachrichtenzug* received an important order to "destroy all radios and documents". Another order was soon received to "prepare to defend the bunker". I was called again to see the signals officer, for what I cannot remember, but as I hurried with my gun to the bunker exit I came across two armed American soldiers. I was directed outside, where my comrades from the *Nachrichtenzug* were already in a group surrounded by American soldiers.

A negotiator was supposed to be in the bunker conducting surrender negotiations with our *Regimentskommandeur*, *Oberst* Erich Pietzonka. In the meantime, other soldiers who were still squatting in the rubble of the surrounding buildings came over to us. Then our *Kommandeur* came out with the rest of his staff, accompanied by American officers.

Outside, *Oberst* Pietzonka spoke to us once more and then addressed the American commander, handed him his pistol and formally declared the capitulation of the city.[1] Thereupon the American commander, whose speech was translated by an interpreter, spoke words of recognition of our troop's accomplishments and then returned the pistol to our *Regimentskommandeur*.

Now it was our turn to give up our weapons, although we had already made them partially useless. So we took our pistols, which the Americans were particularly keen to have, stripped them, stamped on the parts and then threw them into the rubble of the buildings. In the presence of their officers, the American soldiers let this happen, although they would have certainly liked to have taken such souvenirs if the officers were not present.

While American fighter-bombers bombarded targets on the nearby Crozon Peninsula (where our *Divisionskommandeur Generalmajor* Hermann Ramcke had been ferried out to two days earlier), we climbed over the rubble of ruined buildings accompanied by American soldiers to the outskirts of the town to wait for a truck column. Before we were removed by truck, we were told "extend your left arm". Then two American soldiers stepped forward, and one of them felt for watches under the tunic sleeves. The watches were taken off and thrown into a helmet held by the second soldier. I held out my right arm to the American. "No watch?" he asked. "*Nein*," I replied. That's how I kept my wristwatch.

The POW cage

Then we were loaded on to trucks and taken to a makeshift camp on a meadow far out of town. In this camp, in my estimation, were several thousand prisoners all crammed together. There were no facilities in this barbed wire camp except several latrines in the form of excavated trenches.

Fresh water was not available, but later tanker trucks came to the camp. These vehicles were immediately stormed by fellow prisoners, wasting a lot of water in the mad rush. The guards were forced to fire shots into the air in an attempt to restore some order. We paratroopers did not get any water that day because we did not want to offer such a spectacle to our watchers. As it was raining we used tent quarters (*Zeltplane*) that some of us had to catch rainwater and feed it into our cookware.

---

1   General Walter M. Robertson of the 2nd US Infantry Division.

After two or three days we received American rations, which impressed us very much. I remember a can of Irish stew, as well as a packet of biscuits and some cigarettes. In the constant rain we could not lie on the soaked ground. Anyone with a *Zeltplane* created a makeshift shelter, but everyone else had to get wet.

I remember one event very well. One morning the camp gate opened, and in the midst of a number of American officers we were visited by our *Divisions Kommandeur, Generalmajor* Ramcke. He remembered the fallen and thanked us for our service, and said in the presence of the American officers: "Well, you are now prisoners of war and have to obey the rules! From now on you work for the Americans. But what if your clumsy butts upset the work of your hands? You are not responsible for your sacred ass! And: if there is a god in heaven, he will make sure that there is no giant's magical palace at the end the beanstalk."[2] [This speech was translated by Volker Stutzer. Ramcke is clearly lecturing his men on how to behave in captivity using *'umgangssprachlich'*, an informal, casual manner of speech. Ramcke seems familiar to sayings in both English/German, so he was sure to be understood. A literal translation was not possible; the meaning of the message had to be conveyed. The reference to the story of Jack and the Beanstalk would have been familiar to most of his audience.]

Through the visit of 'Papa' Ramcke – as we called him – we learned for the first time that he too survived the action in Brest.

Meanwhile, rumours circulated in the camp that German forces were already making a stand in front of Paris and the Americans were thus involved in heavy defensive battles. Escape plans were forged and some comrades who dared to make their way through to the alleged front went through the barbed wire fence during the night. To divert the guards, we sang previously agreed songs; for example, when the guards approached the spot where the comrades wanted to go through the barbed wire we sang "come back" to the tune *J'attendrai*.[3] Many comrades managed to leave the camp. How far they got I do not know. I also witnessed one who came back. He walked up to the guards standing at the gate and said "let me in again". So they did!

To England and America

How long we spent on this wet meadow I do not remember, but I guess it was more than one week. One day, we paratroopers were separated and trucked to a tented camp on the Cotentin Peninsula. On the way there, stones and other objects were thrown at us as we passed through the French villages and towns. Some comrades were seriously injured. It should be noted that our guards were mostly black soldiers, who tried to protect us as much as possible.

We only stayed a short time in this camp, and then we were trucked out again to a port (Caen or Le Havre?). There we saw the big American landing craft, which brought a locomotive and several loaded railroad cars to the mainland on three internal tracks. We were embarked on one of these landing craft, the bow door was closed, and it was very dark in the hold of the ship and we saw nothing of our surroundings. Because of its shallow draught, the boat danced in what was probably a stormy sea, with the vast majority of my comrades becoming seasick. We were frequently slipping back and forth on the vomit.

---

2   Ramcke's own recollection of this speech is slightly different to that recalled by Herr Schulte. See Ramcke, p.89.

3   French for 'I will wait', a popular French song recorded in 1938 by Rina Ketty.

After landing in Southampton, we boarded a train and were taken to an American POW camp, presumably in central England. We had the opportunity to take a shower and then, while naked, we were led into a long corridor.

There we stood in line and slowly moved towards an illuminated room, not knowing what to expect. As I entered the room I was grabbed by two burly black men, vaccinated in the left and right upper arms, and then my body was intensively processed with a DDT spray so that no place remained unpowdered.[4] Also in this camp we were registered for the first time. We did not stay long and soon found ourselves on a train to Liverpool, where we boarded a large troopship. We were taken below decks. It was clean and everyone got a canvas-covered bed in a stack of three. The only exit to the deck could be secured by a barbed wire-covered hatch. At the top of the steps there were always two armed guards. In good weather we were allowed in small groups once a day, for about a quarter of an hour, on deck to get some fresh air. And so after a two- or three-day journey we realised that this troop transporter had been placed in a convoy of other large ships and that we were probably being taken to America.

Then we encountered rough seas. On deck there was the sound of creaking and groaning. Where we once a day shuffled to a warm meal in the dining room, more and more comrades were seasick in the heavy seas and could not eat anything, so the kitchen staff gave us large portions and also filled any cookware we brought with us.

I had never taken part in such a long voyage, and it was a great experience. When we were allowed on deck to look at the ships, they would disappear behind or ahead of us on the peak of a large wave and I thought that they would surely fall on top of our ship that was in a trough, and vice-versa, then we would soon be on the peak of a wave in the rough swell.

We also worried that our ship, which did not fly under the Red Cross flag, would be attacked by German U-boats. We had already experienced the U-boat alarm three times on this trip. Through loudspeakers we heard in our room the warning, which was repeated three times, "All men on station, attention, German submarine". Then the barbed wire hatch was closed over the single staircase to the upper deck. We listened to the propeller sounds of the accompanying warships and the detonations of the depth charges, which were certainly thrown far from us but made a frightening noise through the steel hull of our troop transporter.

If our ship had been hit by a torpedo, none of us would have had a chance of survival under those circumstances. I do not remember today how long we were on this ship, but it must have been under three weeks before the machinery noise became quieter and then finally fell silent.

Hours later we were allowed to leave our accommodation, and when got to the upper deck it was early morning. We saw Manhattan with the Empire State Building in front of us. We left the ship and were escorted to a building that was equipped to handle immigration or livestock transport. Here we were searched again. Things that we had kept before, such as soap, cookware, cutlery and odds and ends, were taken from us and thrown into large trash cans. "Piss off, you'll get everything new" was a common remark made in German. Then again we had to take off our clothes, shower and endure the DDT treatment. Our clothes were de-loused, but when we got them back everything was one size smaller.

After this procedure, barges took us to the opposite bank of the Hudson River, where a passenger train was already waiting for us. This train began to move in the late afternoon. According to our observations, we first travelled west, then south. The destination was unknown to us.

---

4   DDT was a colourless, tasteless and almost odourless crystalline chemical compound originally developed as an insecticide. It was used in the Second World War to control malaria and typhus amongst troops and prisoners.

The train was very comfortable, but we lacked in food. I do not remember if we received anything to eat that day. The next morning, paper cups and later paper plates were issued. Then there was some bread and jam, and then the paper cups and plates were collected from us. We were not satisfied. At noon the same procedure: paper plates, paper spoons for a sweet broth in which a few raisins floated around. We thought that was just the starter, but then the cardboard items were collected again. There was plenty of food on the train because we had seen the supplies being loaded. For how long we were travelling on this train I do not know today. It was at least three days, if not more.

Camp Chaffee, Arkansas

One night we finally reached our destination. We left the train and were driven in Army trucks to a nearby brightly lit POW camp.

We were received by an officer. He apologised, as the barracks had not yet been fully prepared for us. They had been notified of the arrival of the transport too late. Therefore at first only mattresses were provided in the accommodation so we could rest. All other items would be supplied when they arrived.

I looked around the perimeter of the camp and found that it consisted of at least two areas separated by 10ft-high wire fences. At the corners of the area were wooden watchtowers for the guards. Then I noticed an early riser in the adjacent camp, so I called him to the fence. I learned from him that the camp was part of Army Camp Chaffee in Arkansas. He had gone into captivity in North Africa. Since I was hungry, I asked him how the food was. He complained that the food was not as good as it used to be. I turned away without another word because I was very hungry.

About 0800 hours, after roll call, we went to the kitchen barracks, where there was a large dining room. The German kitchen crew had prepared breakfast for us, with coffee, tea, cocoa, milk and fruit juices of your choice. There was also bread, butter, cold meats and scrambled egg with bacon. We could not believe the variety, the quality and the amount on offer. Upon leaving the dining room, I saw on a blackboard the menu for lunch and dinner. I still remember two dishes from that first menu I saw: French-style chops and diplomatic pudding.[5] Since I had the rank of *Feldwebel* at that time, I did not need to work under the provisions of the Geneva Convention, but you had to do something. You cannot play sports all day long. We had a relatively good library in the camp, with German and English language works, so I began to borrow books. In addition there were men in the camp who were willing and able to give lessons. Among my comrades was a foreign trade merchant from Hamburg, who had been the director of a private bank in Buenos Aires before the war. He offered to give Spanish lessons to interested parties such as myself. He was a good teacher, and despite all the jargon of Spanish grammar, the lessons were very practical in terms of business and private correspondence.

So during the day I would run along the fence line, making my rounds and studying hard the Spanish vocabulary. Later on I added the 'Advanced English' course because I was taught four years of English during my school years. We were treated very well and fairly by the Americans at the time. When our comrades died, we were allowed to participate in their burial outside the camp on the adjacent site. The coffin of the deceased was draped with the German battle flag, and at the graveside American soldiers fired an honour salute.

After the foreseeable military collapse of Germany, a lot changed in the camp. Our food rations were cut and we were increasingly asked to volunteer to work. These requests were then followed by

---

5   Bread and butter pudding made from bread, raisins or candied fruit, rum/liqueur and cream.

Standing at rigid attention in contrast to the bowed heads of the Catholic chaplain, the POW chaplain who served as an interpreter, the mortician and the German priest, said that the departed comrade had done his duty as a soldier according to his vows. (Fort Chaffee Museum Collection at the Pebley Centre at University of Arkansas – Fort Smith)

At the compound gate, a bell tolled in the custom of the Catholic Church. The casket was placed upon an Army vehicle commandeered for that purpose. Four US Army officers snapped to attention and saluted in honour of the dead German soldier, in keeping with international military customs. (Fort Chaffee Museum Collection at the Pebley Centre at University of Arkansas – Fort Smith)

As the vehicle bearing the casket rolled away from the compound gate, Staff Sergeant Carl Engberg barked out a command and the American guard of honour presented arms. Another command and the American soldiers swung down the road leading the solemn procession, followed by the vehicle with the casket. In the rear, the dead prisoner's company marched three abreast in full uniform out the compound gate and down the road, passing in front of the barracks which quartered the American guards. At the camp gate, the MPs on duty there presented arms and the procession turned into a main road which passes the camp. (Fort Chaffee Museum Collection at the Pebley Centre at University of Arkansas – Fort Smith)

Throughout the ceremony, the Company's leaders standing stoically before the German military band, did not so much as blink an eyelid, even when the choir to their right and the band behind rendered 'Dear Comrade', a beloved song on such occasions. The leaders did not appear moved. They were excellently trained soldiers of the Third Reich carrying on in the tradition of German militarism. (Fort Chaffee Museum Collection at the Pebley Centre at University of Arkansas – Fort Smith)

Whilst at attention, the German band render 'Dear Comrade' as part of the funeral service. (Fort Chaffee Museum Collection at the Pebley Centre at University of Arkansas – Fort Smith)

German POW and former member of Rommel's *Afrika Korps* makes hamburgers at Camp Chaffee. (Fort Chaffee Museum Collection at the Pebley Centre at University of Arkansas – Fort Smith)

visits by several officers. I was called to see an American major who asked me in German: "Willi, do you not want to work?" I replied: "If I work then I replace a man and you will send him to a bomb factory and then you will drop that bomb on my parents' heads. You would not do it either!" "Ok, you can go," he replied.

Then the war was over. The food was very bad after that. We would only receive meat once a week, a fish as big as a herring! At that time we were placed under heavy guard in a barrack lecture room, where we were shown a film about the concentration camps. Naturally we were shaken. Everyone had heard that there were camps where criminals had to work hard, but none of us had seen such a camp. As a result we were asked repeatedly if we wanted to work, but the majority of us still said no.

One day we were asked to provide evidence proving our level of service. I presented my *Soldbuch* as others did, and these documents were collected for an alleged review. A little later there was another document inspection by other Americans. When we told them that we had already submitted our identity documents for review, they did not believe us. I withstood this and another check by showing receipts such as an old vacation coupon and an envelope addressed to me showing my rank.

After most of our comrades had already been transferred to the enlisted men's camp, I and a few others were able to spend a short time in our NCOs' camp. One evening the rest of us, about 40 men, were ordered outside. We were led toward the camp gate between the fences, where we had to stand on an assigned preordained square of about 1.5m x 1.5m and 3m apart. We were told we would have to stand in the dirt until we agreed to work. How long we stood there I do not remember today.

After one or two men fell down, we held a consultation in view of the hopelessness of our situation and we agreed to work. Then an American master sergeant came who spoke a little German, and he said: "So now you will work and then you can sing 'Germany, Germany above all, above all in the world' [from the then German national anthem, *Deutschlandlied*]."

We moved to the enlisted men's camp, where I cut grass with a short sickle, living on some white bread with jam and beans in the evening. When the first payday came there was another row with the Americans, as we refused to accept the money on the grounds that we were forced to work. We later took the money!

We also caught copperhead snakes, which were mainly found in the haystacks. Some comrades had perfected this practice. They killed the snakes, cut off their skins in the camp and made knots for attaching scarves.

I did not belong to the grass-cutting work detail for long. I found a book in the library called *Rheumatism, its recognition and treatment*, and I acquired [faked] the relatively rare disease 'intercostal rheumatism', with which I wanted to achieve premature release from captivity. I reported myself sick, complaining of pain in the sternum, but that was probably not enough to sway the German doctor to the diagnosis of intercostal rheumatism. My chest was brushed with iodine and a day's rest was arranged, and then I had to work again. I did that two or three times, but I did not get along with that doctor.

One morning at roll call the Americans were looking for an interpreter. I reported immediately, certain that I would be spared having to cut grass, at least for one day. I was assigned to the 4th Company as the replacement for an injured interpreter. At the company office, Americans worked on one side and German POWs on the other as clerks. I was assigned a desk, and on the desk sat a triangular bar that said 'Interpreter' in English and German. There was nothing to do yet. Then the first American soldier came to me and began to speak. I could not understand him. He was a southerner and his pronunciation had a nasal mumble sound that I had not been used to. I asked him to repeat and speak a little slower. It did not help when one of the other German scribes said: "Why don't you give him the typewriter?" I only asked him to repeat what he had said.

Then came the US company commander, a *Captain*, to whom I was introduced. "Howdy, howdy!" he said, and then he distributed some cigarettes. The German and American typists had made themselves very comfortable, put their feet up on the desks and smoked with pleasure.

My work mainly consisted of translating German, American, British and Russian military reports from the *New York Times*, which I then attached to a pin-board in German to inform my comrades. For this activity I had a good dictionary at my disposal and the work became routine.

It was not long before the 4th Company was moved to Texas to help with the cotton harvest. I remained in Camp Chaffee. Afterward I was used at a coal yard, shovelling coal. As the railroad cars full of coal would arrive, an excavator unloaded the coal until such a point where it could not fully empty the cars. We would then shovel the remaining coal into the excavator bucket until the car was empty. So I discovered my rheumatism again, but was never written off sick for very long.

One morning at roll-call, an electrician was sought who could handle large electric motors. Immediately my hand went up. Although I knew nothing about electric motors, it might be a day away from the coal yard. I was driven in a Jeep to the American camp and introduced to an engineer, who was glad we could converse in English, and learned from him that I was to be used as an electrician in the engine room of a cold store. We drove to the cold store and he showed me the layout. It was a very large room with three large electric motors and many fitting and instruments. He asked me if I could get used to it and I told him that I had done repair work in a cold store with my boss in Germany before, but every facility was different. He understood that and I was accepted.

The next morning I was driven to the American camp with the other workers and went to the cold store. In a small room next to the machine hall, I met two mechanics who were messing about rolling from one wall to the other in their swivel chairs, pushing their feet off the walls. My request to come in was ignored; neither of them said a word to me. After a while I sat down and took part in this wordless game. At 0900 hours, one of the mechanics looked at his watch and said: "Time for breakfast." They went to their lockers and took out small portable metal boxes where they kept their breakfast. I also fetched my food ration for the whole day; four slices of white bread spread with a little jam. One of the mechanics asked me if this was my breakfast (I later learned that his name was Lewis and he was of Russian origin). I said yes and told him it was also my ration for the rest of the day. Then he got up without a word and left.

After a while he returned and gave me a big bag of pastries, which he must have brought somewhere nearby. After breakfast he invited me, like him, to put on a thick padded overcoat and showed me around the cold rooms.

With Lewis I went through all the cold rooms, changed defective bulbs, and he told me that tomorrow I would have to do it all alone. I was more overwhelmed at the sight of the stored goods; huge rooms with cattle and pork halves, rooms with bacon, eggs, fish, lobster and fruit. Wonderful prospects for me! Back in the engine room, I was told the function of the machines, fittings, rules, regulations and measuring instruments. It was very interesting.

One day when I was outside the cold store, I was approached by a fellow inmate who asked: "Are you new here?" When I said yes, he told me that he worked with some other comrades in the bakery and that I could get cakes, pastries and milk from him! Then he asked me what I could offer in return from the cold store. I told him there was fruit, lobster, fish, eggs and sliced beef fillets. We agreed to place the goods that were to be exchanged in a specific waste bin, which we had marked. The waste bin would then be picked up by other comrades in the garbage truck, and our goods would be delivered to us. Of course, these comrades also had to be supplied with goods from both of us. Relationships were soon established around the camp with comrades in the uniform store and the steam laundry, and a trade in natural products became more and more extensive. In the meantime, I did not have to wash my underwear anymore; I just used brand new ones.

After about six months I had to give up this job because an American dismissed from the Army took over my job as a civilian. After another sick leave due to my rheumatic complaints on the breastbone, which of course brought me light duties within the camp, I was called to the American office. The offer: due to my language skills I was supposed to take charge of some comrades who operated the coal heating systems to the office barracks and accommodation in the American camp, and who worked in shifts. Each of my comrades had to operate heaters in three blocks. I was assigned a boiler room in an office barracks just opposite a large kitchen plant. My task was to report damage to the heating systems and order coal. In addition I received an ID card, which allowed me to move freely in all the areas where my comrades were employed. It was a very good job.

I already mentioned that my boiler room was opposite a canteen kitchen. This kitchen was occupied at night by one American and about 20 Germans. My first shift was a night shift. As a rule, the American supervising the kitchen staff would go to sleep and between 2300 and 2400 hours would leave. My closest comrades and I then went through a side door, past the dishwasher and put on aprons, and therefore became kitchen staff.

The comrades employed there then served us a complete meal, as food was already prepared to feed Americans during the night. Special requests were fulfilled where possible. Of course, you could also take food. I had three cats in my boiler room and they were so spoiled that they only took milk and chicken thighs.

From time to time we were approached by American soldiers, whom we would talk to, where possible of course. They would offer us cigarettes and alcohol. I remember one of my comrades who came into my boiler room during a night shift. He almost fell over and said, "Willi! You have to pay attention to the heating", then promptly collapsed next to me, drunk! I immediately went to his boiler room, and there I met about six to eight American soldiers from Puerto Rico who offered me rum and were more than happy to speak in Spanish with me. This was total fraternisation. Although I tried to drink a little rum, I was no longer used to alcohol, and I drank too much. I felt miserable the next day, and could not smell rum, let alone drink it, for many years afterward.

During the night shift, at around 0500 hours, I would regularly watch a Jeep driving to a nearby snack bar, where a dairy truck had recently unloaded several boxes of bottled milk. One of the three occupants of the Jeep wore a helmet and the other two did not. The soldiers would load a box of milk and then drive off. Only later did we learn that the milk-snatchers were POWs who worked in the steam laundry at night and were being driven around by an American soldier.

Then my comrades and I would also borrow this milk. One bottle for self-consumption and another for the day shift. We threw the empty bottles into the stoves, where the evidence would melt into the embers. Later, during a day shift, I was approached by a comrade who worked at the snack bar. He said: "You get the milk you need for the night shift, we have nothing against that. If necessary we cook the cocoa with water for the Americans, but you have to return the empties, otherwise you will cause trouble for us." So we began to return the empties. The dayshift was also a pleasant experience. For breakfast and lunch we went through the side entrance of the American canteen kitchen, put on a scarf and then ate food offered to us by our comrades.

An interesting show was put on by the plumbers. After an agreement with comrades working in the scullery, who would isolate the drain lines, the plumbers would drive back to the workshop, where the boss was standing outside. He had been alerted by a phone call about a blocked drain and sent the plumbers to an adjoining kitchen. Three of them dragged their toolboxes (emptied in the scullery), tore open an inspection cover and got to work on the drainage pipes. The German kitchen staff would then load food stores into the Jeep toolboxes outside. I will never forget that in an adjoining room, an American cook had prepared 10 or more meatloaves on a large table ready to cut into portions. One of the plumbers saw that he was leaving his desk, put down his toolbox on the table, picked up a large meatloaf and stuffed it into the toolbox before disappearing with it. The American cook came back, stopped, counted his meatloaves several times and evidently did not know how many he had before.

After the plumbers had taken care of themselves, they opened the stopper valve and the water flowed again normally. One American thanked the plumbers and donated a nice meal. We then joked that the camp was firmly in German hands. At some point at the end of the heating season, the work detail was disbanded.

From a newspaper we had learned that the then US President Truman had said in a speech: "The war is not yet over [...] but that does not release us from the moral obligation to send home the Prisoners of War." In the camp, several Austrians distanced themselves from us as they hoped they might be released early. So then it happened. We were separated, but according to the new Allied zones of occupation. With the prospect of release I did not continue with my rheumatism. First to leave were those who came from the American zone of occupation, and sometime later came the turn of those, like me, who came from the British zone. We finally left the camp and were taken to Camp Shanks near New York, and after a few days we boarded a Liberty ship in New York harbour.

Return to England

This time the Atlantic crossing was much faster, and I think we landed in Liverpool after about one week. Some still believed that we would return home to Germany. Having boarded a train, we thought we were headed for another port on the east coast to be transported to mainland Europe from there.

During the trip I saw the sea on the left side of our direction and said they must be taking us to Scotland. They almost lynched me. Some men could not stand the truth. We stopped somewhere in the north, possibly in southern Scotland. The next morning we discovered that a comrade had hung himself. The disappointment was probably too much for him to take.

After a few days I was transferred with two or three other comrades to the Information Bureau at Middleton Manor in Sussex, England, where I was employed in the POW central file station. There were lots of mail for the POWs in England that could not be delivered because the prisoner's files were not up to date. We then noted on the index cards the camp numbers according to the current checklist information, and then later marked the post with the correct camp number.

The treatment by the English personnel was very good, but we had to get used to the military forms and rules of conduct that were different to those we had experienced in America. The accommodation and food was definitely not the same as Camp Chaffee.

In the meantime, I had received a letter from my parents. They informed me that they had been bombed out and they were living in a nearby damaged house. My Father was transporting bricks to our garden with a small handcart. He had to collect the old bricks from the rubble in order to build a makeshift home for our family.

Repatriation

Now I had to help my Father. I rediscovered my intercostal rheumatism and reported sick. After repeated unsuccessful reports to the camp doctor, I was finally taken on a stretcher to the infirmary. I was examined several times, and a short time later my name was added to a discharge list and I was sent to a camp near Hull. Here I was handed a miracle: in addition to my medical history documents from the US, which certainly contributed to my current situation, I also received a military pass. After a very short stay in this camp, we were embarked in Hull. I had adopted a stooping posture, and on the way to the ship I was overtaken by an English soldier who saw that I had difficulty in carrying my duffel bag so he carried it for me to the ship.

After a sea voyage past Heligoland, which we passed at night, we landed in Cuxhaven. I took my duffel bag and boarded a train that was waiting to take us to a discharge camp on the Lüneburg Heath. The next day there was a train to Münster, my home town. I received my discharge permit, and late in the afternoon of the next day I reached the outskirts of Münster and was accommodated in a former cavalry barracks, where I also received something to eat.

I could have gone home that same evening, but it would have been very difficult trying to find the house where my parents were now living in the darkness, so I spent the night in the barracks.

The next morning I walked through a totally destroyed city. I walked over cleared roads to the left and right of the huge rubble mountains, and passed the destroyed house facades until I finally found the house I was looking for.

Epilogue

My parents were well and the reunion was indescribable. It was a very emotional and joyous occasion. Unfortunately, the misery was not yet over and the celebration was marred by the fact that my parents had not receieved any sign of life from my younger brother. He had been serving on the Russian Front and we feared the worst. Although I was now home, we still had to rebuild our shattered lives.

(Wilhelm Schulte passed away on 28 December 2003, aged 83.)

6

Friedrich 'Fred' Wilhelm Kranefeld

Military service as a *Fallschirm-Sanitäter*

Fred was born on 12 May 1922 in Westhofen-Westfalen. He shared the following story with me during a two-hour-long phone conversation from Canada, which had been arranged by his daughter a week or two earlier. This gave Fred time to reflect and remember the anecdotes you are about to read. Fred started at the beginning and finished at the end, sometimes rewinding to another period as he remembered another anecdote, and I hastily made notes during the interview and produced the following text from it. In 2018, I made contact with his son Derek and he was able to furnish photographs that were meant to accompany the original interview. Fred had been a keen photographer and took many photos both during and after the Second World War. Fred volunteered to become a Fallschirmjäger *and was subsequently selected to become a* Sanitäter *(medic). He served in Crete, Russia and was captured in Sicily in 1943.*

Fred in training fatigues with an ammunition bandolier around his neck. (Derek Kranefeld)

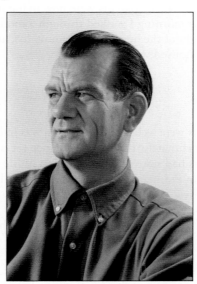

This studio portrait of Fred was taken some time between 1968 and 1970. This photo was selected by his son Derek as an image that he and his sister best remember their father. Fred was a keen photographer both during the war and in the years afterward and spent much of his time behind the lens. (Derek Kranefeld)

Sanitäter training

I was trained as a musician and could play the piano and the oboe. One of the reasons that I volunteered for the *Fallschirmtruppe* was the extra pay and double rations of food. When I was inducted as a *Fallschirmjäger*, the selection went by professions. As I was a musician I was selected to be a medic. Training was conducted at the Spandau barracks, followed by parachute training at Stendal, and upon completion I joined *Sanitäts Kompanie 2*.

Our senior officers were Dr Carl Langemeyer and Dr Adolf Stimpfl. Both of them were skilful doctors and surgeons. Dr Stimpfl was not snappish, he held back and did not socialise, and he would leave at the end of the night. Dr Langemeyer (Lang) was

Oberarzt (senior physician) Dr Carl Langemeyer at the Sennelager training grounds in early 1941. He was awarded the *Ritterkreuz* on 18 November 1944. (Derek Kranefeld)

Men of *2/Fallsch.San.Abt-XI Fliegerkorps* during field training. Fred is second from the right. (Derek Kranefeld)

Fallschirm-Sanitäter board a JU-52 transport aircraft before a training jump. (Derek Kranefeld)

completely the opposite. He would say: "From now on I am your father and your mother." We all felt like he was an older brother to us.

In Brandenburg there was a restaurant that was used by *Fallschirmjäger*, infantry, artillery and cavalry troops. Lang would walk in and always order a light beer and a schnapps chaser. He always paid for the drinks and would pay for everything all night. He was a good man.

Sanitäts Kompanie 2 was as unmilitary as you could get; the only thing soldierly about us was the uniform. All day we would attend medical lectures and conduct training. Stopping blood was the limit of our training.

None of the medics in *Kompanien 1–4* of *Fallschirm-Sanitäts-Abteilung-XI Fliegerkorps* were covered by the Geneva Convention. We had a small piece of paper in our *Soldbuch* which gave name, number and the fact that we were members of an armed unit. A red cross was allowed over a hospital or aid station, as these were covered by the Geneva Convention. We were only covered in the rear at a hospital or aid station, and not in the front line. This only applied to paratroop-medics. We were not allowed to wear a Red Cross armband. Basically, as a medic we were unarmed, but when we joined the 'yellows' [nickname for the paratroops with their yellow collar tabs] we were armed.

Crete

Our aircraft left the Topolia airfield in Greece during the afternoon of 20 May as part of the second wave.

I was number 13 and Dr Stimpfl was number 12 in our aircraft. The weapons and supply containers were released as the sixth or seventh man jumped. There was a serious updraft when we jumped, and it felt an age to come down. I am not sure exactly the height at which we jumped from our aircraft, but I believe it was about 90m and very hot. There were about 20 holes in Dr Stimpfl's parachute canopy. He yelled out to me: "They're using actual bullets here." My only medical kit was a small first-aid package with some dress-

In Greece prior to the invasion, men from *2/FSA* clean and prepare their weapons. From left to right: *Feldwebel* Josef Griese (WIA on 20 May), *Sanitäts-Gefreiter* Otto Loop, *Sanitäts-Gefreiter* Eberhard Sanger, *Sanitäts-Gefreiter* Herbert Lecher and *Sanitäts-Gefreiter* Hermann Paus. (Jose Ramon Artaza Ibañez)

ings and adhesive tape. I carried a P08 [Luger] pistol and jumped without a main weapon. Only later in Sicily did I jump with a rifle.

The majority of *2. Kompanie* of *Fallsch-San-Abt* (*2/FSA*) jumped with *III./FJR1* at around 1730 hours near Gazi, west of Heraklion.[1]

---

1   At 1500 hours on 21 May, two *Züge* from *2/FSA* along with *5 & 6/FJR2* were dropped into the coastal strip west of Platanias. One *Zug* under the command of *Oberarzt* Dr Dieter Hartmann was decimated after landing. Hartmann was killed. Twenty men from the second *Zug* managed to escape to friendly forces near Maleme. See Golla, p.467. [Authors note, several sources state a smaller force, possibly a reinforced platoon.]

Three *Sanitäter* from *2.Kompanie* ready to board their JU-52 at the Topolia airfield in Greece on 20 May 1941, prior to their jump near the harbour town of Heraklion later in the afternoon. The man on the left is holding a lifejacket that was issued to all paratroopers for the flight to Crete. (Derek Kranefeld)

Dr Dieter Hartmann, who was killed on 21 May when his *Zug* was dropped onto well-camouflaged Allied positions near Platanias, east of Maleme. This photo was taken after the operation at the Corinth Canal. (Derek Kranefeld)

Sanitäts-Gefreiter Otto Loop on the flight from Topolia to Heraklion. He was killed on 27 May and is buried in block 1 grave 958 at the Maleme cemetery. (Jose Ramon Artaza Ibañez)

The grave of *Gefreiter* Otto Loop at Maleme. (aretecrete.com)

Dr Dieter Hartmann at the Sennelager training grounds in early 1941. (Jose Ramon Artaza Ibañez)

The grave of *Oberarzt* Dr Dieter Hartmann at Maleme, buried with another comrade from *2/FSA*. (aretecrete.com)

Soon after we landed we captured an English officer. He immediately informed us: "You were half an hour late!" He was right; we were late. We had to dig our JU-52 out of the sand as it was buried up to the axle on the Greek airfield. Apparently the British had good intelligence about our attack!

I landed in a vineyard and I was not in a good mood. Suddenly something appeared in front of me, obscured by vines. I pulled out my pistol and BOOM, I had shot a donkey. As the day went on, more and more men were in my position. Lang was furious with the stench and demanded to know who shot the donkey. We could not bury it as the ground was clay and very hard. It wasn't until we returned to Greece that I owned up to Lang that it was me who shot the donkey.

We were positioned close to a bridge that spanned a fairly deep dry ravine.[2] The bridge was not very long and was south of the highway to southern Crete. On the north side were the British forces, and we were to the south. Heraklion was a fortress town with big gates and thick walls. There was no sense in shooting at the walls, so we lay back and enjoyed the sunshine.

One of Fred's comrades from *2/FSA*, *Sanitäts-Gefreiter* Walter Rahn. (Jose Ramon Artaza Ibañez)

---

2   A local historian pinpointed this bridge to an area known as 'The Bridges', or *Ta Gyofirakia* in Greek.

The bridge was the apple in Lang's eye. One hundred and fifty yards east of the bridge was a landing place and 50yds further east was our aid station. The bridge was the only way the British troops could get to us from the south.[3] Lang had an idea. One day he was wheeling and dealing with the yellows and they gave him some explosives. I was not involved as I was situated on a hill about 1km away, but all the boys were talking about it afterward. Lang's idea was to blow the bridge himself. Lang knew no more about explosives than that you light them and they go bang. At night time when it was quiet, the charges were set. The plunger was pressed but there was no bang. He had obviously done something wrong. As daylight approached, no-one dared wander out to examine the explosives due to the Scots Highlander sharpshooters. We all had diarrhoea due to the greasy food, so we were more than happy to remain in our holes and shit all day.

A short time later we heard a dog barking near our positions. Someone shot it as it was raising an almighty din. Cigarettes again ran low, so two men walked down to one of the gates on the city wall with a white rag and asked the soldiers on the wall if they could get some. This was a strange episode and they were told: "You have no business here, you have to leave!"

Our food rations were subsidised with olives that we found in barrels and British rations, which seemed to be made up of tins of corned beef. We finally met up with German troops [*Gebirgsjäger*] coming from the west. One of them was an explosives expert. He and Lang went to take a look at the bridge as no-one had yet dared to inspect the explosives. The soldier spent 15–20 minutes inspecting

the bridge, and when he returned he said: "Who did that?" "We did," came the reply. "You had better sit down and hope it does not go off; there are too many explosives for such a small bridge!" It was very lucky that the bridge did not blow up.

Once the British evacuated the city, Lang ordered us to move in. He repeated the need for us to be careful. What bothered us most were the Greeks and Cretans, not the British. We were afraid of the natives. One of the *Fallschirmjäger* doctors and a medic had allegedly been found nailed to a barn door near Maleme.[4] They had been mutilated, as had many other men. All photos were ordered to

Lang and his famous black umbrella. He was instrumental in setting up a *Hauptverbandplatz* near Heraklion to deal with the heavy casualties suffered by *FJR1*. Behind him is a *Feldwebel* and a *Gefreiter* with ammunition belts. (Derek Kranefeld)

---

3   The 1st Battalion of the Argyll & Sutherland Highlanders.

4   Fred believed that this was *Oberarzt* Dr Hartmann; however, according to Kurowski, pp.123–24, Hartmann was killed by a sniper, as were several of his men, and the survivors were captured by British troops.

be confiscated as these incidents were not to go public. Someone showed me photographs of the horrific incidents when we were in Russia.

Whilst on the bridge area, our radio operator spent two days sending encrypted messages. We needed help and were getting nothing from the mainland. Lang broke protocol and sent an 'open voice' communication. He got a reaction. Bombers turned up some hours later and dropped what appeared to look like pianos.[5] One thing I must say about Lang: he knew no fear. At one point during the battle for Heraklion he showed himself in full view of the defenders carrying a black umbrella. Some thought he was mad, but he was a brave man.

I remember another time when we ran out of cigarettes. Men were asking: "Got any fags." Someone knew where they were, they were with the logistics officer; loads of them had been collected from supply containers. We requested some to be issued, but we were told we had no business having them. Lang said: "I will keep him busy, and you steal the cigarettes." We stole a great many of them and distributed them to the men.

When we returned to Greece, many of us were still suffering from diarrhoea. Out of 130 men, 36 were killed, 5 missing, 18 wounded and 2 injured from the jump. Two of those killed were my best friends. Many of them were killed in the air.

This the first of three photographs of makeshift graves photographed by Fred. These were his comrades from 2/ FSA who jumped on 21 May. He must have gone to the Maleme area to visit these graves and pay his respects after the battle for Heraklion was over. From left to right: *Oberarzt* Dr Dieter Hartmann, aged 27; *Uffz* August Geisberger, aged 25; *Uffz* August Schrumpf, aged 26; *Uffz* Gerhard Löffler, aged 22; *Gefreiter* Günther von Hohenhau, aged 19; *Gefreiter* Georg Ruske, aged 21; *Gefreiter* Fritz Geihe, aged 21; unreadable marker; *Gefreiter* Anton Müller, aged 21; *Gefreiter* Robert Förster, aged 21; an unknown *Fallschirmjäger*; unreadable marker. (Derek Kranefeld)

---

5   Fred never elaborated on what these 'piano' objects were. It may have been a heavy weapon such as a 37mm anti-tank gun or recoilless gun attached to multiple parachutes.

Eight graves of men from *2/FSA*. From left to right: *Gefreiter* Alois Flommersfeld, aged 20; *Gefreiter* Josef Kropp, aged 21; *Gefreiter* Erich Noack, aged 19; *Obergefreiter* Herbert Thiessen, aged 24; *Obergefreiter* Herbert Fiebrantz, aged 24; an unknown *Fallschirmjäger*; *Gefreiter* Hermann Kurz, aged 21; *Obergefreiter* Hartmut Werner, aged 20. (Derek Kranefeld)

Two men from Dr Hartmann's *Zug* from *2/FSA* who were killed near Platanias on 21 and 22 May 1941 respectively. They are *Obergefreiter* Joseph Streit, aged 23, and *Obergefreiter* Franz Mettenmeier, aged 21. They are buried alongside each other in the cemetery at Maleme. (Derek Kranefeld)

Memorial cross erected on 29 May 1941 to the men of
I/FJR1 who were killed in the fighting for Heraklion.
(Derek Kranefeld)

The grave of *Gefreiter* Ernst-August Winkelmann
from *2/FSA*, who was killed on 20 May. He now
lies in block 1 grave 877 at the Maleme cemetery.
(Jose Ramon Artaza Ibañez)

The grave of *Gefreiter* Ernst-August Winkelmann at
Maleme. (aretecrete.com)

Unlike many of my comrades, I never
received the *Kreta* cuff title and never
enquired about it, nor was I ever reprimanded
for not wearing it.

I was, however, awarded the Iron Cross
2nd Class on 26 June 1941 via *FJR1*.

I don't know how it started, but when
we returned from Crete all of the men were
singing and whistling 'It's a long way to
Tipperary', a popular British song at the
time. One day Lang blew his stack: "I've
had it; I know it and I don't want to hear it
anymore. I will order 14 days bread and water
if I hear it again." Whilst we were in Russia a
few months later there was an injured yellow
Feldwebel on the operating table under full
anaesthetic. Lang was ready to start, and as
he made the first incision the man bellows
"It's a long way to Tipperary". Everyone in
the operating room stood back, expecting
Lang to explode. He dropped his scalpel and
laughed. That was a relief to all of us.

The *Kreta* cuff title was instituted on 16 October 1942 to reward all *Wehrmacht* personnel who had taken part in the battle of Crete in May 1941. The cuff title was worn on all uniforms and was sewn on the left sleeve at a prescribed distance from the seam of the cuff. For paratroops to be awarded this cuff title they must have taken part in a parachute or glider landing (or the seaborne forces) between 20 and 27 May 1941. (Ian Alexander Sandford)

Award ceremony for the men of *2/FSA* upon their return to Greece. Derek Kranefeld believes his father is third from the left in the front rank. (Jose Ramon Artaza Ibañez)

2/FSA in Germany after Crete. Fred can be seen in the sixth rank on the building side. (Jose Ramon Artaza Ibañez)

Our base in Brandenburg/Havel

I was out one night in Brandenburg and I thought I saw a parachute, and someone else also saw one in the night sky. The alarm was raised and we had to guard a factory in case there were saboteurs operating close by. I spent all night checking IDs of the factory workers. I encountered several loudmouths who refused to show ID and were therefore refused entry into the factory. Of course this action was noticed by the manager, and I almost found myself in trouble for interrupting the war effort.

My close friends Herman Paus, Apfelbaum, Lecher and I were regarded as the bad boys in Brandenburg. If anything happened in the town, we always got the blame. Every time I came up for promotion I was held over. I was always in trouble. Most NCO *Sanis* did not survive, so naturally I did eventually get promoted. I was a loudmouth and was not good at taking orders; I had to digest it first, and ruffled a few officers' feathers in the process. Yellow officers often complained about me.

The barracks at Brandenburg Havel. (Derek Kranefeld)

Russia

At the beginning of December 1941, we were sent to Army Group North and took up positions east of Schlüsselberg on the River Neva. There was a fortress island at the mouth of the river held by the Russians. The Russians used artillery barges on the river, but they were not very accurate. Only the Russians in the fortress were killed by Russian artillery, as they were surrounded on three sides. Every three days the Russians received ammunition, so on the first day it was hell on earth and then nothing for the next two days. We would go underground to our bunkers on the first day. Russian troops built a bridge across the Neva, but the yellows on the other side would hit everything that moved, causing massive casualties. The bridge was destroyed, but the next night the Russians would build another one. They were not worried about casualties; it was bloody murder, and more reinforcements would turn up to take the place of the dead.

The lice were known as '52 Tonners', you couldn't kill them. Washing alone was no good. Dr Langemeyer found he had lice. It turned out that his orderly had seen them crawling around in his pants. Boiling them was the only way to kill them, but to be sure we froze them solid first and then boiled them. The lice did not like that.

In Russia we had our own operating room and recovery ward. Once the doctors finished their surgery, the casualties were passed on to me. There were lots of stomach wounds. I used wet rags to wet the lips of those men who could not eat or drink. All of the casualties were yellows. My own brother died of kidney failure in the East. A Dr Gowolka in Stendal sent him to the *Ostfront* 15 days before the capitulation. He should never have gone.

Fred (third from left) with his comrades in Russia in December 1941. The men went east with only greatcoats and snoods. Proper winter uniforms had not yet been issued. (Derek Kranefeld)

Lang speaks to his men on the Neva Front in Russia in December 1941. (Derek Kranefeld)

One evening at about 2100 hours, Lang came to me with a little job. He wanted me to look after a casualty suffering from extreme gangrene. He was not expected to last the night. I made his last night as comfortable as possible. I never even knew him, but I kept him going until he closed his eyes for the last time. I looked at life differently after that.

Luckily we were in Russia for less than four weeks. When we returned in late December 1941, we organised a Christmas party. Because I could play the piano, Lang asked me to play for the party. "No way," I said, "it's not my duty." "Why not?" Lang asked. "I did not get promoted," I replied. I was promoted within the hour. We had a bloody good time and Lang supplied all of the Christmas presents. I still have mine at home after all these years.

Sicily and capture

Prior to the operations on Sicily we were based in southern France. Before being flown to Venice we had to hand in all our personal items except for our ID. My *Fallschirmjäger* badge was taken and I never got it back. In Venice we were confined to the base and had to stand guard on the aircraft.

In Sicily we would defend our positions and move back under strong opposition. I was wounded in the ass by a grenade and painfully managed to pull out the shrapnel. To ease my situation I had found a box of cigars, and offered one to a *Feldwebel* I was with before we began to walk/hobble towards Palermo. We slept during the day and walked through the night. I only had five rounds of ammunition in my pocket. We came across a shack in the darkness and thought it a good place to sleep, as we were exhausted. We bedded down, and when we woke up we had a shock. We were in the middle of what looked like a supply depot, so we walked in and were confronted by British soldiers. Surprised by our presence, they asked "What are you doing here?" Of course we gave up, as we had no weapons! The commanding officer at the depot spoke perfect German: "How can you just walk in, it's impossible, the guards must have been asleep." The guards had been asleep, as we saw no-one. I had a shoulder sack with a few items inside. I opened the sack when we were searched, and I pulled out a lovely sheath knife. The sergeant searching us said "I wish I had one of those", so I gave it to him and he had tears in his eyes. I had no idea where I had picked it up. It wasn't even mine.

All meals were given to us by Italian soldiers. On the second day my *Feldwebel* kicked one of the Italians in the ass. "I hate them," he said.

POW

My group of POWs were shipped off to the USA and landed in Norfolk, Virginia, and taken to Mississippi. We were split up into two groups. One went cotton picking and the other group cut trees with saws and axes. We were not accompanied or watched, so we used to sleep until it was time to go. This went on for weeks until the old civilian responsible for us saw what we were doing. Things changed after that and we had to work.

We were then sent to Alabama to take part in the peanut harvest. On the first morning the farmer came to meet us. "Grab a pitchfork," he told us, and he threw them on the ground in front of us. I caught up with him and asked him why he threw the forks. "I don't want to get closer in case I get eaten by you Nazis," he replied. The camp was commanded by a senior Army NCO. His wife used to visit him at midday with his lunch. We used to talk. She asked me to show her where the Nazis were. "Look around," I said, "wherever you see someone with a shirt off, that's it." She turned to me and said: "I want to see the ones with horns!"

Whilst a POW in America I had lost my ID and could not prove that I was a medic. I sent a medical personnel request to the Swiss Red Cross. I received a reply in the shape of a one-sided postcard signed by Hermann Goering confirming my identity.

In 1946 I was repatriated and sent to Liverpool in England. I remember being on the ship for eight hours listening to a song called 'Begin the Beguine', sung by Artie Shaw, that was played over and over through the speakers. It was torture. Once we were finally ashore we were taken to Braintree in Essex.

Whilst we were in Braintree, one of the prisoners fell in love with a local English girl and he would disappear every night. During one of his forays he was caught, and I had to interpret. He explained the reason why he kept disappearing: "I am in love." He was given four weeks' close detention and the girl was given 14 days' house arrest for fraternising with a German prisoner of war. Four weeks later the prisoner was gone! The girl's father had come down to the camp and demanded to see the commander. Apparently he put his foot on the table and asked: "How much do you want for him? I want to buy him." The prisoner was released and we never saw him again.

I was interrogated in Braintree, but a week later I was repatriated to Dortmund.

My return to Germany

Once I had returned to Germany I had to see a doctor for a medical to work in the coal mines. I didn't want to do this, but I had no choice. I had to work him over. It was a young doctor, and after my examination I was made exempt from working underground, and with no hard work at all in the rain or damp weather. My Father laughed when I told him the story. He said: "Now I've heard everything!"

I joined an insurance company and was transferred to Mannheim, but I had no money. Shortly afterward I applied for a new medical job working for the occupational forces. I took an exam and passed. My medical knowledge obviously helped. I was instructed to immunise four companies of men, basically pushing needles into arms. Whilst working my way through the lines of men, the CO comes in. "Who is the best man for immunisation?" he said. "Fred is," came the reply. I immunised him and he was happy. Later that night there were only 50 men left, but I managed to finish them all. Just after finishing this long job, a colleague asked me to translate a document. I suddenly became excited and asked him for another form. It was an immigration form to enter Canada. I filled in both forms, but unfortunately my colleague's form was refused due to a drink problem. That is how I ended up in Canada, where I went on to run an electronics business and I retired in 1987. I never returned to Germany for 42 years.

On reflection after the war, I can personally say that quite a lot of us did not consider the severity of war. We only more or less remembered the good times. We always maintained our sense of humour and made fun during many dangerous situations, and often came close to getting caught up in that fun.

(Fred Kranefeld passed away in January 2008, aged 85.)

7

Helmut 'Bolle' Bollmann

Memories of Italy and Normandy

Helmut Bollmann was born in Mansfeld, Germany, on 6 May 1921. Bolle was the first veteran whom I corresponded with via email. He kindly permitted me to use some short stories from his memoirs entitled Der Mansfeld kommt – *memories of war and peace, which he kindly translated for me. Helmut Bollmann was an officer candidate and* Zugführer *in 1/Fallschirm Panzerjäger* Abteilung *of FJD1. The following accounts took place near the city of Battipaglia, several days after the Allied landings at Salerno, in the Bay of Naples, Italy, in September 1943. After surviving the fighting at Cassino, Fahnenjunker-Feldwebel (and soon to be Leutnant) Helmut Bollmann along with 25 other battle worn men were transferred to Brittany in France where they provided the cadre for three new* Kompanien *of Fallschirm-Panzerjäger. The* Panzerjäger Abteilung *of FJD3 saw action near Saint-Lô soon after the Allied invasion, where they were credited with destroying many American tanks. Bolle was captured by US forces in April 1945. After his release from captivity in 1946, Bolle went to work for a new home newspaper as a journalist and political editor, and later became a senior editor at the Associated Press in Frankfurt, retiring in 1984.*

Bolle as a senior editor in the early 1980s.
(Helmut Bollmann)

I stumbled upon this photo on German eBay and instantly recognised Bolle. The photo is a postcard probably produced to send to family members. On the reverse it has the address of the photo studio in Eisleben, which is 16km from Mansfeld, Bolle's home town. Bolle, a young *Unteroffizier*, wears the parachute badge, wound badge in black and the EK2 ribbon. (Author's Collection)

Salerno

On 9 September 1943, the Allies landed with strong forces near Salerno in the Gulf of Naples. They established a bridgehead, which had to be eliminated as soon as possible. Due to the huge Allied armada in the Gulf of Naples and their air superiority, this was not going to be an easy task.

The attack from Eboli in the direction of Battapaglia was an easy ride for me. Our *Bataillon* had already retaken most of the town when my *Panzerjägerzug* arrived. However, the soldiers were not successful in crossing the small river that flowed through the city.

When I finally reached the market place, something amazing happened. An English [*sic*] *Major*, who had been taken prisoner, ordered the other POWs to line up as though they were on the parade ground in England and place their rifles together in pyramids. Then he reported to the German *Kommandeur* that they were ready to leave, before marching off in step. These Tommies were terrific men and showed exemplary discipline.

Later on I learned that a German staff officer, who was on a reconnaissance ride to the front line, hastily turned around when he caught sight of the marching English column. He caused panic with the staff in the hinterland when he reported, "the enemy was advancing towards Eboli". He was in so much of a hurry that he must have missed the eight *Fallschirmjäger* who were escorting the column on foot.

My three guns stood in the southern outskirts of Battapaglia. Under a hail of bombs and naval artillery, the city was soon reduced to rubble. Huge craters littered the landscape. A dud naval artillery shell, which I nearly stumbled over, had a massive 40cm calibre. It was the biggest hunk of metal that I had ever seen.

Helmut Bollmann as a senior NCO and officer candidate. (Helmut Bollmann)

Bolle as an *Unteroffizier* stood beside a staff car. (Helmut Bollmann)

During one of my excursions I came across a long zig-zag-shaped air raid shelter, which appeared to be empty. I thought I had found the ideal command post, but it all looked too good to be true that nobody was in. That was odd; there had to be a catch to it.

I walked down the staircase. Behind the second corner was a beam of light, which came from a hole in the concrete ceiling. At my feet lay a 100kg bomb. I held my breath, stepped very carefully over the damned thing and tiptoed away.

At dusk, the fighter-bombers stopped for the day and the mosquitoes began to buzz around us. I could now lean back in my ditch and look forward to the magnificent firework display which was performed every evening. Four or five German bombers made an appearance at nightfall and tried in vain to sink the mighty Allied fleet, which sat majestically in the Gulf of Naples. Wisely, they dropped their bombs somewhere in the water and turned back, before they were caught in one of the countless searchlights. Anti-aircraft guns from the armada were firing endless amounts of tracer skywards, which burst with a loud bang. It was great entertainment for both sides.

At dawn the fighter-bombers reappeared and took turns to fire all day long at anything that moved on the ground. There had only been sporadic fire from the fleet artillery during the night, but now it rained down again. Tanks had not yet disembarked; at least none could be seen.

Beside the shelter containing the bomb lay a mortar and some ammunition, which had been left behind by some English [sic] soldiers. I aimed it at their positions and sent them some of their own shells. However, I did not continue this for long. The English mortar specialists knew their business better than the German *Panzerjäger*. They soon located our position and began to bombard us with shells. Well, the wiser man soon gives in and I took to my heels as fast as I could.

After we had tried in vain to eliminate the Allied bridgehead near Salerno, we were ordered to retreat.

The Hummel

On the side of the road sat an abandoned Hummel, a German roofless, tracked, self-propelled artillery piece with a large-calibre 15cm gun. We *Fallschirmjäger* did not have such heavy weaponry at our disposal. This gun obviously belonged to the *Artillerie Bataillon*, which had taken part in the attack that night.

Sd.Kfz.165 Hummel self-propelled 15cm gun. (Musée des Blindés, Saumur)

To my surprise I found no crew. The vehicle was as empty as my water bottle. There was a shell crater near the right-side track. When the shell exploded it must have scared the crew to death. They must have scattered in all directions and then not been able to find their vehicle in the dark. There was no other explanation.

I ordered my deputy to return to our start point with the *Kompanie*. I sat between the control sticks of the Hummel and started the engine, with the intention of delivering this lost vehicle to the command post of my *Kompanie*.

On the way back I began to think about the situation. I throttled back on the engine and thought it over. On my return I would have to write out a report, which the *Kompaniechef* would pass on to *Bataillon*, *Bataillon* would pass it on to *Division* and *Division* would pass it on to the Armee-Korps. At the end of it all there may even be a court martial, with me as the chief witness. After all, a Hummel like this was not a small, insignificant military item.

I shuddered at the thought and I decided: GET RID OF IT!

I stopped at my command post and ordered an *Oberjäger* to follow me on a motorcycle combination. After giving the *Kompanie HQ* a wide berth, I drove through Battapaglia in the direction of Eboli to a huge road junction, where I parked the troublesome Hummel on the roadside.

Then I swung myself into the sidecar and returned to my command post to get some sleep. When I passed the road junction five hours later, by sheer chance of course, the Hummel was gone. It must have been found by its lawful owners. Whether they had found it or not, it was no longer there. Good riddance!

The enemy

In the morning grey of the following day, a counterattack took place. After an attack by several bombers, followed by some artillery salvos, English [*sic*] infantry began to move across the open field in front of our positions. But this time they were not experienced Tommies. One could tell by their spiritless movement across the ground that these were young lads with no front-line experience at all.

I squatted in a ditch with my machine pistol, waiting for things to happen. The enemy was still out of range of my weapon, but all of a sudden I became puzzled by some movement and could hardly believe my eyes. About 50 yards in front of me, a real big fatty rose to his feet and looked around completely bewildered. He wore a helmet, but he had no weapon, not even a belt, but a Red Cross armband could be seen on his upper arm.

Both sides ceased fire. For a short moment a strange hush descended on the battlefield. Panting for breath, the man approached in a gallop and dropped exhausted into the ditch. He took off his helmet and his neckerchief, and wiped the sweat from his scarlet-coloured face. He had simply lost his way and had run in the wrong direction. He was still shocked and looked at me as though he was seeing a ghost.

The noise of battle started again.

"May I have a cup of tea?" was his first polite question after he had slowly recovered. I looked at him, still dumbfounded, and hurriedly tried to remember the English I had learned at school. "No tea, only coffee," I told my unexpected guest. The soldier declined with a shake of the head and began to unpack his bread bag.

The enemy made no progress and had requested artillery support. When the first shells hit the ground, I pointed my finger towards a drainage pipe, which connected the ditches on both sides of the road. "Get in there!" I shouted. The POW obediently squeezed himself into the narrow tunnel, but he did not stay in this shelter. He crawled through the tunnel to the other side, and there, as cool as you please, began to make a mess tin of tea on his spirit stove. The way back underground obviously seemed too strenuous to him.

Between two bursting shells, he jumped across the road and offered me, a little embarrassed, a mug of tea. The other side had entrenched itself, and the fight dragged on. In broad daylight the prisoner could not be sent behind. So I made the most of this time to brush up on my English.

The fat man showed me some photos of his family; he had a wife and two children at home, and told me that he was a musician by profession. In the band of his regiment, which was now a medical platoon, he used to play the bass drum.

Tapping his paunch, he said a belt was not in stock for the size of his belly.

In between making tea, he now and again offered me a Navy Cut cigarette. The German malt coffee he justly disdained, but the pea soup from the field kitchen was consumed with relish; a second helping was alright with him. We were both a bit sorry when we had to part company in the evening.

The next morning, tanks appeared on the battlefield for the first time since the landings had begun. It was a hot day and the attackers suffered heavy losses. Towards evening, enemy representatives waved a white flag and met with German staff officers between the lines. A ceasefire until midnight was arranged in order to recover the wounded. In addition to the ambulances, enemy tanks with muzzle caps fitted rolled forward and participated in the salvage operation.

On 19 September 1943, I was wounded for the second time. I suddenly dropped my binoculars. A short, sharp whiplash hit my left forearm and blood began to flow from my sleeve. I packed the wound with a bandage, reported by field telephone to the *Kompanie* and was driven to the dressing station on a motorcycle. The medical officer examined my wound: "Off to the hospital." "But …" I replied. "No buts," interrupted the doctor as he pulled a piece of material out of the wound with tweezers. In the field hospital I slept in a beautiful white bed for the first time in many weeks.

Close combat and a close encounter in Normandy – July 1944

The Americans made an advance without artillery preparations on the right of the road on a broad front over hedges and meadows. More than 30 tanks rolled over the German *HKL*.

I was in the middle of one of the meadows when one of the tanks, a Sherman, ploughed through the low earth barrier of a hedge at full power with its machine gun rattling.

I immediately dived into a foxhole, but it was too late. The Sherman, as big as a barn gate, had spotted me and came straight ahead in my direction. I knew exactly what would happen next. The metal colossus would roll over the foxhole and turn on its axle. Death and funeral would take place at the same time. For a split second, a lightning flash of frightened paralysis ran through me. No time to panic though. Fractions of seconds would now count, but it could be done. Others had

The tank destruction badge was awarded for the single-handed destruction of an enemy tank using a hand-held weapon and was worn on the upper-right sleeve of the uniform tunic. (Gerard van Pul)

done it before. When I was in the dead angle of the tank's machine gun and when it braked in order to complete its cruel game, I jumped like a weasel from my hole, ran around the beast and boarded it from the rear. I pulled out a hand grenade, counted slowly '21, 22, 23', opened the turret hatch and let the explosive fall. As I jumped off, I heard a dull bang and the turret flap broke open with a din. The Sherman was now a harmless wreck.

Afterwards I was awarded the highly respected tank destruction badge, which was sewn on the upper right arm of the tunic. I had unexpectedly survived from pure instinct of self-preservation and with a lot of shit in my pants – as it were!

The American attack ended in a fiasco. The opposing infantry had been stopped in the *HKL*. The tanks that had broken through were destroyed in the first catching position and the remainder took to their heels.

In Rennes, Brittany, were some supplies of protective shields for our *Panzerschreck* rocket launchers. These shields made a gas mask unnecessary when firing the weapon, as it protected you somewhat from the smoke and fumes when fired. Along with a few good men, I received the order to fetch them and was allowed the use of the only amphibious vehicle in the detachment for the journey.

Bolle's certificate for the tank destruction badge in silver, dated 12 November 1944. (Helmut Bollmann)

My own car had recently been destroyed by the devil in the shape of an American *Jabo*.

My *Kommandeur* told me to "bring it back undamaged" as he parted with his favourite toy.

The mass of the men on front leave drove in an open truck to Rennes. During the overnight return trip, I and my amphibious vehicle were squeezed into a *Panzer* column heading for the front. I had a Tiger tank in front and another behind me. Overtaking was out of the question, only stop and go, everything without lights.

The Tiger behind drove close to the one in front. I turned and looked anxiously at the following monster. The driver's hatch was open, but in the darkness nothing much could be seen; certainly not a small amphibious vehicle in front. The driver relied on the *Panzer Kommandeur*, who was equipped with headphones and a throat mike in the open hatch.

Finally the tank crept closer; at a snail's pace, but closer. Everything now took place in slow motion. The tank crunched against the amphibious vehicle and it slowly began to fold up, squeezed like an accordion. There was enough time to jump out of the vehicle, and within seconds I had climbed aboard the tank and entered the turret hatch.

I roared furiously at the completely blank faces of the crew: "Where were your eyes, were you asleep, who made you the *Kommandeur*, you are incapable, and you negligently destroyed *Wehrmacht* property, you do not have this god-damned can under control."

But what use was this outbreak of rage? The *Oberfeldwebel* had fallen asleep for a few seconds: why did it have to happen now. This trip to Rennes ended very badly.

The fatal shot

On 17 July 1944, I had recieved a leave pass to return home and get married. Before I left, however, I had been tasked to conduct a reconnaissance of the Saint-Lô to Bérigny road so our troops could follow. My replacement could not be trusted to conduct such a mission because he had come from the *Flak* troops and was inexperienced. Once the mission was complete, I was to catch a train home from Rennes.

I drove ahead with a *Melder* to explore the terrain, and from a farm on a small hill I could observe the Saint-Lô to Bérigny road.

The second tree to the left of the gate had recieved a direct hit and the trunk blocked my way. As I started to jump over this obstacle, a sledgehammer hit my left knee. I fell back behind the trunk, my leg was numb and my pants turned red. With my *Kappmesser* I cut off the trouser leg, and the hole in my knee was the size of a chicken egg. An entire bandage fitted easily into the wound, with a second wrapped around it. I used the leather strap of my *Kappmesser* as a tourniquet and applied it to my thigh above the knee.

But who shot me and from where? They came out of the ditch on the other side not 30 yards away from, one white and one coloured soldier (the coloured solider later told me they had become lost in the rubble of Saint-Lô). They could have shouted "hands up!"

Now they crouched around the tree trunk. I drew my pistol. The white soldier reached for the trigger, but before he had time to aim, my bullet hit him in the stomach. The coloured soldier dropped his rifle and threw himself to the ground, holding both hands in front of his face. He was still lying there when my *Melder* finally arrived. Together, they dragged me behind the next hedgerow, and then, supported by both men, I was taken to the nearby farmyard and driven to the dressing station.

After a general anaesthesia and emergency surgery, the leg was immobile. My stay in the hospital lasted two unbearably long and painful nights until I was transported to a hospital in Paris. When a young doctor on a Paris platform saw my wound badge in silver, he graciously gave me his last available morphine injection and assigned me to the naval hospital.

In any other infirmary an amputation would have been carried out without much consideration. Not so in the naval hospital. The attending orthopaedist, a lecturer at the Kiel University Hospital, looked at the injury and said: "The knee is beyond saving, but I still want to try and save the rest of your leg. What you need now is a lot of patience."

He wrote the following letter to my father:

As you will know, your son was sent to the Marine Hospital Fieldpost Number M09267 on 20 July 1944. He had been treated for a war injury to his leg but despite immediate immobilisation I have

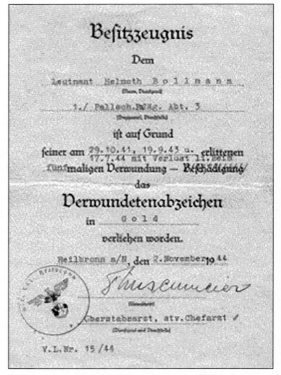

Certificate for the wound badge in gold, dated 2 November 1944. Bolle had been wounded five times, including the loss of his left leg. (Helmut Bollmann)

made up my mind to do a knee resection because your son's life was in danger. Your son has recovered well after the operation and most of the unbearable pain has gone. The fever continues and he will experience it for some time. I have told your son that I will write to you. You can be sure that everything is being done for him in terms of medical and nursing care. The naval hospital is quiet and has all the modern resources at its disposal so you do not have to worry about him.

I lay with my right leg plastered to the knee, my left leg hung on tension wires attached to the bone above and below the knee as well as above the ankle. I was constantly feverish and suffered terrible pain, only able to sleep with morphine. With time I became better, and the fever subsided. The sun shone into the room and somehow the world became more colourful.

I was transported to Heilbronn, where my Father came to visit me. I had a fever again, the wound had become infected and the left leg had to be amputated. After a transfer to the home hospital in Eisleben I recieved further operations, followed by a period of recovery. In April 1945, as the fronts closed in, the Americans came, followed by the Russians after the war ended. I went into captivity on crutches, and was released in 1946, when I immediately headed to the Allied zone and eventually worked for a new home newspaper called *Werra-Rundschau*, which was first published on 2 January 1948 and is still in print to this day.

(Helmut Bollmann passed away in October 2006, aged 85.)

8

Karl-Heinz 'Charlie' Pollmann

The Parachute Combat Engineer

Charlie was born on 26 August 1924 in Lüneburg. On completion of his Fallschirmjäger *training in the summer of 1942, Charlie was sent to North Africa with Rudolf Witzig's* Pionier *unit as part of the famous* Ramcke Brigade. *Later, in 1944, he served in Lithuania with I/Fallschirm-Pionier-Regiment 21, where he was wounded and evacuated back to Germany. Charlie was one of the very few veterans who, by a stroke of luck, never became a POW.*

I met Charlie in Lüneburg in 2000 and was greeted from the train by a spritely man in his late 70s, who took me to lunch and then we walked to his apartment to meet his wife and talk about his experiences during the Second World War. When the time came to leave, Charlie escorted me to the bus stop and bid me farewell. In the summer of 2001, Charlie was honoured with the Verdienstkreuz am Bande *(Cross of Merit), which was presented to him by the Mayor of Lüneburg.*

Charlie was awarded the *EK2* on 19 February 1943 and soon returned home to Germany on leave. (Karl-Heinz Pollmann)

Fallschirm-Pionier training

My apprenticeship as a mechanic ended in February 1942 and I received my journeyman's certificate. The following day was call-up.

To avoid duty in the *Reichsarbeitsdienst*, I volunteered for service in the *Fallschirmtruppe*. The next day I travelled by rail to Dessau-Kochstedt for a three-day entrance examination, which consisted of writing essays, mathematics and sport. I was lucky, as I was accepted. On the next Monday, 8 March 1942, my service began.

On that date, Kurt Behr, Egon Rabe and I, all residents of Lüneburg, were summoned to *Fallschirm Pionier Bataillon 1* in Dessau. The first thing we were taught was that all movements around the barracks had to be made in double-step. Later on we were shown to our rooms and given uniforms. Training could now start.

From the outset, *Leutnant* Hans Kaths, our *Kompanieführer*, put matters straight; we were to relinquish our daily cigarette ration to the older, more experienced soldiers, who in return would give us their sweet rations. This did not worry me as I knew that smoking was a health hazard.

The next three weeks were extremely hard. I was posted to a mortar section of a *Schwere* (heavy) *Kompanie*. At the end of April, our *Bataillon* was shipped off to Normandy in France. Our *2. Kompanie* was billeted at Saint-Remy-sur-Orne, while the *3. Kompanie* (to which Kurt Behr and Egon Rabe belonged) was located at Thury-Harcourt.

It was at Saint-Remy-sur-Orne where we acquired the skills of our future trade. Our *Zugführer* was *Leutnant* Gerhard Mertins, the future *Kommandeur* of *Pionier Bataillon 5*. After the war he made a fortune as an international arms dealer.

Our training included shooting, handling explosives, making sailor knots and building pontoon bridges across the River Orne. We also had plenty of opportunities to sample the local spirit, the famous Calvados brandy.

Fallschirm-Pioniers form up in training fatigues prior to an exercise. (Roland Höfer)

Men of *2/Fallschirm-Pionier-Bataillon 4* marching back to barracks after a field training exercise near Perugia in Italy. Leading the men is *Leutnant* Otto Schäfer. (Roland Höfer)

One day, my feet were aching badly after a 30km forced march. I was cared for by a nurse who lanced one of my blisters. I swooned. With a 40-degree fever and an infection of the lymphatic vessel, I was admitted to the Caen hospital for two weeks.

In *3. Kompanie* served a *Gruppeführer* who was none other than Harald Quandt, the stepson of Dr Joseph Goebbels.[1] During an important celebration, *Leutnant* Quandt had the privilege to welcome a theatrical group, among whose members were such famous actors as Albert Florath, the sisters Hedi and Margot Höpfner, as well as other well-known comedians who had all been sent by the *Reichspropogandaminister* himself to entertain us. In the early summer of 1942, our *Kompanie* was incorporated into *Fallschirm-Korps-Pionier-Bataillon* and transferred back to Dessau-Kochstedt.

From there we carried out an additional course at Dessau-Rosslau and later on the Altengrabow-Magdeburg training ground. After this we started training at the Wittstock/Dosse Parachute School.

Fallschirmschule

At Wittstock we were introduced to the harsh realities of a parachute school. First came the ground exercises: ground rolls (forwards and backwards), jumping into soft sand from an aircraft hatch, and finally, being dragged along the rugged surface of the exercise yard by a parachute blown by the propeller blast of two powerful aircraft engines. These were the first things we were taught.

We then learned to meticulously fold our own parachute, which we would use on our first jump. Only two days before, a motorised glider carrying 12 men had crashed on the airfield. There were no survivors. One of the comrades in my barrack began to turn paler each day. He might still have refused to jump, but found another way out. During a long and arduous march, he slipped a small stone into one of his boots. On returning to base, he suffered from a spectacular foot inflammation and was thus declared unfit for duty.

On the next day, as we were returning to the barracks after one of the numerous parachute folding sessions, we noticed that a small, agitated crowd had gathered in front of our building. We were told that a young man was holed up in our room. He first fired a shot at the ceiling and then, placing the rifle barrel into his mouth, pulled the trigger again. Because of this tragic event, the jump was postponed until the next day.

Our first jump was made from 250m. The orders were: "Get ready"; "Hook up"; "Get ready to jump".

The aircraft door was wide open. A green light was turned on and a shrill sound filled the air. The jumpmaster gave the final order: "*Ab!*" (Away).

Ten men, one behind the other, rushed out through the door. One more deep breath and the show was on!

The world tumbled about. Then a sharp jolt as the parachute deployed. I felt on top of the world. Luckily everything went as planned, otherwise I would have reported to the depot to get a free parachute!

During the next 45 seconds, we were dangling from the harness as the ground rushed up to meet us. Meanwhile our instructors kept shouting into their megaphones: "Keep your feet together!" Then came the impact of touchdown, followed by a landing roll. We were safely back on the ground.

---

1   Quandt himself was captured by Canadian troops in Italy in September 1944. After the war he became one of the wealthiest men in Germany. He was killed when his light aircraft crashed in Italy in September 1967. (Correspondence with Carl Bayerlein)

Fallschirm-Pioniers prior to a training jump at the Avignon airfield in France in the summer of 1943. They are training for Operation Valkyrie, which would be implemented a year later as part of the 20 July bomb plot. (Roland Höfer)

Fallschirmjäger land after a training jump. Their landing is scrutinised by instructors on the ground. (Kate Eichler)

During the next week, we made another five jumps, with and without weapons, from various types of aircraft: Dornier 23, Junkers JU-52 and Heinkel 111. I felt proud to wear the paratroopers' diving eagle badge on my chest, and showing off a little, I returned to my *Bataillon*.

Charlie proudly displays his paratroopers' badge on completion of his training at the Wittstock parachute school in 1942. (Karl-Heinz Pollmann)

To Africa with the *Ramcke Brigade*

We moved to Wittenberg and our *2. Kompanie*, led by *Oberleutnant* Cord Tietjen, was assigned to the *Ramcke Brigade* in July 1942, which was part of Rommel's *Afrika Korps*. The *Kompanie* mission was to lay mines. The rest of the *Bataillon* would soon follow.

Excerpts from K-H Pollmann's diary:
Tunisia, 7 November 1942 – 6 January 1943

7.11.42	At 2am, we were issued with tropical clothing. At 10pm, we entrained.
8.11.42	We travelled by train across Germany to Munich.
9.11.42	We crossed the Alps passing through many tunnels en-route. We skirted the city of Bolzano in Southern Tyrol.
10.11.42	Journeyed through the heartland of Italy along the Apennine range and on to *Florenze*.
11.11.42	Continue through Naples and on to Lecce near Brindisi. At 1800 hours, we took up our quarters in an Army barracks.
12.11.42	Waiting to be flown to *Afrika*.
13.11.42	Emplaned and then flown out in JU-52s from Lecce to Trapani in Sicily. In our circuit pattern, our aircraft nearly collided with a JU-88. At Trapani, we were served an excellent meal with peas. At night, guard duty at the airport.
14.11.42	Milk soup. Flight to Bizerte in Tunisia. We pitched our tents in an olive grove. We were attacked by British fighter planes.
15.11.42	In the morning we struck the tents. Italian anti-tank vehicles drove us 32km to the south, by Lake Garaet el Ichkeul south-west of Bizerte. We dug foxholes and felled the trees which blocked the view with explosives.
16.11.42	We slept in hay wagons. On waking up, we caught a white rabbit, which we stewed in two mess tins on an Esbit portable cooker and ate at 3pm. Unfortunately we had no salt.
17.11.42	We pitched three 4-man tents with individual shelter quarters.
18.11.42	Everything was quiet
19.11.41	We slaughtered a sheep and cooked it on a spit. Later on, an Arab came along to complain. What could we do about it? Supplies were long overdue and we were starving.
20.11.42	Everything was quiet.

21.11.42	Our positions were moved 300m back. We pitched tents for four and eight men. A black native gave us some straw.
22.11.42	We improved our individual tank shelter. It rained during the night. The left-hand pole collapsed and the hole was flooded.
23.11.42	We pitched the tent again. Today, quite unusually, I have shaved.
24.11.42	We moved our position 3.5km ahead, by the destroyed bridge. We pitched our tents and this time I was on guard duty. In the north, I watched an air attack on Bizerte. Anti-aircraft guns, searchlights and bombs.
25.11.42	We bought eggs from Arabs and then we were caught in a sudden downpour.
26.11.42	We moved our positions to Ferryville-Mateur, 16km in the direction of Teboura. Near a farm, we were surrounded by enemy armour. At night, we fell back 10km.
27.11.42	In the morning we mounted armoured vehicles and drove to the farm. We came under attack from our own *Stukas*, and then were fired at by the enemy tanks, a few of which we knocked out. A German *Panzer* ran over one of our own Teller Mines. One of his tracks was shattered. *Obergefreiter* Dräger was killed.
28.11.42	About midnight, back to the ford, 10km away, by Wadi Tinja, between Mateur and Bizerte. We took up position on the left side of the road. The ground was terribly hard. In the afternoon we moved closer to the road. The 1st squad left us.
29.11.42	During the night, from midnight to 3am we laid T-Mines. At 11pm, we were exposed to enemy artillery fire for 90 minutes. We took shelter by the mosque and laid mines on the bridge.
30.11.42	Our group captured a British officer and withdrew in the afternoon to Bizerte. *Unteroffizier* Hartung with *Pioniers* Hörsting, Häublein and Pollmann stayed behind to blow up the bridge in case the enemy came. *Spieß* Jenal turned up and brought some supplies he had salvaged from a freighter sunk in the harbour. Each man received a sausage and a few other things.
1.12.42	The 2nd squad of the *Luftlande-Kompanie* took over our quarters. We cooked doughnuts we had made from corn flour.
2.12.42	I got hold of three hens and cooked hen broth with millet.
3.12.42	I walked and then rode a horse to Mateur. I bought 100 francs worth of bread, oranges, cheese, sweets and matches.
4.12.42	With Häublein, we dug a foxhole on the right side of the road. In the afternoon, a Bristol-Blenheim bomber was shot down and crashed 500m away from us. *Oberst* Barenthin, commanding the *Pionier* troops of the *Fallschirm-Korps*, arrived in his *Kubelwagen* and waved at me. He said: "*Pionier*, there are a few unexploded 250kg bombs by the wreck. Blow them up!" I grabbed a few 100gm explosive charges, fuses and cord, and carried out the order. The most spectacular explosion I have ever seen.
5.12.42	In the morning I blew up the third bomb. Later, I lobbed a hand grenade into the river: the catch was excellent: 41 fish, measuring from 12–30cm. I cooked them with millet.
6.12.42	For today's meal I shot a chicken with a P08 pistol. The Arabs were over-charging us and besides, we were flat broke.
7.12.42	Hörsting got hold of a small sheep, which was skinned, gutted and cooked.
8.12.42	The wet season began. Our hole was flooded. We changed position and moved into the farm, with the Italians.
9.12.42	The supply motorcyclist brought us a 30-litre container of warm wine. Never before have we been so drunk.
10.12.42	The three Italians departed. On guard duty during the night.

11.12.42	We switched the pieces of furniture in the sleeping room. I got kicked in the pants by the grey horse. The pain was such that I hardly slept a wink that night.
12.12.42	Today 150 slave workers were sent to mend the road. They cleared the manure from the road.
13.12.42	Marching order. We removed the explosives and cleared the minefield. We boarded trucks and on through Mateur and Bizerte to the airfield and an olive grove. I slept beside the rucksacks on a layer of 20–30 woollen blankets. Had some wine during the night.
14.12.42	I put on clean underwear, then visited the Djebel Kebir fort.
15.12.42	Guard duty for two hours. Afterwards, I gathered my belongings and went back to the *3. Kompanie*.
16.12.42	In the morning, off to the medical officer at Bizerte to fetch anti-mange powder. In the afternoon, rifle maintenance.
17.12.42	In the morning I washed my trousers and tunic. In the afternoon, machine-gun practice.
18.12.42	Blast duties: Blew up French T-Mines. Cleared and defused 280 mines. In the afternoon, swam in the sea.
19.12.42	Around 10.30pm, I was sitting on the barrier while on guard duty. *Feldwebel* Beckmann turned up unexpectedly and berated me for misdemeanour on duty.
20.12.42	I reported to the *Kompanieführer, Oberleutnant* Friedrich. Five days of hard detention in Germany. I received the balance of my pay for 1942: 1,900 Francs, I felt like a rich man. I received a small parcel from my Mother. Who could ask for more?
21.12.42	Orientation exercise with compass, to the sea, followed by a swim in 16-degree warm water. The swell was rough. On the beach, we found a French portee [truck with a gun mounted on its bed], the gun of which was aimed at the sea. We operated the breech and suddenly, the piece went off, scaring us out of our minds.
22.12.42	On guard duty again.
23.12.42	In the afternoon, I got hold of a Christmas tree for tonight's celebrations.
24.12.42	Christmas Eve. On guard duty.
25.12.42	Christmas Day. Roasted goose for lunch.
26.12.42	Boxing Day. Transfer to Ferryville.
27.12.42	Guard duty on the bridge to Ferryville.
28.12.42	On guard duty again until 4pm. During the night, two Italian airmen arrived from the Ferryville brothel. They had to walk all the way to Caruba (18km) as there was no transport available.
29.12.42	Drill. "You want to be soldiers? Lie down, stand up, march, march!" For lunch, noodle soup with goulash and boiled potatoes. Guard duty at 4pm.
30.12.42	Guard duty until 4pm.
31.12.42	New Year's Eve. In the morning, we conduct weapon maintenance. In the evening, the New Year was cut short by an alert. Four sentries are placed on each bridge. At midnight, loud crackling of rifle fire and machine guns as flares shot skyward. Welcome to the New Year!
1.01.43	New Year's Day. Air alert at 3am. The heavy *Flak* opened up, chunks of plaster fell from the ceiling. In the afternoon, guard duty on the bridge.
2.01.43	We took up positions at the Ferme Michaud, 10km away from Mateur. We pitched tropical tents.
3.01.43	In the morning, kit inspection. In the afternoon, I am on guard duty at the *Bataillon*.
4.01.43	The *Kompanie* set off on a forced march: 30km with all of the equipment.
5.01.43	British Spitfires strafed the tents in the camp. We removed and camouflaged them.

6.01.43   During the night, at 00.45hrs, immediate standby. We returned to the front. At the Jefna Pass we built shelters in the ravine. Friendly and enemy shells were crisscrossing overhead.

Here ends my diary ...

On 30 December 1942, at night, the *Pioniers* of *3. Kompanie, Witzig Bataillon*, were delivered by parachute and two gliders behind the French and British lines in eastern Algeria to destroy airfields and bridges. The operation, however, was a failure. Only two men, one of whom was the *Kompanieführer, Oberleutnant* Friedrich, returned to the German lines.[2] As they were being driven away by their captors, *Oberleutnant* Friedrich and a Tunisian scout jumped out of the truck and made good their escape. Several days later, they were back in our camp in the Ferme Michaud, near Mateur.

I was delighted when on my return from a mission, I found that both had come out of it in one piece! But *Oberleutnant* Friedrich did not trifle with regulations, and instead of sharing my joy at being reunited, was quick to point out my boot laces, which were not properly secured but tied around the shaft. Friedrich had not been away two days and discipline was beginning to slacken. After the unfortunate experience of the night jumps, we suffered more casualties in the Djebel el Azzag region during an encounter with British paratroopers led by *Colonel* John Frost.[3] Back at Michaud for some rest, *Feldwebel* Johannes 'Hannes' Meist decided to raid enemy lines and carry out a few strikes at Beja and towards Algeria. I took part in two of these missions, and on 19 February 1943 I was awarded the Iron Cross 2nd Class. I was promoted to the rank of *Gefreiter*, while *Feldwebel* Meist was awarded the *DKiG* on 25 May.[4]

On 26 February, the *Division von Manteuffel*, to which the *Witzig Bataillon* was subordinated, launched an offensive westward in to the Sedjenane Valley. We boarded trucks and headed for the front. I had placed my rifle behind the bunk on which I was sitting.

Suddenly, as we came across another vehicle, our truck ran into a pothole and tilted. My rifle was knocked over and caught between the two trucks. A sharp crack and the barrel was bent. What was I to do? Fortunately, during a halt, I swapped my rifle for that of a wounded soldier who was about to be evacuated.

At dawn, the British attacked the hill on which we were posted. Suddenly, I felt a sharp pain in the thigh: I had been hit by a bullet. I was taken to the *Hauptverbandplatz*. From there I was flown out in a Feisler Storch light aircraft to the Ferryville [Menzel Bourguiba] Hospital. The bullet, however, fell to the ground as I dropped my trousers.[5] An operation was thus unnecessary. Four weeks of care and rest ensued. With every meal, my liking for French food grew stronger. We had white bread, wine and sometimes artichokes.

---

2   This operation was designed to disrupt the Allied supply routes into Tunisia. It was cold, windy and there was no moon. The poorly trained pilots dropped their human loads miles away from the drop zones. The *Fallschirmjäger* were rounded up by British paratroopers. See Lucas, p.89.

3   One of the first British paratroopers, later captured at Arnhem in September 1944.

4   See Scherzer, p.214. In 2018, I tracked down Ernst Meist, the son of Hannes Meist. He could remember very little about his father's wartime story. He could only remember hearing about Suda Bay in Crete, where the sea was full of white 'balloons', the parachutes of drowned *Fallschirmjäger*. As Hannes touched ground, his JU-52 was shot out of the sky above him. He also lost his ID disc near Maleme and his wife was informed that he had been KIA. After the disaster in Tunisia, Hannes escaped in a dingy and paddled from Tunis to Sicily. He was later promoted to *Leutnant* in Italy and was captured at Monte Cassino. He died in 1991, and later his wife destroyed all material relating to his wartime service.

5   Charlie kept the bullet, and in 1998 it was examined by the Imperial War Museum and was found to have two rifling grooves, so it could only be a round fired from a British .303 Lee Enfield No4 Mk1 bolt action rifle.

Return to Germany before the collapse in Tunisia

On 1 April 1943, after convalescing, I was returned to my unit. *Major* Witzig then gave me my first leave, telling me: "Call at the *Spieß*, he'll give you four weeks' leave!" Never before had I turned about so quickly.[6] Later, with two comrades, also from northern Germany, we hitch-hiked on the road to Tunis, which was about 150km away.

At Tunis we could afford a *Droschke* (taxi cab), which took us to Carthage airport, where we waited to be flown home to Germany. A few Italian aircraft were landing and we were told that of the eight which had taken off, only three had made it to their destination. As we found the venture rather risky, we chose instead to board a JU-90, which had just arrived and had some spare room. Mail was loaded and the aircraft took off. During the flight, ready to fight it out with the Tommies, we posted ourselves behind an *MG15* machine gun. In the evening, we arrived at Grossetto, and from there, via Rome, headed for the Motherland.

In Munich we received new tropical uniforms, and then headed home to Lüneburg. I enjoyed my first leave, but just before my time was up, I received a telegram which stated: "After leave you are to report to Wittenberg." The *Bataillon* was being restructured there. Veterans of the old *Kompanien*, new recruits and *Luftwaffe* soldiers formed the new *Bataillon*. I was now a veteran of *Afrika*.

One day, I was called to the *Spieß*: "Pollmann, tomorrow we will send you to the Helmstedt driving school; there you will gain the class-A driving licence!" The course had already started when I arrived, and I had never before driven a car. Two days later was the examination, which I missed, so I returned to my unit and reported to the *Spieß*, to be told: "Pollmann, do you know, you still have to make five days' calaboose (jail/prison)." I really had forgotten about the incident the previous December. I did my five days and reported back to the *Spieß*. "Pollmann, you are a good soldier, instead of a *Schirrmeister* [Motor transport NCO]; we will make a parachute warden out of you!" My training was to start the next week at the *Flugtechnische Schule IV* in Bayreuth. The next six weeks were spent training to fold all kinds of parachutes.

Routine life in France

After undergoing several training courses, I rejoined the *Bataillon* and in late 1943 we moved to Dreux, west of Paris.

Quartered at Marcilly-sur-Eure with my *Kompanie*, I was transferred with an *Oberfeldwebel*, two *Oberjäger* and several *Jäger* to the *Bataillon HQ* at Yvry-la-Bataille. My group was tasked with equipment servicing and maintenance duties. We had a small cottage and a large shed at our disposal. The field latrines were located by a small brook.

In May 1944, I was promoted to the rank of *Obergefreiter*. The *Korps Fallschirm Pionier Bataillon* was transferred to Moulins-sur-Allier from our HQ in the Dreux-Evreux region in France. Our parachute packing tables were laid out in the schoolyard of the *Lycée Théodore Banville*, the same school where Coco Chanel lived when she was a neglected child before she went to Paris.

On 1 May 1944, the *Bataillon* was renamed the *I/Fallschirm-Pionier-Regiment 21*, commanded by *Major* Rudolf Witzig.

On 6 June 1944, the Allies landed in Normandy. We expected to be deployed in that region, but the marching order never came. Finally, in early July, we were ordered off to Salzwedel, supposedly

---

6   Every member of the Wehrmacht was entitled to 14 days annual leave. An additional leave up to 21 days could be given for convalescence or a family death. At any one time, approximately ten percent of the German military was on home leave. See Villahermosa p.143.

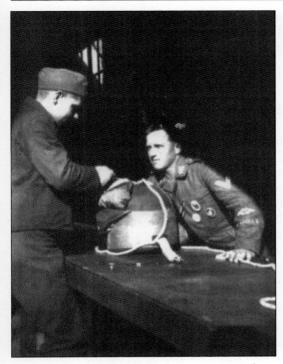

Fixing the static line of an RZ16 parachute. (Karl-Heinz Pollmann)

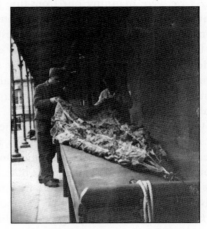

Karl (left) with *Obergefreiter* Pinggera, a comrade from the South Tyrol, who like Karl is a veteran of the Africa campaign. Karl is packing a parachute used for the *Waffenbehälter*. All parachutes had to be repacked every six to eight weeks to avoid a failure upon opening. (Karl-Heinz Pollmann)

Preparing the canopy of an RZ16 parachute. (Karl-Heinz Pollmann)

Packing the RZ16 parachute. (Karl-Heinz Pollmann)

Packing a cargo parachute. (Karl-Heinz Pollmann)

for night jump training. However, the shrewdest ones among us were convinced that instead, we would seize the iron mines in neutral Sweden.[7] But by mid-July, we were deployed between Kovno (Kaunas) and Dünaburg (Daugavpils) in Lithuania to help the beleaguered *Kampfgruppe Schirmer* (*FJR16 Ost*) break through the Russian lines.

I/Fallschirm-Pionier-Regiment 21 in Lithuania

I was assigned to *3. Kompanie*, because our parachutes were left behind in Salzwedel.[8] My *Zugführer* was *Leutnant* Graf Bernstorff from Wehningen. In the meantime I used an old *MG34* instead of the newer *MG42*, because it was more sparing on ammunition and better suited to sustained fire.

As we were manning our front-line positions, we were often exposed to enemy propaganda. Through loud-hailers, the Russians would shout: "German soldiers, come over to us. You will get vanilla pudding, a large helping, not just enough to fill the lid of your mess tin."

Rumours were rife about the 20 July coup to overthrow Hitler, but none of us had any accurate information about the event. One day, around midday, I was slumbering in a ditch when I was brutally startled out of my sleep by a loud detonation. A 15cm howitzer shell had exploded hardly 2m away from me. All around, the ground was strewn with red-hot splinters, but luckily I was unhurt.

One night, a Russian sneaked into the ditch where we were posted, stabbed one of my comrades to death and abducted another. Even though this took place about 25m away from our own trench, none of us noticed anything. On another occasion, a Russian T-34 tank fired in my direction. I only had time to shelter in a hole. The tank fired again, it was close by, but this time its shell hit a wooden shack, which caught fire immediately. The alternatives were to be either shot or burnt alive, and I did not know which to choose. Fortunately, the T-34 left the scene and I was safe.[9]

On 21 August, I was lying prone behind my *MG34*, ready to reload, when an explosive bullet, fired by a Russian sniper, hit me in the left arm. Dazed with shock, I felt no pain but stared at the wound, from which a bubbly trickle of blood was flowing. I swooned. When I came to, I was lying on a garden gate, which three of my comrades were using as a makeshift stretcher to take me to safety. My wound was dressed and I was led to a *HVPl* in the rear. In the evening, I was loaded onto a freight train, whose destination was Eidtkau and Gumbinnen. There, naked under a blanket, I was taken off the train. Several *BDM* girls, compassionately, offered their help and said: "The poor soldier, he must be sweating profusely." But as they pulled off my blanket, they started to scream, and in no time covered me up again.

In the hospital train, to make up for the loss of blood, I was given a large glass of red wine, mixed with one egg and some orange juice. It felt good to be alive!

---

7   This demonstrates that rumours were rife about forthcoming operations.

8   The *Bataillon* under the command of *Major* Rudolf Witzig had an authorised strength of 21 officers and 1,011 NCOs and enlisted men, and had been conducting night parachute training at Salzwedel when the movement order to Lithuania was recieved. Upon arrival in Lithuania, the *Bataillon* took up positions only 10km from the East Prussian border. See Villahermosa, p.167.

9   The *Bataillon* were involved in heavy fighting between July and October, when they were pulled out of the front line and relocated to Bützow in Mecklenburg. On 26 July, for example, Soviet forces in regiment strength, with tank support, attacked positions held by the *Bataillon*. After a long day of fighting, the Soviets lost 30 tanks and suffered heavy losses. The *Fallschirm-Pionier Bataillon* also suffered heavy losses. *1. Kompanie*, under the command of *Leutnant* Kubillus, came away from the fighting with only 26 men. See *Gemeinschaft der Fallschirmpioniere*.

The end of the war is nigh

In Brandenburg, on 1 April 1945, during my monthly check-up the staff medical officer granted me a further four weeks' leave as 'unfit for duty'. On 13 April, the men fit for duty were ordered to report to the depot and collect *Panzerfausts* to defend Berlin. The men in my situation were allowed an extra two weeks' furlough. Too good to refuse!

Obergefreiter Müller, who shared my room, was a native from Hannover, a city which was already under Allied control. As the railway station had been destroyed, we set off together, on foot, to Neustadt an der Dosse, in the direction of Lüneburg. The Americans had already reached the banks of the Elbe at Magdeburg, and it was rumoured in Hamburg that Lüneburg was to be evacuated. We decided to go there and lend a hand. We found our way to Lüneburg. The train station had been wrecked in the bombings. We rummaged around for some food.

On 18 April, as we were sitting at a table eating baked potatoes, my sister, Ilse, entered the room and told us that the British were at Am Sande. I replied: "Are you kidding?" But at the same time I saw a British soldier riding down the street on a motorcycle. "Müller, guess what? The war is over. Let's take our uniforms down to the cellar!" Which is just what we did.

Epilogue

Müller went home two weeks later. He was caught by the British, but because of his wounds he was soon discharged in Munsterlager. He died in 1997. Kurt Behr and Egon Rabe were both repatriated from the POW camp in 1945. Both men died in the 1960s, at less than 40 years old.

And as for me, British soldiers entered my house shortly after they had taken the town. They were looking for men who had been members of the *Wehrmacht*. I was asked if I had been a soldier, and I replied "No". They turned and saw a portrait of me in uniform hanging on the wall. They asked me who the man was in the picture. "My brother," I replied. In the dimly lit room they could not make a comparison, so they about-turned and left the house. I never became a prisoner of war.

Karl was awarded the Cross of Merit by the Mayor of Lüneburg in the summer of 2001.
(Karl-Heinz Pollmann)

(Charlie Pollmann passed away on 1 January 2018, aged 93.)

9

Kurt Engelmann

Belgium – Crete – Tunisia

Kurt Engelmann was born in Bleicherode on 11 April 1919. He was a first-generation Fallschirmjäger, *joining the* Regiment 'General Göring' *in November 1937, followed by I/FJR1, which was formed from the IV-Regiment 'General Göring' in April 1938 under the command of Oberst Bruno Bräuer. He undertook his training at Stendal and subsequently took part in the ground campaign in Poland at Pulawy and Deblin. Engelmann was assigned to Rudolf Witzig's* Pionierzug *in late 1939, and after extensive training for an upcoming secret mission, he took part in the famous glider assault on the Fort at Eben Emael in Belgium on 10 May 1940, one of the operations that signalled the invasion of the Low Countries. After assignment to 10/LL.St.Rgt, Engelmann jumped into Crete on 20 May 1941 and was briefly captured. He went on to serve as a* Zugführer *in a heavy mortar platoon whilst serving with FJR5 in Tunisia, where he was captured again and became a POW of the Americans until 1947. After the war he returned to East Germany, and it was not until many years later that he was finally reunited with his former comrades who had taken part in the glider assault at Eben Emael, the airborne assault on Crete and the ground fighting in Tunisia.*

Oberjager Kurt Engelmann in 1941 wearing the
LW parachute badge, EK2 ribbon and EK1.
(Frank Engelmann)

Kurt Englemann in 2004, aged 85.
(Kurt Engelmann)

The early days

In 1936, I became fascinated by an article which had been published in a copy of the *Berliner Illustrierte Zeitung*.[1] It featured photographs and interesting comments on the *Fallschirmjäger* of the *Regiment 'General Göring'*, which was based in Berlin.

These men were at the peak of their physical fitness and were especially good gymnasts. In 1937, I applied to become a *Fallschirmjäger* in the *Regiment 'General Göring'*.

However, after my schooling it was a requirement that I completed six months' Reichs Labour Service, which took place from April to October 1937 in Geisa/Röhn.

During this time I received the dates for my flyer fitness and physical tests. My summons to the *Regiment 'General Göring'* came on 30 November 1937, and I subsequently travelled to Berlin to begin my training.

Along with many other civilians like me, we were briefly greeted by the staff and then thrown in at the deep end. No sooner had we walked in the gate, we heard "down, down, march, march", all the time being filmed by reporters from *Die Deutsche Wochenschau*.[2] On the next day we travelled to Stendal to join *I/FJR1*.[3]

Basic training was from 1 December 1937 to 27 February 1938. It consisted of training with rifles, pistols, machine pistols, light and heavy machine guns as well as light and heavy mortars. The *Sandplatz* at Stendal/Borstel was an ideal exercise area, which we would often curse.

On 1 March 1938, our *Fallschirmjäger* training finally began on the airfield at Stendal.

The DFS-230 light assault glider was the second secret weapon to be used at Eben Emael. The glider could deliver a well-equipped squad of men right to the heart of an objective, unlike paratroops who were scattered upon landing and had to find their weapons containers before they could become a fighting unit.
(MHM-Flugplatz Berlin-Gatow)

1 Long-running illustrated weekly news magazine that became a propaganda tool during the Second World War.

2 Kurt may have confused a pre-war newsreel series with *Der Deutsche Wochenshau*. These early newsreel series were amalgamated in 1939, and *DDW* ran from 1940 until 1945

3 The parachute *Bataillon* of *Regiment General Göring* was redesignated as *IV/Fallsch.Jager.Rgt General Göring* on 1 September 1937 and redesignated again on 1 April 1938 to *I/FJR1*. See Golla, pp.37-38.

My great ability at gymnastics paid off. For four weeks everything went well. I made a single jump from 250m with the RZ1 parachute. I made a further six jumps from 120–150m, and finally a dawn jump from 120m.

On 15 May 1938, with the parachute school finally behind us, we were allowed to wear the *Fallschirmjäger Regiment 1* cuff title and the Parachute Rifleman's badge.

After the parachute school, the normal training continued.

From 16–19 June 1938, we went to Burg near Luxembourg to train with the new DFS-230 light assault glider. The first exercise was to be carried out in the presence of *General* Kurt Student. Eight men wearily climbed aboard the fabric-covered crate. For us *Fallschirmjäger* this was a very unusual experience. After a successful landing, *General* Student came over and asked: "How was it men?" "Shit, *Herr General*," came the reply. We would get to know the glider very well in the near future.

Poland

On 1 September 1939, we were flown from Stendal to the concentration area at Seifersdorf (Raszków) in Lower Silesia. We remained on standby for an airborne operation to seize the vital bridge at Pulawy in eastern Poland. However, we never made an airborne assault as the Poles blew up the bridge beforehand. Early on 20 September, we were transported by truck through Wilun-Radom-Pulawy to occupy and defend Deblin, and we took part in the removal of vital materials from the Deblin airfield across the Vistula River. All around us we saw the effects of the war in Poland. On 28 September, we began our return journey to Germany via Oppeln, arriving in Stendal in early October.

On 2 November 1939, 1/FJR1 under the command of *Hauptmann* Walter Koch, was transferred from Stendal to Hildesheim. The following day, I was transferred to Hildesheim to join the newly formed *Sturmabteilung* 'Koch' where a new assignment awaited me, one that would go down in the annals of military history.[4]

Sturmgruppe Granit

I was assigned to *Pionierzug Witzig* (from *II/FJR1*), under the command of *Oberleutnant* Rudolf Witzig, and had to pass *Pionier* training. From November 1939, during the preparatory phase before our new mission, we carried out countless towed glider flights during the day and night. During this training phase we had no idea what the target of all our training would be.

In December 1939, we carried out training in the snow and cold weather of the Adler Mountains. We carried out bridge demolition and field demolition training, and we also trained on Polish fortifications in Gleiwitz with a new secret weapon, the 50kg and 12.5kg hollow demolition charges.

On 19 March 1940, our *Zug* was moved to Köln-Ostheim, where life was very slow going. We were under curfew for six days a week and only allowed out on Sundays.

By now it was well known to us that the mission was against a large fort. A scaled-down plaster model of Fort Eben Emael was always available as a training aid for us to examine, and we played

---

4   *Sturmabteilung Koch* was named after its commander, *Hauptmann* Walter Koch, and formed from *1/FJR1* and the *Pionierzug* from *II/FJR1*.

A German engineer prepares a 50kg hollow charge for detonation. The photo was taken in late 1939 or early 1940 in Czechoslovakia. The tests for these charges were carried out on the bunkers of the Benes line, and also the casemates and bunkers on the Polish border near Gleiwitz. This testing was invaluable in assessing the performance of this new secret weapon. (Dr Cord Tietjen)

The result of a 50kg hollow charge test on a concrete and steel casemate. The 50kg hollow charge was a circular dome charge in two pieces for ease of handling. The top half comprised a priming charge, igniter and fuse. The bottom half had a concave underside with a TNT filling. When the charge detonated, the resultant focused blast energy could penetrate 25cm of steel and 35cm of steel-reinforced concrete. (Dr Cord Tietjen)

Contemporary photo of *Trupp 4*'s objective Mi-Nord, a machine-gun casemate, showing the damage caused by the 50kg hollow charge suspended against the embrasure on the right of the structure. (Martin Vlach)

The steel observation cupola atop the MG bunker, which still shows the damage caused by a 50kg hollow charge. (Martin Vlach)

One of the MG embrasures of Mi-Nord. (Martin Vlach)

over the mission every day.[5] Absolute secrecy was ordered by *General* Student. There was no home leave and we were only allowed out of the barracks in groups.

Within our *Sturmgruppe* codenamed '*Granit*', I was assigned to *Trupp.4*, an eight-man squad under the command of *Feldwebel* Helmut Wenzel. The deputy *Truppführer* was *Obergefreiter* Karl Polzin and our glider pilot was *Unteroffizier* Otto Bräutigam. Our target was Objective 19, or *Mi-Nord* [*Mi* being short for *Mitrailleuse*, or machine gun], a heavy machine-gun bunker on the surface of the fort in the north-east sector close to the Albert Canal.

We also had orders to prevent hostile attacks from the north and south, to penetrate and defend and make contact with *Oberleutnant* Witzig in *Trupp.11* as soon as possible. If we were to fail, then *Trupp.11* was to take over our objective.

Our DFS-230 assault gliders were situated in hangars at Köln-Ostheim, which was secured by an electric fence. We provided guards day and night, and it was us who decided which superior officers had entry to the airfield.[6] One incident occurred when two airfield craftsmen walked past an open window in one of the hangars and saw the gliders lined up inside. They had been repairing something in an adjacent hangar. Whether or not they saw something did not matter, and both were immediately taken into protective custody and only released later in the day on 10 May in order to retain complete secrecy.[7] After several practise alerts, the genuine alarm was sounded on 9

5   Glider pilot Erwin Ziller from *Trupp.6* built the plaster model of Fort Eben Emael on 2 March 1940. See Gonzalez, Steinke & Tannahill, p.62.

6   The glider was the second secret weapon to be utilised for the mission, in addition to the hollow charge. See Mrazek, p.37.

7   Engelmann recalled that two men from the beacon platoon had been overheard talking about the mission and found themselves sentenced to death, but were acquitted again after the operation.

May. Several of our gliders were transported to the airfield at Köln-Butzweilerhof, where the JU-52 towing planes awaited them.

The glider assault on Fort Eben Emael

At 0230 hours on 10 May, we were woken up. It was time to prepare. Nobody could sleep that night. At around 0400 hours, everything was ready for launch. At 0430 hours, 32 tow groups from Köln Ostheim and 10 tow groups from Köln Butzweilerhof began their flight to their assigned targets: three bridges over the Albert Canal at Kanne (*Sturmgruppe Eisen*), Vroenhoven (*Sturmgruppe Beton*) and Veldwezelt (*Sturmgruppe Stahl*).

At 0435 hours, our *Sturmgruppe* set off for the target – the fortress of Eben Emael. The fort was alledged to be the strongest in the world at that time and considered to be impregnable. It was built in the early 1930s, and the location was chosen after the construction of the Albert Canal, with its 60m-high north-east/east wall. Steep concrete walls connected the fort to the steep sloping embankment of the Albert Canal. Its diamond-shaped surface was covered with barbed wire entanglements and tank obstacles. A 400m-long water-filled trench lay below the formidable west wall fortifications. The surface of the fort was 900m in length from north to south and approximately 700m at its widest point. On the surface of the fort were armoured cupolas housing large-calibre guns and concrete casemates with multiple smaller-calibre weapons and machine guns, as well as *Flak* guns and searchlights. Below ground level there was a command post, a hospital, ammunition storages and generators that delivered the energy for the artillery traversing and elevating systems, lifts and lights, and it also housed a communications centre. The lowest level of the fort contained the garrison barracks. The required strength of the fort was over 1,000 soldiers. On the day of our insertion, the strength was 650 men plus a relief force of over 200 troops who were stationed outside the fort in the nearby town of Wonck.

We took off from the airfield at Köln Ostheim, 86 men in 11 gliders, which followed a line of beacons on the ground that showed our pilots the way up to the Dutch border. After a flight time of 31 minutes and a distance of 73km from Köln, we reached an altitude of 2,600m, and when we reached the Vetschauer Mountain the glider was released. The glider pilot of *Trupp.4*, *Unteroffizier* Otto Bräutigam (who held the world record in glider flying before the war), had, like most of the other gliders pilots, a rough flight during the tow.

On our release we could see the Rhine and the sillhouette of the cathederal in Köln. At regular intervals we could see the flashing beacons on the ground that showed us the way to the border. Upon releasing at 2,600m, it was dawn and very cold in our glider, its thin fabric skin offering us no protection from the elements. After release, the flight became smoother and on our right we could see the lights of Maastricht. The first tracer bullets appeared in the distance, but none of the gliders of our assault group were hit.

After a gliding time of 20 minutes, in which we covered 25km, we could see the outline of the fort and the Albert Canal from a height of 800m. Our glider pilot pointed the nose of the glider towards the ground as the anti-aircraft fire started to come up from the fort.

Bräutigam kept the stick forward and we took up a steep dive. The ground came rushing up toward us, and after a short and very hard landing our glider came to a stop directly in front of our target. The time was 0525 hours. On our left we could see our objective, Casemate 19, its machine guns firing from openings in the bunker wall. After the hull of our glider dropped, our *Truppführer*, Helmut Wenzel, jumped out with two men, who each carried one half of a 50kg hollow charge, and rushed to the casemate in order to prepare it for detonation. Wenzel threw a 1kg charge into the opening of the periscope, and then ignited the 50kg charge on the steel observervation cupola situated on top of the casemate. In the meantime, the rest of our *Trupp* had taken up position in the bushes in front of the rampart, and our machine-gunner, Karl Polzin, took the casemate openings under fire. I and another man each took half of another 50kg hollow charge and rushed toward the bunker. The second 50kg charge was suspended and ignited in front of a machine-gun embrasure. We threw ourselves behind a rampart 4m away, but we still felt the enormous shock wave when it detonated.

The charge blew a very big hole into the concrete wall of the casemate, so that an entry into the bunker was now possible. An awful view awaited us when we entered the casemate. Casemate 19 had been destroyed and was no longer able to offer any resistance; our *Trupp* had accomplished its mission within 15 minutes of landing on the fort. We proceeded to drape a flag onto the bunker as a marker for the *Luftwaffe* to indicate that the casemate was in our hands. Now we had time to take a closer look at our surroundings. The detonations from the other positions had almost ceased by this time.

Our objective was equipped with three heavy machine guns, two armoured searchlights, one artillery observation cupola and one light machine gun to cover the entrance.

Our *Truppführer*, *Feldwebel* Wenzel, then set up his command post against the rampart next to Casemate 19 and put the seven of us into a defensive position. This location was chosen for a command post because of its excellent observation of the entire fort, with the exception of the southern and western positions, which were located on slopes and could not be seen due to thickets.

Wenzel himself went to the next positions to find out which of them had not yet been destroyed, and at the same time find our assault group leader, *Oberleutnant* Witzig, and report the capture of Casemate 19. On the way he met one of our radio operators, Leo Gilg, who was also looking for Witzig to receive orders to set up the radio post. None of the other runners who had been sent out to find Witzig or members of *Trupp.11* had been successful. Wenzel concluded that *Trupp.11* had not landed on the fort.

Witzig's second in command, *Leutnant* Egon Delica, had flown in the glider of Hans Niedermeier's *Trupp.1*, which had landed approximately 400m south of Casemate 18, where heavy fire could still be heard.

Wenzel decided that *Leutnant* Delica was unable to assume command of the assault group due to his current position on the fort.[8] Wenzel decided to act and he took command himself. He had the radio team set up their position at the northern rampart and established the dressing post there, as the initial fighting had already cost two dead and 12 wounded.

Wenzel arranged for radio contact to be established with *Sturmgruppe Beton* at Vroenhoven, where *Hauptmann* Koch had his command post. He managed to give his situation report and also called up *Stuka* support to supress the positions at the entrance and prevent supplies being brought up from the village of Eben Emael. Within 20 minutes, JU-87 and HS-126 aircraft appeared in the sky above and put on a show of precision bombing. One He-111 flew over the fort and dropped several *Waffenbehälter* filled with fresh ammunition.

It was around 0900 hours when a lone glider flew over the fort and landed not very far from the northern rampart. In it was *Oberleutnant* Rudolf Witzig and *Trupp.11*, who had been forced to land on a meadow beside the Rhine when the tow rope broke shortly after take-off. In a relatively short time, Witzig had quickly organised a replacement JU-52 tow aircraft, which was able to land on the meadow and take off again with the glider in tow.

---

8   Egon Delica was a *Luftwaffe* aerial reconnaissance officer employed to direct air attacks. He was not para-troop trained and was allegedly unpopular amongst the men. When Witzig failed to arrive, Delica should have taken command, but something 'odd' occurred and *Feldwebel* Wenzel took over. Delica was awarded the *Ritterkreuz* for his part in the mission, whereas Wenzel was not. See Gonzalez, Steinke & Tannahill, p.165.

Witzig was quickly briefed by *Feldwebel* Wenzel and assumed command of the assault group. In the meantime, it had been established that Max Meier's *Trupp.2* had not landed on the fort. His pilot, Fritz Bredenbeck, had been forced to land near Düren close to the border. During the course of the day, *Trupp.2* had fought its way to the edge of the fort, but were unable to penetrate the fort's defences, with the result that Casemate 24 had not yet been destroyed.[9]

Fritz Heinemann's *Trupp.7*, whose target was an armoured cupola on the northern tip outside the blockade belt, which turned out to be a dummy installation, was unable to join the fighting within the fort. Due to these setbacks and the losses, our fighting strength had been reduced to 60 men, who were facing a force of approximately 600 Belgian soldiers in the fort and casemates.

By midday things had quietened down. The sun was beating down and the men were becoming very thirsty, particularly as everyone had expected to be relieved by this time. A bunker in the south-east outside the fort suddenly began shelling our positions on the northern tip with shrapnel rounds, which was repeated at intervals throughout the afternoon.

Heavy gunfire broke out in the south-west of the fort shortly after 1300 hours. Witzig ordered *Feldwebel* Wenzel to move up with some men, but they were unable to locate the enemy in the difficult terrain. For a short time we had to take cover in *Trupp.3*'s Casemate 12 as the fire became heavier and heavier. *Feldwebel* Wenzel was at this time wounded by a bullet, which grazed his head.

Several times we had to move against the Belgians in the vicinity of *Oberjäger* Peter Arent's Casemate 12, as fresh troops had been moved up from Wonck. Although we suffered some losses, the Belgians were unable to make a successful co-ordinated attack. The shooting had stopped in this area after 1800 hours, and *Feldwebel* Wenzel returned to the northern tip with his men. *Oberleutnant* Witzig deployed his further depleted Trupp to the defensive position at the northern rampart, particularly as it was becoming dark and it was uncertain whether the Belgians would launch a counter-attack on the fort. All of us were extremely nervous in the dark; everyone stared into the darkness with their weapons at the ready, expecting an attack at any minute.

Some artillery began firing at about 2200 hours, but we were lucky and did not suffer any further losses.

Casemate 17, a bunker in the canal wall, illuminated the canal with its searchlights and had successfully prevented the Army *Pioniers* from crossing until then. During the afternoon, Witzig had already seen how dangerous this position was and sent *Oberjäger* Siegfried Harlos and *Trupp.6* to tackle it. On three occasions, charges were lowered on a rope and detonated beside the bunker, but its 60mm gun continued to fire. In the north-east we frequently saw flares, which encouraged us to believe that the Army was not very far away. In spite of this, the night seemed endless, particularly as the artillery fire also kept flaring up against us. Finally dawn approached, and it seemed to us like a miracle that the Belgians had not launched a counter-attack and that we had survived the night.

At around 0600 hours on 11 May, the 1st Platoon of Army *Pionier Bataillon 51*, under the command of *Oberfeldwebel* Josef Portsteffen, had fought its way to the fort. We were glad to see that German relief forces were finally close.

It began to get light and our mood picked up again; we became aware of our hunger and above all, our thirst. We suddenly came under fire again from Casemate 23, and from the northern tip we were able to watch two German anti-tank guns duelling with Casemate 17 on the canal wall.

---

9   *Trupp.2* finally reached the bridge at Kanne (one of *SA Koch*'s objectives to the north of the fort) after a road trip from Düren, but the *Truppführer*, *Oberjäger* Max Maier, was killed. His deputy, *Oberjäger* Walter Maier, crossed the wreckage of the destroyed bridge and made contact with his comrades near the fort before returning to the east bank of the Albert Canal. See Gonzalez, Steinke & Tannahill, pp.275–76.

10 May 1940. *Trupp.2* after their premature landing near Düren. From left to right: Fritz Bredenbeck (glider pilot), *Truppführer* Max Maier (killed at the Kanne bridge), Walter Meier, Paul Bader, behind him Fritz Gehlich, with Gerhard Iskra at the back and Wilhelm Ölmann on the right. The photo was taken by Hans Comdür. (Kurt Engelmann)

Trupp.3, from left to right: Erwin Franz, Helmut Stopp, Josef Müller, *Truppführer* Peter Arent, Alfred Supper (glider pilot) and Paul Kupsch. (Reinhard Wenzel)

Trupp.4, from left to right: Karl Polzin, Eddi Schmidt, *Truppführer* Helmut Wenzel, Otto Bräutigam (glider pilot), Fritz Florian and Kurt Engelmann. (Reinhard Wenzel)

Trupp.6, from left to right: Hans Grigowski, Peter Zirwes, *Truppführer* Siegfried Harlos, Fritz Köhler from *Trupp.4* Erwin Ziller (glider pilot), Walter Kipnick, Richard Bläser and Werner Grams. (Reinhard Wenzel)

Trupp.7, from left to right: *Truppführer* Fritz Heinemann, Aloysius Passmann, Wilhelm Alefs and Wolfgang Schulz. (Reinhard Wenzel)

Trupp.8, from left to right: Heinz Weinert, Johannes Else, Hans Distelmeier (glider pilot) and Herbert Plietz. (Reinhard Wenzel)

Trupp.9, from left to right: Günter Schulz, Anton Wingers, Ewald Neuhaus and Hans Braun. (Reinhard Wenzel)

From left to right: Peter Gräf (*Trupp.1*), Hans Grigowski (*Trupp.6*) and Fritz Köhler (*Trupp.4*). (Reinhard Wenzel)

From left to right: Wilhelm Ölmann (*Trupp.2*), Wilhelm Stucke (*Trupp.1*) and Richard Drucks (*Trupp.1*).
(Reinhard Wenzel)

The shells fired from the canal bunker hit the village and church at Canne, but after a short time it was finally knocked out.

Time passed very slowly and we kept on hearing shots from the unclear area in the south-east, but there was no enemy to be seen.

At noon on 11 May, photographs were taken of the men who had assaulted Eben Emael.[10] The photos clearly show the effort and high tension under which we had stood for two days. One must remember that none of us could sleep during the night of 9–10 May. We had gone to bed at 2200 hours, but sleep was unthinkable and impossible as everyone had the outcome of the mission on their mind, especially since we were informed that in case of failure there would be a massive bombardment by *Stuka* dive-bombers regardless of our results on the ground. 10 May was a hot day. Our water bottles were given to the wounded and were empty. The heat, thirst and tension of one day of war with almost constant shelling kept us on edge. Then there was the everlasting night at the north wall, where we expected a counter-attack by the Belgians and could not close an eye. It was no wonder that we appear exhausted in the photos taken on 11 May. Not all of my comrades could be photographed, as they were entrusted with special tasks so it was impossible to take uniform photos of the *Truppen*.

---

10   The photos were taken by Helmut Wenzel, who took a Leica camera with him into combat. He took photos in Poland, Eben Emael, Greece, Crete and Tunisia. According to his son Reinhard, Helmut Wenzel destroyed his photo albums later in life. Helmut Wenzel presented Kurt Englemann with copies of these photos at his first *Sturmgruppe* reunion in 1986.

At 1315 hours, the fort was finally handed over to *Oberstleutant* Hans Mikosch by the fort commander, *Major* Jean Jottrand.[11] The garrison of almost 1,000 men began the trek into captivity. Our assault group had suffered six dead and 18 wounded. Belgian casualties were 23 dead and 65 wounded. After burying our dead comrades at the fort, we marched away, with some of the wounded having to be carried on improvised stretchers. This turned into a problem between the bushes and trees on the steep ground leading to the entrance position, particularly as shooting broke out, which was apparently caused by some of the Army *Pioniers*.

We finally reached the entrance position and were able to take a short break. Some men rushed into the destroyed village, searched a bar and found the water that we had been longing for. We quickly quenched our thirst and took as much as we could for our wounded and other comrades.

We continued along the canal, with the wounded transported some of the way on inflated bags. We became soaked when we had to wade part of the way through the floods.

We were then attacked by French bombers, and since there was no cover we had to throw ourselves flat on the ground. Fortunately for us, the bombs fell into the water about 40m away from us. We then continued north toward the village of Kanne, where we handed our wounded over to the medics at the dressing station.

Our march then continued to Maastricht, which took us two hours. We spent the night on the floor between the classroom benches in a local school, where we were able to forget the sounds of screaming shells and gunfire.

We took part in a funeral march to Maastricht to honour the fallen of *Sturmabteilung Koch*, and on 12 May we received our first cup of coffee; what a pleasure! Only then did we realise that it was Whitsun. Our trucks turned up at around midday and we set off on foot towards the Maas bridge to meet them. There we had to withstand an attack by some 20 British bombers before our journey could continue. We were then transported by truck back home to Köln-Dellbrück, where we arrived at about 1800 hours, and after a short break we continued on to Köln-Ostheim, where a large reception and medal award ceremony awaited us and we were all awarded the Iron Cross 2nd Class. On 13 May we were taken to Münster, where another reception was held in our honour. We were presented to the commander of *Luftlotte.II*, *General* Albert Kesselring, who awarded us the Iron Cross 1st Class.

On 14 May, we returned to Hildesheim and were given a well earned 14 days' special leave, which helped us to forget the harships we had endured at Eben Emael.

Epilogue

In further correspondence with Kurt Engelmann I enquired about his wounded comrade Willi Windemuth and how the men felt when they heard that six of their comrades had fallen in the fighting

"Windemuth was not seriously wounded and he came back to the *Trupp* after a short stay in hospital. I knew all of the men in *Sturmgruppe Granit* and we were shocked when we heard that six men had been killed."

---

11   Hans Mikosch was the commander of *Pionier Bataillon 51* and awarded the *Ritterkreuz* for his part in the campaign.

What was the fate of the men of Trupp.4?

"Helmut Wenzel saw action on Crete, where he was wounded, and he was later captured by British troops in Tunisia and was a POW in the USA until January 1946. He passed away on 24 January 2003.

Otto Brautigam was killed in 1941 whilst flying a Messerschmitt Gigant glider.

Karl Polzin was mistakenly shot dead by *Oberleutnant* Horst Trebes in Halberstadt in 1941.

Eddi Schmidt died in 1991; his further military service is unknown.

Fritz Köhler lives in Baierbross but he never attends any of the *Sturmgruppe* reunions.

Fritz Florian died in 1989. He was captured by the Americans in Tunisia. We shared the same POW camp from 1943–1945. I only saw him again in 1986, when as a citizen of the DDR, I participated in my first *Sturmgruppe* reunion. My invitation was camouflaged as a silver wedding anniversary as old comrades meetings were forbidden in the DDR. These events brought the unwelcome attention of the Stasi.

The grave of *Oberjäger* Ernst Grzechza of *11/LL.St.Rgt* at Maleme. (aretecrete.com)

As for Willi Windemuth, I had not seen him since 1940. He is supposed to have deceased in the meantime.[12]

Rudolf 'Ralf' Witzig died on 3 October 2001."

Were you informed about the incident involving Oberjäger *Ernst Grzechza, the deputy squad leader from* Trupp.5 *who was supposedly drunk during the mission?*

"This story was serious. His canteen was filled with rum in order to give the wounded some relief. Ernst could not resist the temptation and drank too much of it himself. He sat drunk astride a large-calibre gun barrel which was still functional and was thus turned around with the gun. *Feldwebel* Wenzel threatened him before he came down again! It is true that Ernst only received the *EK2* and not the *EK1* like all the other men of the assault group. Ernst Grzechza was later killed in action on Crete on 20 May 1941."

What do you remember about the equipment you took with you to Eben Emael?

"In addition to the two 50kg and 12.5kg hollow charges, we took an array of smaller explosive devices of different sizes as well as a short ladder and flamethrowers. In my opinion, our equipment was not properly secured and it is still a mystery to me how we managed to accommodate it inside the cramped confines of the glider."

---

12   Willi Windemuth did not survive the war. He died on 6.2.45 in Saarburg, Germany, as a *Feldwebel*.

What of the surviving veterans of Sturmgruppe Granit?

"In previous years the 16 surviving veterans of *Sturmgruppe Granit* have met on the day of employment at Eben Emael on 10 May. We meet at Xanten and from there travel by car to the soldiers' cemetery at Ysselsteyn in the Netherlands in order to lay wreaths on the graves of our six fallen comrades. In the meantime, however, only a few veterans are able to make this journey."

In memoriam to my comrades killed on 10 May 1940

+ Max Maier   + Karl Unger   + Willi Hübel
+ Fritz Kruck   + Helmuth Bögle   + Kurt Jürgensen

On 1 June 1940, I was promoted to *Oberjäger* and until August instructed at the parachute school in Braunschweig-Broitzen.

At the end of August 1940, I was sent to Halberstadt to join *III. Bataillon* of the newly built *Luftlande-Sturmregiment.1*, which was under the command of *Major* Otto Scherber. I joined *10. Kompanie* under the command of *Oberleutnant* Rudolf Schulte-Sasse. The *Bataillon* was filled with very young *Fallschirmjäger*, and it was up to us, the old hands, to train them up in the forthcoming months.

Memorial cross for the five men who fell at the Fort. Max Maier from Trupp 2 was killed at the Kanne bridge (Authors collection)

10/LL.St.Rgt and the Invasion of Crete

At the end of April 1941, we were moved by train through Prague and Vienna to Hungary, then by truck through Saloniki and Thermopylen to Megara in Greece.

After the successful operations of 1940, many young men had volunteered to become *Fallschirmjäger*. Full of excitement, they wanted to be just like the old ones.

After hard, strict training, the young ones again and again asked: "When are we going to see battle?" We, the instructors, tried to calm them down, but it was in vain.

Nobody thought that on 20 May 1941, most of the young volunteers from *III. Bataillon* of the *Sturmregiment* would give their lives for the Fatherland!

I will never forget young *Jäger* Hans Ramstetter, with whom on the day before the battle, I swam to an island off the coast near Megara and had struggled to reach the shore on the way back. Despite the hard work, it had been

The grave of *Jäger* Hans Ramstetter of *10/LL.St. Rgt* at Maleme. (aretecrete.com)

a nice day for us. For *Jäger* Ramstetter, it was the last day of his young life. He was only 20 years old. I found his grave in the soldiers' cemetery at Maleme on the 50th anniversary of the invasion in 1991, when I paid my respects to my other comrades who are laid to rest at Maleme.[13]

In all war diaries, the fate of *III/Sturmregiment* is described in a short passage: "Dispatched two hours too late, landings much dispersed and landed amidst enemy entrenchments east of Pyrgos. The major force of *III/Sturmregiment* was destroyed; nearly all the officers were killed."[14]

From my point of view, the *10.Kompanie* drop zone was not suited for a landing at all, with rolling hills and olive groves.[15] Upon touching ground, none of my comrades could be seen, only enemy fire coming in from all directions.

Forming a *Gruppe* or a *Zug* and finding the weapon containers was impossible under heavy fire in that landscape. I crawled up a hill to get an idea about the situation, and was hit through the upper leg, but I found four other comrades from my *Kompanie*, among them our medic, who dressed my wound.

All day long we held the hill against enemy attacks, owing to a machine gun which we had found in a *Waffenbehälter*. We found our *Kompanieführer*, *Oberleutnant* Schulte-Sasse, dying nearby but we could not help him.

I tried to save ammunition with the *MG* by firing short bursts. Lying behind a thorn hedge, the only cover I had from sight, the New Zealanders had spotted this target and sniped off one thorn branch after the other, right above my head.

A thought crept into my mind: exactly one year ago I was engaged to be married, and today my life will end.

In the afternoon, all ammunition for the *MG* was spent and soon enough the fire on my position ceased. I played dead! When the evening was approaching, our *Oberfeldwebel* (the highest-ranking soldier of our five comrades on the hill) shouted that there was no sense in resisting further and that we had no option but to surrender.

So we came into the hands of the 23rd New Zealand Battalion, who brought us to their base south of Pyrgos. From them we finally received water, because our supply was long dry.

The grave of *Oberleutnant* Rudolf Schulte-Sasse of *10/LL.St.Rgt* at Maleme. (aretecrete.com)

---

13   *10 Kompanie* suffered heavy casualties on 20 May, with 64 killed and 14 missing. These figures consisted of two officers, seven NCOs and 69 enlisted men. If *10 Kompanie* had a similar complement to *9 Kompanie*, i.e. 144 men, then it suffered 54 percent fatalities. (BDF Archive).

14   *III/LL.St.Rgt* was unable to start from its airfield in Greece until 0715 hours due to the dust clouds created by the aircraft. The aircraft should have taken off at one minute intervals, but this was increased to five minutes due to the dust clouds; therefore the aircraft did not reach Crete until after 0900 hours. As strong winds were blowing over the coast, it was feared that many paratroopers would be blown out to sea. There was also strong *Flak* fire from the coast. It was decided that the *Bataillon* would jump further inland into difficult terrain dotted with stone walls, olive trees, dried-up irrigation ditches and rocks. The landings took place in the middle of positions held by the 21 & 23 NZ Battalions. *Major* Otto Scherber, the *Bataillonskommandeur*, was shot in the air. Many other officers shared the same fate or were killed shortly after landing. The *Bataillon* suffered 400 casualties. See Richter, p.113.

15   *10.Kompanie* were dropped south of the Maleme to Platanias coastal road between Gerani and Modhion. See Davin, pp.80–81.

Among the New Zealanders were armed Cretan civilians who openly showed their hatred for us, but the New Zealanders said they would protect us from those who wanted to murder us. Despite these assurances, we gave nothing for our lives anymore.

During the afternoon of 21 May, we watched from our prison hut as more *Fallschirmjäger* were dropped to the east towards Platanias. Like us they were dispatched amidst the enemy and partly landed in the sea. They suffered similarly to our own *Bataillon*.[16]

In my opinion this operation was a crime! At this time, the operations staff knew that this area was firmly in the hands of the New Zealanders; why didn't they land the troops where *IV/LL.St. Rgt* had landed almost without casualties and had managed to establish a bridgehead?[17]

During 22 May, we prisoners were brought to a rallying point near Chania in open trucks. Our guards asked us to give them a written statement to say that they had treated us well, which they actually had.

From this camp, we marched, in most cases hobbled, towards Chania (most of us were wounded). The civilian population was full of hatred: they spat at us, threw stones at us and if the Allied guards had not been there, the Cretans would have lynched us! Now I realised for the first time that our attack on the freedom-loving, self-respecting Cretans was not just and that our leaders had not taken their attitude into consideration.

We were glad when our hobbling bunch finally arrived at the former Turkish casemates in the port, which were used as a prison camp and where we were protected from the angry civilian population.

In 1991, Kurt returned to the Turkish casemates in Chania, where he was held prisoner by New Zealand troops 50 years earlier. (Kurt Engelmann)

16 Engelmann was unaware at the time as to which formation had jumped at 1500 hours on 21 May. They were the remnants of *II/FJR2*, namely *5.* and *6.Kompanie* under the command of *Oberleutnant* Thiel and *Oberleutnant* Nagele respectively, along with two *Züge* of *Sanitäter* under the command of *Oberarzt* Dr Dieter Hartmann.

17 The greater part of *IV/LL.St.Rgt* was dropped between the villages of Tavronitis and Kamisiana. See Golla, p.435.

Here, we witnessed by day and especially at night the air attacks of our *Luftwaffe* on the port and the ships anchoring there, which ripped out some of the iron grids from the casemates.

While our officers were taken from the island by boat during the early hours of 27 May, we were set free later in the afternoon.[18] Fifty years later, I could still recognise the casemates (from the outside) on my first visit to Crete. I was surprised about the friendliness of the Cretan people towards the Germans; they held no resentment against their former aggressors. To the contrary in fact, the Cretans were very helpful in keeping our dead in the Gonia monastery near Kolimbari and the upkeep of the soldiers' cemetery at Maleme.

The return home and departure to Tunisia

We returned to our barracks at Halberstadt to train replacements for our casualties sustained on Crete.[19] In May 1942, *III/LL.St.Rgt* was redesignated *III/FJR5* and was soon transferred to Mourmelon near Reims in France, where we trained for the airborne invasion of Malta (Operation Hercules), and after the mission was cancelled, we patrolled the Channel coast.[20]

After the November 1942 Allied landings at Oran and Algier in North Africa, *III/FJR5* was transferred to Naples/Caserta on 9 November, and on the 13th we flew over Caserta to Tunis/La Marsa.

After a night in the Marshal Foch Barracks, where we had to survive a furious battle against lice, we continued to march to Madjez-el-Bab the next day.

On 19 November we attacked Medjez. Until 12 May 1943, we operated between Goubellat, Medjez-el-Bab and Bou Arada. Our *Kompanieführer*, *Oberleutnant* Ullrich Jahn, was killed on 30 November 1942 in the fight against British paratroopers who had jumped in behind our lines at Depienne, 50km south-west of Tunis, on 29 November (in the battle of the Red and Green Devils).

During this time, I discovered my love for Tunisia, the friendliness and helpfulness of the Arabs towards us Germans, but also their faith in Allah when they held out in their homes in the middle of battle. Allah was going to protect them.

Christmas 1942 was spent in a French farm near Goubellat. In April 1995, I and three comrades of the former *10.Kompanie* went to see our old entrenchments at Wadi Sehbarka and the farms in which we had lived in 1942/43, among them, the so-called Christmas-farm.

Now some Arabs lived there, but after we had explained our intentions to them and said that we had spent Christmas 53 years ago in that place, they showed great hospitality. They brought us tea, baked flat bread, brought eggs and gave each of us a goodbye-present. They showed us great hospitality, although they were poor by our standards.

---

18   *Hauptmann* Gustav Altmann, *Kompaniechef* of *2/LL.St.Rgt* and veteran officer from *Sturmabteilung Koch*, was captured on 22 May in the Akrotiri Peninsula and was one of 17 German officers to be shipped off the island to Egypt. See Pissin, p.213.

19   Although the majority of the *Sturmregiment* saw action in Russia in the latter part of 1941, only two *Kompanien* from *III/LL.St.Rgt* were available and were sent to Rshev/Sobakino in central Russia from January–April 1942. The presence of *10.* & *11.Kompanie* in Sobakino was confirmed by another *10.Kompanie* veteran who was there. Engelmann's *Kompanie* was now commanded by *Oberleutnant* Horst Vogel. It would appear that the refitting of the *Bataillon* after the casualties sustained in Crete took longer than expected. Engelmann did not take part in these operations, and more than likely remained in Halberstadt to train new replacements.

20   *III/FJR5* carried on the traditions of *II/FJR5 (II/LL.St.Rgt)* was transferred to Afrika in June 1942 as part of the Ramcke Brigade.

Kurt Engelmann and his comrades at the Christmas Farm in Tunisia, April 1995. (Kurt Engelmann)

After the fighting in Tunisia had ended, we retreated to the Cape Bône peninsula, where we became prisoners of the Americans.

Captivity & the post-war tears

From Oran we were transported to Newport in the USA, and from there by train to Livingston in Louisiana. In September 1943 we went to Brady, Texas, in May 1944 to Swift, Texas, and in August 1944 again to Brady.

In May 1945 we were transported via Florence, Arizona, to Rupert, Idaho. There we were working to harvest sweet potatoes. On 22 December 1945, we were taken by bus to Stockton, California.

On 1 May 1945, we were supposed to travel home via New York, but were transferred north in the Channel to England. From 1 August 1946, we were in Camp 188 at Stuartfield in Aberdeenshire, where we worked in the agricultural industry.

On 10 June 1947, we were transferred to Camp 19 at Happendon, then on 6 July 1947, we went to Hull, were loaded on to ships and finally transported home to Germany.

My hometown of Bleicherode was part of the Soviet occupation zone, where talking about the time of the war was taboo, so I had no contact with my old comrades for a few years.

In 1986, the organisers of a meeting of former members of *Pionierzug* Witzig contacted me and invited me on the pretence it was a golden marriage celebration. As a pensioner since 1984, I was allowed to travel to the Federal Republic, so I could meet those comrades of our first action at Eben Emael who were still alive. At the next meeting I joined them for a visit to our first objective, the fort, where we celebrated a reunion of friendship with our former enemies.

So my secret wishes during the GDR (German Democratic Republic or East Germany) era had been fulfilled. I could visit my main theatres of operations during the Second World War: Eben Emael, Crete and Tunisia.

(Kurt Engelmann passed away on 28 March 2019, two weeks short of his 100th birthday.)

Portrait photo of *Feldwebel* Kurt Engelmann taken in 1942 whilst serving with *10/LL.St. Rgt.*(Kurt Engelmann)

10

Josef 'Sepp' Jendryschik

Memories of Combat on Crete

Sepp Jendryschik was born on 26 April 1912 in Kattowitz (Katowice), Poland (Upper Silesia). He joined 12/FJR1 early in the war and served on Crete in May 1941, the Neva Front near Leningrad during the winter of 1941/42 and took part in the relief of encircled Army units at Velikiye Luki in January 1943.

In Russia, Sepp was severely wounded in the stomach and hip by a mortar round and could not take part in further fighting. After recovering from his wounds, Sepp was sent to Stendal but soon received a transfer order from Oberkommando der Wehrmacht (OKW) and was assigned to a Foreign Armies East front-line reconnaissance detachment. He was now in a real 'Himmelfahrtkommando' and his Fallschirmjäger *days were at an end.*

Sepp Jendryschik was part-Polish, and with his language skills and knowledge of Poland was useful in tracking down partisan units operating behind the German lines. He spent most of the rest of the war in Russia, and in the last days of the war attended an officer course. Events overtook him and he briefly found himself in British and then Russian captivity.

In June 1945, he was employed as a pianist in a Berlin bar, entertaining American and British officers, and later played piano concerts in the officers' casinos. Before the rise of the Berlin Wall he also played for Russian officers.

Sepp went on to write a book called Zgoda *about a Russian concentration camp in Poland where his father had been interred. This is Sepp's story of combat on the island of Crete from 24 May 1941 with* 12 *(heavy)* Kompanie *of* Fallschirmjäger Regiment 1.

Portrait photo of *Oberjäger* Sepp Jendryschik in late 1942. He wears the *Kreta* campaign cuff title on his left sleeve; on his left breast he wears the paratrooper badge, wound badge in black, *Luftwaffe* ground assault badge and the *Ostvolk* medal. He also wears the *EK2* and *Ostfront* medal ribbons through the second buttonhole of the tunic. (Sepp Jendryschik)

To the best of my memory and conscience, I will tell you something about my impressions of the preparations and the subsequent combat actions around the harbour town of Heraklion and its vicinity.

Whilst training at the parachute school, we were not only instructed in the 10 commandments of the soldier, but also told about the experiences of those paratroopers who had participated in the Polish campaign in a ground role alongside the Army. Sometimes, these men had stepped on mines, which caused severe wounds and later resulted in the amputation of the extremities, which incapacitated the soldier militarily and physically.

In great detail, we were taught to watch out for these dangers, as well as those occurring while searching buildings for hidden weapons; however, it was important to move with appropriate intervals between the men. We were to follow safety guidelines, look after ourselves and protect our comrades.

The experiences of combat-tested soldiers were spoon-fed to us: to be aware of booby-traps in suitcases, wires connecting explosives with door knobs and other cunning devices which detonated upon the slightest touch. These warnings were not one-offs, but followed up in later actions, too.

We were supposed to write a last will and deposit this letter in the *Kompanie* office, upon which we were ordered not to send postcards or letters or make phone calls until further notice. The order not to compromise operational security was like an oath to us. We were also confined to the compound.

In early May 1941, we left the barracks at Gardelegen according to Prussian standards of order and cleanliness and were brought to the train station in unmarked vehicles of the Army, where we were seated in railway coaches of the *Reichsbahn*.

With ample provisions of food and drink, we reached the airfield of Tanagra in Greece, after a rather long journey through the Balkans.

The dirt and dust whipped up by the departing and arriving aircraft quickly crusted our faces upon arrival, which made us spit like lamas, so we were happy to be told to rest near the perimeter fence line. We all had the odd feeling that the dice had already fallen, but the uncertainty did not last long.

"The old man is coming," one of the comrades shouted, speaking of our *Kompanieführer*, *Oberleutnant* Karl Vosshage.

He wiped the sweat from his forehead and ordered: "Form up around me, all of you!"

"Did you have a good journey?" was his first question. We responded with *"Jawohl Oberleutnant."*

"Now listen up good: we are here for a short break only. Looking at you, I cannot remember having told you to put on camouflage. Had I known it was so dusty around here, I'd have brought a compressor along to blow this war paint off you!"

We laughed aloud. This was just like we knew him ever since he was appointed as instructor to us in the barracks.

"We are supposed to wait here at the fence line until further notice, but you are allowed to walk over to the fresh water reservoir, fill your helmets with water and wash those exposed body parts. You will go in groups of 10 under the supervision of an *Oberjäger*. Do not stay longer than 10 minutes though. Fall out!"

Indeed, we looked like a completely new human race, and as the dust had gone down our throats as well, we gurgled in contest with each other to cure our dry coughing. The cool, fresh water was like a divine gift.

Back at the fence line, we started various activities to kill time: as far as I remember, we played skat and 'seventeen and four' (also called blackjack). The latter was formally prohibited, but this way some increased or spent their salary, to which a danger addition had been paid. Even the pilot participated; he was well versed in card games. "When are we going to leave?" one of the comrades asked him.

"Even if I knew, I couldn't say," he replied. "I have orders to take my plane back."

After two hours, the order to fall in was given.

I just had a grand with four aces and three jacks, and said to my comrade Paule: "What's the old man up to now? Didn't he say we were to rest here?"

With a strange smile, Vosshage pointed at a JU-52, which had just landed minutes ago. He told us to run over to the plane and unload crates of beer. "One bottle per man or do you think a waiter will bring you the drink?"

Like Arab stallions, we galloped over to the aircraft. This was like balsam for the dry throats, and at once we sang: "*Bier her, Bier her oder ich fall um ...*" (Beer, beer or I will fall over ...)

Obviously, Vosshage had been informed about this supply flight, because he put some bottles for the staff into his bag. He smashed his empty bottle on a rock and buried the broken glass shards with the heel of his boot:

> Shards bring luck! Good luck to all of you, but do not imitate me. This is not a *Polterabend*.[1] After supper you will take your parachutes from the tent. Some units of our Regiment have already jumped into combat. By order of the command staff, I am to tell you that we are to go into combat, soon. You as an elite force have the order to defeat the English enemy with your courage, determination, iron will and combat-tested weapons. The eyes of all Germans, wherever they may be, are set upon you. You are to uphold the honour of the Fatherland. Use the night to sleep and to rest. Good night.

Our *Kompanieführer* left at a fast pace for the command post.

After supper, we picked up our parachutes while the JU-52s stood in a row like pearls on a string waiting for their passengers, ready to take us to our destination.

Even if I am off a serious topic, the mentality of some young comrades who were something between 17 and 20 years old back then and who were acknowledged sports aces, I am trying to record their words as good as I can memorise them.

We had a unique character in our ranks, born in Berlin, who with his native dialect and wearing his heart on his sleeve was quite amusing to us, and hence informally was called 'Paule'. He was always making fun of everybody regardless of rank and social standing, but without malice and only to express his personal points of view.

It was 24 May 1941 when we finally moved out at dawn in groups of 12, with full combat load and parachutes strapped to our backs, and took our places in the JU-52s full of knowledge of what was about to happen.[2, 3]

---

1   *Polterabend* is a German wedding custom conducted the night before a wedding, where porcelain is broken to bring good luck to the bride and groom.

2   According to the *12 Kompanie* casualty list for Crete, eight men were killed during the fighting. Five of them were killed on 20 May, indicating that some elements of *12.Kp* jumped in the second wave. The other three were killed on 26 May when the *Kompanie* provided rearguard for the attack on Hill 296. Richter, p.194, states that the remnants of *12/FJR1* and other *Fallschirmjäger* regiments on the mainland became part of a 400-man *Bataillon* under the command of *Hauptmann* Gustav Vogel that jumped in the early morning of 24 May to reinforce *FJR1*. The jump area was south-west of the town of Heraklion, about 1km south-east of the western hedgehog positions held by *Major* Schulz, the commander of *III/FJR1*. In Nasse's book, *Fallschirmjäger in Crete*, p.122, Dr Adolf Eiben, the regimental doctor, recalled that *12.Kompanie* was grounded because of a lack of aircraft. *Oberleutnant* Vosshage was furious and told Eiben before take-off: "I hope you don't regret leaving the heavy *Kompanie* behind."

3   Approximately 600 of the 2,300 men of *FJR1* had to be left behind on 20 May due to a lack of aircraft. See Nisbett, p.87.

A typical scene at one of the airfields in southern Greece on 20, 21, 24 and 28 May 1941, as young *Fallschirmjäger* prepare to board their JU-52 to fly to Crete. This *Gruppe* is from the *Fallschirm-Panzerjäger-Abteilung*, who were dropped as reinforcements between Kolymbari and Tavronitis at 0745hrs on 21 May. (Kate Eichler)

We were armed only with a holstered pistol model 08, our pockets full of ammunition, grenades and cigarettes. This made sitting somewhat uncomfortable, but we were young and fit and could stomach the strain quite easily.

Fallschirmjäger in the cramped interior of a JU-52 on their way to Crete, 20 May 1941. (Author's Collection)

"I think it was a great idea of the heavy guy in Carinhall to buy us a beer. Make room!" our clown Paule said.[4]

The noise of the plane increased notably as it lifted off the ground.

"Are we supposed to pray a rosary now or chatter?" Paule asked those who were sitting by his side and across the aisle.

"Let's tell stories!" Karl replied, and everybody agreed.

"So what are you thinking about right now, Karl?"

"If somebody shoots my balls off, I'm going to be impotent for the rest of my days."

"Hey, if they only shoot one off, you're still okay, but when a splinter rips it all off completely, the medics can get you a new pair, too. Just keep crawling low until the water boils in your arse like they taught you on the acres at Gardelegen."

Paule to Alfred: "You got any brothers and sisters?"

"Only one sister, who is married to a gentleman horse rider."

"Why don't you call a gay guy a gay guy?"

"What's on your mind? My brother-in-law has horse stables with breeding and training. If you want to know for sure you can come and visit us any time."

We were roaring with laughter.

Paule to Horst: "Now it's your turn: what's it like at your home?"

"I am the only heir to the family. My creator is already dead and after the service I am to attend university and take over the factory. My mother wants many grandchildren. I've told her, I'd convert to Islam so I can have four wives. My mother became upset and said that none of them will ever cross her doorstep!"

Paule to Emil: "Now what's on your mind?"

"Nothing's on my mind. My buddy Hans wrote me that he has lice downstairs and now has his hands more often in his pockets instead of on the lathe."

Paule to Adolf: "You are going to be a veterinarian; do you have any good recipes for Emil's buddy?"

"There is some radical method: you shave off every lock of hair between your legs and cook your bedding."

Paule to Otto: "You're the last one I'm asking today: you are a Bavarian, right? Don't you call us pig-Prussians? You got a sweetheart?"

Otto replied: "With looks like this, I can have half a dozen girls if I want. You know, with real big boobs! You can come down for a visit if you like. But now it's your turn, Paule."

Paul replied: "Serious now: do you know that this is going to be one hell of a job? Don't think they will roll out the red carpet for us. If we were not in this smoke chamber, I'd sing you a Berlin traditional [song]: 'Wait, wait just a little while …' I tell you, it's in my piss, we will be on the ground pretty soon."

This dialogue might sound funny to the reader. They were intended to be that way and they were intended to cheer us up. They were held in the language of the *Landser*, which then as now is pretty rough in tone. We did not have to overlay fears with mockery; we knew well enough that life had to end someday and that this day might not be far away.

"Silence in the woods!" the navigator shouted as he came out of the cockpit and said aloud: "By higher order, I am permitted to inform you that we will descend upon the island of Crete in 1½ hours. As far as I know, you will jump near the harbour town of Heraklion!"

---

4   Carinhall was the country residence of Hermann Göring, located north-east of Berlin and named after his first wife Carin, who died in 1931.

He looked around and asked: "Who is the senior rank among you?" Without hesitation, I raised my arm. "Come over here, then. I will instruct you how to operate the weapons containers." He stepped over to the containers, shook my hand and explained the function of the retaining bolts, which held the four containers in place.

"It is my job to pull the bolts and push the canisters out after you jump.[5] This is a routine which my grandmother could do if she was here."

"But why are you telling me? I've not been trained to pull bolts in whatever time," I replied to the navigator. He put his hand on my shoulder, saying at me with a smile: "You're jumping last. I will leave the cockpit door open and when it is time; I will hand-signal you and shout 'Off they go'!

A contemporary photo of an *Abwurfbehälter* reproduced by a living history group. Many variations of air-dropped container were used by the *Luftwaffe* to supply the *Fallschirmjäger* on the ground. This example is a multi-purpose container as denoted by the marking *FL 29680*. This mobile container was introduced in 1940 and was suitable for weapons, ammunition, food and equipment. The contents were secured with four internal straps. Handles were fitted externally for easy lifting and carrying. Inside the container was a tow bar, two wheels and two chest straps that could be fitted for mobility. See Veltzé, p.334. According to Pissin, p.209, some 5358 airdrop containers were utilised during the Crete campaign. (Andy Darby)

"Then you pull the bolts and shove the containers out. By the way: if you want to see our destination from a distance, you can come forward in a little while and have a look. We have photos next to the pilot's seat, but they have been taken from quite some height, so they are somewhat blurry. We are sure that the region is sprinkled with hills though."

---

5   This refers to the retaining bolts for the four vertically dropped canisters loaded into the racks from the underbelly of the aircraft, also known as bomb shafts. Once the retaining bolts were removed the canisters would drop. There may have been additional canisters ready to be pushed from the exit door once the men had jumped.

Fallschirmjäger exit from three JU-52s over Crete. (Kate Eichler)

A *Fallschirmjäger* is positioned in the door of a JU-52 seconds before jumping. This is a training jump. A dispatcher holds back two static lines from the previous jumpers. (Author's Collection)

I replied: "Do we know anything about the height from which we will jump? It is important for the men."

"It depends on the situation. We have to keep in mind that the Tommies will try to shoot us out of the sky. But don't worry old chap, if this doesn't go to plan then we are all down the drain." He took his seat up front, saying: "When we are approaching the island, you may come forward and have a look and get yourself orientated. I'll give you a signal so you know when to come to me."

"What did the navi say, come on, tell us," my comrades demanded to know, so I briefed them in great detail and ended with the words: "I don't know any more myself."

"Amen!" Paule added. "Does anybody know what that word means? I'll give you 10 Reichmarks if you tell me."

Of course, all answers were wrong, so somebody said. "Alright Paule, enlighten us!"

"So be it." Paule said. "An old Jewish man once told me. He was a vendor with his cart full of tomatoes, onions and what have you. Sometimes he gave me a carrot. The word is Hebrew. Now you assholes know what the Pastor means when he says the word."

I sat down until the navigator motioned me to come forward and have a look over his shoulder. I saw the town of Heraklion. The area looked like sugar cubes on a tabletop to me. These were buildings, whitewashed with narrow paths and alleyways between them. He then told me to stand by the weapons container racks.

I told my comrades that we were already approaching the drop zone.

With great discipline, everybody checked the 'chute harness and prepared for the jump. When the dispatcher shouted "Make ready!" and the horn sounded three minutes later, everybody formed up, slapping the back of the man in front with the words *"Glück Ab!"* (Happy landings).

Then they jumped and I was alone.

As ordered, I pulled the retainer bolts, but only one unlocked, so I shouted for the navigator. He yelled at me: "Up and get out, NOW!"

I jumped! When my 'chute opened, I checked 360° to see where my comrades were. Around 500m away I saw white spots on the ground; the parachutes of my comrades who had already landed. My landing took place on a rich agave tree and I felt a sting in my buttocks. I thought that a bullet had hit home. I pulled out my gravity knife and cut the parachute cords. Later on I was told that the unknown plant was used by the Mexicans to make liquor called Pulque.

As soon as I had dropped the harness and opened my smock, I pulled the thorn from my butt. Lying down, I noticed that the storm of steel was already on and the shots were not falling far from my position.[6]

In the unspeakable heat, the sweat was running into my eyes and blinded me for a moment. I crawled up a hill and saw unidentified individuals running around 400 or 500m to my front.

In order to keep a low profile, I weasled through bushes and thickets for several hours and finally reached a comrade, a *Sani* who doubled as a staff runner. He pointed me in the right direction so I could find my comrades from *12.Kompanie* and said: "*Oberst* Bräuer has ordered that everyone is up to himself now. All for one and one for all! Every position is to be held until further notice." Before he left, he said: "Get going, run and crawl, it will be dark soon." He slapped my helmet and went off.

To my greatest relief, I reached my comrades, who were all unhurt and well.

"Get some rest and when you have caught your breath, you can tell us why you have come late," I was told.

---

6   This was an attack by men of the Agyll & Sutherland Highlanders. As they were approaching Heraklion from the south/south-west, the paratroops were organising themselves on the ground. See Richter, p.194.

"Please, give me a drink!" I said. My tongue was swollen in my mouth so I could hardly speak. In one large swig, I emptied the canteen like a Bavarian empties his beer stein, then relieved the comrade at the mortar who stuffed one round after the other into the barrel just like the Polish when they stuff their geese. (Like the humour, swearing was part of the rank-and-file soldier's dictionary.)

We were fortunate enough to scout a deep well nearby where we could draw water with the helmet. Otherwise, we would have died from dehydration or been killed by partisans in our dehydrated state.

Our positions were not connected with each other, but we could shout for our other comrades who were firing their syringes (*Landser*-term for machine guns) until the barrels were red hot. We had plenty of ammunition as several Waffenbehälter had been dropped on us. Through the steady fire, neither us or the Tommies managed to get much rest.

"This is like a slaughterhouse," one comrade remarked. "I've been told that on the other side of the island, partisans are having one bloodbath after the other."

Oberst Bruno Bräuer, the commander of *FJR1*. He was the first German paratrooper and referred to as the victor of Dordrecht and Moerdijk in Holland in May 1940. He was executed by the Greeks on 20 May 1947. (Author's Collection)

We tried to give the gentlemen on the other side hell, so they would surrender. The drumfire was so hard on our ears, we stuffed our ears as good as possible so we had to shout at each other.

The combat command ironed out plans for further strategies. Everybody knew that defeat meant annihilation. For the time being, the English [*sic*] could not penetrate our positions. So the first days passed.

The JU-52s circled high above. They parachuted in any supplies we requested. Logistics were working well. Although the provisions were not substantial, we did not have to starve for one moment.

One day, we were surprised by rifle fire from a different direction. We could not see much due to the rolling hills in our area, but we doubled the sentries and had to get up several times during the night in order to relieve our comrades.

"Follow me; we are under fire from partisans," an *Oberjäger* told me. "Stuff your pockets full of hand grenades …"

Hindered by the underbrush, which made a silent low crawl almost impossible, we closed in on the enemy. They were hidden behind a slight hill and just waiting for one of our comrades to expose himself so they could snipe at him.

My comrade lay on top of a piece of raised ground so he could see them well. He fired full auto on them, wounded or even killed one of theirs and shouted: "I'll cover your flank. Don't stand up! Throw your eggs to their left!" Which is what I did.

He came to me at a run: "Don't throw any more grenades. They have taken to their heels."

I noticed that my grenades had all detonated too far behind them as I had been only 4m away from them and their sangar had been a metre deep. Except for a spade, they had taken all weapons with them.

"I'll have the *Sani* look after him," my comrade said, pointing at the wounded partisan. "I'll go and report to staff."

Myself, I have no love for partisans. There are other ways to show patriotism; by donning a proper uniform, for example. These men were just robbing bandits.

We had not taken anybody's freedom. One day we would go home, just like the Romans, Turks and every other nation which had ever occupied Crete.

Upon our return, we shook hands and brushed the dirt from our smocks.

The front lines had proven quite impossible to penetrate during the last few days, so we thought that we had to hold the ground before acting again and dug in deeper every time the firing stopped for a moment.

It was to our surprise that we were ordered out of our positions by nightfall, to fill up the canteens and take a new position on top of a designated hill to the east.[7]

Many comrades nearly collapsed when they heard about the climbing expedition through rough, broken, steep terrain with little if any sight of a nearing enemy.

A lost donkey, which some comrades had caught in order to carry the mortar base plate, had to be pulled along by the ears and pushed by his butt so he would move.

The first English [*sic*] troops were overrun just before we reached the hilltop. We were surprised to see how much weaponry, ammunition and supplies they had at their disposal.

As soon as we had them disarmed, we fell to the ground, weak as if our bones had been removed. Some fell into a coma-type sleep. Our officers had offered to do sentry duty for them so they could rest. So we slept until the warm sunrays woke us up.

Below our hill, we saw the town of Heraklion, not knowing what was yet to come.

"We'll soon be visited by a JU-52, so we must clean this plateau of all rocks." If I remember correctly, it was *Oberleutnant* Horst Kerfin (*Ritterkreuzträger*) who gave us this order.

Even if we had not believed that this was possible, we soon saw the aircraft landing and taking off again after debussing its cargo. The skills of this pilot who had landed on an airstrip which had never been used before, and the risk of the enterprise, made us compare him to Udet.[8] We shouted encouragement and waved our arms in a frenzy as the aircraft left the ground. Unfortunately, the daring pilot has never been mentioned in any book.[9]

After nine long days, the fighting had stopped in Heraklion.

I want to tell you about one of many crimes committed by Greek Partisans. We were ordered to take intervals of 50m and collect the parachutes on the drop-zone. I think it was a *Sani* from the *III Bataillon* who, coming from the other side, took a lot of photos with his own camera.

"I'll write a book when the war is over," he said, and took off in the direction of the coast.

We came back to our garrison at Gardelegen, received the Iron Cross after the parade and went for a well-deserved home leave.

After my return, I ran into the *Sanitäter* in the compound. He asked me to wait at the doorstep of his room as he was on duty. He presented me with a photograph to thank me for having half-emptied my canteen on that day on Crete. "I'll drop by *12. Kompanie* one of these days, so we can have a beer together," he said. The photo showed mutilated comrades, butchered by partisans.[10]

---

7   Hill 296, also known as Apex Hill, south of the airfield, which was assaulted on 26 May.
8   Ernst Udet was a First World War fighter ace and later a *Luftwaffe* general
9   See the account by Sebastian Krug, p.90.
10 These paratroopers were killed in the public toilets on the harbour mole by Greek soldiers with hand grenades after refusing to surrender and killing a Greek officer. See Prekatsounakis, p.183.

Inside the public toilets on the harbour mole in Heraklion. During the research for his book *Crete: The Battle for Heraklion 1941*, Yannis Prekatsounakis discovered that the men in this photo are probably from *13/FJR1* as mortars were found outside the public toilets. It is interesting to note that the body on the right of the photo has piston rings on his tunic sleeve, indicating that he is a *Kompanie Spieß*. The *13 Kompanie* Spieß was *Oberfeldwebel* Karl Brückmann, who was killed close to the public toilets, so his body may have been moved here by Greek or British soldiers. The photo was probably taken after the town was finally occupied by German forces on 29 May 1941, eight days after these men were killed. There are apparently several other bodies out of picture, so the public toilets may have been a collection point for those killed in the immediate vicinity.
(Sepp Jendryschik)

I never did see that *Sani* again. Later, in Russia, I was wounded by mortar shrapnel and after long treatment in various hospitals, I was transferred for assignment at Stendal. From Stendal I was ordered to report to Foreign Armies East and spent most of the rest of the war in Russia.

Only after the end of the war did I go into British and then briefly Russian captivity.

(Sepp Jendryschik passed away on 22 May 2001, aged 89.)

11

Bernd Bosshammer

Prelude to Crete and the Gran Sasso raid

Bernd Bosshammer was born on 3 September 1919 in Rölsdorf, near Düren, and was a pre-war Fallschirmjäger *volunteer who saw action in Poland, Holland and Crete during the early part of the war. In Crete, on 20 May 1941, Bosshammer was seriously wounded shortly after landing and spent the next nine days sheltering in a donkey stable with two comrades before he was eventually rescued by fellow paratroopers. The diary he kept from this ordeal is featured in part two of this book. Bosshammer later went on to serve in the* Fallschirm-Lehr Bataillon *and took part in* Operation Eiche *(Oak). This was a glider-borne operation in September 1943 to rescue Mussolini from his mountain-top prison on the Gran Sasso d'Italia in the Appenine Mountains. Later in the war he saw combat in Holland and north-west Germany, where he was wounded several times, and was captured whilst in hospital recovering from his wounds.*

Oberjäger Bernd Bosshammer,
5/Fallschirmjäger Regiment 1. Photo taken
at Tangermünde/Elbe in October 1940.
(Bernd Bosshammer)

Bernd Bosshammer at the 2003 *BDF* (*Bundestreffen*)
meeting. (Bund Deutscher Fallschirmjäger)

Pre-war

In 1937 I volunteered for service in the *Reichsarbeitsdienst (RAD)* and served for six months in Much near Overath. In 1938 I volunteered for the *Fallschirmtruppe* and was subsequently sent to *3. Kompanie, Fallschirmjäger Regiment 1* in Stendal under the command of *Oberleutnant* Henning Freiherr von Brandis. At *Fallschirmschule 1* in Stendal-Borstel, I completed my jump training and in 1939 was posted to *III/FJR1* at Gardelegen and joined *9. Kompanie* under the command of *Oberleutnant* Otto Gessner. My *Zugführer* was *Oberleutnant* Rauch, who came from the *SA Regiment Feldherrnhalle*.

Poland

On 12 September 1939, we *Fallschirmjäger* were transported in JU-52 transport aircraft from the airfield at Lichtenwalde to Radom in Poland. Near Wola Gulowska, my comrade Alfred Asbach and I were captured by Polish troops. After one-and-a-half days in captivity we managed to make a night-time escape and return to our *Kompanie*.

In early October 1939, the *Kompanie* returned to Germany by road but the barracks in Gardelegen were occupied so I was privately quartered with a family near Kleinbahnhof. At the end of April 1940, the unit was on the move once again, this time to Gütersloh in western Germany.

Holland

On 10 May 1940, I took part in the landings at the Waalhaven airfield near Rotterdam and was lightly wounded by a grazing shot to the head during the assault. I also took part in the fighting at Dordrecht, and after the fighting was over I was quartered with an elderly Dutch couple in Katwijk am See.

Continuation training

At the end of May 1940, the *Bataillon* once again returned to Gardelegen, where I was able to take a week's leave with my parents and siblings in Hochkirchen. When I returned in June, I reported to *Leutnant* Rausch and learned that we were to conduct more training at the *Fallschirmschule* at Braunschweig Broitzen. Once again we practiced falling forwards and backwards, rolling forwards and backwards as well as packing the RZ1 parachute. I became well acquainted with the packing equipment called *PW7* (*Packwerzeugtasche 7*, packing equipment bag 7), which came with bags of lead shot, scissors, packing forks, olive green and red cord, wooden paddles and a rubber cable. I also remember the stamps on each parachute. There was an equipment stamp, a factory control stamp and an air transport inspection stamp. The RZ1 parachutes were made by the firms Schröder & Co in Berlin, Autoflug in Bernau and Köhler & Stelling in Brandenburg.

During this training period, I also qualified as an aircraft dispatcher, parachute supervisor and examiner, and also conducted several test jumps using new camouflage parachutes. By the end of the training I was able to pack a parachute in less than 10 minutes and knew all of the technical values of the 'chute itself. Meanwhile, I had been promoted to *Obergefreiter* and had been awarded the Iron Cross 2nd Class and the wound badge.

Since the training halls at Braunschweig could not accommodate all of the training *Kompanien*, a two-shift day was established, which meant that the early shift would be on the way into the city at 1300 hours to eat at Börner am Böhlweg or at the train station, both famous restaurants in the town.

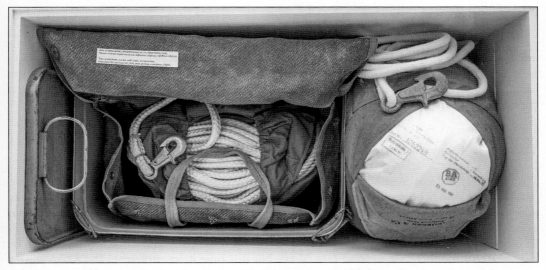

Two parachute types. On the left is a parachute for personnel in its burlap sack and storage container. The other is a parachute used on an *Abwurfbehälter*. (Yannis Prekatsounakis)

Operation *Seelöwe* – The invasion of England

In September 1940, we were suddenly recalled from the *Fallschirmschule* as plans were being made for a new assignment, Operation Sealion, the invasion of England. Karl Siebert and I had to report to *Hauptmann* Burckhardt, commander of *II/FJR1* at Tangermünde. At the Kasernhof Barracks in Tangermünde, a unit was conducting training and from a distance I recognised my former No.2 *MG* gunner, Alfred Asbach. As I went to greet him, I heard a shout from behind. I turned around to see an *Oberleutnant*, and on closer inspection I recognised Harry Herrmann, whom I had known in Stendal one year before. He asked me what I was doing in Tangermünde, and when I told him I had to report to *Hauptmann* Burckhardt he informed me that I would be joining 5. *Kompanie* and to prepare for the planned invasion. I was made a *Gruppeführer* and Karl became deputy *Zugführer* under *Feldwebel* Frieherr von Berlepsch, who was also introduced to us. The other *Gruppeführers* were Ernst Pfister, Hein Tappe, Hein Weiland, Wilhelm Reuter and Alfred Grünhagen.

The first days were spent packing parachutes for the invasion, and I personally packed over 200 of them in the sports hall in Tangermünde.

When Harry Herrmann jumped into Crete on 20 May 1941, he was temporarily blinded by a head shot but continued to lead his men, albeit occasionally losing consciousness. For his actions he was awarded the *Ritterkreuz* on 9 July 1941. (Prof Dr Heinz Bliss)

We were deployed to the airfield at Stendal, where we learned that Operation Sealion would no longer take place.

The *Kompanie* returned to Tangermünde and was brought up to full operational strength. Now we began training, which included forced marches, live firing exercises, blowing up bunkers and field training. NCOs were transferred to the military training area to train on sand tables, and we also conducted a mission during the flood disaster on the Elbe. Meanwhile, von Berlepsch was promoted to *Leutnant* and the *Kompanie* was brought up to a very high standard of training.

Prelude to Operation Mercury

On 14 April 1941, I was duty NCO when an alert was issued by *Oberleutnant* Herrmann at 0120 hours. The men had already been subject to a curfew for several days. The *Zugführers* received a brief and the *Kompanie* was given the order to relocate by truck, and in addition the trucks would be loaded onto railway wagons and we would require jump equipment, so the men recieved their parachutes.

Despite the late hour and lack of sleep, we were pleased to finally know that we might soon be deployed. All too often we recieved false alerts, but this time it was different. The *Kompaniechef* returned from the commander's briefing and ordered a transfer to our operational base at Stendal. The trucks arrived, backpacks were packed, parachutes and weapons were loaded and march rations were issued. Everything went as practiced many times before. I wrote a letter to my parents and siblings with the remark "it starts, where?", and handed it over to the troops remaining behind. From the clothing store I generously received three pairs of socks, a set of underwear and I marvelled at a brand new *Oberjäger* tunic with collar liner. The whole *Kompanie* then mounted the trucks. My place was in the cab of the Opel Blitz truck, next to the driver, *Gefreiter* Kuhnert, who was much older than us. We were transported to Stendal, approximately 12km from Tangermünde, where the trucks were loaded on to the railway wagons. The trucks were secured and a full roll call was carried out. We began our journey at 1000 hours, going on through the day and night to an unknown destination in the south.

On the march to Greece, *Oberjäger* Bosshammer oversees transport preparations. (Prof Dr Heinz Bliss)

The locomotive was changed twice a day and we were fed twice a day. Our clothing was plain and did not identify us as *Fallschirmjäger*. We were all dressed in our aviator tunics, but without any badges, and our *Knochensack* were in our backpacks.

Everything was carried out in the strictest of secrecy. Shortly after passing the Hungarian/Romanian border near Arrad, the train came to a stop. The trucks, luggage, weapons and munitions had to be unloaded again and restowed on the vehicles. From Arrad began a long truck march, and it was a very strenuous journey. We were still unaware of our destination.

The roads were terrible, with the dust and dirt getting worse. I had the task of guiding the driver in the column, as the vehicles in front of us were barely visible through the dense dust clouds. Punctures, ignition failures and engine damage occurred again and again. We stopped, started, touched, pushed and reset, all in the glowing sun.

Days passed until we finally reached the Greek border. If we hoped that the roads would be better here, we had been mistaken, Mountains, passes on steep cliffs, narrow passes and deep gorges were slowly overcome. We only saw the beautiful landscape when the column stopped. Skopje was very badly damaged, the roads barely passable, but the next day we reached Salonika. We stopped at the Gulf of Thessaloniki between Thessaloniki and Katerine, very close to the sea. We were finally able to bathe properly, and also sunbathe. It was wonderful. We wished that this would be our final stop, especially as we also stayed the next day. Unfortunately this was not to be, and also the weather began to turn. On the third day we experienced a terrible thunderstorm.

The *Unteroffizier-Korps* of *5/FJR1* on the march to Greece. From left to right: *Oberjäger* Wunsch, *Oberjäger* Grünhagen, *Oberjäger* Reuter, *Oberjäger* Max Vogel (KIA 21 May), *Oberjäger* Pfister, *Oberjäger* Bosshammer and *Feldwebel* Karl Zimmerman (KIA 21 May). (Prof Dr Heinz Bliss)

This aviator's tunic owned by Yannis Prekatsounakis demonstrates how distinctive the *Fallschirmjäger* uniform was when wearing the qualification badge. In order to maintain secrecy, all paratrooper insignia was removed during the transit to Greece. This tunic for a *Gefreiter* shows that the wearer was a veteran on the Crete campaign. (Yannis Prekatsounakis)

In no time one of our trucks sank into the mud on the unpaved slope down to the sea. Recovering it seemed impossible. Ropes were secured to the vehicle and columns of 30 or more soldiers joined forces to heave ho! To the roar of *Oberjäger* Pfister's voice, we finally pulled the truck from the mud metre by metre until it was on solid ground.

Meanwhile, it was already noon and the field kitchen was not yet in use, so iron rations were issued and replenished the next day.

The following day we reached the final destination of our long and arduous journey. It was a former English colony estate about 60km from Athens. The estate was located in a wide plain with clean fields and a small freshwater river. There were scattered groups of trees which proved to be perfect for pitching our tents. The large tents were quickly set up and expertly connected with roads and paths, fences, front gardens, benches and even a hair salon. The groups had built their own ovens, so the next day our cook, Willi Irrgang, took a day off. The individual groups cooked, fried and baked as we had plenty of time. Duties were few and far between, and mostly conducted in the shade. From time to time you were allowed to ride a truck to Athens to get food. Our *Wehrsold* (service pay) was given to us in Drachmas so we could buy Greek cigarettes, Retsina wine, corn bread and feta cheese.

The days passed by. The weapons and equipment remained packed and only the guards were armed. The men were puzzled about our current existence. What were we doing here? Why were we here? And why did we have it so good? When and where was our mission: would it come at all, because Greece had already been completely conquered?

We had been there for over a week, far from any town or village. Over the past few days we had heard aircraft noise not far from us. There must be an airfield close by. We also saw a tanker truck pass by.

The silence seemed eerie to us. The question why we were there remained unanswered! Were we going to Malta? Were we going to Africa? But surely the JU-52 could only fly so far without stopping? The uncertainty bothered all of us! Mail could be written but it would not be sent straight away. The calm before the so-called storm made us all nervous, restless and uncertain, yet excited.

On 18 May, the platoon and group leaders were called to the *Kompaniechef* and a high alert was issued. Further trips to Athens were cancelled. The boss, Harry Herrmann, said that it will all start soon. Our mission area was explained to us, without actually knowing where it was. Our target was an airfield located by the sea. That was it! The mission should have already taken place a few days previously, but it was postponed twice by the top leadership in Berlin. The mission could now begin.

Once again the guessing game continued: questions and enquiries were the topic of the

One of the men present at the briefings was *Der Spieß* of 5/FJR1, *Hauptfeldwebel* Alfred Kurth. Kurth was killed on 21 May fighting beside his wounded *Kompaniechef* near Karteros, south-east of the airfield at Heraklion. He is buried in block 1 grave 785 at the Maleme cemetery. (Prof Dr Heinz Bliss)

evening. Those of us who were present at the meeting could only pass on what we had heard; there was still insufficient information, except we knew it would start soon.

On 19 May 1941, there was another *Kompanie* briefing, firstly for the officers and NCOs and then for the soldiers. Maps had been made available for the meeting and aerial photographs were shown, which were taken at high altitude with little to see. Sandboxes were built using the available resources to recreate the expected terrain and landmarks.

Now for the first time the word 'Crete' was heard: the island of Crete, a place nobody had even considered, was suddenly on everyone's lips. Where was Crete? What does it look like? Where do people live there? What enemy troop formations are there? Are there larger cities? Which airport is our target? All

The grave of *Hauptfeldwebel* Alfred Kurth at the *Soldatenfriedhof* in Maleme. (aretecrete.com)

of these questions and more rushed through our minds. The only certainty was that we only had one more sleep and then it would begin! There was an unbearable feverish tension, and our heads were full of thoughts but without many answers to all these questions. The only thing that was clear was that it would be a jump operation. Parachute and munitions were unloaded, weapon containers checked, our aviator tunics packed away and the jump smock unpacked.

A final meeting was held between the *Gruppeführers* and the *Zugführer*, and then everything became clear. Our jump was to be conducted at the airfield near Heraklion. Since the airfield was heavily fortified, we were to jump clear of those positions and not directly on to it. Once in our hands, we were to prepare the runway so that our aircraft could land and bring in supplies. *II/ FJR1*, under the command of *Hauptmann* Burckhardt, would jump with four *Kompanien* and the *Stabskompanie* east of the airfield into a depression (Karteros valley) and attack the slightly elevated airfield.

For many of our comrades this would be their first jump mission. We had to fly over the sea at a low altitude so as not to be detected or recognised too quickly. Lifejackets would be issued before entering the aircraft.

The evening was long and the night very short. Only a few slept, and most men thought of loved ones back home. What awaited us on Crete? Would we see our loved ones again? Would we reach our destination without loss? Would we be intercepted by enemy fighters? Or shelled by battleships that might be waiting for us? Would we be dropped in the right location, would we be able to find each other after the jump and fight together as a group or platoon, and would we find the weapon containers?

We were reassured that the airfield would be bombarded before we deployed from the aircraft. The operation would go to plan, the enemy would quickly be overrun and the airfield would be in our hands and supplies could land. How nice if everything should go to plan!

On 20 May the *Kompanie* was woken up by a signal horn at 0500 hours. We ran to the nearby river, washed, shaved, dressed and took breakfast. We checked that everything was properly packed because our backpacks would be returned to Germany. We only kept what we needed for the operation. Soon the whole *Kompanie* were dressed in their jump suits and climbing aboard the trucks. The remaining equipment was also loaded onto trucks and left with the men who would not come with us. These were our drivers and the non-jumpers.

At 0800 hours our trucks moved out toward the nearby airfield at Topolia.

We arrived there at 0910 hours, and were very surprised and disappointed that there were so few aircraft at the airfield. Every *Kompanie* required at least 15 aircraft, some 73–75 for a *Bataillon*!

We learned that the JU-52s had already flown missions to Maleme and Chania in the west of the island. The JU-52s had also suffered losses and some aircraft did not return from their mission. The existing aircraft had to be refuelled from 200-litre barrels using hand pumps. This was a tedious job, especially since we were all fully dressed. We changed locations four or five times before we were finally on the right aircraft. I had eaten a gritty milk soup with raisins, golden yellow in colour from too much butter, and it lay heavy in my stomach. Fortunately, our start was postponed so I was able to empty the contents of my stomach.

Aircraft were still returning and causing huge dust clouds, but there were still not enough machines so every *Zug* had to leave a *Gruppe* behind. These men later became part of *Kompanie Klein* who jumped west of Tavronitis on the morning of 21 May.[1]

We finally got airborne and jumped at 1800 hours near Karteros, south-east of the airfield. Shortly after landing on Crete, I was wounded in the left thigh and spent the next few days laid up in a donkey stable with two comrades, Rose and Gulden, until 29 May. My left thigh was smashed and had a 7cm gash in it. The three of us were eventually rescued and evacuated to a hospital in Athens, where I was told that I would have to lose my leg, but I resisted and threatened the doctors with my pistol. I kept my leg and was sent to another hospital in Wien [see Bernd Bosshammer, 'Nine days between the dead and the living' on page 269].

Recovery and recuperation

In December 1941 I was sent home sent home to Düren with my leg in plaster, and the following month I was again at the hospital in Düren attempting to walk with crutches and slowly recovering from my wounds.

In early 1943 I was sent to recover in Mariazell in Austria, and then to Ospedaletti in Italy, but soon returned to service and was sent to Berlin Döberitz and promoted to *Feldwebel*.

I was then transferred to France, followed by a transfer to Frascati and Albano in Italy. On 12 September 1943, I took part in Operation *Eiche*, the rescue of Mussolini from the Gran Sasso d'Italia.

Fallschirmjäger-Lehr Bataillon at the Gran Sasso

The name of our *Bataillon* was changed to I/FJR7 in order to camouflage us. *Major* Harry Herrmann was relieved for treatment of an illness and command was handed over to *Major* Otto Harald Mors. On 30 September, Mors gave the command back to *Major* Herrmann upon his return and we once again became the *Fallschirmjäger-Lehr Bataillon*.

Until 9 September, we were in tents in Albaner-See, 20km south-east of Rome. From there we went to disarm the 103rd Italian Infantry Division in the area Albano-Genzano. This is where

---

1   Due to the shortage of aircraft on 20 May, *4/FJR1* (*Leutnant* Kiebitz) did not take part in the second wave drop on Heraklion. One of the officers from this *Kompanie* was *Leutnant* Hans Klein. According to the *Gefechtsbericht* of *XI Fliegerkorps*, Klein led a *Kompanie* made of of men from *FJR2*. It is possible that this formation also included Gruppen from 4/FJR1. *Kompanie Klein* was dropped with the *Fallschirm-Panzer-Jäger-Abteilung* at 0745 hours on 21 May west of Tavronitis. Klein was killed on 23 May in the vicinity of Agia Marina between Gerani and Chania.

Leutnant Hannes Weber was killed (there were two officers named Hannes Weber). We occupied accommodation of the Italian 111th Infantry Regiment, and from there went on to disarm an Italian Artillery Regiment in the area of Arricia. The *Bataillon* became motorised with the capture of some Fiat lorries, as many of our vehicles were still in France. Everybody not familiar with a truck was trained as a driver, which was good because the next day we travelled to Frascati.

Feldwebel Franzen was killed when he tried to defuse a hand grenade. It was sabotage, as some of the grenades had been equipped without time delay fuses. On 9 September, the *Bataillon* command post put *1. Kompanie* on alert. We were not informed of the reason. Everybody spoke about the elimination of high government officials and Italian officers. Throughout the whole day, weapons and equipment were checked. The captured vehicles were checked and refuelled.

Jupp Vieth, our parachute warder, prepared and loaded the parachutes. I spent the whole day in the command post with Lambert, Klein and Nadler. We had a lot to do as we were passing on orders. The men were allocated by a wireless and telephone group under the command of *Feldwebel* Ripke. Munitions were handed out to the men. In the command post, a captured vehicle with a field telephone, we were allocated another *Gefreiter*, whose name I did not know. It was now very cramped and I spent most of the time looking after the soldiers on guard duty.

Late in the afternoon, *Oberleutnant* von Berlepsch had to go and discuss the situation with the *Bataillon* staff. He returned at about 2200 hours with some documents and aerial photographs. I was in the command vehicle at the time. Every *Zug* and *Gruppeführer* had to muster in the big tent. The guards were reinforced and alert phase one was given. We were told that all of the information was strictly secret and it was to be a mission without parachutes; it would be a glider operation.

In France, near Laval, we had been trained to use the DFS-230 glider, especially in quick landings. The skids were wound round with barbed wire. The wheels were dropped after take-off, and on the DFS-230 Type B we had a braking parachute. The aims and objectives of this operation were still secret. They did not tell us any names or places. The aerial photos were not very good. It looked like a big house on a hill.

They always talked about one man who was guarded by 200–250 soldiers. The expected places to land were marked with a cross. There were also drawings of the inside of the building. *Feldwebel* Abel had to be well acquainted with these plans. Abel spent a long time with *Oberleutnant* von Berlepsch, perhaps because his Italian was very good (he had been an Italian teacher).

After that, we had a talk in our command vehicle about rationing, weapons and munitions. *Oberjäger* Willi Irrgang, our cook, and also Vieth had to take part in the operation, but not to fight.

The following night was short; we had to get up at 0500 hours. At 0555 hours, the trucks were ready to go. Every *Zug* and *Gruppeführer* had to report their full attendance, and after a short delay we started at 0700 hours. We left behind some of the *Bataillon*. The other *Kompanien* started at 0300 hours with captured trucks and some tanks, led by *Oberleutnant* Hannes Weber to Assergi. We drove in the direction of Rome and stopped at the airfield at Practica de Mare. There for the first time we were told that our mission was on the Gran Sasso and that we were to capture [*sic*] *Il Duce*. We were only allowed to shoot when the occupying forces opened fire, and then only on the orders of Von Berlepsch.

One of our *Gruppen* had to stay at Practica de Mare as *SS Hauptsturmführer* (Captain) Otto Skorzeny was to fly with seven of his *SS* men. It was the *Gruppe* which had problems with their truck, but they arrived just before the take-off.[2] Some men from *1. Kompanie* also had to stay

---

2   Skorzeny, a *Waffen-SS* officer, conducted several commando-style operations during the Second World War, and was known as the most dangerous man in Europe by Allied forces.

behind because the gliders could only hold 10 men and our *Gruppen* consisted of 14 men. The men who had to stay behind were very annoyed. Our pilot and commander of the glider group was *Leutnant* Meyer-Wehner. The pilot of the HS-126 towing plane was *Oberleutnant* Johannes Heidenreich.

Then we were told that two planes had broken down and another 18 soldiers would have to stay behind. It was a hard decision to decide who was coming and who was staying. *Oberleutnant* Georg Freiherr von Berlepsch was looking for a car because he sent his back to the broken-down lorry. Now the lorry was with us but not his car, with all of his equipment. At 1200 hours, the anti-aircraft fire started, signifying an air raid. We could see the British planes in the sky and hear the bombs. We were lucky. The car belonging to the *Kompaniechef* now turned up. It had broken down. Von Berlepsch picked up his equipment and proceeded to the glider. Some *Luftwaffe* soldiers brought out a high-ranking Italian officer, the police general Soletti whom they had taken from Rome. He had to come with us because his presence might avert needless bloodshed. Soletti turned pale and wanted to shoot himself, so we took away his pistol. He reluctantly climbed into the glider with Meyer-Wehner. There were 10 gliders altogether.

The planes started at 1300 hours, precisely on time. In the first plane was *Hauptmann* Langguth, who knew the area from his reconaissance flights. In one glider was von Berlepsch, in another Eugen Abel, in another *Leutnant* Gradler, with their men. In another glider were Meyer-Wehner, Otto Skorzeny, an interpreter, Soletti and seven *Waffen-SS* soldiers.

At 1400 hours, we saw the mountain of the Gran Sasso and the sporting hotel of Campo Imperatore. We landed about 120–150m away from the hotel. There were many soldiers in front of the hotel, but they did not look dangerous or alarmed. They thought we were English or American soldiers who wanted to pick up Mussolini. Our cook inadvertently fired a shot and we were lucky it went without consequences. Abel went inside the hotel, and after a few minutes we could see Mussolini in front of the window. We overcame the Italian soldiers and they gave us their weapons, and afterward they were herded into the big dining room.

One of our gliders (with Matthias Heck on board) crash-landed, injuring seven soldiers, but fortunately all of them except one could walk. The wounded soldiers were transported down the mountain by cable car and were treated at the bottom. After about 15 minutes, *Il Duce* came outside with Abel. Behind *Il* Duce was Skorzeny.

Major Mors, *Oberleutnant* Schulze and *Oberleutnant* Kurth, along with other officers and men, came up the mountain by cable car. *Il Duce* said he did not want the guards to be treated as prisoners. The Italian soldiers were glad that nobody had fired on them. The hotel was surrounded and nobody was allowed inside or outside.

Il Duce was transported by Feisler light aircraft to the airfield at Practica de Mare. All Italian soldiers and *Fallschirmjäger* not guarding the hotel escorted Mussolini to the plane. Skorzeny wanted to accompany Mussolini, but the pilot, *Hauptmann* Gerlach, said no. He was obviously persuaded, as he did fly out with *Il Duce*.

I stayed at the hotel to guard it. We brought the last soldiers into the valley by cable car. We could not bring the gliders back, so we destroyed them where they had landed. Our mission was a success and there were no dead. Every time we brought soldiers down from the mountain we always took some Italian soldiers with us.

We stayed the night in bivouacs in the Gran Sasso valley. The liberation of *Il Duce* from the Gran Sasso d'Italia went down in the history of the *Fallschirmtruppe*.

The last year of the war

After the Gran Sasso raid, I was transferred to Cita de Castello, where the *Bataillon* was being formed into a *Regiment*. The *Kommandeur* was once again *Major* Harry Herrmann.

In 1944 I saw service at Anzio/Nettuno, and in March 1944 was sent to France with the *Regiment* and became '*Der Spieß*' of *4. Kompanie* under the command of *Leutnant* von Gliga.

From April to May 1944, I became '*Der Spieß*' of *Nachrichtenzug Köhler* in *I/Fj-Lehr Regiment*, the *Bataillonskommandeur* was *Hauptmann* Zuber and we were stationed at Amiens-Abbeville. In August 1944 I saw action at Pontoise-Beauvais near Paris. It was here that a large part of the *Regiment* went into captivity. At this time I was promoted from *Oberfeldwebel* to *Hauptfeldwebel*.

In September 1944, the remainder of the *Regiment* was sent to Hastenrath in the area of Aachen. They were to make up part of a *Kampfgruppe* before being sent to Köln Wahn. There was not much rest to be had as we were in action on 17/18 September at Mook in Holland, where I was heavily wounded again and was taken to hospital in Bedburg and then to Düsseldorf, and on again to Berlin. I had suffered serious blood loss (my wife donated blood five times), but recovered in time to go into action again in January 1945. Again it was Holland, in Brüggen and Roermond. Once again I was wounded in the leg by a shell splinter and was evacuated to a hospital in Arnsberg. In April 1945 I was captured when the Americans captured the hospital. I was moved around from Menden to Remagen, Koblenz and finally to Bamberg, where I was discharged in October 1945. After my release from captivity I returned to the paper factory in Düren where I had worked as a youth.

(Bernd Bosshammer passed away on 25 November 2011, aged 92.)

12

Carl Bayerlein

Fallschirm-Pionier training, Italy and captivity

Carl regularly corresponded with me using his POW English. He wrote many short articles regarding his wartime service and they were often published in the Pionier *yearbook for other veterans to read. He had intended to write a book, but this never came to fruition. He was interviewed several times by TV production companies and authors regarding his experiences during the battle for Ortona in December 1943 and the battle for Monte Luro in 1944, which features in this account. Born on 1 January 1926, Carl was a volunteer* Fallschirmjäger *who joined up when he was 17 and saw active service in Italy at Ortona, Cassino and other locations on the Gustav Line before being captured by Canadian forces at Monte Luro after intense fighting on the height he was defending. The following reports focus on Carl's training, deployment to Italy, eventual capture on Monte Luro in the Gothic Line and his subsequent captivity.*

Jäger Carl Bayerlein in
the summer of 1943 at
Tangermünde/Elbe with
13.Ausbildungs Kompanie.
(Carl Bayerlein)

A meeting of former combatants in Ortona, Italy, in December 1998.
Carl Bayerlein (left) is with three Canadian veterans. The Canadian
veterans are from the Royal 22nd Regiment (Van Doos) and the
Loyal Edmontons (Loyal Eddies). (Carl Bayerlein)

Fallschirm-Pionier Training at Tangermünde

In 1942, as a member of the *Hitlerjugend* (Hitler Youth), I attended a preliminary recruitment evaluation, and when I came to the table to give my personal details I saw an index card and written below my name was "to the *Waffen-SS*". When I saw this I told the lady that I had already reported to the paratroops, even though it was a lie. She then deleted *Waffen-SS* and made a note "volunteer to report to the *Fallschirmtruppe*". My father, who was on the Eastern Front, had strongly advised against going into the *SS*. He said: "In case we lose this war, it could get unpleasant."

The following day I wrote to the responsible military district command and requested the volunteer documentation. After receiving these documents and obtaining my parents' signatures, I sent the forms off and was soon summoned to the Rudolf-Herzog barracks in Munich for the physical examination and suitability test.

My apprenticeship would normally have been completed on 30 March 1943, but on 30 January I was able to take the early joining tests and in early March was summoned to the beautiful alpine countryside at Hallein near Salzburg, in the former Ostmark, to undertake my Reich Labour Service.

My three months' labour service was not very intense because it was aimed at pre-military training. After a few days at home I received a call-up order to attend the main inspection centre of the General Command of *XI Fliegerkorps* in Gardelegen on 20 June 1943.

It was a huge difference in comparison from cosy Austria to the sandy north in Prussia.

In Gardelegen there was a huge barracks camp which was swarming with men in various uniforms, men in civilian clothes and men in their *RAD* uniforms who had received their call directly from the labour barracks. A selection took place soon after my arrival, and men with craft trades were assigned to the *Pioniers*. That's what happened to me!

After further physical and mental testing, we were kitted out with uniforms and equipment and were soon transported by rail via Stendal to Tangermünde on the Elbe to join a *Pionier-Ausbildungs-Kompanie*. Tangermünde was built in the so-called 'red brick Gothic' style and was known as the Rothenburg of the north, but we did not see much of the town at first.[1] Our accommodation, an ugly barracks, was a former brewery (known as the old brewery) and was located 19km south of the town towards Tangerhütte. The accommodation was depressing and our dormitory could accommodate 52 men, where I was unfortunate to endure sweaty feet, snoring, teeth grinding and sleepwalking.

My new compatriots represented every region of the great Fatherland: comrade Stege from Heidelberg to comrade Dugnat from Memel (east Prussia now in Lithuania), comrade Hans Gimpel from Romania to comrade Kunze from the Sudetenland (part of former Czechoslovakia), and comrade Podzswardowski from the Magdeburger Börde (fertile lowland area near Magdeburg), who had to repeat his name several times with each report he made.

A lot of the men were from Saxony-Anhalt, and in particular the town of Aschersleben, so many in fact that there was a *Fallschirm-Ersatz-Bataillon* named Aschersleben. Southern Germans were in the minority. In the case of the training staff, Prussians were the majority and were distinguished by their dashing appearance and particularly loud shouting, as if they could only scare off the enemy by shouting at them.

---

1   Rothenburg is a medieval town in Bavaria.

The following several months were filled with nonsensical drills mixed with popular frolics such as masked balls, which could have served the author Hans Helmut Kirst as a template for his book *08/15*.[2] To elaborate on this could fill a whole book in itself!

Only those who were lucky enough to find employment as a batman to an NCO or became a recruit *Gefreiter* were better off. During the training period, such recruit *Gefreite* soon became little godfathers!

After about four weeks the swearing-in took place. Before this oath ceremony there had been no leave pass, so the first pass took place under supervision. The *Pionier Ausbildungs Kompanie* was then under the command of *Oberleutnant* Gerhard Mertins and my *Zugführer* was *Feldwebel* Weidner. The dreaded *Spieß* was *Unteroffizier* Schlüter. Despite missing a lung due to a serious wound in Crete he could roar so loudly that civilians would quite often stop and feel sorry for us.

Our drill ground was not far from the barracks. It was a rectangular area strewn with black coal slag and the place where we received our basic training. After a few hours on the training ground our nostrils were black with coal dust. Here many a recruit secretly cursed the Army and Tangermünde.

Right at the beginning of our training we had to clear up a building in the town. The personal luggage of the *Fallschirm-Pioniers* who had been killed in Crete and those still in the hospitals was stored here. For example, there was a whole box of P38 pistols as well as rifle and pistol ammunition. Since I had only fired at the shooting range with a few assigned cartridges up to that point, I took a short machine-gun belt back to the barracks.

After we had returned to the barracks, a table had been set up as a drop-off point where it was requested that anyone who had taken something from the building should leave it, but apparently nobody had taken anything! I hid the live ammunition in my straw mattress, but I carelessly told my comrade Hans Gimpel about it.

Just outside the town was another barracks camp which belonged to the 'old brewery'. This was where our *Pionier* equipment such as vehicles and bridge construction equipment was stored. The camp was guarded by First World War veterans on behalf of the North German *Schließdienstes* (private security or guard service).

The nearby Elbe River served as our water training area, which had to be guarded at night. Guard detachments were always on the move from the Elbe to Tangermünde, and since the barracks gate was also constantly guarded the barrack room was busy as men came to and from their watches. The food was adequate: a lot of mixed vegetables, barley and milk soup, common in the north, which I had not seen until now. There was also pasta cooked in milk and sweetened. We got used to the food, but we were constantly hungry because we were kept on the move day and night. When the men were allowed into the town they would pay for a main course in the 'Black Eagle' for 75 Pfennigs.

Our assault exercise area was in Schönhausen on the *Reichstraße 107*, about 10km from Tangermünde and the birthplace of Bismarck. Our *Kompaniechef* would ride ahead on his horse while we marched behind in the summer heat. In extreme temperatures one or two relief stops were granted. It was our duty to wear long underpants even in the summer.

Not far from Tangermünde was a huge iron bridge that spanned the Elbe. On the left was the then largest German sugar factory, the Feodora-Falte factory, which supplied us with our favourite spread, artificial honey!

2   A German trilogy of novels written in the 1950s about a fictional German Second World War soldier called Private Asch. The title *08/15* refers to a German First World War machine gun, the MG08 Model 15.

The training area at Schönhausen was nothing but sandy hills and trees, and now in July the sand was very hot. It was a damn strenuous thing to run around here and in no time the shoes were filled with sand.

In a nearby valley was a female Reich Labour Service camp. Our *Kompaniechef* began to disappear after a short time; he was having a relationship with the camp leader. She later became his wife. Now it was a little quieter in his absence.

We conducted practice attacks with blank cartridges. I had taken a couple of live rounds from my supply and fired at a nearby windmill as I was fed up with always banging away with blanks. At noon food was delivered to us in canisters, and to drink there was the so called *Fliegerbier*, but nobody knew what it consisted of![3]

In the afternoon we would return on foot to Tangermünde. Once we reached the town the command came for a song, and we would sing songs such as 'In a bar in Mexico', the '*Burenlied* (a war has broken out)' or the 'Three birch trees that stand smashed on the heath'. Even the song 'We are *Pioniers*, the pride of the Army' was often sung, which then became macabre, "and then a bullet hits me, dying we call to the enemy in defiance, hurrah *Pionier*!" The reality looked a bit different later on!

The Feodora sugar factory had a large foreign labour camp attached to it. It was reported that a disturbance had broken out in the camp, so we were ordered to move in and search it, but nothing dangerous was found. It was probably nothing more than an exercise to intimidate the foreign workers.

After this exercise it was announced that our *Kompanie* was destined to act as a reserve unit in the event of unrest in Berlin. In the context of 'Valkyrie', we might have been misused to obey the rebels during the coup to depose the Reich government.[4] This failed uprising of the Army officers took place exactly one year later on 20 July 1944.

Despite the constant pressure of time, it must be said that we received a very thorough and intensive period of training. During our *Pionier* training, great importance was given to the knowledge of mines and the laying of them. We were also introduced to enemy mines, which were described and shown to us. Training took place on light mortars, but only with training ammunition, and our targets were often herds of grazing cows in the meadows. For days the 'bride of the soldier', the *Karabiner 98K* (bolt action rifle), was handled until we knew it by heart, even down to the last screw. Although we had been shown the newly developed *FG42* (*Fallschirmjägergewehr 42*, or paratrooper rifle 42), we never actually handled it. Later, we went to war with the weapons that our fathers had used in the First World War! Our current weapon, the *Karabiner*, was good at long range and ideally suited, but it was found that difficulties arose during a parachute jump because of the weight and length.

Training was also conducted on the 2cm anti-tank rifle with the tapered barrel, but it was already outdated. We also trained with hollow charges and the various existing *Pionier* demolition charges. These included 3kg and 10kg containerised box charges and ball charges, pole charges, containerised tree charges, 100g borehole cartridges and all the various safety fuses, igniters, detonators and primers. In addition we learned about explosives such as grenade filling 88 (made from TNT and ammonium nitrate) and filling powder 02 (either TNT or Donarit and used in stick grenades), and commercial explosives such as Donarit and Ekrazit, with their corresponding charge calculations. Then we dealt with timings, detonating cord and electric demolition cable.

---

3   Flyers' beer was a low-alcohol drink usually available in the airfield canteens.
4   A plan to ensure continuity of government in the event of an uprising, which was activated in a failed plot by high-ranking Army officers to overthrow Hitler's government.

We then conducted exercises with rubber inner tubes and assault boats under combat conditions, ferry crossings under smokescreens, makeshift bridge making and underwater blasting. We were fully engaged in our training. On several occasions short-notice night exercises were conducted involving street fighting in the neighbouring Kabelitz, where the inhabitants were delighted by the chatter of our weapons. Afterward in the local tavern, the jumpers from the permanent staff would demonstrate for us the *Fallschirmjäger* fall forwards on the tavern floor.

In Rathenow on the River Havel, a multi-day water exercise was scheduled and we were accommodated in the local *Flak* barracks. A wooden bridge was built over the river, and upon completion it was visited by a *Major* Rosenbruch and his entourage for approval. As soon as the convoy of visitors disappeared, the bridge collapsed. The props had not been driven deep enough into the sandy bedrock and had been weakened by the water flow. There were a few long faces afterward, but the main thing was the sightseeing inspection went well.

For the evening pass in Rathenow we were told that "anyone who is encountered in the city without a girl will spend a day in the stockade". Because of this there were several fist fights with the *Flak* soldiers.

During water training in Tangermünde I once turned up in the wrong footwear. As a punishment I had to drag a heavy rusty anchor whilst running at full speed. I was about to collapse. I found this to be an arbitrary part of the training. When we returned from our battle duties in Schönhausen, we were suddenly told to form up: "First rank six steps forward, second rank three steps forward, open your ammunition pouches." Although I had fired a few live rounds, I had thrown the empty cylinders away. I had used the windmill again as a target.

One day towards the end of our training, our *Kompaniechef* was searching for carpenters to manufacture bedroom furniture. Since I had learned this profession, I volunteered. In a joinery owned by a soldier, we were able to produce the furniture we needed. However, the others were not in such a hurry, they were more interested in getting away from the barracks. Instead of furniture, they started to build a boat, which later proved to be unseaworthy. Of course, first we cut the boards and glued the sides in case the *Kompaniechef* came and enquired about the progress of the furniture.

In the meantime, a festival took place in August on the Elbe, which was organised by our *Kompanie* and to which the population of Tangermünde was invited. Our training was demonstrated with dingy rides, a swimming demonstration and assault boat exercises and attacks. For this purpose, plenty of drill ammunition was used. It was an impressive military spectacle. Beer was served, the *BDM* were in attendance and the celebrations were conducted as if it was peacetime.[5]

My service in the joinery was soon over, and when I returned to the dormitory in the evening I found my straw mattress torn apart and lying on the floor. Of course the machine-gun belt with the remaining live ammunition was missing. What was not known to me was the following: the owner of the windmill at Schönhausen had visited the *Kompaniechef* and complained that his windmill had been fired at with live ammunition. Our boss informed him that we only fired blank cartridges, but the windmill owner insisted that they were not blanks as there were marks consistent with live ammunition. After all he had been a soldier in the First World War and knew what bullet holes looked like.

First I was summoned to *Spieß* Schlüter. He threatened me with an incident report, and although I denied any guilt he knew otherwise. Then he asked me where the other live cartridges were hidden. I relented and said that I threw them in the latrine, but that was even worse than damaging the windmill blades. Now I was expected to scoop out the latrine located in the yard.

---

5   *Bund Deutsche Mädel* (League of German Girls), the female wing of the Hitler Youth.

It was a *zwölfzylinder* and that would have taken days.[6] Finally, I had to take up the matter with the *Kompaniechef* wearing my steel helmet. He condemned me to eight days of strict arrest. My dormitory comrade Hans Gimpel had reported me for having live ammunition. That's how they found out.

Since the cells in the old brewery were constantly occupied, I could not begin my detention straight away. But when the *Spieß* saw me walking around free, he made sure that I served my sentence immediately. *Gefreiter* Werner Schuricke escorted me to the barracks camp, walking a few metres behind with his pistol holstered on his belt.

The guards in the camp were glad of the distraction. In the evening they opened the cell door and I came to them in the guard house. The informer was plagued by his conscience, and since he was busy working in the kitchen he would send an extra portion of food to the brig.

On the fourth day, when I had made myself comfortable on the cell cot, the keys clinked and a *Gefreiter* from the barracks told me to pack my things immediately. The next morning we were to depart for the jump school. By train we travelled via Wittenberg, Perleberg and Heiligengrabe to Wittstock an der Dosse in the Uckermark. I did not cry a tear for Tangermünde, and the other men felt the same way!

Parachute Training at *Fallschirmschule II*, Wittstock, 1943

After our basic and *Pionier* training with *13/Fallsch.Aus.Rgt.1* in Tangermünde, we were transported by train to *Fallschirmschule II* at Wittstock. In contrast to our former barracks, we now had modern spacious accommodation. In Tangermünde I shared a dormitory with over 50 men, with all their special habits and noises caused by the Prussian pea soup, but here in Wittstock there were only four men to a room. However, I had the misfortune to share a room with a bed-wetter.

The jump area and barracks were far out of town. Unnecessary drills did not occur here, even if everything was conducted on the run. Our service began very early with daily morning exercises, a 5,000m run at 0400 hours, but we were free in the afternoons.

I was assigned to *4. Schüler-Kompanie* under the command of *Hauptmann* Henschel, who wore a large Bulgarian Order on his chest. He also trained men from the *SA (Sturmabteilung)* units. We received the special clothing required for our parachute training: jump trousers, combat boots, helmet, knee pads and ankle bindings, as well as the *springerkombination*, also known as the bonesack.

The trainee is suspended from a training harness and swung through the air by an instructor. The trainee will then attempt to counter the movement to adopt the correct posture for landing. (Author's collection)

---

6   A 12-seat common toilet area.

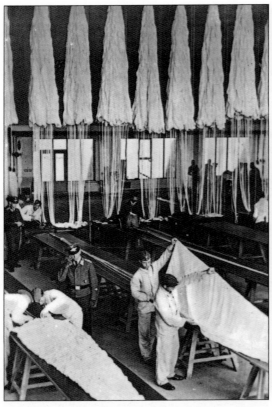

Each paratrooper was required to pack his own chute with the aid of a helper (servicewomen packed the chutes of British paratroops). This was a good incentive to ensure the parachute was packed properly and opened correctly. (Author's collection)

A crucifix jump position was adopted where the parachutist would launch himself spread-eagled, horizontally, out of the aircraft by means of two handles either side of the door. This reduced the swinging motion when the canopy opened and thus reduced the risk of the parachutist getting tangled up in the shroud-lines. (Author's collection)

First we conducted individual exercises on the ground using thick crash mats: falling forwards, falling backwards, rolling forwards and rolling backwards, as well as jumping in the sand from a JU-52 mock-up. Then we conducted a jump from a tether line to a mat with a roll forward or backward, depending on the current posture at the time of release.

I felt like a performance artist. The trainees were divided into groups for the duration of our jump training. Each parachute group had 10 men, since the capacity of the training aircraft was focused on this number of men. Each pupil soon received his own parachute, at that time the *RZ20* (*Rückenfallschirm Zwangsauslösung modell 20* – back parachute forced release). Some pupils ahead of our course still used the older *RZ16* model. Each parachute came with a lockable metal case in which the parachute was housed, because each student was responsible for his own parachute and its packing.

The folding and packing of the parachute was practiced by using certain tools like the so-called packing forks, and the packing was conducted in a large hall on tables that were several metres long. On completion of the packing process, the pack was sealed with a length of cord and secured.

Soon the training became more serious and the practice jumps could begin. My first jump was conducted at 250m from a Dornier DO-23, known to us as the 'flying coffin'. Since we often

When the canopy fully developed, the wearer would be exposed to the huge jerking effect as the shroud-lines finished paying out (Author's collection)

The parachute was designed to fully deploy after approximately 100ft. (Author's collection)

experienced warm air pockets over the sandy jump area, the aircraft would suddenly pitch, which was not a pleasant feeling on my maiden flight.

The jump was executed out of the right side door, in contrast to the JU-52 (left side). The static line (*aufziehleine*) was engaged onto a three-point fixture. I firmly held on to the handles by the exit until the Bosch horn sounded. Then my hands reluctantly let go, I gritted my teeth, overcame my weaker inner self and jumped from the aircraft.

It was quiet for a few seconds, peaceful almost, until I felt the strong sudden jerk of the parachute deployment and I found myself suspended in the straps with the open canopy above me.

The Earth approached me quickly and I could think clearly again. Each jump was controlled and commented from below, and commands were given with megaphones. My first jump was a success and all my bones were still intact.

The next two jumps were performed again from a DO-23, but this time in a group. In a group jump we had to stay as close as possible to the man in front, so the distance between us upon landing was as short as possible. Of course with every jump you also had the *Karabiner 98*, so depending on the aircraft you would jump using a different method.

Now the jump height was reduced slightly each time, from 200m to 180m. The latter jumps took place from a Heinkel HE-111 and the height was again reduced. My last jump on 24 October 1943 was from a height of 120m. With each jump your perception became clearer, and we gradually became accustomed to this 'extreme sport'.

Trials had shown that 13 well-trained parachutists could exit a JU-52 in eight seconds. At an altitude of 330ft and an aircraft speed of 120 miles per hour, their dispersal distance would only be approximately 25 yards between each man (Author's collection)

The crucifix jump was not the best position for landing; it called for the parachutist to land on all fours, which resulted in a high proportion of serious ankle and wrist injuries, even when wearing padded protection (Author's collection)

It was imperative that the *Fallschirmjäger* could disengage himself from the parachute as quickly as possible, particularly if he was being dragged. Improvements were made to the early parachutes to enable the men to quickly remove their harnesses. (Author's collection)

This *Fallschirmjäger* is carrying the single line that connected to the canopy lines, which gave the man no control over his descent. (Author's collection)

The following jumps were recorded in my log book:

1. 6 October 1943   0916hrs 250m   Single   DO-23
2. 7 October 1943   1343hrs 200m   6 men   DO-23
3. 8 October 1943   0858hrs 180m   6 men   DO-23
4. 12 October 1943   0823hrs 150m   10 men   HE-111
5. 13 October 1943   0825hrs 130m   10 men   HE-111
6. 24 October 1943   0851hrs 120m   10 men   HE-111

My last jump, like the previous two from the Heinkel, took place from the floor hatch in the converted bomb-bay. I had the *Karabiner* swaddled as required with the right arm. In order to get out of the hatch, a small hop forward was required. As I did this the static line became entangled around my neck and in no time began to strangle me. I momentarily lost consciousness and dropped my rifle out of the aircraft. My landing was also not very skilful. Then I heard an announcement through a megaphone: "The man who lost his rifle, march here, march here now!" I reported to the control point and showed them the abrasions on my neck, and was then ordered to immediately search for the rifle. This was no easy task on the huge jump area, because the parachute jumps continued whilst I searched. After searching much of the surrounding terrain, I noticed a piece of wood sticking out of the ground. It was my rifle and it had drilled itself into the soil. The butt had broken off and the rifle now consisted of two parts, which were only held together by the sling.

The following day I had to attend training with a broken rifle. Although I had crudely fixed the two pieces back together, the rifle fell apart again on the order *"Gewehr umhängen"* [slinging the rifle on the right shoulder]. For this I was awarded 10 press-ups. In addition I was threatened with 100 Reichmarks in damages, but fortunately this was only a threat.

Since the jump training was almost over we were now often assigned to guard duty. During this period of inactivity, a Turkish military delegation came to visit Wittstock and they were treated to a parachute jump demonstration. Several *Züge* jumped in front of their eyes, accompanied by pyrotechnics which were installed by us. At that time it was hoped that Turkey would join the war on the side of the Axis powers and we Germans courted them accordingly, but despite arms deliveries we had little success. Turkey later declared war on the German Reich.

In another barrack block lived a unit of the *SA Standarte Feldherrenhalle* who were also conducting jump training. Since I was a non-smoker, I would exchange some of my daily ration of cigarettes for milk soup, which I had become accustomed to during training.

There were lots of stories told at Wittstock, and one involved parachute packing where a packing fork had not been removed during the packing process. This caused the parachute to malfunction, leaving the jumper hanging by his static line and dragged through the air behind the aircraft. The pilot immediately flew 20km to the Rechlin airfield near Lake Müritz, where the secret *Luftwaffe* test facility was located. There a boat was waiting on the lake. The static line was then cut at the lowest possible altitude and the man was fished out of the water. I did not see this incident, but that is how the story was told to me.

Another story that was commonly talked about regarded experiments with camouflage parachutes, where some of the folds stuck together due to the coloured dye and they did not fully open. Attempts were made to conduct jumps from the large Messerschmitt Me-323 '*Gigant*' transport aircraft, where four men would jump simultaneously from different exit points, but these camouflage parachutes never fully opened, became entangled and resulted in several deaths.

Soon a *Marschkompanie* was put together from our advanced training course.[7] This meant that our transfer was imminent. We recieved new rifles (my carbine had the number 9618) and dog tags. Before we left, our instructors had given us their addresses in Germany in the event that we should be transferred to France. If there was a possibility to shop there and buy things cheaper, we could post them back to Germany, but with payment made of course.

Deployment to Italy

The day of departure came quickly and we left for the station in Wittstock, where a transport train was already waiting for us. First we went through the Thuringian forest, then via Regensburg to Wörgl in the Tyrol. We stayed in Wörgl for several days and nobody knew why. Of course, there was wild speculation as to our destination. The boldest were of the opinion that we would be used on the island of Gibraltar to chase away the Tommy (Englishmen) [sic], but we soon continued our journey south over the Brenner Pass to Bolzano. We stopped in Bolzano and saw the pile of parachutes used by the *Fallschirmjäger* who jumped into Sicily in July. We continued through the South Tyrol during the ongoing grape harvest, where the farmers waved to us as we passed.

Our wagon was a converted freight car. In order for everyone to sleep, planks were available and these were fitted at night to create bunk beds. An opening in the floor of the wagon made it possible to conduct the necessary ablutions whilst underway.

The next stop was at Incisa-Figline in the Arno Valley, south of Florence. Half of the train was uncoupled and returned to Germany, and our half remained. Those comrades who returned to Germany were soon deployed to the Eastern Front and I never saw any of them again.

In my freight car there was a box filled with our *Wehrpasses* (military pass). I opened the box and picked out my *Wehrpass*. Inside the front cover was a piece of paper and it stated that I still had to serve four days in the stockade! Now I will mention something that shows how things worked in the greater German *Wehrmacht*! At the beginning of May 1944, I was permitted to go on leave from the Cassino front. When I got back to Roccasecca behind the front line and reported to '*Der Spieß*' (Helmut Lotze) about my leave, he told me that I still had four days in stockade before I could return to Germany. So, in the absence of a cell I had to spend four days employed with the vehicle drivers before I could go home.

---

7   A *Kompanie* of trained replacements.

After an adventurous journey we reached our final destination, the city of Sulmona in the region of Abruzzo. Here we were divided into the different *Kompanien* of *Fallschirm-Pionier-Bataillon 1*. I was assigned to *3. Kompanie* and it became my home for almost one year!

Carl took part in the bitter house-to-house fighting in Ortona in December 1943. Between February and March 1944 he was posted to the Cassino front on Hill 575 to the north-west of Monastery hill on the Gustav defensive line.

The following account takes place after returning from leave granted at the Cassino front, where Carl and his unit are used to conduct demolition work to hamper the Allied advance towards the Gustav defensive line in northern Italy. As the front line moved north, Carl and his comrades found themselves fighting for survival in one of many fierce defensive battles for the Gothic Line.

Retreat through central Italy

My home leave from the Cassino front lasted from 8–30 May 1944. When I returned home to Germany, I heard on the radio that fierce fighting was once again raging at Cassino and after a few days I heard the news that Cassino had to be evacuated. After completing my rest vacation, I headed south again to rejoin *3. Kompanie* of *Fallschirm-Pionier-Bataillon 1*.

The leave train took me first to Florence and then continued further south. On 5 June, the day the Italian capital was taken by the Allies, I was already in Perugia in the province of Umbria. I stayed here and recieved my march rations before hitchhiking to Terni. I had been unable to find out the exact location of my unit, so I stayed in a vacant house somewhere between Terni and Rieti. The next day I entered Rieti and spent the night in the Mussolini barracks located in the centre of town. At a busy intersection, retreating traffic was being controlled by a military policeman who informed me that the *Fallschirm-Pioniers* were close by. He was even able to tell me that *3. Kompanie* were located in a monastery only 7km away. It was a pilgrimage called 'Convento di Fonte Colombo' and it was hidden away in a forest on a hill. Since I did not have a vehicle, I organised a bicycle from a farmhouse. Next to the house was a cherry tree full of ripe fruit, which satisfied my vitamin requirements. The path to the *Kloster* was uphill on a dusty road, and after a long walk in the June heat I reached my destination.

Convento di Fonte Columbo, a 13th-century Franciscan monastery and in June 1944 the temporary HQ of *3/Fallsch.Pi.Btl.1*. (l Luoghi del Silenzio)

There was great astonishment at my sudden unexpected arrival. Nobody even knew that I had been on leave. I could have stayed away until 8 May 1945 and nobody would have missed me. During the sudden retreat from Cassino, our trucks were mistakenly attacked by German aircraft and the trucks contained all the unit paperwork. I also met several comrades who had escaped the collapse of the Cassino front.

Horst Rausch had returned from the hospital. *Unteroffizier* Reinhard Schumacher had recovered from his wounds sustained in the defensive fighting.[8] Rolf Sichting, Christian Brüning, Matthes Kusper and Edusch Bottor were all here. From these old comrades I learned what had happened during the fall of Cassino and the subsequent defensive battles.

Most of my former comrades had been captured, killed or wounded. Before I left Germany, I recieved a letter from the parents of former *Zugführer* Werner Issmer as I had written to them when I returned to the Reich. They had asked me how their son was doing as they had not heard from him in a while. Since it had been reported that he had probably been killed, I informed his parents, but it was premature. I now found out that Issmer had been badly wounded but he was still alive.

Even our comrade Asino, who was able to imitate our donkeys so well, was no longer there. It was reported that he bravely led the *Zug* for a while until he himself was badly wounded. Our machine-gunner Arno Köhler was reported to have been killed and *Gefreiter* Fuggerer, who had taken over the flamethrower from me, had also disappeared in Cassino. There were a lot of new men in the *Zug* and I had to get used to new names and faces. Some were older comrades but most were young, and there were also a few men who had been demoted for various reasons. *Uffz* Schumacher took me into his *Gruppe* immediately after my arrival.

The Convento di Fonte Columbo was still occupied by numerous monks, but many of the *Klosterzellen* were empty.[9] I quartered myself in one of the barest of these cells. Horst Rausch and I examined our surroundings at the monastery. On one side wing I discovered the Ossuary, where for centuries the bones and the skulls of the deceased monks were kept. In the dry air the bodies were mummified; hundreds of skulls grinned at us, truly a scary sight (today the Ossarium is bricked up except for a small window). Our stay in this monastery lasted about eight days, and then it was back to serious work.

Our Henschel trucks were loaded, one of them with explosives, then we left the well-camouflaged monastery and headed north, first through Rieti and over the high pass towards Terni.

Here on the pass came our first order. A well-camouflaged power plant had to be prepared for demolition. We placed the charges on the pipes and ducts, but the actual demolition would be conducted by follow-up units.

Our *Zugführer* was *Feldwebel* Heinz Schumacher, the elder brother of my *Gruppeführer* Reinhold. *Feldwebel* Hobeck, the former *Zugführer*, was at a training course at Kriegsschule. Of course we lacked the experienced ranks and comrades like *Uffz* Langheim, Schorsch, Georg Römer, Paul Hasselfeld, Willy Zarth, Horst Schröder, Werner Klockmann, Bernhard Rebers or the *Obergefreiter* Meyer and many others who were no longer with the unit. Rolf Sichting was summoned into the *Zugtrupp* by *Uffz* Kahle.

Now the actual retreat through central Italy began. We returned the same way I had come a few days before. We were now split up and recieved our demolition assignments, and we would often go days without seeing each other. Sometimes you were alone for several days and nights at the

---

8   Equivalent rank to *Oberjäger*, but *Fallschirm-Pioniers* often used the rank of *Unteroffizier*, abbreviated to *Uffz*.

9   A *Klosterzellen* is a small bare room no larger than a cell used as accommodation for monks.

respective blasting sites, under bridges, in houses or out in the open. When the last German unit had passed your assigned site, the demolition could commence prior to retreating to the next one.

We used commercial explosives such as Donarit, Ekrazit and dynamite, and later we also used aerial bombs when there were no aircraft to drop them. Mines and grenades were also used. Everything of military significance was chosen as a suitable blast site: roads, bridges, towers, sunken roads, railways, fuel and ammunition storages, factories and other manufacturing facilities as well as tunnels. It was important that the enemy was suppressed and weakened for as long as possible. It was envisaged that the Gustav Line would not last forever in southern Italy, if only because of the considerable supply difficulties.[10]

After the Allies had taken the airfields intact in the south of the country, they were able to cause considerable damage to the railways and roads supplying the Gustav defensive line. Further north, the Gothic Line, or Green Line as it was later called, was still under construction and was destined to become the strongest defensive position before the Po Valley. To the south, a defensive line was planned near Florence called the Arno Line and a second one to the north of the Green Line in the heart of Tuscany (Genghis Khan Line)

On 17 June, in a small town called Piegaro in the province of Perugia, we were assigned to blow up a row of houses and the road leading into the valley. On the way to Piegaro we had blown up an ammunition warehouse. When the clouds of smoke rose into the air, the enemy *Jabos* came to investigate but we had found cover in a nearby forest. I would often sit on the fender of the truck and act as an aircraft observer.

At noon we reached Piegaro. Several men under the command of *Uffz* Gutheil brought explosive charges to the town gate and the houses. A winding road led down to the valley, so we hacked holes in the bends of the road to accommodate the demolition charges. It was hard work in the midday heat of that June day to dig out holes in the stony ground with a pickaxe. Here I once again cursed the pioneering life. In the meantime, our Henschel trucks were waiting in a quarry down in the valley. After we had filled the holes with explosives and placed the fuses, *Uffz* Gutheil planned to blow everything up together at the same time from the town exit. Soon the shout "fire" was heard. Gutheil and another man came running, but there was no follow-up detonation. They waited a while longer to ensure that the fuses had burned down, and they returned to the town gate. Suddenly, there was a huge explosion, the town gate and the houses collapsed and a huge cloud of dust rose up into the sky. I was positioned some 500m way from one of the road blast sites. *Uffz* Gutheil and his companion did not reappear. I only knew this man fleetingly, as he arrived shortly before I did. The mystery of this event is still not solved, and will probably remain so forever. It was suspected that the two men wanted to stay behind and conceal themselves in the small town after they had carried out the demolition. We waited helplessly for a while, but as a result of the explosions we came under enemy fire. The remaining road blast sites were detonated before making for the trucks and finally driving on. According to my information, Gutheil and the other Pionier did not report from captivity.

After passing the picturesque Lago di Chiusi, we now went to Pozzuolo in the province of Arezzo. Pozzuolo was also a small town with a distinctive tall bell tower. From that location the enemy could see everything for miles around. Two men were assigned to me to form a demolition team. They were both new comrades without any practical demolition experience. One was called Kissel from the Palatinate and the other, Jupp (his first name), came from Luxembourg and would later become a Nazi Party district speaker. But first he had to do his duty at the front.

---

10 The Gustav Line was a defensive line that ran from west to east across Italy and included Monte Cassino and Ortona within its defences. This line held up the Allies for several months in 1943/44.

The houses on the left and right of the street had already been prepared for demolition, but the church tower was yet to be blown up. A motorcycle arrived with some Teller Mines, and with the help of some Italians I managed to get the mines up into the tower. I asked in advance if the T-Mines would be enough to destroy the tower and was assured that the charge calculation had been worked out correctly. The fuse hung down from the tower so it could be lit from below. During these preparations, Kissel and Jupp were nowhere to be seen. They had discovered a cellar full of wine bottles.

The front line was now only 10km away, and one afternoon a motorcycle drove through the town. An enemy aircraft flew overhead. Suddenly it dipped one wing and rushed toward the town, firing at the motorcycle with its machine guns. At the same time it dropped a bomb on one of the houses. Suddenly there was a larger second explosion. The blast must have detonated some of our charges, as a row of houses exploded at the same time. A bomb crashed onto the street near me but luckily it failed to explode. Italian civilians now began to come out of the houses where they had been sheltering. I pulled out a metal splinter from the head of a wounded Italian woman and sent her to the dressing station on the outskirts of town. More *Jabos* were now appearing and dropping bombs onto the town, so the soldiers moved out of Pozzuolo until the bombing stopped.

In the middle of Pozzuolo was an abandoned police station. It had been used to store a large quantity of hunting weapons. The former owners were required to hand them in. I took a beautifully decorated rifle and some ammunition, which I used to shoot wild pigeons that were in abundance. I left the birds with an Italian family whose hiding place I had discovered. They would pluck them and fry them up. There was also an iron box anchored to a wall in the police station, so I returned with a borehole charge and detonator and blew up the container.

I found several Beretta pistols and a revolver with ammunition in it. I gave one of the weapons to Kissel and kept one for myself. As Kissel handled his pistol, a shot rang out. The bullet had penetrated the middle finger of his left hand. Now he came crying and asked what he should do. I sent him away to find a dressing station where he could be patched up. He asked me what he should say as a reason for his wounding. I advised him to tell the truth, perhaps that it happened when cleaning the weapon. He must have stated in the hospital that he had been shot in the town by strangers. I had not thought about this incident for a while when two members of the Military Field Police paid me a visit later in August and asked me about his story. I described it as it happened; but I had not witnessed it. In the hospital there had been traces of gun smoke on the wound, indicating that it must have been fired from close-quarters. This led to the suspicion that it could be a case of self-inflicted injury. I did not hear any more from Kissel!

Now I was alone with Jupp. After two more days the last of our own troops passed through the town. The town was now under heavy artillery and mortar fire, so we decided that night we would blow up the church tower and the remaining houses. Since the fuse in the tower was quite long, I had enough time after the ignition to assist Jupp and afterwards we ran off to a safe distance and waited for the detonation.

With lightning and thunderbolts the street crashed down and a violent explosion also took place at the tower, but in the darkness I could not see that the tower had withstood the explosion.

A few miles away we took over a new blast site in a ravine on a hill. As we were leaving, a motorcycle came to meet us despite the onset of enemy harassing fire. I was told there was still ammunition in a garage that needed to be destroyed. The motorcycle rider supplied me with the appropriate detonator. These grenades were apparently intended for the Eastern Front but had been incorrectly delivered to Italy. In any case, a demolition had to take place. Now we went back to the garage, which was located on the edge of town. It was locked, with an iron roll-up door. We opened it and there was at least a few tons of ammunition lying there. They were mainly mortar shells. I initiated a charge and we moved away as quickly as possible. The rider was waiting on a nearby hill as he had to report on the orderly demolition of these highly explosive shells. At some distance we stopped and waited for the explosion. There followed a loud bang and fireball, followed by the howl of dozens of mortar shells, countless detonations spitting and breathing fire through the air. It was a firework display like I had never experienced before. I almost got hit myself as a few shells exploded in my vicinity, resulting in splinters and iron parts whizzing through the air. We had thrown ourselves to the ground hoping that the firestorm would soon pass.

Jupp left with the rider and I went to a new blast site. I slept for a few hours in a nearby farmhouse, which had clearly served as lodgings for German soldiers. Cuts of Army bread and rifle ammunition were still lying on the table.

The next morning, one of our *Kompanie* motorcycles approached carrying our *Kompaniechef*, *Hauptmann* Arno Jacobeit. He had come personally to question me as to why the church tower had not been blown up as ordered. I told him that I used all 12 T-Mines for the demolition and that we blew it up the night before. Through his binoculars I could see that the tower was still standing. When making the charge calculation, consideration had not been given to the fact that it was a relatively new structure with reinforced supports. I could only testify that it was not my fault.

After the threatened repercussions, I was informed that a re-blasting with more T-Mines should be attempted. I had to go back to Pozzuolo and the motorcycle would bring the required explosives. I waited a while before heading to the town, but it was impossible to re-enter due to heavy artillery and mortar fire landing nearby. Even the motorcycle carrying the mines had to turn around. I occupied my old blast site on the hill nearby, and from there I had a beautiful view of Lago di Trasimeno and in the distance the towers and walls of Perugia, which towered into the summer sky. However, I had no time for the scenic Tuscan countryside; military matters had to take priority.

Hauptmann Arno Jacobeit, *Kompaniechef* of *3/Fallsch-Pi-Btl.1* and later *Bataillonskommandeur*. (Carl Bayerlein)

Firstly, suitable cover had to be found and ways to block or delay the enemy's further advance. Pozzuolo was now almost completely in the hands of the enemy and they were concentrating their fire on the hill where I was now located. German Army units had withdrawn slowly under enemy pressure. Only a few metres away from me on an embankment was a Tiger tank. The crew informed me that the *Panzer* had fired at the tower, but the turret could no longer rotate due to mechanical problems. I told the commander to take the *Panzer* into cover in the ravine, but if they could not head back they should manoeuvre it directly to another nearby blast site. The *Panzer* would then be destroyed in the remaining demolition because in the blast hole was a 250kg aerial bomb. I gained the impression that the *Panzer* soldiers had no great desire to rescue the vehicle and they secretly disappeared.

When it became light the enemy discovered the steel colossus and directed fire upon it. A splinter hit me, but got stuck in the wallet of my *Soldbuch*. Now I unscrewed the fuel cap on the *Panzer*, ignited an egg grenade and threw it into the [fuel] tank in the hope that the fuel would ignite, but it just gurgled and the grenade was drowned.

After hurriedly leaving this blast site, I marched for several kilometres under harassing fire and eventually found my comrades and our truck, which took us on what felt like a long journey, driving only at night to avoid the enemy *Jabos*. Several times during the journey we had to stop and reinflate the tyres. Due to continuous use, the inner tubes had become porous. South-east of Siena, in one of the most beautiful landscapes in Italy, I was again assigned a new blast site.

This time I was partnered with a new comrade called Preuss, who had just been assigned to us. The blast site was an important bridge that was to be blown up when the last German soldier crossed. The charges had already been installed, so we only had to make the ignition. We pitched our quarters under the bridge, and above we set up a wooden board with 'demolition unit' written on it and an arrow pointing down. From a neighbouring deserted farmhouse we found some mattresses. Behind the farmhouse I discovered fresh tracks on the ground. I dug where the tracks ended and found a large buried box. Inside were several hams, canned goods, sugar, honey, olive oil and a typewriter. After a few days of relative calm, the main battle line also approached our location.

An Army officer informed me that he was the last man of his unit, so the bridge could be blown up. Under enemy fire, our brave Henschel truck arrived to pick us up. We set the igniters and ran for the truck, where the remaining men of my group were already sitting. As we drove away, the bridge exploded with a thunderous crash. Of course, there was more interest in our food treasures and everyone recieved some of the good stuff we had found. Again we returned to Siena, far back in the peaceful hinterland. Here the factories still worked, seemingly unaffected by the war.

Our next stop was Castelfranco di Sopra, set in a bizarre landscape with deep ravines. This medieval town was surrounded by walls and there were several town gates. We found accommodation in a police station where the whole *Zug* could be accommodated. We had to develop defensive positions in the olive groves to stop the enemy from advancing on the high mountains. We dug foxholes, shelters and connecting trenches. There was also a nearby bridge called Ponte di Mandri which spanned a gorge, and this too had to be prepared for demolition. Whilst digging the blast holes, we came across a water pipe that provided drinking water from the mountains of Pratomagno. A section of pipe was damaged during the digging and water began to leak out. This water also supplied a hospital in the town, but since it would be a long time before the enemy reached this location I decided to find someone to repair the water pipe.

We heard rumours that partisans were operating in the mountains. Sometimes we would see women walking up the slopes with loads on their heads, probably food for the partisans. Several times in the town we searched homes in the early morning for male workers as helpers in the construction work. After a few days they had mostly disappeared without a trace. They had moved into the mountains.

Because of the danger posed by the partisans, extreme vigilance was therefore necessary. In the town, shops were open as in peacetime, so we could at least go shopping. Early one morning I went to a bakery and brought fresh white bread and some nice towels. Our pay was in the local currency and the rate was one *Reichsmark* = 10 Italian *Lire*. We had a peaceful time here without the thunder of guns and *Jabos*. Whilst we were in Castelfranco, one of our sentries shot and killed a woman for failing to comply with the night-time curfew period.

We were not used here for defensive duties or demolition work, and after about 14 days we returned to the heart of Tuscany. We travelled via Figline and Incisa, where our transport train had stopped back in the autumn of 1943. Then we moved on toward the Mugello area via Rufina in the Chianti wine region.

On 8 July, we arrived at a small village called Caselle, which consisted of about 20 houses, a church, a small school and a wine business. There were many people living here, several families having fled from Florence hoping for some respite from the Allied bombing. The high mountains towered up behind the village.

The rear defensive positions were still under construction here before the actual Gothic Line. Bridges were to be made ready for demolition, trees were cut down to create fields of fire and positions were dug into the mountain slopes.

It was here that we heard news about the 20 July attack on the *Führer*. From now on the German greeting with outstretched arm was introduced into the *Luftwaffe*.

Whilst we were in Caselle I fired the first *Panzerfaust* in our *Kompanie*, as I had previously attended a training course on this weapon. The outline of a *Panzer* had been painted on a rock face and the entire *Kompanie* was assembled in a semicircle at a reasonable distance. A steel drum was used as cover for me. I aimed at the *Panzer* outline and squeezed the triggering device. With a jet of flame, the warhead flew toward the rock face, but there was no detonation. Ironically, at the point of impact was a soft layer of earth and the warhead simply stuck in it! It was a huge embarrassment. With a detonator and fuse, we blew up the dud warhead. There were no other *Panzerfaust* available to repeat the demonstration.

I was awarded the Iron Cross 2nd Class and appointed deputy *Gruppeführer* for the dangerous demolition of a railway bridge on which enemy tanks were approaching. It was not easy in this new appointment because we had several former *Feldwebel* who had been demoted within our groups.

On 25 July, there was a sudden alarm: the *Zug* should move immediately. The trucks arrived and we loaded everything, but after a few kilometres we stopped. It was a false alarm. The residents of the village, who had been happy about our departure, now made long faces when we returned. It was suspected that the *Kompaniechef* had given the alarm in a wine-induced mood. Around 1 August, the final departure took place and we travelled across country to the Adriatic coast at Urbino.

We reached Fano on the coast during the night. Whilst driving through the town it came under attack from the air. It was a miracle that we were not hit, even though the bombs were falling around us. We spent the rest of the night on a mountain embankment where we dug in. Our next task was the demolition of the coastal railway lines, construction sites and mining of the coastline.

It was assumed that there would be an enemy landing from the sea. Although the Gothic Line already had many bunkers, minefields and shelters, it was still largely under construction. It would have been the last line of fortifications in front of the Po Valley and the northern Italian industrial centres. The Allied forces' advance to the north had to be stopped here.

The defensive line ran south of Cattolica on the Adriatic, toward Pistoia, Pisa and La Spezia on the west coast. In the middle of the country was the heavily fortified and insurmountable Futa Pass; therefore, the enemy would only be able to make a breakthrough on the Adriatic side.

Between Fano and Pesaro we moved to protect against enemy landings with a new type of mine. These were made of concrete, with nails, screws and other iron parts poured into it. They were placed on wooden poles just above the ground and secured with tension wires. These mines were intended for landing troops. Everything was green in colour and therefore camouflaged in the grass. The effect of this mine was devastating.

Our next destination was Pesaro, which was the home of the Benelli Company. Our *Kompanie* occupied some houses on the outskirts of town where the Benelli directors used to live. Organisation Todt had already begun to transport machinery, tools and materials from the factories to the Reich or northern Italy, where production could begin again.[11] Some of the machines were so firmly anchored into the ground that disassembly would have done more harm than good. As a precaution, the machinery was prepared for demolition. For this purpose, a new explosive called Plastite was used. This compound was kneadable and had the advantage that it could be pressed into corners and cracks.

---

11   Organisation Todt was an engineering organisation that used both conscripted and forced labour on construction projects such as the *autobahns*, the Atlantic Wall and the Siegfried Line.

At the beginning of August we had recieved a new *Kompanieführer, Leutnant* Harald Quandt, the stepson of Reich Minister Dr Joseph Goebbels. With him came a large amount of market goods, Scho-Ka-Kola, chocolate, schnapps and fine cigarettes. Since the plague of mosquitoes was almost unbearable in the midsummer, we also recieved mosquito nets and tents. Atebrin tablets had to be taken daily to prevent malaria.

For the construction of positions near the coast, I commanded a work detail of about 30 Italians. As the enemy *Jabo* attacks intensified, I was left with eight men after the first week. It was only after I confiscated the remaining ID passes and told them that anyone without an ID could be shot that the number of men remain constant. The enemy tried everything to disrupt work on the fortification sites. As soon as vehicles or labour columns showed up, the *Jabos* dived down, firing their guns and dropping bombs. Every farm that was suspected of housing German soldiers became the target of their attacks. Our *Flak* barely fired, as they preferred to remain in cover undetected. The airspace was clearly dominated by the enemy and the sky was filled with circling aircraft, the chatter of machine guns and the impact of bombs. Sometimes the planes flew directly to their objective like a remote-controlled device. They must have had the most accurate of intelligence. By using targeted bombing, whole minefields were destroyed and for miles the sky was full of smoke.

I was the target of one such *Jabo* attack. We were digging a tunnel into an embankment. The earth was sandy and easy to dig there, and the men were already several metres in so perhaps the piles of fresh earth outside were visible from the air. Suddenly there was a howl in the air. I looked up and saw a *Jabo* rushing towards us. At the last moment I was able to push two men inside. The aircraft guns were already firing and the cannon rounds hit the ground just outside the entrance. It was precision work. My Italian helpers were not prepared to continue after the attack, despite the fact that I had confiscated their ID passes (later in hospital I found a bundle of these passes with my belongings).

Around 20 August we relocated from this dangerous area. In order to ward off any possible landing attempt behind the Gothic Line, we were employed as a coast watch in the seaside resort of Cattolica. Here we found peace for some time and performed guard duties. There were pedal boats on the beach, and we would pedal out into the warm blue Adriatic.

We found lots of ripe tomatoes, so we were able to produce fresh tomato salad every day. Vinegar, oil and salt were also available. The first grapes began to ripen and melons could also be found. The civilian population had been evacuated from the entire coastline area, so the lodgings and hotels were empty. I found letters from two German ladies. They were writing to ask if naked swimming was allowed nearby. I wrote back to them immediately and informed them that they should come at once as everyone bathes naked here. Whether or not I ever recieved a reply to my *Feldpostnummer* L25475, I will never know!

We were happy and relaxed here. Since the autumn of 1943 we had been constantly on the go. First we had climbed like *Gebirgsjäger* in the stony Abruzzi and Apennines. We had then passed through several Italian provinces as state tourists from the south near Cassino, retreating through Umbria and Tuscany to the north in the Le Marche region.

In one house I found some artists' paints and I began to paint the blue sea and the boats. It was truly idyllic here in Cattolica.

In the late afternoon of 31 August we were suddenly alerted. We were told that the enemy had broken through inland, so the entire *Kompanie* would have to launch a counterattack. Our sentries were collected and ammunition was issued. Little did we know that on this sunny August afternoon it would be the end for many of us, either through wounding, capture or death!

Final battle and finale

We were driven in our trucks close to the village of Tomba di Pesaro (Tavullia). Our *Zug* came under murderously accurate mortar fire near a ravine. There were some immediate casualties, including the indestructible *Obergefreiter* Matthes Kusper, who was one of the few 'old hands' still with us.

Before midnight we had reached Monte Luro to the north-east, and with artillery support we were able to storm this dominant hill. We were dug in on the north-east slope, and at midnight the enemy began to fire their own artillery barrage. The first impacts fell too short, causing only a few casualties. Through the vineyards I slowly worked my way up the hill with a *Panzerfaust* on my shoulder before another barrage by our own artillery. When it stopped we began our assault on the height. Just before we reached the summit, *Uffz* Karl Sonnabend took the *Panzerfaust* from me. He wanted to crack a tank with it, but when he stepped out of a cornfield with the *Panzerfaust* he was spotted in the glow of a fire and was immediately hit by a bullet and dropped dead on the spot. Nearby were some enemy tanks.

After a short time the hill was in our possession. Tanks were in flames and the ground was strewn with the dead and wounded. Prisoners were gathered and some captured tanks were taken to the rear. It was a Canadian unit that was surprised by our counter-attack. They had not experienced such a strong counter-attack for a long time. At night our *Zug* withdrew to the base of the hill in the valley below to sleep for a few hours.

The terrain was hilly, crossed by hollows, fertile cereal fields alternated with vineyards. Abandoned farmhouses were scattered around. Beside a dusty country road piles of cereal sheaves were placed in a harvested field, and this offered us some cover so we hid ourselves. In the morning I was plagued by an intense thirst. I told the *Zugführer*, *Leutnant* Heinz Schumacher, that I wanted to look for a well in order to fetch some water for us. With several flasks I went down a hollow to a farmhouse, but only found water in one further away. When the bottles were full, a low-flying observation aircraft passed overhead. I could clearly see the observer's face. On the way back I happened to look at the foot of the hill that we had stormed the night before, and from the bushes came a row of soldiers.

At first I was in doubt as to what troops they were because they appeared to have the same yellowish-coloured tropical uniforms. Their rifles were slung or carried casually in their hands as if they were going hunting.

It had probably been reported by aerial observers that the enemy (that is, us) was undetectable, so the patrol was sent to find us. We were indeed perfectly camouflaged in the sheaves. When the observation plane had gone, I left my cover and returned to the *Zug*. I reported to my *Gruppeführer*, *Uffz* Reinhold Schumacher, that I saw a troop of foreign soldiers near the bottom of the hill. He went off to find out if these were our own soldiers who were scattered around the base of the hill. The binoculars showed beyond doubt that it was indeed an enemy patrol or vanguard of a larger force.

We made a report of our observation to our *Zugführer*. Now more soldiers were visible with the naked eye. We were put on alert, with orders to keep in cover in order to draw the enemy in as close as possible. In a loose line, they came towards us unaware. When they approached to about 50m from our position, we opened up with all weapons. The enemy was surprised and they ran back and forth, aiming to the left and right, as they also recieved fire from an elevated position.

The majority were killed or wounded and the rest quickly retreated. More ammunition was issued and I recieved another *Panzerfaust*. If we had retreated to an area more suitable for defence, or if anti-tank weapons had been requested, most of our *Bataillon* would have been spared from the forthcoming annihilation!

Aircraft flew over us again without spotting us. In the late afternoon, engine and track noises could be heard. The enemy tanks were coming! Side by side they headed towards us, the infantry following behind at a distance. *Uffz* Makiffka fired an *MG42* from the hip at the tank hatches. Comrade Richter ran away, which made me angry.

I stood up, aiming my *Panzerfaust* at a tank that was racing towards me. There was an officer standing in the turret holding a revolver in each hand. He fired without hitting me. I steadied the *Panzerfaust* and squeezed the firing lever. With a jet of fire, the warhead shot toward the tank and hit the turret. At the same time I felt a blow to my right arm and the *Panzerfaust* tube flew out of my hands. I had been hit! My uniform sleeve was torn and blood spurted from my right arm. I applied pressure with my other hand and ran back to our positions. At the radio position the *Sani*, Franz Gscheider, gave me provisional treatment. Next to me was *Uffz* Schumacher, who had also been hit in the arm. I then ran back to the dressing station. The enemy was firing tank shells at anyone who was trying to escape to safety.

I was soon wounded again when a splinter penetrated my lungs. The blood loss made me weak and I stumbled into a farmhouse. Several wounded from our unit were lying on the straw-covered floor. I lost consciousness and was only awakened by intense heat: the straw was burning and the house was on fire. I managed to crawl outside and lay there. There were strange voices. I vaguely heard that the house was lit on purpose, with the wounded burned inside.

Now I was a prisoner and was searched, with awards pulled off, money and photographs taken. I was left lying there, severely wounded. Troops later searched me again, but then I was marched back to their positions under threat of a rifle butt. The route crossed over vineyard wires and I could barely walk in my state of weakness, and found myself being hit with a rifle butt into the small of my back.

In a shallow depression I found Christian Brüning from my *Zug*, who was whimpering with pain. He told me loudly in agony: "The pigs shot me after my capture." He asked me to send a *Sani*.

At a crossroads all of the wounded were gathered and locked in a house. Here I recieved a morphine injection from a German medic, which dampened the worst of the pain.

After a few hours some medical vehicles arrived. More and more Canadian and Polish wounded were brought in. We were taken to an open area and placed on stretchers. First the enemy wounded were taken care of and loaded up, and as this was happening there was a sudden howling in the air followed by a hellish crash. The whole area was under fire from German *Do-Werfers*.[12]

The guards hastily fled to find cover as we lay defenceless on the stretchers. We thought that our last moments had come, so powerful and terrifying was this firestorm! A Polish soldier lying next to me had his buttocks blown off by shrapnel. He later died in an ambulance next to me. The Canadians had exacted their bloody revenge on us for our successful attack on Monte Luro the day before.

In the POW hospital in Taranto, I later met a comrade called Alois Hocke from Birkenhain in Upper Silesia. He told me how he too was initially taken prisoner unwounded, but was then shot with a burst of fire along with several other men. Since then his arm was lame. The large number of missing German soldiers from 1 September 1944 was probably due to acts contrary to international law and inhumanity.

---

12   Multi-barrel rocket launchers.

British Captivity

In the evening I was taken by ambulance to an English [*sic*] dressing station near Fano. Most of the wounded here were *Jäger* from *Fallschirmjäger Division 1*. Since my injury was severe, I could not be treated here so I was transported at night by ambulance to a field hospital near Ancona. During this journey in the ambulance, two other men died of their wounds. Doctors were already waiting in the hospital, and I was taken straight to the operating theatre. My uniform was simply cut off me with big shears. When I saw them approach with the shears I became scared, but they reassured me. At this time I had managed to keep hold of a beautiful Italian pocket watch. An English medic wanted to take it from me, but despite being weak due to blood loss, I protested, so he gave it back. After waking from the anaesthesia the next day, the watch was gone!

After a few days we were registered at the hospital by representatives of the Red Cross. Then came the interrogators, who were German-speaking Jews, and they came to my bedside. To my astonishment, they knew the names of all our officers and even the location of our quarters on the Adriatic.

Here I learned that my *Kompanieführer*, *Leutnant* Harald Quandt, had also been taken prisoner. He had apparently used a pseudonym when he was captured so as not to be identified. From hearsay, I learned that a former *Gruppeführer*, a *Feldwebel*, had informed the Allies of their new prize. I heard this from various sources.

Fortunately for us, we were treated in the English [*sic*] military hospital with the newly developed Penicillin, so many of us survived our severe injuries. At that time it had to be injected so that the level of Penicillin remained constant in the body.

After 11 days I was ready for transportation to a regular hospital. From the port of Ancona we went by ship to Taranto (Tarent) in southern Italy. There I was admitted to the 22nd British Field Hospital. This prison hospital was built in an olive grove and the tents were intended to hold 24 patients. At that time it was a hospital almost fully occupied by *Fallschirmjäger*, and was secured accordingly. It was surrounded by a double barbed wire fence, lit up at night, with watchtowers at the corners and guards patrolling the grounds. The English [*sic*] still considered the German paratroopers particularly dangerous. The large main building served as a hospital for English [*sic*] and Canadian wounded, as it had already been used as such by the *Luftwaffe*. The existing x-ray equipment came from Germany and was left behind during the rapid evacuation of southern Italy. The more complex operations were carried out in the main building by mixed medical professionals. The chief physician was British and was assisted by senior physician Dr Schubert, as well as junior physician Dr Riess.

Treatment and medical care was excellent and the food was also good, as long as the war lasted of course. They did not differentiate between friend or foe when it came to treatment. There was an English head nurse who as a result of her resolute appearance was nicknamed 'Montgomery'. Anyone who had a run in with her could find themselves at the shipping depot even if their wounds had not completely healed. This happened to me, and despite the plaster cast sleeve I was moved out.

The local sports stadium had been converted into a shipment warehouse. Hundreds of prisoners from all corners of the *Wehrmacht* were camped here in small cardboard tents. The sanitary conditions were miserable and the men just waited for ships to take them halfway across the world, as far away as possible where they could no longer pose a threat.

The camp doctor was a Jew called Weinberg. Since I was without shoes, I went to him and told him I had no footwear. He answered: "Then go to Hitler, he will give you shoes!"

The shipping commission was appalled when they found me here in the camp with a dirty plaster on my arm, under which lice were now quartered. I was immediately classed as a bed patient and returned by ambulance to the field hospital. 'Montgomery' was not pleased to see me return. In the officers' section was my former *Kompanieführer*, Harald Quandt. The British did not know at first how important a prisoner he was, or they handled it as a secret. He was part Jewish and his father, divorced from Magda Goebbels, was a big industrial boss back in Germany. Quandt had been taken prisoner wounded. He was hit by a salvo of bullets, but they were only flesh wounds. They apparently removed 14 bullets from him, and the doctors allegedly asked him after the operation if he would like a magazine for his bullets!

The first guards we had were Indian soldiers, who sat bored in their watchtowers or grudgingly walked the grounds. There were several escape attempts from the military hospital. No sooner were men restored to health, than they would try to reach the German lines and return to their units. These activists were *Fallschirmjäger*, and with homemade Red Cross armbands, two of them were able to pass themselves off as medics at the gate. They also managed to organise an ambulance and disappear. Most of the escapees were, however, caught. In part they often betrayed themselves, as they habitually walked in step with each other. The English [*sic*] secret service had apparently drawn an invisible line across the Italian peninsula, with guard posts and check points specifically to recapture escaped POWs on their way north. I found this out from one of our men who had been recaptured. For those willing to escape, I made simple maps of Italy on which the possible control line was marked. Soon my activities were betrayed, my belongings were checked and a bush of chilli peppers, which might possibly serve as a weapon, was taken from me. This was followed by an immediate transfer to a regular prison located on a hill outside Tarent. This camp contained various sections, with one for *Fallschirmjäger* and a separate one for Austrians, who not did not want to identify as '*Östmarkers*'. The Upper Silesians now suddenly identified themselves as Polish, and then there was a specially guarded camp for the Russian '*Hiwis*'.[13] These men were under the command of a loyal Russian *Kommissar*. Under strict supervision, they had to make daily route marches because they had to return to Russia in a healthy state to face the consequences of their betrayal of Mother Russia. In one of the camp areas were high-ranking Italian officers, who enjoyed a lot of freedom. As I spoke Italian, they asked me about the chances of the outcome of the war so they could establish how long they might have to spend in captivity.

At that time England was under fire from the V-weapons, so there was still the possibility of a German victory.[14] Full of conviction and optimism, I was still left in no doubt about our victory; however, the nearer the Allies approached the borders of the Reich in both the east and west, a sinking of morale and discipline became noticeable. Some men were already removing the national insignia from their uniforms.

In December 1944, the *Wehrmacht* had its initial successes during the Ardennes Offensive and suddenly the national insignia was sewn back on, as if by magic!

Because nothing could be done for me in this camp, I was taken to a military hospital in Grottaglie. It was a hospital that had been set up in some houses, and I was placed on the upper floor with a wide view over the countryside, and unlike the previous camp it was not cold.

Next to me lay a young Luxembourger, who had been forcibly conscripted into the *Wehrmacht*. He had a hand wound with severe nerve pain, and he whimpered day and night. I wrote his mail for him as best as I could with my other hand. A commission appeared whilst I was there to select severely wounded men for an exchange for Allied wounded in Germany. Since I could definitely not fire a gun any more, my name was added to the exchange list.

Meanwhile, the Ardennes Offensive had failed and parts of the Reich in the west and east had been conquered and occupied by the enemy. The *Wehrmacht* were now in full retreat on their own soil. Thus the planned prisoner exchange faltered.

---

13   *Hilfswilliger*, or willing helper; auxiliary volunteers from Eastern Europe who served in the *Wehrmacht*.
14   *Vergeltungswaffe*, or revenge weapons, more commonly known as the V-1 & V-2 rockets.

The 22nd General Hospital now became the 55th, which I was transferred back to once again. German *Sanis* were now employed as nurses and the guards were young Jewish soldiers. It was decided to carry out a bone transplant on me as an experiment.

On 20 April 1945, the *Führer*'s birthday, I went under the knife. One part of the bone was removed from my right leg and transplanted into the right arm. I was informed that this was the first such operation to be carried out in a military hospital. After the operation I was handcuffed to the bed until the leg wound had healed. In the following days, different groups of physicians came to my bedside and looked at x-ray pictures, happy with the success of the operation.

The end of the Second World War

On 8 May 1945, I was sitting on a tree stump in the sun near the fence-line. A guard was making his rounds of the grounds. He turned and said: "Do you know that the war is over? Germany is *kaputt* and has capitulated!" But then he continued: 'It may be that we need you again soon!" I often had to think about these prophetic words later!

Masses of Italians came to our hospital from the Mediterranean area. They were half-starved. It was the garrison from the Aegean islands. They had simply been left there by the English [*sic*]. For weeks they had fed only on grass, and had not received replenishment for a long time.

Until the end of the war, our food was monotonous but sufficient: three months of mutton, three months of goose meat and three months of American beef tongue. There was also plundered food prepared by German cooks, so we once again made our acquaintance with barley and cabbage.

Our camp interpreter, a South Tyrolean, had been released and sent home, so I took his place. I now had it much better. I would go to the main house every day for treatment, and whilst I was there I would help with the Italian soldiers' correspondence. Some of them had recieved letters, but many of them could not read and write. Most of these men had become sick from raiding the

Ortona 2004: Carl (left) speaking to Gabriele Delizio, who as a child remained in Ortona during the fighting in December 1943. (DDF)

trash cans. That's how I was able to improve my vitamin needs, because the Italian work provided fruit and onions. Our food was white bread and canned foods.

At the beginning of June 1945, some prisoners suddenly showed up with white beards and splendid ornate uniforms. They were the foresters from Hermann Göring's hunting estate and had been captured by the British and brought to Italy.

At the beginning of September 1945, a transport train was put together and the return journey to Germany began. In Innsbruck, which was occupied by the French, the reasonably healthy prisoners were sorted out and sent to France. Some men jumped off the train rather than serve more time as a POW. In Bad Aibling, we came to a camp without any protection from the elements. It began to rain and my plaster cast broke up. On 13 September, the camp gates opened for me for the final time and I could return home.

Epilogue

I wrote most of my war memories after the war by hand, and later I visited Italy many times to refresh my memory. I could remember most of my war experiences exactly as they happened, because the war for us (and me), as young boys, was a big adventure (at first). When I close my eyes today, I see most of my experiences like a movie registered in my brain. I will never forget my POW number: 191 906.

(The author recently found out from the Heilbronn town council that Carl sadly passed away several years ago.)

13

Erwin Bauer

A teenage *Fallschirmjäger* in Tunisia

Erwin Bauer was born on 9 April 1925 and volunteered to become a Fallschirmjäger *at 16 years old. His call-up papers to join the parachute school at Stendal arrived on his 17th birthday. Whilst assigned to Mont-Saint-Michel in Brittany, Bauer committed a minor disciplinary offence which saved him from the Russian Front, and was instead mobilised to Africa with* FJR5. *As the final battles in Tunisia came to an end, Bauer surrendered and spent the next four years in American, French and Belgian captivity before returning home to Frankfurt in 1948. He was shocked by the situation in Frankfurt, as the whole city had been destroyed. After working in the black market for one or two years, he continued his education and became a master craftsman, working for several companies until his retirement. In 2018, I attempted to contact a member of his family and recieved an email from Ronald Bauer, one of Erwin Bauer's sons. He informed me that Herr Bauer was still alive and in fine health at the age of 93, and still residing in Frankfurt am Main. Ronald sent me several video messages from his father, and Erwin reviewed the following material. Unfortunately, Herr Bauer only had one wartime photo as they were taken from him in captivity; however, I managed to obtain some photos from the Aliceville POW camp museum in Alabama, where he had been interred after the war.*

Erwin Bauer in Tunisia, 1943. This is the only wartime photo still in Erwin's possession. All other personal possessions were taken from him after capture. (Erwin Bauer)

9 April 2019: Erwin Bauer at home in Frankfurt am Main celebrating his 94th birthday. (Erwin Bauer)

Initiation

I travelled to Stendal in my best suit; it was only four weeks old. At the barrack gate I was met by a non-commissioned officer, who welcomed me and led me to a small *Truppe* of eight other newcomers.

It was a rainy day and the barrack yard was scattered with small puddles. The NCO made us stand in a line; we had already learned that in the Hitler Youth.

Then the dear NCO held a small welcoming address. Afterwards, he informed us that we were going to carry out a bit of Prussian drill. We had to run around the barrack yard; if we ran through a puddle the NCO would shout, "Get down!", then we would carry on and roll forwards and backwards in the damp soil, until we had satisfied the NCO. When we finished my best suit was completely ruined. My enthusiasm for *Führer*, *Volk* and Fatherland had already wained.

Fallschirmjäger Regiment 5

Following my recruitment time I was assigned to a unit on the island of Mont-Saint-Michel in France but was soon transferred for disciplinary reasons to a new unit at Mourmelon, south-east of Reims. The new unit consisted of a newly raised *I. Bataillon* along with *II & III. Bataillon* from the famous *Sturmregiment*, which had just returned from Russia. With these Bataillone, the new *Fallschirmjäger Regiment 5* was set up in May 1942 under the command of *Oberstleutnant* Walter Koch.

Spring 1942 near Mourmelon in France: *Oberstleutnant* Walter Koch (with white cap) oversees training on a 75mm LG40 recoilless gun mounted on a hedgerow. (Alfred Genz)

The *Kommandeur* of *I/FJR5* was *Hauptmann* Hans Jungwirth, and with this unit I went to the jump school at Stendal. The school was a clean, sporty affair and their motto was 'pack chutes for jumping'. With an NCO instructor supervising, we learnt the art of folding chutes properly. *II/FJR5* was sent to Africa in July 1942 to become part of the famous *Ramcke Brigade* who fought near El-Alamein. In the meantime, *I* and *III/FJR5* were transferred to Mourmelon to train for Operation Hercules, the airborne invasion of Malta, which was supposed to take place in mid-July 1942.

Tunisia

Not long after Operation Hercules was cancelled, we were informed that we were going to Africa. My old unit from Mont-Saint-Michel, on the other hand, was moved from France to Russia. Thankfully my disciplinary offence saved me from the Russian front.

On 8 November 1942, Allied troops landed in Morocco and Algeria, and in order to protect the flank of the *Afrika-Korps*, who were withdrawing westward, new units were to be sent to North Africa. At the end of October 1942, my unit, *I/FJR5*, was flown to Naples in Italy. Whilst en-route we learned of our new employment in North Africa; however, it was not to be a jump mission. Our stay in Naples was a short one. On the airfield at Naples around 70 JU-52s were available and our *3. Kompanie* was divided amongst 10–15 aircraft.

The *Kompanie* landed at the El Aouina airfield in Tunis on 11 November to provide an advance guard prior to the arrival of the remaining two *Bataillone*.[1]

Shortly before we landed at Tunis, the Allies bombarded the airfield. It was lucky that we landed a few minutes later. It was a very warm day, the weapons were unloaded from the aircraft and I was chosen to stand guard, probably because I was the youngest.

We were accommodated in the Marshal Foch barracks, which had been vacated by French troops only a short time before.

After a short stay it came to our first mission near Djedaida. Here we suffered our first casualties: two dead. One of the dead was Poldi, a friend of mine from Vienna. After Djedaida, we took part in several small engagements.

I think it was December 1942 when my unit, *3. Zug* of *3. Kompanie*, penetrated into the Atlas Mountains on a two-week mission. It was only meant to be a short mission and we only took equipment for a few days. Already during the first day it began to rain heavily. This supposed short mission lasted two weeks, and so did the rain. Our foxholes were full of rain water and our equipment, including weapons and ammunition, were waterlogged. The only foxhole which had a roof was the radio post. I remember this time exactly. Another attack in the Atlas Mountains was planned and it should have been a surprise attack. Our *Kompanie* was dispatched with the necessary weapons and equipment for an attack in a mountainous area. We moved in complete silence, like Red Indians, one behind the other, in a 1km line up the mountain. Talking was forbidden. It was not far to the hostile positions.

The most forward of our unit had positioned themselves a short distance from the enemy line. Everything looked as though it would be a successful breakthrough.

The whole area was very steep and suddenly one of the *MG* crews dropped an ammunition box to the ground. The box rumbled down the mountain with a loud echoing din. The front was suddenly wide awake, and from all sides flares shot up into the sky and turned the surrounding

---

1   Whilst en-route to Tunisia, the aircraft flew over Mount Etna on the east coast of Sicily. Erwin recalls that the aircraft circled the volcano several times to allow the men in all the JU-52s to see the sight below.

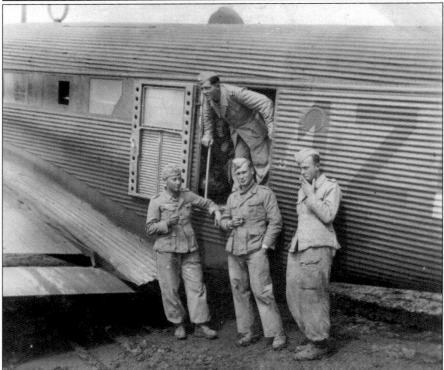

Fallschirm-Panzerjäger pose by a JU-52 from *KG zbV.1*, which provided air transport of men and materiel across the Mediterranean to North Africa. (Kate Eichler)

terrain into daylight. From all sides *MG* fire started up. Our position offered us no prospect of a successful assault, so the attack failed. We could not afford the losses, so we hastily returned to our old positions.

In January 1943, *3. Kompanie*, under the command of *Oberleutnant* Dewet Klar, was employed in the area of Bou-Arada. We did not take part in the attacks on Hills 221 or 231; the number designations of these heights are no longer in my memory.

However, it was always the same procedure. In groups of 10–12 men we would start our attacks with rifles, *MPis*, *MGs* and every man would have a few hand grenades. Our attacks were surprising and most of the time successful. Unfortunately we only enjoyed success for a few hours.

The Allies requested tanks, which were always positioned in our line of advance. We were not prepared to fight tanks and we often had no chance. It was very rare that we destroyed a tank with a hollow charge.[2] One condition was the terrain and that the tanks did not position themselves as to cover each other. If they were on their own in an area with cover we had a chance.

These senseless employments against tanks naturally also demanded their victims.

In mid-March 1943, we attacked Ridge 331 near Bou Arada. We were assigned a sector near the height. In the morning grey, our group of 10 men moved close to the hostile positions. Our only protection from the hostile *MG* fire were the isolated boulders on the ground. The start of the mission was successful, but within the middle range of the height the attack was stopped. The area no longer provided protection against enemy *MG* fire. At this time six men of the group had already fallen. Amongst the dead were the young Schneider twins. One brother lay heavily wounded and called out to his sibling, who lay nearby. The other brother left the protection of his cover and with a jump came to the assistance of his twin. This jump was fatal. He was cut down by *MG* fire and he fell to the ground lifeless next to his brother.

I would also like to mention the courage of our medics. They carried out their work with outstanding bravery, and where assistance was possible they would protect you without regard to their own lives. I had to admire these men.

The battle for Ridge 331 was lost when Allied tanks intervened around midday. *Obergefreiter* Tillmann and I were the only ones who reached our *Kompanie* command post in the evening. We only managed to escape when I used a smoke grenade at the right time. It gave us the opportunity to escape the enemy tank fire. Those who lost their lives on Ridge 331 remained. One of those was *Oberjäger* Josef-Franz Rösgen: we had seen much together. All Franz wanted to do was destroy an enemy tank with his hollow charge. No words could hold him back from it.

A few hours later we tried to retrieve the dead from Ridge 331. Of the young soldiers that we had left behind, only a cruel sight of mutilated blackened bodies remained.

On our way back from Ridge 331, Tillmann and I ran into *Oberleutnant* Klar, who had a machine-pistol in his hands. He ordered us both to return to Hill 331 and fight on. We ran a short way back, and once out of view we stopped and took cover. We had not eaten or drunk anything since the morning.

We spent the next few days doing punishment drill with *Oberleutnant* Klar, and in the following weeks the *Kompanie* was filled with young soldiers from the *Division Hermann Göring* (*HG*), who arrived in Tunisia between mid-February and early March.[3]

The war in Africa was coming to an end. There were only two opinions amongst the men: those who believed in victory and those who saw no more hope. The newcomers of the *Division HG* had

---

2   The *Panzerfaust* was not available until late 1943.
3   On 14 March 1943, *FJR5* was redesignated *Jäger Regiment Hermann Göring* and incorporated into the *Division Hermann Göring*. See Bender & Petersen, p20. Erwin had no knowledge of this redesignation in name or the issue of a *Hermann Göring* cuff title.

not yet experienced war and could not see that the fighting was useless. Likewise, we could not suffer the continuous loss of men.

There was an attack in late March 1943, which is still good in my memory. I had a machine-pistol and the pockets of my jump-smock were filled with grenades.

We *Jäger* advanced in line formation and carefully climbed the height towards the hostile line. The number of the hill I can no longer remember. I soon lost contact with the *Jäger* on my left and right, but I had already worked out my own tactics: forward, stop, rip out the igniter cord from the grenade, throw, storm forward, down into cover, wait for the detonation, then jump up and again forward always shouting "hands up, hands up!".

Suddenly, as I rose from the ground, two British soldiers emerged in front of me. I was so frightened that I dropped my machine-pistol. The Tommies held up their hands, so I had my first two prisoners. With the Tommies beside me, I stormed on further upward. On the height another eight Tommies emerged with their hands up. The Tommies gave me a certain amount of protection because they constantly shouted "stop firing, stop firing" to their comrades.

On the height I met other comrades, and together we had approximately 50 prisoners. We spent the following hours with the Tommies in their old positions. It was here that something marvellous happened. From war we became friends. Communication was achieved with our hands. We had put our weapons away. We ate and drank alcohol together, of which we found sufficient quantities. Before long it was already the afternoon.

Suddenly, a shout came from one of the observation posts: "Hostile tanks are approaching." We had to move. The Tommies showed us routes through the barbed wire and ways back to our starting positions.

20 April 1943 – *Unternehmen Fliederblüte (Operation Lilac Blossom)*

We were safe in the knowledge that the war in Africa was nearing its end. What followed was a futile retreat and the senseless sacrifice of lives.

It was Hitler's birthday, 20 April, and one heard: "In order to honour Adolf Hitler a large-scale attack will take place." We old hands of the *Kompanie* were awarded with the Iron Cross and an Italian Bravery Medal.

Fighting was already a few hours old in the next objective, that of Medjez-el-Bab. The remainder of the *Bataillon*, or perhaps only sections of it, were ready for this battle. About 60–70 *Panzers* from the *10. Panzer Division* and *Schwere Panzer-Abteilung 501/504*, the last in Africa, were stationed with the *Fallschirmjäger* in a waiting position. We drove 30km through the night on the backs of the tanks and broke through the enemy line without encountering any considerable resistance. Then came the command to dismount. The *Panzers* went their own way and we ours. Our *Zug* was under the command of *Oberleutnant* Müller.

The *Panzer* unit became engaged in a tank battle and was totally destroyed. I heard later that about 400 Allied tanks faced our *Panzers*. It was an unequal fight.

Our *Zug* was attacked by jeeps fitted with MGs. We then heard a shout from one of the *Jäger*: "*Oberleutnant* Klar, our *Kompanieführer*, is here with some men." *Oberleutnant* Müller gave the command for the new arrivals to open fire on the jeeps.

Tanks now joined in the hunt for us *Jäger*, and we had no chance with our light infantry weapons. We separated and each man went alone to try and find his own way back. I had completely lost my orientation. I tried to hide, but my only real chance was to wait for darkness. We had not eaten or drunk anything all day. Hunger, thirst and a lack of ammunition made me feel helpless, and still the jeeps came closer. I threw the two hand grenades I had brought with me; they brought peace for a while.

Surrender and captivity

Then three English [*sic*] jeeps appeared suddenly in front of me and made it clear that it was the end. I surrendered.

I spent my last days in Africa at a POW camp in Oran.[4] In a convoy of 70 ships we set sail for the USA, protected by warships. I spent four years in the USA at camps such as Aliceville in Alabama, picking cotton and mining.

Camp Aliceville under construction in 1942. It was initially called Aliceville Internment Camp, and changed to POW Camp in July 1943. At that time it was the largest camp in the US, with a capacity of 6,000 prisoners. (Aliceville Museum Collection)

View of the road through one of the six POW compounds at Camp Aliceville. There were 26 camps in Alabama, with over 500 in total throughout the US, holding almost 500,000 prisoners, mostly German. (Aliceville Museum Collection)

---

4   The parachute forces suffered approximately 10,000 casualties in North Africa, the equivalent of an entire *Fallschirmjäger* division. See Villahermosa, p.159.

POWs marching on 3rd Avenue in Aliceville on 2 June 1943. These are some of the prisoners from the first train to arrive in town. (Aliceville Museum Collection)

Another photo of the first batch of prisoners to arrive in Aliceville. The prisoners in these photos were all captured in North Africa, many in Tunisia in the spring of 1943. They are *Afrika-Korps*, Hermann Göring Division and some members of *Strafkompanien*. All arrived in the uniforms they were captured in. (Aliceville Museum Collection)

German POWs marching through the front gate of the camp on 3 June 1943. (Aliceville Museum Collection)

More POWs march to camp on 3 June 1943. (Aliceville Museum Collection)

The camp printing press used to print *Der Zaungast* (The fence post), the prisoner's camp newspaper, and other publications. It was a second-hand machine, purchased with profits from the camp POW canteens. (Aliceville Museum Collection)

CAMP ALICEVILLE, 1944
AMPHITHEATER, COMPOUND A

Drawing of an outdoor concert produced by one of the POWs (Aliceville Museum Collection)

der Zaungast

Edited and published weekly by and for the German Prisoners of War at Prisoner of War Camp Aliceville-Alabama
ZEITSCHRIFT DES KRIEGSGEFANGENENLAGERS ALICEVILLE/ALA · 3. JUNI 1945 · NUMMER 24

Eine Rheinfahrt zum Drachenfels

Koelner Skizze

Die Sonne verkuendet einen herrlichen Tag. Der Dampfer „Loreley" liegt abfahrtbereit am Leystapel in Koeln. Frau Schmitz, schon auf der Landebruecke, ruft im Gedraenge dem zurueckbleibenden Gatten ihre letzten Anweisungen zu: Die Eier nicht laenger als 4 Minuten kochen lassen! Fuer das Kaffeewasser 2 Lot Malz und 1 - ein !- Lot Bohnen! 3 Messerspitzen Fett fuer die Bratkartoffel! - Die Kinder, Hermaennche und Baerbelche, trippeln ungeduldig um die Mutter herum. Jetzt ertoent die Schiffsglocke. Baerbelche haengt sich aufgeregt an Frau Schmitzens Rockschoss; Hermaennche, noch aufgeregter, laeuft voraus. Gluecklich gelangen sie aufs Schiff. Ein letztes Winken, und schon gleitet die „Loreley" unter der Haengebruecke durch. Die Menschen am Ufer verschwinden. - Frau Schmitz laesst sich aufatmend an einem Tisch nieder, oeffnet resolut das Kleid am Halse und laesst sich den frischen Morgenwind um den Busen wehen. Neben sich stellt sie die grosse Tasche mit den Einmachglaesern voll Kartoffelsalat, den hartgekochten Eiern und den vielen Butterbroten. Da sieht sie auch schon eine Bekannte. „Och, wie nett, de Frau Monnerjahn!"

Waehrend Baerbelche brav neben der Mutter sitzt, strolcht Hermaennche mit anderen Jungen auf dem Schiff herum. Sie legen sich weit ueber den Schiffsrand, winken vorueberziehenden Kaehnen zu, lassen Papierschnitzel im Winde tanzen und spucken herzhaft in den Rhein. Jetzt scharen sie sich um die Schiffskapelle. Der Trompeter blaest gerade „Gruess mir das blonde Kind vom Rhein", und sie lachen ueber seine dicken Backen. Stumm und betreten schauen sie in den dunklen Maschinenraum, aus dem ihnen eine heisse Luft

entgegenstroemt. Am Kapitaen druecken sie sich vorsichtig vorueber. Als er aber in gehoeriger Entfernung ist, rufen sie kraeftig „Heidewitzka, Herr Kapitaen!" hinter ihm her und verschwinden dann schleunigst, um sich bei der Mutter schon wieder ein Butterbrot zu holen. „Nae, Frau Schmitz, wat haet de Jung 'ne goode App'tit!"

Bonn kommt in Sicht, und schon gruesst das Siebengebirge herueber. „Nur am Rhein da moecht' ich leben, nur am Rhein geboren sein" blaest der Trompeter. Die Kinder blicken aufgeregt zum Drachenfels. Frau Schmitz hat endlich alle haeuslichen Themen von der Grossen Waesche bis zum Hausputz mit ihrer Bekannten besprochen und macht sich nun fertig. In Koenigswinter steigt sie mit den Kindern aus. - Und dann stehen sie am Fuss des sagenreichen Berges und damit vor drei Moeglichkeiten: man kann mit der Zahnradbahn, mit einem gemieteten Esel und zu Fuss auf den Drachenfels gelangen. Baerbelche will mit der Zahnradbahn, Hermaennche mit dem Esel, Frau Schmitz zu Fuss! Die Mutter entscheidet, Hermaennche

Blick rheinabwaerts auf den „Drachenfels"

knottert und Baerbelche heult. Frau Schmitz wird kribbelig! „Maach mich nit jeck, domme Put!" Baerbelche heult noch mehr. „Mamm', ich muss emal!" - So steigen sie auf den Drachenfels.

Oben angekommen, setzen sie sich in die Gartenwirtschaft. Frau Schmitz bestellt ein Glas Bier und fuer die Kinder Limonade. Dann verzehren sie den Kartoffelsalat. (Nirgends schmeckt Kartoffelsalat so gut wie auf dem Drachenfels!) - Die Kinder spielen nun. Frau Schmitz ist allein und geniesst die hertliche Aussicht. In der Tiefe sieht sie den alten Vater Rhein. Wie lieblich Spielzeuge erscheinen ihr die Schiffe auf dem Fluss. Dort, ueber dem Rhein, liegt Rolandseck mit seinem Rolandsbogen. Der Blick geht weiter ueber die Berge bis zur fernen Eifel, die sich dunkel am Horizont abhebt. Im Norden sieht Frau Schmitz ploetzlich den Koelner

1

Front page from an edition of *Der Zaungast*. A German language professor at the University of Alabama studies the newspapers from Aliceville. She has expressed her amazement that there appears to be no propaganda or hidden messages in the papers. It appears to be a reflection of things that meant something to the POWs, such as home, family, sports, etc. (Aliceville Museum Collection)

A Christmas card made by the prisoners, quite possibly on the camp printing press. This card celebrates Christmas 1943 and was no doubt made by a former *Fallschirmjäger* of *FJR5*, as it features the comet, the original insignia of the *Sturmregiment* whose traditions they inherited (Erwin Bauer)

A simple Christmas message is printed on the reverse: Glory to God in the highest and peace to men on earth. (Erwin Bauer)

Afterwards I was sent to France as a farmer and miner. Then I escaped, but was caught and sent to a mine in Belgium. I escaped again, and at the beginning of 1948 finally made it home to Frankfurt.

Epilogue

When I look back, I think of the good men I served with. *Oberleutnant* Klar was a good officer in all the attacks he had taken part in. I had experiences with other officers during missions. Among others were *Leutnant* Erich Schuster (KIA 11 January 1943, near Djebel Rihane), *Oberleutnant* Wilhelm Kristofek, *Oberleutnant* Walter Gasteyer and *Oberleutnant* Archikowski. They will always have a place of honour in the history of the *Fallschirmtruppe*.

I write this in memory of *Obergefreiter* Josef-Franz Rösgen, killed on Hill 331 on 18 March 1942 and buried in Bordj-Cedria; a man and a friend whom I shall never forget.

Wachvergehen (Watch offence)

I have two short stories I would like to tell. The first is from my time on Mont-Saint-Michel in France. Offences whilst on duty were considered a mortal sin and were punished accordingly. It was autumn. Our *Zug* was quartered in small groups in Saint-Michel. Our day began at 0600 hours with exercise for those of us who were not assigned to guard duties.

Our *Zugführer* approached from the large entrance gate. On the way he blew on his whistle at short intervals. This was the signal for us to be on the street in our sports kit to begin our morning run. On completion of the run there were exercises down by the large gate. Afterwards it was breakfast for the whole *Zug* in one of the hotels. After breakfast the daily watch plan was announced. Guard duties were mainly conducted at night. The night was divided into watches: two hours' guard and three hours' rest. It was a scary business in the dark through the church on the way up to the highest peak. There were no stairs in the last few metres and you had to climb up through the turret. From this location you had a fantastic view over the sea to the west.

We would regularly see enemy reconaissance aircraft and would occasionally come under attack. My last watch on this particular night was from 0400–0600 hours, and for a split-second I fell asleep. At that exact moment I became the victim of the *Feldwebel* who was also on watch. There was no negotiation with this man. He told me that on the weekend I would undertake a punishment drill on the tidal flat.

I was astonished when I turned up for the drill. Suddenly, *Jäger* Rutkewitz emerged equipped with four heavy *MG* ammunition boxes. His offence was unknown to me. After one hour of the worst harassment came the order to change equipment. I had normal combat gear. It was hard for me, but sometimes when *Jäger* Rutkewitz came into my view I saw him struggling with his boxes. Then the equipment change and *Jäger* Rutkewitz took over my gear, consisting of rifle, ammo belt, gas mask and light combat pack. Whilst handing over, I quickly realised what a perfect actor Rutkewitz really was. His ammunition boxes were empty! So I kept up the illusion and moaned and groaned for the next hour. The whole show went in our favour, but I dread to think what would have happened if we were discovered.

After a few days I had to march to our *Kompanie* command post for a new assignment. Together with five other comrades we were transferred to another *Fallschirmjäger* unit. We received our marching order, but no transport or food, and our new unit was 35km away. After a very long walk we reached our destination without a warm reception. My new unit was destined for Africa and the one I had just left ended up in Russia.

Feldpost (forces postal service)

Lili Marlen was a well-known term for both friend and foe. It is a story about a *Landser* who meets his sweetheart under a street lantern.

I was still 17 years old and also dreamed of a Lili Marlen. I wrote a long letter to Berlin and asked the post office to forward the letter to a girl's school in the hope it would reach someone of my age. After four weeks I received a reply. The writer was a 17-year-old student. She told me that my letter had come into the hands of her teacher and that she had read it to the class. So I finally found my 'Lili'. Even today, after so many years, her name is unforgotten: Gerda Schnur of Beußelstraße, Berlin. We exchanged many nice letters. Contact was lost when the war in Africa was over, followed by the post-war turmoil. I never found out what became of Gerda.

(Erwin Bauer, now aged 94, still resides in Frankfurt am Main.)

14

Robert 'Bob' Frettlöhr

Monte Cassino

Robert 'Bob' Frettlöhr was born on 28 March 1924. He became a high-profile Fallschirmjäger veteran due to his experience during and after the battles for Monte Cassino in the Italian peninsula, the most costly Allied campaign of the Second World War. Bob participated in many reunions, and featured in many TV programmes, documentaries and books. He wanted to send a clear message to the younger generations about the futility of war and the resultant senseless waste of life, which he experienced first-hand. The same sentiments came from his Allied comrades, and at Cassino there were no barriers, no blame, no prejudice; only forgiveness and support. In 1946, whilst a POW in England, Bob was part of a dance band and played at RAF Lindholme, where he was to meet his future wife, Sally. After his repatriation to Germany, he soon returned to England under POW status and married the lady he met in the NAAFI social club, and gained his British citizenship in 1964. He became a successful musician in the post-war years, was well known within the jazz community as an accomplished double bass player and played well into his retirement.

Cameo photograph of Bob taken prior to his deployment to the Cassino front. (Sue Doubell)

Portrait taken in 2009, when Bob was a member of the civilian committee of No868 (Mirfield) Sqn – Air Training Corps in West Yorkshire. (Sue Doubell)

Training at Wittstock

I joined the *Fallschirmtruppe* in the early summer of 1943 having previously joined the *Luftwaffe* in April 1942 as an aircrew radio operator. While I was in Dresden, we were shown a film depicting the role of the *Fallschirmjäger* and it inspired me to enlist. I think part of the reason was that we were promised good quality food. But in all seriousness, that film and the message of being part of an elite was the reason I most remember.

Photo taken in Dresden in 1943 that Bob sent to his mother. (Sue Doubell)

Studio photograph taken in 1943. From left to right: Willi Schmitz, Karl Zobotka, Ferdinand ? and Bob. Two of his comrades in this photo were killed and the fate of the third is unknown. (Sue Doubell)

I carried out my training at the Wittstock *Fallschirmschule*. Here we were all taught to pack our own chutes and we worked in teams of two. We worked either side of a very long table, with the chute laid out on top. One of the trainees asked an instructor: "What happens if the chute does not open?" The instructor replied: "You go back to the stores, make a complaint and get another one!" I completed two jumps from a Dornier, two from a Heinkel He-111 bomber and my last two jumps were from a JU-52.

Jumping from an aircraft at low altitude, well obviously the first jumps were very scary, the action jumps being the worst to get used to. We had three-quarter-length boots that were fastened at the side, and your ankles were strapped. Despite these measures, my ankles have since become a weak point and will sprain easily. We were taught above all, to always keep our feet and knees together, with the knees bent for impact.

You were given the option not to continue your training if you felt that you could not jump, but once you had sworn your allegiance, you were expected to jump, no matter what. They did not accept refusals very well.

After each jump, the chutes were hung in a huge drying room ready to be packed. There was always only one chute, with no reserve or safety chute. Once my training was completed I was awarded the *Fallschirmschützenabzeichen* (the paratrooper's badge).

To Italy and Monte Cassino

I was then posted to Italy and based on the Adriatic coast in a mountain village called Germanico. Many *Fallschirmjäger* reserves were based there.

From Germanico I was sent to Tollo near Chieti to join *Fallschirmjäger Division 1*.

There, I received my training with *Pionier* equipment, explosives, mines etc. I was with the *15.Kompanie* of *FJR4* and we all moved in early February 1944 to Monte Cassino. We stayed in the rear area for a week or so before finally taking over. *FJR3* went into Cassino town to relieve the *Panzergrenadiers* and our *Regiment* was behind Monte Cassino, sealing off the valley, where the French Canadians were trying to break through. After the bombing of the monastery in February, we remained there. When the New Zealand tanks tried to break through over the Albeneta Farm, we were detailed off with anti-tank equipment to attack and disable them. Out of approximately 16 tanks, only five got out. One of the tanks was occupied by my now dear friend Jim Moody from New Zealand, who still calls me Bazooka Bob.

I was wounded at Cassino during the withdrawal on 17 May 1944. We left Rocca Janula and were moving to the other side of the valley. When I reached the top, a grenade exploded nearby. I saw a bright flash and the next thing I remember was coming around with a badly swollen and injured left leg. I crawled into the first-aid station in the crypt of the monastery ruins. My leg was cleaned up and bandaged during the night of 17 May. In the early morning of 18 May, the rest of the *Fallschirmjäger* evacuated, leaving the wounded behind.

At around 0930 hours, a Polish platoon under the command of *Leutnant* Kazimierz Gurbiel entered the monastery and took us as prisoners. Three of us who could not walk stayed there; the walking wounded were taken away. When I saw the Polish soldiers and realised that they would not harm me, I saw them as liberators, as if I had been born again, and that's why it was very important when later I was able to meet up with Kazimierz.

At lunchtime we were joined by several officers and among them was an American reporter. The reporter was called Mr Tetlow and he was immaculately dressed in a white trench coat. He spoke with me briefly in German. You must remember, I was in pain, hungry, exhausted, dirty and feeling lousy, and I was very angry with the nerve of this clean, well-fed reporter, who had no idea about what we had endured.

Un saluto da Montecassino.

Im Felde, den 2.5.1944

16771

Meine liebe Mutter!

Die besten Glückwünsche zum

Muttertag sendet Dir Dein

Sohn Robert.

MONTECASSINO · Interno della Basilica.
(Arch. Cosimo Fanzago 1591 - 1678)

I was well treated by the men who captured me, and indeed met with Kazimirez many years later and we remained in contact until his death on 27 January 1992.

Two of us were helped down the hill as best we could; the third I have no idea about. He did not end up with us. I was taken to a US field hospital about 6 miles behind the lines before being sent to Aversa near Naples. After two to three weeks in a US hospital, we were loaded on to a Liberty transport in Naples, which took us through the Mediterranean and a 21-day voyage to the USA. My final destination was Norfolk, Virginia, and then Lake Erie, and at one camp I became a lumberjack and was also allowed to issue the petrol, earning me the nickname Gazzo. Although we were very well looked after and well fed, the commandant of the camp was verbally abusive to all of the POWs, called them all sorts of names and tarred them all with the Nazi brush. We were all young lads – we were not Nazis, my family were not Nazis, but that did not matter to the commandant. If I was ever to meet him again, I would kill him for what he said.

Bob found postcards in the ruins of the Monte Cassino abbey and kept them as souvenirs. He sent one to his mother. The message reads: "In the field 2 May 1944, My dear Mother, I am sending you the very best wishes on mother's day, your son Robert." (Sue Doubell)

It was not until April 1946 that we were shipped back to Europe. In Ostend we were sent to POW camps 21 and 28 near Brussels. After a call for *Pioniers* we were sent from Ostend to Tilbury in England, from there to Scotland, and from Scotland we were sent to a US air force base and from there to Doncaster. We finally ended up at the RAF base at Lindholme in South Yorkshire.

I had been away from home a long time. We were allowed to write letters, but that was not the same. I was finally released in early 1948, given 40 *Deutschmarks* and sent to Münster. I was finally able to visit my parents. My home town had been flattened during the war. There was not a lot left, as most of the buildings had gone. Hitler had taken everyone's money, including my parents' savings, and only the rich were able to save their funds. My parents were still alive, but like everyone else they had to start again from scratch.

Whilst at RAF Lindholme I met a girl named Sally who worked in the NAAFI. Of course, fraternising with a German POW was frowned upon. My future wife's sisters and their respective husbands never had any prejudice, even though one of them, Tom Carter, was a British paratrooper who had served at Cassino. I had to write a letter to the king to get permission to marry. I was issued with an Alien ID and settled down in England with my wife.

Bob as a POW at RAF Lindholme in 1948. The clothes he stood in were made for him as he had nothing of his own. (Sue Doubell)

Two meetings of former enemies

Bob sent me the following article written by Zenon Andrzejewski, which is based on the transcripts of the letters sent between Bob and Kazimierz and gives an interesting perspective from the Polish officer who liberated the monastery at Monte Cassino and the part that Bob Frettlöhr played in clearing the name of former Polish Army officer Kazimierz Gurbiel and his men who entered the ruins on that morning of 18 May 1944. These men had been accused of war crimes in the aftermath of the battle, 39 years after the event supposedly occurred.

In the morning of 18 May 1944, *Lance Corporal* Szczepulski and *Major Sergeant* Antoni Wróblewski entered the courtyard of the monastery of Monte Cassino. They were greeted by a headless statue of St Benedict and a solemn silence. They gave a signal and the rest of the patrol arrived along with their commanding officer, *Lieutenant* Kazimierz Gurbiel.

Lance Corporal Wadas ran to a half-opened door and shouted: "*Hande hoch, oder wir schiesse!*" (Hands up, or I will shoot!). After a while the German paratroopers started to come out with their hands up. They presented a picture of misery and despair, bandaged and in rags, dirty and unshaven. Such was the appearance of the "heroes from Crete, Stalingrad and Ortona, the flower of Nordic youth – *Nibelungen*, the German semi-gods", wrote the writer Wankowicz.

There were 18 of them in all. When they noticed the Polish eagles on the uniforms they turned pale from fear. Through Wadas I told them not to be afraid, we don't shoot prisoners of war. We gave them cigarettes and I asked *Sergeant* Zapotoczny and *Lance Corporal* Wadas to escort them to the Regimental Headquarters. *Lieutenant* Gurbiel remembered years later: "I went downstairs into the basement and I found myself in the crypt of St Benedict used by the Germans as a small field hospital.

In 2009, very little had changed in the monastery crypt since 1944. This is the place where Bob lay wounded, praying he would survive. (Sue Doubell)

"What I saw here in the light of two wax candles was macabre! Near the altar, among the boxes filled with the corpses on golden chasubles lay three severely wounded young parachutists, almost boys! Their comrades had left them bread, water and tinned food. Sacks and rucksacks were filled with corpses or remnants of corpses of the German soldiers who could not be buried during the fighting. There was an intense stench from decaying bodies." The wounded paratroopers were looking at the Poles with fear in their eyes, uncertain about their fate. But hate and revenge on a defeated enemy were foreign to the Poles.

Lieutenant Gurbiel ordered his soldiers to take care of the wretches, to give them cigarettes, and he delegated a German hospital orderly to do what could be done. Gurbiel then quickly left the crypt for fresh air outside, and he sent a soldier for stretcher bearers in order to remove the prisoners from the crypt. One of the three parachutists taken prisoner by Gurbiel was *Gefreiter* Robert Frettlöhr. In the afternoon, after Gurbiel's patrol had left the monastery, Frettlöhr and the other wounded prisoners were transported to the hospital in Aversa near Naples. Then he was evacuated to the USA for further treatment. For him the war was over.

The war would also soon be over for *Lieutenant* Gurbiel. After murderous fighting for Piedmonte, he took part in the Adriatic campaign and on 7 July 1944 was severely wounded and lost a leg at Capelle San Ignazio. After the war, Kazimierz Gurbiel settled in Scotland and then emigrated to the USA before returning to Poland many years later.

Robert Frettlöhr did not return to his birthplace in Germany. He settled in England after the war, where he married and worked until his retirement. Both Gurbiel and Frettlöhr would probably pass their lives without knowledge of each other but for a chance event that caused their paths to cross again after 41 years.

On 18 March 1983, West German television aired a programme called 'War crimes on the basis of the archives of the *Wehrmacht* Commission for Investigations of War Crimes'. The producers of this programme informed the viewers that during the Second World War, war crimes had not only been committed by the Germans but also by the Allies, who had violated International Law. After this introduction, a certain Manfred Franz Hoflehner appeared on the screen, a former *Feldwebel* and an alleged participant in the battle of Monte Cassino. To millions of viewers, he stated that the Polish patrol that took the monastery on 18 May 1944 brutally murdered the wounded German paratroopers with machine guns and then cut their throats. The main person responsible was said to be, of course, the commanding officer, *Lieutenant* Kazimierz Gurbiel.

This slanderous accusation shook Polish public opinion, both at home and abroad, and created an international scandal. The baseless accusation against the 'Podolian Lancers' caused indignation, particularly amongst the Polish veteran organisations worldwide. Ex-soldiers and their sons protested all over the world. Protests were sent to the German embassies in London and Washington, and to the television company in Germany.

A meticulous investigation was carried out by the German publicist and historian Alexander Tiplt, proving that the Polish Lancers did not commit any crime when they occupied the monastery of Monte Cassino. However, crucial evidence was still missing: a living witness to those events!

Help came from an unexpected source. In Yorkshire in England lived an ex-soldier who took part in the battle of Monte Cassino on the German side. It was former *Gefreiter* Robert Frettlöhr from the 4th Parachute Regiment, one of the three wounded paratroopers captured by Gurbiel in the crypt of the monastery. Finding Robert Frettlöhr was a sensation. He was one of those wounded prisoners who allegedly had his throat cut by the Poles who entered the monastery.

On 30 March 1985, at the Polish Combatants Association in Huddersfield, England, a meeting takes place between representatives of the Carpathian Association in London and the 'resurrected' Robert Frettlöhr. Looking at a photograph taken near the monastery, Frettlöhr is sure he recognises *Lieutenant* Gurbiel, the officer who took him prisoner all those years earlier.

On 13 July 1985, Robert Frettlöhr made the following statement under oath:

I, the undersigned Robert Frettlöhr, born on 28 March 1924 in Duisberg-Meiderich, now a British citizen, having received the information about legal consequences in case my statement is faulty – due to conscious intention or due to lack of prudence – I declare that as a soldier of the 15th Company of the 4th Regiment of the 1st Division of Parachutist Riflemen, as a *Gefreiter* on the 18 May 1944, I was lying wounded in my left leg, together with other parachutists in the field hospital in the ruins of the monastery of Monte Cassino. This hospital was the only one in the precincts of the monastery. Between 9 and 10am, the Polish soldiers entered the ruins of the monastery and took over the hospital. I and two friends, one of them severely wounded, stayed for some time in the hospital. Others were conducted away under an escort. Only in the afternoon we descended with one of the Polish soldiers very slowly from the monastery mountain and [were] then taken in an ambulance with English soldiers. We were transported to the hospital for prisoners of war in Aversa near Naples. We were treated well by the Polish soldiers. Food was good too. We talked a lot. In addition I state that none of us was shot nor lost his life by having his throat cut.

On 19 August 1985, Kazimierz and Frettlöhr finally met for the first time since the events of 1944. They met at the airport in Frankfurt am Main whilst Kazimierz was on a stopover from Washington to Poland. They promised to meet each other again at Monte Cassino for the 45th anniversary of the battle.

Frankfurt airport 1985, the first meeting since 1944 of Bob and Kazimierz. They met for a few short hours, and both men were clearly moved by the meeting. (Sue Doubell)

Before the meeting, there was an exchange of letters between England and Poland, which resulted in a permanent friendship between the two former soldiers, enemies in a previous time. Bob wrote:

Dear Kazimierz, during sleepless nights my thoughts often turn to Monte Cassino. It is sufficient just to close my eyes to see you and your people entering the crypt where I lay wounded. I remember every word spoken to me at that time. Our meeting in Frankfurt after 41 years seems to be a dream ... I wanted then to tell you so much and two hours was not long enough ... I am counting the days to our next meeting at Monte Cassino. We took part in the greatest battles of the last war in which many young Germans and Poles lost their lives and we survived. Why this senseless war? My heart aches when I think of those boys killed there at Monte Cassino. In the cause of what? The Generals, far from the battlefield, were giving their orders and we had to obey and die ... Let it never be again that Germans and Poles shoot at each other.

Gurbiel replied:

Dear Robert, I thank you from my heart for your defence of the honour and dignity of the soldiers from my patrol, unjustifiably accused of committing a multiple murder. You know best how it was on the 18 May 1944 when we met for the first time. Myself, although I ended the war mutilated, I do not feel hatred towards the Germans. This feeling is foreign to me because it is impossible to build the future on hate. Therefore I propose to you a soldierly friendship, whose foundation will be deeper than the foundations of the monastery at Monte Cassino. They will be deeper, because they are in the heart of man. When we meet again on the Monastery Mountain we will manifest before the whole world that our nations will never again stand against each other with weapons.

On 18 May 1989, at the left entrance to the Monte Cassino Basilica, a not too young gentleman with dark spectacles and a large moustache was standing. Resting on a walking stick, he was attentively observing the entrance as if he was waiting for someone. Impatient, he leaned on a railing nearby and listened to the sermon. After the holy mass, when people were leaving, someone suddenly shouted: "Gurbiel!" "Who are you?" asked the gentleman, looking around. "It's me, Frettlöhr!" They fell into each other's arms. After a brief conversation, they went down into the crypt of St Benedict, where they had met 45 years ago at the same hour in exactly the same place: the prisoner of war with somebody who had the power to decide his fate. On 18 May 1944, this place was a heap of rubble, with corpses and a smell of decay. A 20-year-old paratrooper, Robert Frettlöhr, was lying wounded, left to the mercy of a Polish officer, six years his senior, Kazimierz Gurbiel, who was taking him prisoner. Today, in a beautifully restored crypt, two elderly men were meeting, both with a cruel load of wartime experiences. Then they were enemies in the heat of the battle. Now they were friends. A German and a Pole. Kazimierz Gurbiel said to Frettlöhr: "You were lying in this place here and I took you prisoner!" Frettlöhr had tears in his eyes, which was understandable. They left the crypt together. In the meantime, in the monastery courtyard appeared a delegation of German paratrooper veterans, who 45 years earlier defended fiercely against the Poles' attempt to access the holy mountain. Robert Frettlöhr introduced his comrades to *Lieutenant* Gurbiel. The Germans then proceeded to the Polish cemetery to lay a

German graves at Monte Cassino photographed during a visit in 1986. (Sue Doubell)

wreath. The Poles did the same at the German cemetery. This second meeting after 45 years on the Monte Cassino mountain, of former *Gefreiter* Frettlöhr and *Lieutenant* Gurbiel, was a symbolic act of reconciliation of the Polish and German soldiers. Robert Frettlöhr said: "Many German soldiers were sucked into this monstrous war machine against their will."

The day of 18 May 1989 passed quickly, as if a moment. After the official ceremonies and many social meetings, both Gurbiel and Frettlöhr cordially took leave of each other but decided to meet again at Monte Cassino on the 50th anniversary of the battle. Alas, *Lieutenant* Gurbiel passed away on 27 January 1992. He was buried on 30 January in Przemyśl, Poland. There were no delegations, no orchestra and no farewell salvo. Such was the departure of the commanding officer whose Lancers were the first to enter Monte Cassino 50 years earlier.

(Bob Frettlöhr passed away on 4 January 2014, aged 89.)

Remembrance Sunday in 2010 in Mirfield, West Yorkshire. Bob is assisted by a British Parachute Regiment veteran and a *Fallschirmjäger* veteran after laying a wreath for fallen comrades. (Sue Doubell)

Elvington in Yorkshire, 2000. Bob and a comrade speak to men of a *Fallschirmjäger* living history group. (Sue Doubell)

15

Rudolf Müller

Two winters in Russia

Rudolf Müller was born in Würzburg, Germany, on 24 September 1923. At the end of 1940, aged 17, he joined the Wehrmacht *and recieved his* Fallschirmjäger *training in Stendal and Wittstock. Rudolf Müller participated in the military campaigns in Greece, Crete, Russia (Mius, Volkhov, Zhitomir and Kirovgrad), Italy and France (Brest), where he was captured by US forces on 6 September 1944. After several wounds and four years of captivity in the USA and England, he returned to his homeland in 1948 at the age of 25. There he married and began working as a police officer in Wildflecken and Oschenfurt, and retired as an inspector.*

In the post-war years, Rudolf Müller set out to visit all of the areas where he had served during the war. In his free time he devoted himself to several volunteer activities such as the missing search service, VDK and the Bund Deutscher Fallschirmjäger. *On trips to Russia and the Ukraine, and with the co-operation of local nationals, he tracked down war cemeteries, was committed to the search for war graves and instrumental in ensuring that fallen comrades were reburied. For his commitment he was awarded the Federal Cross of Merit in 1976 and the European Peace Cross in 1986. Herr Müller found many friends around the world, among them former opponents, many of whom attended his 90th birthday celebration in 2013. He also worked as a volunteer archivist at the LL/LTS school in Altenstadt and later the Freiburg archive. The following reports describe two harsh winters in Russia with 7. Kompanie of Fallschirmjäger Regiment 2.*

Oberjager Rudolf Müller in 1943, aged 20. (Bund Deutscher Fallschirmjäger)

Rudolf Müller in 2009, celebrating Franz Rzeha's 90th birthday. (Rudolf Müller)

Fallschirmjäger in the winter of 1941/42 on the Mius Front

In November 1941, *II/FJR2* was based in the barrack camp at Tangermünde. On 6 December we were loaded on to trains at Stendal and eight days later, on 14 December, we arrived at the Dnipropetrovsk (Dnipro) terminus. A few days later our unit was taken by train to Stalino (Donetsk) and Charzysk (Khartsyz'k), about 300km to the south-east. We mistakenly believed in a peaceful Christmas in warm quarters, but were bitterly disappointed. On the first day of the holiday (25 December), the order came to prepare for the march to the front. The men of 4. *Zug*, *7/FJR2* recieved sledges because the heavy equipment (*sMG* and mortars) had to be transported in addition to the necessary ammunition, explosives etc. In the dark early hours of 26 December, we began a march of about 40km to our goal, Stoschkwo. In temperatures of minus 30 degrees, in snow drifts with an icy east wind and wearing our normal cloth uniforms, the men dragged themselves through the deep snow. More and more equipment had to be taken from the sledges and carried because progress in the knee-deep snow was otherwise impossible. Superfluous things were discarded, and at each short break my comrades lay down in the snow to rest. Getting up and marching along became more and more difficult. Comrades would often reach into the snow and used it as refreshment. The *Kompaniechef*, Horst Zimmermann and, *Zugführer* Franz Hetzel were constantly in the column to prevent the men from eating the snow and lying down. The slogan "only a few more kilometres" spurred me on again and again to the last of my strength.

By dark we reached a horse stable and desperately wanted to rest. After a short time we were expelled from our shelter by Russian fighter planes. By using some cord, a connection was made to the man in front (from waist belt to waist belt) to ensure that no-one was lost in the freezing snow. Shouting contact to the *Jägerzug 1–3* was lost and our *4. Zug* became separated in the snowdrift. Our *sMG Gruppe* with the comrades Willi Hermann, Franz Riedel, Rudolf Müller, Adolf Zimmermann, Willi Grosch, Heinz Strobel, Peter Winters, Heinz Potschun and Rudolf Walter could not follow with the heavy equipment. We had a lot of trouble staying together at night in the deep snow. In this condition we were challenged in the dark by an infantry unit, and were lucky to be picked up without knowing the password.

On 27 and 28 December, our *sMG Gruppe* participated in two attacks and we supported the Infantry *Kompanie* with effective fire. On the afternoon of 28 December this unit linked up with a *Fallschirmjäger* unit and released us to them. An Infantry officer gave us a written statement concerning our combat mission actions. Towards evening and completely exhausted, we reached a single-track railway line, which led to Nikitino further to the north. We ran in the snow across the railway embankment until we came to a forest, in front of which was a Kolchose [farm] where we met comrades from the *Fallschirm-MG-Bataillon*. We were able to rest in the straw of a stable building whilst an *MG Bataillon* officer notified our *Kompanie* by radio. It was as though we were cursed, because we were not left alone. That night the Russians attacked the farm, and we defended one side of the fenced yard with all our weapons. Our comrades of the *MG Bataillon* were very appreciative of the reinforcement. After the failed attack, we received a good meal and the news that our *7. Kompanie* was in Petropawlowka.

At daybreak on 29 December, we marched with an escort in the shape of 15 captured Red Army soldiers whom we had to deliver to Petropawlowka. The snowstorm had subsided and for the first time we could see the big wide snowy expanse. On the way across country we came to a homestead which housed a dressing station. A large number of fallen *Fallschirmjäger* and Red Army soldiers were lined up outside. The *Fallschirmjäger* doctor gave us some lightly wounded Russians, which increased our marching formation. We were wearing snow shirts for camouflage in the white environment, but our prisoners were wearing their brown jackets. Our motley crew did not remain hidden on the snowy surface from Russian fighter planes. With bombs and guns, they tried to destroy us regardless of the presence of their recognisable comrades. Three Russians were badly wounded, one of whom died.

Around lunchtime on 29 December we arrived in Petropawlowka, where we were greeted with a warm welcome by our comrades of *7/FJR2*. The first thing we recieved from the Italian '*Bersaglieri*' Infantry, who were also in the village, was a hot meal. We also learned that our *Kompanie* was involved in battles during our absence and had suffered their first losses. Our comrades led us to two stable buildings and showed us dead Italian soldiers lying there on the floor. I was shocked to see the murdered and mutilated men. During a Russian attack a few days before, the Italian units had vacated Petropawlowka and left behind over 150 comrades in the large dressing station collection point. On 27 and 28 December, German *Fallschirmjäger* attacked the village and found the dead. The wounded had all been murdered with headshots. In the post-war years I recieved photos of the morgues and the cemetery there from several comrades. I sent copies of the photos to the Italian burial service in Rome, the *VDK* in Kassel, the *Fallschirmjäger* archives in Altenstadt and the *Bundesarchive* in Freiburg.

Our *Gruppe* did not receive a well-deserved rest in Petropawlowka, and on the night of 30 December were ready to move out again. We were loaded onto trucks heading towards the railway embankment when one of the vehicles drove over a mine, leaving us to the deep snow again. We moved into a *Kolchose* but were immediately thrown out by heavy Russian artillery and mortar fire. After moving to a new position in the evening, I discovered that we were lying in front of the farmstead that we had defended during the night of 29 December with the comrades of the *MG Bataillon*. A *Jägerzug* from our *Kompanie* had replaced the *MG Bataillon*, and we moved in with the *sMG* on a hill behind the homestead. From this position we could clearly see the Russian trenches and could deliver fire over the heads of our colleagues in the *Kolchose*.

On 31 December, the first big Russian attack on the homestead took place. The Soviet soldiers came down the slope in several waves, running against the *Kolchose*. The combined fire of all weapons from the *Jägerzug*, our *sMG Gruppe*, mortar fire, as well as the strong fire from *Fallschirm-Artillerie*, resulted in heavy losses to the attackers. Three comrades of one *Zug* and a *Sani* were killed, and several men were wounded. These fallen soldiers and the 15 comrades of *7. Kompanie*, who had fallen in the previous days, lay frozen for days on the railway embankment because they could not be buried in the rock-hard frozen snow-covered ground. Many days later the fallen were brought back with sleds, so only the dead Red Army soldiers were still lying on the ground. Temporary snowfall produced a white sheet over the dead, and only the limbs protruding from the snow gave an indication that the dead were present.

Our *sMG Gruppe* moved into a shot-to-pieces hut about 200m behind the previous position. A piece of wall was missing on the enemy side, so we used an old door and some wooden boards as a windbreak. On the floor in the hut we had an open fire, which was vital. In the period from 31 December 1941 to 6 January 1942, we had greater than minus 40 degrees of cold in this position. An icy wind blew over the wide, flat snowfields and the occasional blizzard forced the guard to stand in the cover hole. It was a time of suffering. The *sMG* was covered with a tarpaulin. The men of the *Gruppe* had only one fur coat and a pair of fur overboots, which were used by the guard at the *sMG* and handed over when he was relieved. In this Siberian cold the guards were replaced every hour, and for a long time none of the men could stand it in the position. Everyone had to take care of each other, because an alleged feeling of warmth was the first sign of frostbite. When one comrade of the *Jägerzug* returned early from an overnight watch at a *Horchposten*, his comrades had to take off his boots. The socks were stuck in the boots and the toes lacked flesh; only sharp bones were visible. He and other comrades had to have their limbs amputated at the field hospital.

Where were our winter clothes? The frost protection cream that we recieved did not protect us from the Russian winter. The watch-free comrades were able to warm up a bit by the open fire in the hut. That too took skill. Firstly, the front and then the back of the body was warmed up. You turned like a pancake from one side to the other. Those who fell asleep by the fire usually woke up to the stench of their burned boots or the warming feet, which could be seen through a hole in the leather. The burned boots were repaired with pieces of old car tyres and the scorched *springerhosen* with string and safety pins stapled together. The coats were greasy, torn and burned. Not to mention the dirt and lice. The Army bread came to the front frozen – frozen solid – and had to be cut into pieces with a meat cleaver. Each piece of bread was placed on a knife and held over the fire until it was black and edible. The bread was also softened when dipped into the heated 'iced coffee' that was delivered to us. How beautiful did a piece of meat sausage look when the ice still glittered on it? Nowadays everyone would get sick if they recieved such food!

Leutnant Werner Dygutsch, *Zugführer* in *7. Kompanie*, was wounded by shrapnel on New Year's Eve in front of our *sMG* position on a railway embankment. Three days later it was another *Fallschirmjäger* officer who was wounded in the same place. Our *sMG* was repositioned on a hill (a snow-covered coal dump) and thus had a good field of fire, but was also visible to the Russians. From the right, a *Fallschirmjäger* came to our position in the morning. I said: "Well buddy, who are you looking for?" He introduced himself as *Oberleutnant* von Pretzmann and said that he was the *Kompaniechef* of *12/FJR2*, the unit in the neighbouring position of the *MG Bataillon* and that he wanted to take a look at his left-flank neighbour. I apologised for calling him 'buddy' because I did not recognise him as an officer as he wore a snow shirt over his uniform, as each of us did. He showed great joy when he finally recognised me. As a *Leutnant* he was, in December 1940 and from February to April 1941, my *Zugführer* in *4/Fallschirm Ersatz Bataillon* in Stendal at the <u>Kaserne</u> (barracks) 'Albrecht der Bär'. My comrade Franz Riedel, whom I had relieved at the *sMG*, remained briefly in the position and asked *Oberleutnant* von Pretzmann to take cover behind the hill as our position was visible to the Russians. He remained standing because he intended to return to his *Kompanie*. It took less than two minutes before the first Russian greetings arrived, and a massive mortar attack on our *sMG* position began. Franz Riedel and I immediately took cover, and I was surprised that the *Oberleutnant* did not jump into our foxhole. Between the impacts I lifted my head and saw the officer lying in front of the hill on the railway embankment. Franz Riedel and I jumped from our cover to Pretzmann and saw that he had been wounded by shrapnel in his neck. The blood flowed intermittently from the wound, on which I pressed a bandage pack. The mortar fire continued, and I lay with the wounded man without cover on the snowy surface. With each impact I squeezed deeper into the snow, all the while squeezing the officer's neck wound. Only when I heard a breath rattle did I realise that he was suffocating due to the excessive pressure. In the meantime, Franz Riedel ran to the nearby *Kompanie* of the *MG Bataillon* for help. The *Fallschirmjäger* came and fetched the wounded *Kompaniechef*. After the war, I learned from *Leutnant* Dygutsch that he had travelled with Pretzmann to a military hospital in East Prussia, and he had survived his severe neck wound.

At the end of March 1942, *FJR2* was removed from the Mius Front and transported home, but we found ourselves travelling north by rail to the Volkhov Front, where we were unloaded on 1 April 1942.[1] The battle raged in Volkhov until 21 June, when the remnants of *FJR2* were almost destroyed.

Epilogue

The combat strength of *FJR2* on 1 January 1942 was 2,797, and on 21 June was only 238 men (15 officers, 223 NCOs and men). On 6 December 1941, *7. Kompanie* moved to Russia with a military strength of 220 men. In operations on the Mius and Volkhov Fronts, the *Kompanie* had the

---

1   Their destination was west of Lipovik.

following losses: 61 killed, 110 wounded and 31 cases of frostbite and disease. Total losses were 202 men. On 11 July 1942, in Diepholz, only one officer, three NCOs and 14 men of *7/FJR2* returned to the garrison.

Fallschirmjäger in the winter of 1943/44 near Kirovograd

On 10 November 1943, our transport train rolled from Italy to Russia via Nuremberg. In Nuremburg our tropical clothing was exchanged for winter uniforms, so it was clear to us where the journey was going. After about 10 days in freight cars, *7/FJR2* was unloaded in the Zhitomir area and moved to a forest area near Radomsyl to the north-east. The *Kompanie* was involved in fighting off Russian counter-attacks there in the mission area of *FJD2* until 9 December. The division was withdrawn from the front line during the night of 9/10 December with orders to move to Kirovgrad.

Building a bunker in a forest near Radomsyl–Zhitomir, 3–5 December 1943. (Rudolf Müller)

Bunker in the forest near Radomsyl– Zhitomir, 3–5 December 1943. (Rudolf Müller)

Bunker building in forest near Radomsyl,
3–5 December 1943 (Rudolf Müller)

Finally, new winter clothing. *FJD2* in Kirovgrad,
December 1943. (Rudolf Müller)

Operational briefing before the attack on Radomsyl-Zhitomir on 7 December 1943. On the right is
Oberstleutnant Hannes Kroh (commander *FJR2*) with *Hauptmann* Karl Tannert (back to camera, and
commander *III/FJR2*). On the left is an officer of *2.SS-Panzer-Division*. (Rudolf Müller)

On 10 December, the *Division* was airlifted to Kirovograd and employed on 15 December with *11. Panzer-Division* near Klinzy.[2]

The Russians had broken through near Kirovgrad and as was the case at Zhitomir, the *Fallschirmjäger* had to clean up the breakthrough at the front. During the battles at Zhitomir and Radomsyl, *7/FJR2* had suffered losses but in the first days of attacks at Tarrasowka and Pervomaisk from 16–20 December many comrades were killed or wounded.

7. Kompanie experienced the worst days on 21/22 December during the attacks on Novgorodka, *Rollbahn IV* and Hill 167.[3]

At dawn on 21 December, the *Kompanie*, together with other *Kompanien* from *II/FJR2*, attacked Hill 167. *Hauptmann* Siegfried Nowarra led the *Kompanie* and *Leutnant* Erich Sachse led *4. Zug*. *Feldwebel* Martin Junge led the *sMG Gruppe* with the gun leaders *Oberjäger* Walter Wilhelm and Rudolf Müller. My old friend Franz Riedel was my *Schütze 1*, Herbert Zeitler was *Schütze 2* and Josef Pfister was *Schütze 3*. With support from two *Sturmgeschütz*, the attack went well. We had reached the top of the hill, rushing forward in the deep snow as Russian tanks attacked the flank and brought our attack to a halt.

I crawled into a Russian *PAK* position whose crew had recently been destroyed by a *Sturmgeschütz* and set up the *sMG* in position there. *Feldwebel* Fritz and *Oberjäger* Heinz Strelow of *5. Kompanie* were already sitting in the hole. A Russian tank had taken notice of us and bombarded the position so badly that nobody could get in or out.

Three of us crawled back to the side of the road, shovelling the snow to one side as our comrades tried to cover us. A *Sturmgeschütz* commanded by a *Leutnant* fired at two Russian tanks at this time, and the turret of one flew up into the sky and crashed in the snow about 20m in front of us. I set up a position with my *sMG* on the road embankment and took the enemy riflemen and *PAK* guns under fire. Single attacking rifle squads in combat formation were fended off with continuous fire from the *sMG*. A shell had torn a hole in the embankment, and in this new breach stood the front support of our *Lafette*. Our belief that 'a shell does not strike in the same place twice' had disastrous results. We heard the call "*sMG* forward", and I ordered a change of position along the *Rollbahn*. Franz Riedel said he wanted to fire off the remaining cartridge belt and introduce a new belt before changing position. At the same time there was an impact and my *sMG* was back on the *Rollbahn*. We had recieved a direct hit from a *PAK*. Franz Riedel and Josef Pfister lay dead on the *Rollbahn*, and Herbert Zeitler was badly wounded. I was covered in large amounts of snow and dirt, and could smell the stench of explosives. After I helped care for Herbert Zeitler, I found myself unresponsive and staring into the snow. For how long, I don't know. Our two dead comrades were covered with their tent canvas and we carried Herbert Zeitler to a *Sturmgeschütz* that took him to the *Hauptverbandplatz*. In short leaps I rushed to the former Russian positions where comrades of *7. Kompanie* were already in cover.

We sat and lay exhausted in the holes, some of which were still filled with dead Russian soldiers, the so called 'Stalin pupils'. We could hear the calls of the many wounded, and finding them in the haze and fog of the coming evening was often difficult. We also carried the dead down to a place where they could be found in the dark. The bodies of our *Kompaniechef* Siegfried Nowarra,

---

2   A large part of *FJD2* were airlifted from Zhitomir in JU-52 transport aircraft over the snowy Ukrainian countryside to Kirovograd. Other parts of the division travelled by road via Vinnitsa and Uman. Trucks belonging to *11. Panzer-Division* transported the *Fallschirmjäger* from the Kirovograd airfield to the staging areas at Klinzy, Kalinovka and Kosyrewka. *FJD2* reported itself combat-ready on the morning of 16 December. See Kammann, pp.126–28.

3   Novgorodka is located 38km south-east of Kirovgrad. Hill 167 was one of the so-called Kirovograd Hills (although closer to Novgorodka). Hill 167, east of Novgorodka, was located on the northern side of the *Rollbahn* and changed hands several times during the fighting.

Head protection and felt boots have arrived. Finally, the *Knobelbecher* jackboots are exchanged for *Winterstiefel* (winter boots). *FJD2* in Kirovgrad, December 1943. (Rudolf Müller)

From 16–22 December 1943, Tarassowka, Gubowka, Rybtschina, Lebedevka, Pervomaisk and Novgorodka were taken by the *Fallschirmjäger* after heavy fighting. (Rudolf Müller)

Oberstleutnant Kroh at the mission brief on 20 December 1943 near Kirovgrad before the attack on Novgorodka. *General* Ramcke said that of all commanders who ever wore the helmet of the German parachute forces, Hans Kroh was one of the bravest and most resourceful combat leaders. (Rudolf Müller)

An *sMG* and carriage (*Lafette*) of *4.Zug* on the endless snowfields near Novgorodka in December 1943. (Rudolf Müller)

Log-lined trench near Novgorodka. (Rudolf Müller)

Hit the deck! (Rudolf Müller)

The former Russian
positions are defended
in December 1943
near Novgorodka.
(Rudolf Müller)

Kompanie Truppführer Oberjäger Heinz Bohn and a *Sani* from *7. Kompanie* were placed one on top of the other. *Hauptmann* Nowarra had been killed by a sniper's bullet; his *Truppführer Oberjäger* Bohn jumped to help him and was also fatally struck. The accompanying *Sanitäter* was killed by a shell detonation. The order came at night for the *Kompanie* to withdraw from the position and dig in at the rear. I spent the rest of the night in a snow hole with my comrade *Oberjäger* Helmut Hartmann. The next morning, 22 December, *II/FJR7* and the rest of *7. Kompanie* had to once again attack Hill 167 because the Russians had reoccupied it during the night. To assist with the attack in our sector there were two Panther tanks. I recieved a light machine gun and had only three men in the *Gruppe*. Halfway to the *Rollbahn*, the tanks were left behind as the *PAK* bombardment was too intense. We now had to storm the Russian positions again without *Panzer* support. Death screams and the call for a '*Sani*' echoed across the snowy landscape. The Russian defensive fire from artillery, *PAK* guns, mortars and *MGs* was so strong that only a few comrades reached the enemy trenches. With a last "Hurrah" we jumped into the Russian positions and threw out the enemy. I saw my comrades Hermann Beutinger, Rudolf Carlsson, Max Lang, Georg Baumert, Anton Milzewski, Gottfried Kunze and others. We immediately set ourselves up for defence because the Russians were always trying to retake their positions. *Oberjäger* Hunze was already safe, but he wanted to jump to another comrade in his cover hole. He recieved a stomach shot from an enemy sniper and died a short time later. Our *Zugführer Leutnant* Sachse was severely wounded by a head shot.[4] The *Radfahrzug* under *Oberfeldwebel* Zausch advanced the attack even further with another "Hurrah", all the while under fire from the Russians.

Late into the night on 22 December we looked for our dead and wounded. An armoured personnel carrier helped us transport the casualties. Since we could not find everyone at night, squads were sent out on the morning of 23 December who found more dead and wounded in snow holes and hollows, including *Gefreiter* Günther Stärker. He was found draped over his *MG* as if he was protecting it with his body. Both forearms had been shot through, so he could not get up off the ground. In this situation a sniper shot him in the head. When we were relieved at the rear slope of Hill 167 on the night of 24 December, about 35 men of *7. Kompanie* were still alive. Exhausted and totally apathetic, we sat in the snow and could not understand how we had survived these last two days.

For the first time, warm coffee, bread and sausage were distributed to the men. Captured Russian soldiers who sat with us stared with longing eyes because they too were starving. We had enough food because it was intended for more than 100 men, so the captive Red Army soldiers recieved a hefty meal. Our padded camouflage suits were no longer white.

4   *Leutnant* Erich Sachse survived Russia but was killed near Duppach/Eifel on 3.3.45 (unit unknown).

On 21 and 22 December 1943, the Russian positions south-east of Kirovgrad were taken by *2/5/6/7/FJR2*.
(Rudolf Müller)

The road north of Novgorodka and captured Russian trenches after the attack on 22 December 1943. (Rudolf Müller)

Christmas 1943, *Fallschirmjäger* from *I/FJR6* rest in their accommodation near Kirovgrad. (Rudolf Müller)

Christmas 1943 in a trench near Novgorodka: letters and parcels have arrived. *Leutnant* Erich Lepkowski (centre) and *Oberjäger* Emil Müschenborn (right). (Rudolf Müller)

Christmas 1943: *Leutnant* Lepkowski and *Oberjäger* Müschenborn from *5/FJR2* in Novgorodka. Müschenborn was KIA near Brest on 5 September 1944. (Rudolf Müller)

They were torn and burned and smeared with dirt and blood. In the evening, the 35 comrades of *7/FJR2* were in a small Russian lodging in Nowo-Andrejewka. There was a solemn mood even though my comrade Georg Baumert and I were promoted to *Oberjäger*. Only an old Russian woman and two small children brought some joy to our small room, in which about 10 men of the *Kompanie* were housed. The assigned *Wehrmacht* alcohol was intended for a full-strength *Kompanie* as it existed before the attacks. Even the Russian grandmother and her two grandchildren recieved a share. The *Kompanie* soon had an increased strength of 45 men due to the return of some lightly wounded comrades. The remainder of the *Kompanie* defended their positions at Nowo-Andrejewka until 5 January 1944.

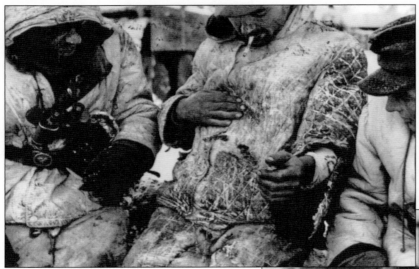

He was lucky: splinters in his left forearm and a splintered winter jacket. (Rudolf Müller)

An exhausted *Melder* from *FJD2* in the Ukraine, at new year 1944. (Rudolf Müller)

On that day the Russians broke through the front with several hundred tanks and numerous rifle brigades. The *Fallschirmjäger* of *FJD2* fended off the attacks in their sectors and cleaned up numerous enemy breakthroughs. In the battle of 5–8 January near Kirovgrad, *Sturmgeschütz Abteilung 286* destroyed 52 tanks, *Fallschirm-Panzer-Jäger-Abteilung* – with 18 guns – destroyed 34 tanks, and the *II Abteilung* from *Flak Regiment 4*, up until the loss of their last gun, destroyed 61 tanks. Thirteen enemy tanks were destroyed by the *Fallschirmjäger* units, including seven with close-range weapons. Until 11 February 1944, the positions at Novgorodka were held by *FJD2*, and by 18 February positions at Nowo-Ukrainka, south-west of Kirovgrad. From 4 March, the *Division* was involved in the retreat battles to the River Dniester. On 10 May, the last big attack at Pugoceni (Puhăceni in Moldova) took place, resulting in the capture of 3,050 Red Army soldiers and the destruction of numerous enemy artillery and *PAK* positions. After suffering heavy losses, the remnants of *FJD2* were withdrawn from Russia on 12 May and arrived in Köln-Wahn (Cologne) on 1 June 1944.

Epilogue

On 10 November 1943, *7/FJR2* went to Russia with 210 men. In the six months of operations, 50 comrades were killed, eight were missing and 129 were wounded. Total losses were 187 comrades. Of the comrades from *7. Kompanie* who were previously transferred to *11. Kompanie*, 25 were killed, two were missing and 10 wounded.

After the war during the period from 1993 to 1998, I visited several of my fallen comrades in the grounds of the former military cemeteries in the Ukraine, especially in the area around Kirovograd. I informed the *VDK* in Kassel annually about the area, condition of the ground, any Ukrainian eyewitnesses and also submitted corresponding sketches and photographs. These documents were for the grave orders of the *VDK*, valuable tools for the reburial of the dead within collective cemeteries. Our fallen comrades in the areas of operations around Kirovgrad are currently being transferred to a new large cemetery at Krupske about 10km west of Kirovgrad. There are about 40,000 German dead who now have a proper grave and permanent rest!

(Rudolf Müller is still alive and resides in Würzburg, aged 95.)

4. Zug from *7/FJR2* training with the new 2.8cm *Panzerbüchse 41*. At the gun are, left, *Oberjäger* Gottfried Kunze, and right, *Obergefreiter* Rudolf Müller. (Rudolf Müller)

16

Volker Stutzer

Sketches of war & death is no laughing matter

Volker Stutzer was born on 9 December 1927 in Ficht, Bavaria. In 1943, at the age of 16, he volunteered for the Luftwaffe *and began his pilot training, at first in gliders. When he was called up in 1944, Volker had already passed four training camps and possessed a 1st Class pilots licence. He was destined to conduct further training on jet fighters, expecting promotion to officer after the prescribed time, but due to fuel shortages rather than a shortage of jets, he was sent to a* Fallschirmjäger *unit with hundreds of other schoolboys to become a tank hunter. After one month of training on anti-tank guns and the* Panzerfaust, *he was now about to march to the Eastern Front.*

Volker recovering at home after being wounded in Pomerania in February 1945. (Volker Stutzer)

Volker in April 2019. (Oliver Stutzer)

Volker's father had served as an Army officer during the First World War and was decorated by the Grand Duke of Sachsen-Weimar himself. Volker's elder brother, Hedio, had been a Panzer *Commander, a recipient of the Iron Cross and was killed in the massive tank battle at Kursk on 8 July 1943, aged 21.*

Volker is the only Fallschirmjäger *conscript to appear in this book, but his story is no less interesting and is worthy of inclusion. He was wounded in the fierce fighting in Pomerania towards the end of the war and was evacuated from the front line. After a short period in American captivity in Regensburg, he returned home. After the war, Volker went on to become a newspaper editor and successful author, retiring in 1990.*

Following Volker's wartime sketches is a poignant article he wrote in 1981 for which he was awarded the Theodor-Wolff-Prize, the journalist prize of German newspapers. More importantly, he received great praise for speaking the truth from families who still mourned their beloved dead.

Introduction

Germany was about to embark on the sixth year of the war against more than 100 nations, and it was very common to see schoolboys join the Army to defend their motherland. Nearly every night and even in the daylight, many Allied bombers gushed into Germany and destroyed the cities, burning people to ash and leaving behind towns in flames. The dictatorial rule became stricter and life was so different from all that we know nowadays. It was unavoidable that an upbringing under the rule of National Socialism influenced us. The tricky brain-washing did the job. The successful economic development made people tolerant for the dark side of the regime. It must have been a happy meeting when the Devils in Hell reported to His Highness, Satan, of their successful doings …

The following sketches sound implausible and fabricated; a tissue of lies. Nonetheless, they are all true and what I tell happened in that way. What I experienced was not at all strange or exceptional for young Germans. But now, casting a retrospective glance on it after half a century, it becomes something like an historical document. Let it be whatever and look back (not in anger) but in wonderment.

Going – coming!

The janitor pushed open the door of our classroom and shouted: "Stutzer to the warden!" The warden stood at the top of the broad stairs waving a piece of paper. Handing it over to me, he said: "The call up paper came for you, go and pack up your stuff!" I was aware of a mixture of feelings: pride, because now would come what I desired so much, to pilot a jet fighter; anxiety, because I did not know what my fate would be; and regret, because I would be leaving my close friends and I was not sure if I would see them again.

Having packed my belongings, I found myself wandering around the sports field behind the boarding school. I sat down on a bench under a tree and fell into deep thought. A man approached me, the lecturer of biology. He had heard about the 'call-up'. He took my hand with both his hands and said: "Boy! Oh boy, come home, come home for heaven's sake!" His eyes shimmered with tears. This man was the only lecturer who bade me farewell, but as I moved off toward the train station, four of my closest friends hurried out of the school and joined me. One of them was my best friend, still too young for the call-up paper. Nobody spoke. I wanted to say something important, like the heroes in our books, but I found my mouth dry as sand, my tongue thick and motionless and my heart unexpectedly heavy.

The train arrived and I boarded. My friends lifted up my bag, stretched out their hands and murmured "May God be with you", and I saw the same moisture in their eyes as I had seen in the lecturer's. I remember seeing the slowly vanishing friends through a veil of mist. My close friend gave me a last glance, and it was something in his eyes that felt like a sharp knife entering my heart. Going – but coming? Back? Where?

I made a short stop at home to deliver my belongings. My mother had roasted a goose as a farewell dish, but we did not enjoy this rare meal. At the moment we sat down at the dining table we heard the roaring sound of several hundred American planes, 'Flying Fortresses' on the way to their targets right above our house at high altitude. The white condensation trails behind them scribbled a bizarre picture on the blue sky. The air was filled with a trembling and rumbling noise, the china and glasses clattered in the cupboard. The gigantic planes followed their course as escort fighters danced around them, and these small planes would often drop to low altitude and attack ground targets. Therefore we carefully tried to hide ourselves under the garden trees, but we could not turn our eyes from the heaven-filling mass of enemies above.

Another going. Not much talking. My mother kissed me, my little brother asking for a picture of the plane I would pilot. My father was at home for a short holiday and he accompanied me to the train station in Passau. He gulped and cleared his throat, and then said: "My boy, you should know that in case of intimacies with a girl you must be careful …" It was the first time in my life that my father said words of this sort, and all of a sudden it filled my heart with bitter pain because I understood how much he feared for me. The second son leaving the family to join the military and face an uncertain future. I replied: "Oh no! No need to say this, I am well aware of all …", and afterwards kept my mouth shut.

The dark, moist early morning! The overcrowded station, the engines steaming and noisy, the flickering lanterns of the railway staff, the stench of sweating, dirty people, their impatience and shouting. My father bidding me farewell and what he very rarely

Portrait of a young Volker taken in 1943 after his brother Hedio had been killed in Russia. (Volker Stutzer)

Wartime Stutzer family photo from 1942. From left to right: mother Bertha, a teacher, aged 47; Dietmar, aged 9; father Paul, a *Hauptmann* of Infantry; Hedio, a *Panzer* soldier; and Volker, aged 15. (Volker Stutzer)

Arbeitsdienst from September to December 1944 in Olmütz in Czechoslovakia, where Volker undertook Infantry training. (Volker Stutzer)

Volker the recruit wearing '*Drillich*', or fatigues, in late December 1944 – January 1945. (Volker Stutzer)

had done to the kid he now did to the grown-up boy: he kissed my forehead and hurried out of the station. I fought my way to the platform and into the carriage, and had to spend more than 24 hours hearing nothing else but the 'tumptata, tumptata' of the wheels and the shrill voices of overtired and hungry people. With paining certainty I knew I was alone, not yet 17 years old and before me service in the military, which did not look so adventurous and thrilling as it had done from my cosy little room in the boarding school.

Finally I reached the air base where I expected to receive my final pilot's training. I had marched for endless hours under a cloudy and dark sky from the station to the barracks, only to hear that there was a shortage of fuel and the training would begin with theory only. Soon the dream of piloting a jet fighter ended. Plenty of jets, but still no fuel. Weeks later I found myself (together with hundreds of other youngsters) becoming a paratrooper. All the young well-trained glider pilots were transferred to the *Fallschirmtruppe*. After our basic infantry training I went with a group of 20 young men to a military training area in Hildesheim. It was here that we recieved our final training. We fired *Panzerfäuste* into old *Panzers*, studied the art of applying blasting agent to a moving *Panzer* and much more. Because the Eastern Front stood strong and the West was about to fall back, we all expected to be sent to the West. We liked that idea because we feared capture at the hands of the Red Army, but did not expect anything bad from US captivity.

The rank

In my *Zug* was a rank, not very high, a junior NCO. One day he came and collected our military passbooks. This was not unusual and nobody took much notice. When he returned and distributed the books, mine was not there. This was a catastrophe, because in a place with thousands of soldiers you cannot get anything without the passbook. I approached the rank and asked him where my book was. He did not care. In despair I walked between the barracks. I wore my blue *Luftwaffe* uniform, the other soldiers already wearing their camouflage field uniform, and officers stopped me and angrily asked why I looked different. From a barrack window came a shout. I approached the voice, which came from a Senior NCO, a man who looked old to me but certainly not over 40. Friendly and paternally, he asked me what was wrong. I explained the matter to him and he called me to his office. He opened his desk, took out a form for the military passbook, asked me for a passport photo (that I luckily had), filled out the form and stamped it, showing me the colonel's signature which was already on it. "Without a passbook you are just half a human being," he said. "You will never get your book back from that drunkard. I know him, maybe he has sold it for brandy." This wonderful man opened his cupboard and gave me one of his field jackets. The paratroopers had special jackets, something like an overcoat called a 'bonesack'. I was now complete and thanked my benefactor a thousand times before returning to my quarters.

My comrades asked me what had happened, and the story was told to them in the toilet. I did not notice, however, that somebody was in one of the cubicles. I told my comrade the story (with swear words) about the rank who had lost my passbook or sold it for brandy. We finished in the toilet and left, but in the cubicle was the rank sitting and waiting to complete his ablution. He had heard it all!

Days passed and I had already forgotten about the episode. Very shortly after, my unit recieved the order to select 100 men for a new *Kompanie*, which was to be sent to the Eastern Front as a special tank destroyer brigade. It was named a 'fire squad' and the ranks said that its members would be sent towards the attacking Russian tanks and forced to jump on them. It would basically be a suicide squad!

The following day, the whole unit was ordered to report and formed a huge square. In the middle was the *Oberst* and his staff. The officer said something about "service for *Führer* and *Fatherland*" and informed us that 100 comrades had been selected for the new *Kompanie* and would march off to the Eastern Front this very evening. The remaining men would stay behind and possibly be sent to the Western Front. Deadly silence! The *Oberst* handed over a list to a *Feldwebel* and told him to read aloud the names. Remembering the scene, I still see the dark and silent block of so many soldiers, breathing in expectation of something bad. The *Feldwebel* shouted: "I will read the names and you will report to me". He read the first name on the long list: "*Jäger* Stutzer!" I went forward and for a short while stood alone in the middle of the unit. I knew this was the work of the rank who had snatched my passbook. It was his revenge. Comrades had told me that he sat in the cubicle and listened to my story. I was about to leave for the East to join a suicide squad. The others would stay here or afterwards be sure not to fall into the hands of the Red Army.

Other names followed, and one man after another stood beside me.

My comrades at the training ground (among them the nice rank) enjoyed only a few days of satisfaction before they were suddenly moved westward. They ended their lives in the notorious Hürtgenwald forest, one of the most deadly places in the history of the Second World War. For many years the bodies of dead German *Fallschirmjäger* and US soldiers lay there unburied because nobody dared go inside the forest, which was filled with mines and all sorts of devil's inventions.

To the Oder River

We left Hildesheim in late January 1945 and were transported in cattle wagons from western Germany to the East, and disembarked in a small, ice-cold Pomeranian village several days later at the beginning of February, where we recieved rifles and ammunition. The German civilians had already packed their belongings and began their journey westward, with nothing ahead of them but uncertainty and wretchedness. We marched on eastward, where behind the horizon the front flickered and roared. For three days we stumbled forward, overburdened with luggage, arms and ammunition. I became exhausted and the faces of my comrades were as grey as ash. The load on my shoulders nearly compressed me and I lost the ability to think clearly.

The daylight waned and we looked for a place to spend the night. The horizon was red with flickering flames and the thunder of guns could be felt in the ears. We tried our very best with the spades we carried with us. I dug and sweated like the damned soul in purgatory! Occasionally a soldier would peep out of his hole, and the red and yellow flames from the near front reflected on his white face and made his eyes glitter.

It was during this time that I saw our *Bataillonskommandeur* for the first and only time. His name was *Hauptmann* Hans von Majer.[1] He arrived in an American jeep, which was a wonder for us to look at! A veteran *Fallschirmjäger* asked him when we would receive more assault rifles, ammo and something warm to eat. The officer looked grave and started to say something, but stopped halfway. I remember an unpleasant feeling in my stomach. I also remember sitting near an experienced *Feldwebel* whose chest was covered in combat decorations, a veteran of many campaigns. Sweat ran from his ashen face: fear of the unknown, or did he know what lay ahead through previous experience?

The next day we marched again and came to a thick forest. Maybe the officers knew where we were and what we were about to do, but they did not tell us. After four more days of marching we reached the front line. It was not like a front in the war books. No trenches, no fortifications, no positions of other troops. A huge army of Soviet power poured inside our country, and here and there German soldiers tried to stop them. We met a *Zug* of *Panzer* soldiers equipped with US Sherman tanks, taken from the Western Front and carried east to reinforce the defences. They had stolen a swine and it was killed with a bullet, and we soon recieved our first warm meal in a long time.

A sketch of Volker drawn by a talented comrade on 6 February 1945 before the battle for Groß Schönfeld. The tension is clearly etched on Volker's face. The picture was found years later by chance amongst lost luggage. (Volker Stutzer)

---

1 Hans von Majer joined the *Fallschirmtruppe* in 1943, having been a *Stuka* pilot. In October 1944 he was a *Leutnant* and a *Kompanieführer* in 2/FJR16 Ost, and in February/March 1945 a *Hauptmann* and *Bataillonskommandeur* in FJR27. Volker believed he was killed in Pomerania, but he survived the war and died on 18 September 1983.

Another night followed and we marched to the end of a forest, and when the morning came, I found myself behind a tree looking out over a wide field, with here and there some snow, the rest brown from the ploughed farmland. The field rose toward the horizon and a village called Groß Schönfeld.[2] It was 17 February 1945. An officer ordered us to create a line, and carefully we moved forward inside the forest under the shelter of the trees. The command was given to fix bayonets and the clicking noise could be heard along the whole edge of the forest. Everything happened so quickly. After a sharp command, the *Zug* jumped forward with a "Hurrah!" and hurried over the frozen field, I with them, my rifle at hand (the heavy luggage was left under a tree). A Russian soldier in a truck was about to cross our path, some of the men fired and the Ivan jumped out, leaving the truck to burn. It was 0700 hours, not completely bright, a bit dim and misty. The Russians began to cry out loud: "*Fallschirmjäger, Fallschirmjäger!*" We had a very fierce reputation! Not all of the Russians fled. We saw them like brown ants running out of the village, pursued by some ranks, firing and shouting at them. Others stood their ground and fired their weapons. I heard the bullets passing me; it was like a soft chirping, the sound of death. I was deadly afraid, 17 years old and now about to die at any moment. Nothing at all prepared me for this. No training, no book, no sentiment, no feeling for the Fatherland. It was sheer horror!

My *Leutnant* fell next to me. I had been his batman. He liked me and I liked and adored him. All of a sudden he was at my feet, sprinkling me with his blood. His head had been torn off by a shell and the body rolled over in the snow, colouring it red. I shrieked and it felt as though an ice-cold hand was clutching my heart. The *Oberfeldwebel* shouted "Forward! Forward" and we hurried to the village. To the left of us, half a mile away, my old *Zug* was involved in close combat with Russian tanks. Nearly all of my comrades from the Oschatz flying school and many others died there on the icy fields.[3] I succeeded in reaching the village, and now began what all soldiers fear: close combat, fighting from house to house, from one side of the road to the other. Tanks arrived, roaring and clanking, and we tried to fire our *Panzerfäuste* at them. Men fell and turned upside down in their blood, pitifully crying for their mothers. Russians hurried out of the burning barns, their bodies in flames, and they roared like devils.

Two days before we reached the forest and formed up to attack, a group of German refugees reached the village, unaware that Russian troops were already there. As I said before, there was no proper front line, just a mixture of advancing or retreating units and vehicles. The Russians took the shrieking and praying women, children and old men, raped and killed and drove the survivors into the cellars of the farmhouses. When we reached the first house we heard the refugees' desperate cries. The ranks shouted: "Forward! Forward, get them out for heaven's sake and take them behind our lines!"

A man-to-man close-range fight began, and it was sheer hell. Between the jumping and falling soldiers – the Russians in brown, the German paratroopers in their characteristic camouflage battle dress – there were civilians running here and there and children crying like tortured animals.

I do not completely remember all that happened during the fight in the village, which took more than two days and nights. Russian tanks arrived and rattled through the burning houses, and we tried to destroy them. Russian infantry were so close that we could see the red stars on their helmets. We attacked, the enemy shrunk back; they attacked and we tried to escape. Corpses piled up in the street and in the fields I saw and heard men shouting: "Help, help, *Sanitäter!*" Nobody came to their rescue, as the *Sani* was the preferred aim for the Russians and the first to fall, shot through the big Red Cross on their chest and back. The wailing waned and finally fell silent. Still

---

2   13km east of the Oder River in the district of Greifenhagen, and now called Żarzyin in Poland.
3   By a stroke of fate, Volker's name was mysteriously removed from his *Zug* Stamrolle and entered into another, and despite trying to have it corrected before the battle he fought with the new *Zug*.

in my mind is the horror I felt when I jumped into a barn to find a better firing position for the *Panzerfaust* I was carrying. I stumbled over something under the straw. I scraped the straw with my foot and uncovered the yellow faces of dead soldiers with wide open, dreadful turned eyes. This really shook me up; what I saw was burned into my mind and is still there.

A German aircraft turned up to help us, but right above me two Russian planes attacked it and he, a JU-87 *Stuka*, lightened himself for his escape and dropped the single bomb from under its fuselage. I observed the round black thing as it tumbled down right to the place where I was positioned. I jumped like a mad man behind a row of field stones, heaped up by the farmer in order to clear his fields. The bomb exploded not more than 3ft from me on the other side of the row and I was covered in a shower of stones. One gave a 'ploomp' on my helmet, and for a second I did not know where I was and I could not hear.

The Russians attacked again with their tanks. An NCO jumped into a shell crater and I followed him, waiting for the tanks to come close enough to fire a *Panzerfaust* at them. Suddenly I heard a voice: "Get out, get out!" It was not the NCO, and nobody else was close. At the same time I sensed something strange under my heart like a hot stone moving up and down. It all happened in a split second as I jumped out of the shell crater.

Hedio, Volker's much-loved older brother, who was killed at the battle of Kursk on 8 July 1943, aged 21. He is buried at the Kursk-Besedino cemetery in Russia. On several occasions during his time at the front, Volker believed he was being watched over by a guardian angel who guided him to safety, avoiding death and serious injury. This was the last photo of Hedio, taken on 6 July 1943, two days before he was killed. (Volker Stutzer)

The NCO shouted "Are you mad, man?" and he tried to get a grip on my battle dress, but slipped. I stumbled out, made it a few metres away and fell to the ground. In that moment a tank shell exploded in the crater and the NCO came out in pieces.

I shrieked in terror and something drove me to a seed drill, left in situ by the farmer. Suddenly another shell exploded behind the steel tank of the seed drill, which absorbed the metal splinters, apart from two that hit me in the shoulder and upper arm, the latter splinter stopped by the rifle butt before it could rip into my body. The rifle fell. I vividly remember the feeling: heat and weakness, but no pain. I saw dead and dying men at my feet and heard the rough voices of Russian soldiers on the other side of the barn. I said to myself: "Oh my God! I will be captured by the Russians, no, no!" I remembered an NCO advising us greenhorns that if we could move our legs we should speed down the fields to the forest, then go on and follow the cart track to the dressing station in Heinrichsdorf. I jumped on and over the corpses and ran, looking over my shoulder for any Russians following me. A comrade wearing our characteristic camouflaged jump suit ran at high speed behind me and was shot, somersaulted and rolled from one side to another. I continued to run for my life, 10 steps, falling and up again. A dead body forced me to stop. I crawled over it. It was a comrade, dead, face down in the mud, his rifle lying next to him. At the opposite side of the field stood a Russian tank, a Josef Stalin 2, the biggest and strongest tank with a 122mm gun for destroying the German Tiger. *MG* fire came from the tank, and its commander stood carelessly in the turret looking around with field glasses. He had seen me moving and I had seen him.

I hope I make it clear in this text that I found myself confronted with a mixture of emotions and more brutal impressions than I could digest. Now on this frozen field in Pomerania, I felt the wish to kill. Obviously hate had me in its grip and the soul gave in. I took the rifle and checked it was loaded: it was. The bolt worked. I estimated the range at 300m. I fixed the sight and avoided any movement. I saw the turret pointing in another direction, the tank man still standing carelessly in the turret. I used the dead body as a rifle rest; I did not care for my wounded arm. I found the enemy in my sight and aimed at his face, hoping to at least hit him in the chest. My index finger was on the trigger but not yet bent. I breathed deep, according to what we had learned. While this happened, my mental order was changed. I said to myself: "You are about to kill someone, how will you live with that? Let him survive! It might be his fate." It is easier to trigger an untargeted salvo as to kill an *individuum*,

In 1992, Volker visited the town of Groß Schönfeld. A local man showed him a paratrooper helmet with part of a skull inside, which was found close to the same location where the seed drill had been in 1945.
(Volker Stutzer)

wide and brassy, squatting in the open turret of a tank. My soul said "no"!

Very carefully, I put the rifle aside and started again the jumping, running and falling on the way to the forest. Gunfire followed my progress. How could the tank commander know that his life had been in my hands? It took several hours to cross the field, crawling like a snake as the Russians fired from tanks and guns at the few survivors trying to escape. I passed the place where my former *Zugkameraden* had sacrificed themselves to destroy the Russian tanks. They were all dead, their wide open eyes staring in sheer terror and desperation. As I finally reached the first trees of the forest late in the afternoon, I was met by two officers and an NCO who had observed my approach from behind a pile of firewood.[4] The first officer shouted: "Fuck off! You'll draw fire on us!" The NCO took me aside under the trees and said: "Oh my god boy, what have they done to you?" He dressed my wound using his own bandage and told me to follow the track to the dressing station in Heinrichsdorf.[5]

Many years later through a third party, a group of young Polish historians used my story to locate and find the forest. After a detailed search they found the bones of three soldiers. With good

---

4   Volker returned to this place after the decline of Communism with a lifelong burning desire to walk there upright, whereas he had once crawled for his life back in February 1945.
5   4km north of Groß Schönfeld, and now called Babinek in Poland.

luck, the *Erkennungsmarke* of an officer was still there. Obviously the three men mentioned above did not leave this spot by the tree line and must have been killed by Russian tank fire or rockets. The bodies lay there for years. Nobody had disturbed the blackberry tendrils or brushwood that covered their remains.

Rain of flowers

I walked alone through the forest to Heinrichsdorf. The dressing station was located in a school and I remember seeing a Soviet tank soldier (he painfully reminded me of my brother) who crouched in a corner of the field hospital covering his partly burnt and bloodied face with his hands, whining and pleading for his life. A German medic knelt down to him, talking in a soft and reassuring voice, using what Russian he knew to convince the poor lad that nobody was about to slaughter him. He recieved the same treatment as we Germans, and after a while it came to light that the communist *Kommissars* had told the Russian soldiers that they would be tortured and killed, and afterwards the Nazi soldiers would make mince-meat of them.

I slept in the gym hall and was abruptly awoken by news that the Russians had broken through towards Heinrichsdorf. The medical staff were to be evacuated immediately. A young doctor approached me and gave me his place on one of the trucks. He stayed behind in order to save me. We finally drove away from hell, driving for hours until we crossed the Oder at Greifenhagen. Our destination was Wartin, 30km further west, far from the front, in western Pomerania, where I recieved medical treatment and a bed.

A few days later one of the doctors arranged for a farmer to take me away on a horse and cart. During this journey we came across a Red Cross train, which had stopped in a wide open space and was full of wounded soldiers from the Oder Front. I was allowed to board what turned out to be one of the last hospital trains out of Pomerania.

The train journey took one week until we came to a stop near Nuremburg, where I received further medical treatment.

Whilst in Nuremberg I had to report to a medical officer. He handed me the papers of four amputated comrades and asked me if I was strong enough to escort them to a hospital in Passau. I was not his first choice for the job. Another soldier, whom I did not know, remembered a comrade from Passau being in the hospital and he gave up this mission so that I could return home. On a wet and cold day in March 1945, I accompanied the four soldiers on a train back home.

We did not fear the arrival of US troops. We expected normal soldierly treatment, so as the war came to an end the wounded in the Passau army hospitals looked ahead with confidence. The military hospital in Passau was full and the walking wounded were sent by train to Wegsheid, close to my home. My father arranged for me to recuperate

Volker's father had served as a young *Leutnant* in the army of the Grand Duchy of Sachsen-Weimar, and in April 1914 he joined the 94th Infantry Regiment and fought at Arras, the Somme and Verdun. (Volker Stutzer)

at home. I had survived, but there was bad news. Treacherous Germans offered to show the Americans the houses where soldiers were living, and this resulted in torched houses, beatings and many deaths.

My father walked to Untergriesbach and asked to speak to a US officer and explain my existence at home. All his life my father had been an honest man and very naive in thinking that others were the same. He spoke *Captain* to *Captain* and was informed that: "Your son may come and report to me. I shall arrange for his treatment in an army hospital and we shall do our very best for him!"

My father returned with the message, and because my mother was even more naive she told me to take nothing with me. "You will get everything you need in the US hospital!" she said.

Therefore I bid farewell to my family and began the walk to Untergriesbach. A US truck passed me, then stopped and all the soldiers pointed their rifles at me, a young, unarmed and wounded boy. "I surrender!" I shouted. I was one man and not a *Regiment*, so I was allowed to continue my journey. A sentry stopped me on the road and I began to explain the matter about the officer promising to take me to hospital, when the soldier struck me in the face and shouted: "Hitler has promised much as well. Shut up, damned bloody Nazi bastard!"

Other soldiers came and pushed me up against a wall and one pushed his sub-machine gun into my stomach. In vain I asked for the officer who had talked to my father. They pushed me into a jeep and we headed east. I passed my home and waved, but nobody saw me, passed through the smoking ruins of Wegsheid and finally found myself in a farmyard in Austria with many other German soldiers.

After I while a GI shouted "One armed man!", and pointed at me. I entered a room and stood in front of an officer. He began to interrogate me and asked me about the 'walking on the road' and 'I surrender' story. I told him that US soldiers burned all the houses where German soldiers were staying and that I preferred to go upright into captivity instead of being pulled out of a house like a rat. He gave a sharp command and said something in US slang, a GI pulled me from the farmhouse, placed me on a truck and we headed west. I left Austria and many months later I learned that prisoners assembled there were sold to the Russians for $5 each.

We were taken to Regensburg, where a huge POW camp had been established. There was a crowd of over 100,000 soldiers covering a square mile, sitting and lying in the mud, without shelter and surrounded by high fences of barbed wire. As I jumped down from the tailboard I heard my name shouted from the crowd. For three days I wandered the camp in search of the 'voice'. Finally I found him: Sepp, an old classmate from the elementary school in Untergriesbach. We flew into each other's arms and wept. He was weak and thin like me, and we held one another's hand like lost children in a dark forest.

After a week or so the US troops started to supply us with a little food. They threw K-rations over the fence like they were feeding lions at a zoo. They came into the camp with 10 jeeps abreast and slowly moved forward, driving the crowds of prisoners like sheep before them. They laughed at the shouting, screaming, stumbling, falling men who desperately tried to save their meagre belongings.

The longer we stayed in the camp, the more news about the conditions in the camp spread out to Regensburg city. Women used to come to the camp looking for their husbands, sons or brothers. The GIs did not permit anyone to come close to the fence, but as more and more prisoners arrived they were forced to enlarge the camp. As the camp grew larger, one green meadow after another changed into wet mud, but before that happened we could go near the fence and graze on the growing green leaves. One sunny, warm day, we became aware of six little girls who carefully sneaked over the fields to the fence. The girls picked flowers and collected them in a basket. We could see their eyes wandering from us to the watchtower and back. They came closer and closer, and suddenly two girls rushed towards the fence. The two little heroines took slices of bread, fruit and other eatables out of the basket and pushed them through the fence into our hands. The girls then snatched up the flowers and threw them high into the air as they skipped along. The flowers danced and whirled down on to our heads and faces like a lovely rain.

Days later our cage was called up for transfer to another camp, where the formalities of dismissal would begin. We were lucky to be able to walk on our own two feet; others were carried but some never saw the desks of the dismissal officers.

They pushed us into trucks and carried us home. We jumped down in Passau and made our way home by foot. I opened the door to my home and my parents gazed at me in horror.

My mother asked: "Have you not been in the hospital for treatment?" "No," came the reply, and I gave them a short sketch of the past few weeks. "I am surprised that an officer did not stick to his promise," my mother said, and that is enough to explain, to whom it may concern, that she and my father have not been of this world …

Death is no laughing matter

On the national day of mourning, I recall three companions and their deaths. It is the national day of mourning and formal speeches fill the air. Our dead are officially mourned. For me, however, the national day of mourning began much earlier this year of 1981; in March to be exact, when I stood in Wegscheid one foggy evening and attended a swearing-in of new troops.[6] The memory of the riots that had broken out elsewhere when soldiers were taking an oath to serve their country was still very fresh.

For fear of disturbances, the ceremony in Wegscheid was first cancelled, but then held after all.

Those who were there, remember that there was only one single note of discord. As the dead were being honoured, a few adolescents laughed provocatively loud.

Laughing at the dead. I have not been able to get this out of my head ever since. One can be against war (I am); one can question the point of armies and of weapons (I do); one can consider military ceremonial to be old fashioned (I do); but can one laugh at the dead?

The cultural eminence of a nation is not least a measure of how it copes with death and of its attitude towards its dead, especially towards those who died an arbitrary, cruel death, a prescribed death, so to speak, whereby nothing was '*Dulce et Decorum est*' toward those who had to drain the bitter cup of sorrow in the prime of their life.

People capable of laughing at the dead, at their memory, must be true fools with hearts of stone, themselves heading inevitably towards this end with the fear of death of the living in their hearts.

When this handful of 17 and 18-year-olds laughed in Wegscheid as the dead were being commemorated, I had a vision. Suddenly I saw before me, standing on the wet grass in Wegscheid, three of my former companions, two of whom were only 17 or 18 years old themselves when they died – had to die, in no way pursuing an ideal, but meeting a cruel fate that had the upper hand.

Myself, how could I ever even conceive of laughing about their deaths, when I am still trying to get over having seen these boys, 17 and 18 years old, live and die, while I escaped from the shadow that enveloped them after they had suffered more than any of these stupid crack-brained fellows could even imagine?

One of them was Jochim. Like myself, he attended the Oschatz flying school and then ended up in *Fallschirmjäger Regiment 27*, the 'fire brigade'. Poorly trained and insufficiently armed, this unit was sent to the East to try and stop the large Russian offensive, an offensive that was to pave the way for the downfall of the Third Reich.

---

6   Wegscheid is a small town in the district of Passau in Bavaria.

Jochim had a timid smile, which I still remember vividly, and he did not talk much. He had just as much difficulty lugging his rucksack as I did; we were both frail boys and almost collapsed under the weight of the *MGs* and the ammunition, whose straps cut deeply into our shoulders. We stumbled forward in the night, advancing east across the Oder River towards the front. Flames flared up on the horizon, and who can say which was louder, the boom of the artillery or the beating of our hearts.

It was February 1945. I can still see Jochim's face before me in the pale night, drenched in sweat despite the cold. We put down our loads and Jochim opened his bags and began to pass around everything he had with him: cigarettes, biscuits, a fountain pen. He said he would'nt be needing them any more, because when the new day dawned, he would die. He was 17 and the word 'die' from his lips sounded unreal, almost like a stupid joke. A *Gefreiter* told him to stop talking, but Jochim continued handing out his belongings. Some of the soldiers accepted the cigarettes and tried to smoke them under the tarpaulin so that the Russians would not be able to see the glow. Boy, was I frightened during this time!

And then I saw Jochim again, this time during the battle for Groß-Schönfeld. The village had been overrun by the Russians. The German women and children had hidden in the cellars and their possessions had already been loaded onto lorries to be carted off by the Russians when we stormed the village. There were flames everywhere, and in addition to the infernal thundering of guns and artillery, we could hear the screams and shrieks of women and children coming from cellars in the part of the village still occupied by the Russians. "Get them out, get them out in the name of God!" we cried, and bolted ahead. Running next to me was Jochim. He didn't tumble to the ground once, just kept running straight ahead down the street in the direction of the shrill screeching from the women and children.

If I could draw, I would hold up a picture of his face for all those who laugh at the dead to see … but I can't, all I can do is conjure up in my mind's eye Jochim, who caught the full load of shrapnel from a tank shell just as he reached a house door, behind which the screaming was especially loud. He slowly fell over forwards and the life drained out of his 17-year-old body, there on the frozen earth in Pomerania. And he had not even fallen in love yet.

After we had taken Groß-Schönfeld, the Russians began taking it back with a concentrated assault of T-34 and Josef Stalin tanks, when the attacking Siberians were so close that we could see the stars on their fur hats. Hans from Amberg died next to me.

He was a jovial, curly haired fellow who spoke in such a strong Palatinate accent that even the NCOs laughed and did not reprove him for it. We had been together from the very first day and had shared almost everything one could share in those days; his face was as familiar to me as my own brother's.

Now, we stood staring into each other's eyes and scarcely recognised one another, so contorted were our boyish faces from the horrors of the battle. Grimy and soaked with persperation, we ran like mad, our eyes bulging with fear and our mouths agape, screaming amid the din of the crashing, echoing tank blasts. Frightened out of our minds, all we could do was fire our guns at random. I was standing at the corner of a house and looked over at a mud-caked T-34, which was turning to shoot as it slowly rattled its way up the street. Suddenly I heard a voice roaring behind me, a voice that sounded both familiar and unfamiliar at the same time. In a tone which strikes terror in my heart to this very day, the voice bellowed: "Give me the *coup de grâce*, please, please, the *coup de grâce* …' And then I saw Hans from Amberg, the curly haired boy with the cute accent, on the ground, grasping his left thigh with both arms. Below the thigh there was: nothing. His leg, starting above the knee, had been torn clean off by a shell splinter, and with each twitch of his heart, his life's blood gushed out of him. He pleaded for the *coup de grâce*, and everyone standing or laying there stared at him, stock still, in horror. In these seconds something was lost inside of me that I have never been able to completely regain. And when I saw another 17-year-old boy laugh during the ceremony commemorating the dead, I again heard Hans from Amberg begging for the *coup de grâce*, his voice growing more and more feeble, and saw him, enveloped by death, sink back in a pool of blood. He was not a hero, not a volunteer, not even a soldier, but a human being, dead, his face twisted in agony. Anyone with the gall to laugh at him must have something wrong with them.

Well, I managed to get out alive, but Jochim, Hans and a host of others were not so lucky. We were 180-strong when we set out; only seven of us survived. Today, when the last remnants of *Fallschirmjäger Regiment 27* assembled, we only numbered five.

But before I had received any tidings from the other ones who were with me on the battlefield, I first had to see another of my comrades die. We both lay in the Bruckberg general hospital near Ansbach, where a guardian angel led me after I was wounded. I have no other explanation. But that's another story entirely. He lay there in his bed, an *Oberfeldwebel* whose name I don't remember. He was older than us all, perhaps even 40, and had a wife and children back home. The NCO was so severely wounded by shell splinters that he could hardly move. He was swaddled in thick bandages, which had to be changed every day. Each time they were replaced it hurt so much that as soon as he heard the rattle of the bandage cart, which the nurses pushed slowly from room to room, he began to whimper and then scream. The mere thought of the excrutiating pain he was going to experience made him despair.

We lay in a large room in a castle formerly belonging to the Feuerbachsche family and stared with fear and horror at the *Oberfeldwebel*, who vegatated there, whining and whimpering, crying loudly "Jesus, have mercy!" when the nurses appeared in the doorway with the cart. I ran without stopping down the long echoing corridor, so I wouldn't have to hear him, hear him scream, so I wouldn't have to watch as the nurses and the few others standing around held him and removed the adhesive bandages from his deep wounds. The faster this was done, the more mercy he was granted.

This went on for days, and the *Oberfeldwebel* became weaker and weaker. No treatment helped. His wounds smelt of pus and he shrieked and hollered. Today, when I hear someone cry "Jesus have mercy!", my heart trembles as I recall those hours. And one morning when we awoke from the confused dreams of our traumatic fever and the wailing of the sleepless nights of the severely wounded, the *Oberfeldwebel* was dead. He lay there with a peaceful, relaxed face, and from one eye the thin trace of a tear ran down over his cheek.

There is little more that I would like to – am able to – say. It was a long time ago, and they have peace. They have preceded us and we will follow them. To whom should this be plainer than to those honouring the dead on this day of mourning?

But the young people who laugh so stupidly at those who died out there being commemorated: have they ever thought even once about what would have happened to them if they had been sent out to die, 17 years old, like Jochim and Hans, or had to leave their families and experience a hell of suffering until their deaths like the *Oberfeldwebel*? How would they die and how would they like it if people laughed at them and their deaths?

Should one laugh at the dead? No, no, Jesus have mercy, no!

The memories of the victims should remain alive in us, as long as we have a heart and a conscience.

(Volker Stutzer is 92 years old and resides in Obernzell in Bavaria.)

1948, and Volker is desperately searching for a job in post-war Germany. (Volker Stutzer)

Volker as a Customs Inspector in Passau in 1961. (Volker Stutzer)

Part II

The following wartime diaries were provided by Bernd Bosshammer, Heinrich Gömpel and Franz Rzeha. All three diaries portray man's survival in the face of extreme adversity, both in combat and during the withdrawal of a beaten army.

Shortly after parachuting in to Crete on 20 May 1941, Bernd Bosshammer was seriously wounded and found himself in no-man's land near the airfield at Heraklion. He sought shelter in a donkey shed with two other wounded comrades, awaiting rescue that finally came nine days after parachuting on to the island. After treatment and medical evacuation from Crete, Bosshammer recalls his continued treatment and finally meets up with his comrades, many of whom were also wounded and in hospital.

Heinrich Gömpel's story takes place in the aftermath and confusion of the surrender of German forces in northern Italy in May 1945. He embarked on an epic journey through the Tyrol region of Italy and the Alps in a desperate attempt to return home, escaping and evading capture by both Italian partisans and the US Army. Gömpel finally reached his family home in Germany on 29 May after a journey of over 800km, mainly on foot.

Franz Rzeha describes his combat experiences during the operation to capture the Corinth Canal bridge and the invasion of Crete in 1941. During both missions, Rzeha witnessed the death of many of his comrades and on Crete found himself as one of a handful of survivors from his *Kompanie*. After a brief period of captivity, he returned to what was left of his unit and continued with operations to defeat Allied forces on Crete.

1

Bernd Bosshammer

9 Days between the dead and the living. My personal memories of the Island of Crete from 19 May to 1 June 1941

These poignant diary notes by the then *Oberjäger* Bernd Bosshammer portray abandonment, hope and desperation of the wounded in no man's land between the front lines during the battle for the island of Crete.

The diary kept on the island of Crete has been preserved, allowing the days, times and events to be accurately reproduced. It will become clear to the reader why the participants in that bloody war pray today for the preservation of peace.

19 May 1941
The entire *Kompanie (5/FJR1)* is situated approximately 60km from Athens in a small forest near Topolia.

In the evening we discussed the *Kompanie* employment during the forthcoming operation. All *Zug* and *Gruppeführers* are gathered in a large *Kompanie* tent.

Oberleutnant Harry Hermann gives the mission briefing. Equipment is distributed, aerial photographs are shown. Food supplies for the mission are handed out.

20 May 1941
We are transported in Opel Blitz trucks to the combat air base at Topolia. We received some milk soup with raisins, which had turned yellow because of too much butter. It lay heavy in my stomach.

It is midday and we sweat in our heavy jump uniforms. We drag around our weapons and ammunition and our heavy parachute. The airfield is covered in a huge dust cloud.

The JU-52s are refuelled from 200-litre barrels with hand pumps. There are not enough machines available for the whole company. Each *Zug* has to leave a *Gruppe* behind which were later dropped in Maleme to the west.

At approximately 1600 hours, we board the aircraft. The heat was now intolerable.

We finally take off; circle the airfield until all the aircraft are assembled for the flight. During the flight there are no attacks due to our fighter planes that give us protection.

We fly 30–40m above the surface of the calm sea and everything is in order.

At 1730 hours the island of Crete came into view. We fly somewhat higher over the island of Dia.[1]

At 1750 hours there is sudden *Flak* and machine-gun fire. We get the indication to jump. I am jumping last. *Oberleutnant* Georg Freiherr von Berlepsch, our *Zugführer*, is first. In front of me is *Gefreiter* Rudolf Freiherr von Suttner from Vienna, who does not want to leave the aircraft.[2] He stands up in the door and collapses; I push him out of the door and jump behind him.

I am shocked by the deployment of my parachute and my machine-pistol flies over my head and my whole face is bleeding. I see stars in front of my eyes.

I make a very bad landing in a vineyard.[3] I can hardly see anything. I loosen off my parachute harness and wash the blood from my face with a cloth.

Now a new stick of paratroops comes over us. They come down fast, one behind the other. A parachute with a *Waffenbehälter* attached to it crashes to the ground nearby.

From all sides we come under enemy fire. I jump up and run in the direction of our objective, a hill in front of the airfield. I can see it approximately 800m away.[4] I cover 200m through the vineyard and come across a weapons container with a mortar and some rifles. I also meet *Obergefreiter* Franzl Klopp.

I run further forward under heavy bombardment for another 120m or so. I see Karl Heinz Siebert and two other comrades that I do not recognise. We run a further 30m and jump over a wire fence. Suddenly I collapse, my leg is burning and I am in great pain. I call for Siebert but it is some minutes before he replies to my calls. He tells me to remain still and calm, they cannot get to me due to the strong bombardment. I lie amongst the crossfire.

My comrades think they can see some English [*sic*] soldiers lying nearby; they are firing on my comrades. I lie still amongst the ensuing gunfire and pretend to be dead. I lie still for 8–10 minutes, which seems like an eternity. The firing suddenly began to die down. My canteen had been shot through, my webbing had been shot through and my jump smock was covered in holes. I rolled myself into a small hollow. I was in agony. My trousers were covered in blood.

At 2000 hours a *Sanitäter* appears, it is *Oberjäger* Blümlein. He tends to me in a primitive manner, applying only a basic field dressing before moving off to find more wounded men.

One hour later at around 2100 hours, I am moved with nine other men to a trench, where we are laid out alongside each other. At 2130 hours an English [*sic*] tank suddenly appears and wildly opens fire.[5] I shout to the other men in the trench to dig in as best they could, to lie on their bellies and try to cover themselves. They must lie still and make no movement whatsoever. The tank drives past us and at 1,000 meters turns around and comes back in our direction. It fires at the trench, once, twice. I hear cries from some of my comrades. *Oberjäger* Hans Fiedler is killed.[6] He suffered a head wound and could not be saved.

The tank finally turns away, meets three other tanks and heads away toward the airfield. We all draw a deep breath, glad that the night had finally come.

---

1   An uninhabited offshore island 7 miles north of Heraklion.
2   Rudolf Freiherr von Suttner was a member of a notable Austrian aristocratic family. He was killed six days before his 21st birthday and is buried in block 1, grave 886 at the Maleme cemetery.
3   *5/FJR1* were dropped south-east of the airfield in the Karteros Valley and were fortunate enough to find cover in the vineyards, but suffered heavy losses in the aftermath of the subsequent heavy fighting. See Bliss, pp.3–4.
4   Agios Ioannis Hill, or East Hill, approximately 500–600m south of the airfield. See Prekatsounakis, p.51.
5   Actually a Bren Carrier (a lightly armoured tracked vehicle) and mistaken for a tank. See Prekatsounakis, p.52.
6   Hans Fiedler is recorded by *VKG* as being killed on 21 May. He is buried in block 1, grave 670 at the Maleme cemetery with the other dead *Fallschirmjäger* from Heraklion.

There are 16 men in the trench, two of them are dead. We all lie together, not all of us are from the same *Kompanie*.

The men with light wounds drag the men with leg wounds to a nearby donkey stable. At midnight we all agree that the wounded men who can move themselves should attempt to find their units. They had orders to find the *Bataillon* or *Kompanie* and report our condition and location. This order was given to *Oberjägers* Bienia and Reuter.

As the men left, only three paratroopers remained in the stable, *Oberjäger* Bosshammer and *Gefreiters* Gulden and Rose. Mutual assistance was impossible; the slightest movement was agony for all three of us. We only have a parachute to cover us. The night grows cold and lasts an eternity.

21 May 1941

At dawn we hear isolated gun fire but we cannot determine where it is coming from. The stable in which we are lying is cast out of concrete to about 40cm and the floor is made from criss-crossed boards. The entry gate is cordoned off, and to allow our access we had to tear four boards away. I am trying to reattach the boards to make the stable more secure.

At around noon German bombers fly in and attack the airfield. I get the feeling that they are trying to bombard us because the impacts are so close to our position.

Aircraft pass overhead all day and later on there is rifle and *MG* fire until it falls dark.

We have no more food supplies or water. About 50m away is a water hole in the vicinity of two houses that face the direction of the airfield. The comrades whom I sent back to the *Kompanie* scouted this out for us. They left us a metal container filled with supplies, but this is now empty.

At night I try to lie on my back and crawl towards the bread bags and water bottles of our dead comrades Hans Fiedler, Max Vogel and another dead para and take the metal container to fill with water.

I have a mad pain in my leg that makes me cry out but I am only concerned with survival. I am gone for four hours and by dawn I return to the donkey stable. I had to drag my bad leg behind me all the way to our old positions and back again. (My thigh had been completely smashed by an explosive projectile and a large amount of bone was visible.)

22 May 1941

A new day has begun. I have not been able to sleep due to the pain. When we see the water I collected we receive a shock. Floating on the top was a green coloured broth and it looks undrinkable. We tear off a strip of parachute and use it to sieve the water into a drinking cup. The drink becomes clearer and so we equally divide it between the three of us. It would be impossible for me to make that journey to the waterhole again. The pain would be unbearable.

We have covered our hole with some wooden boards again from the floor of the donkey stable and try to get some sleep during the day. We decide that one man should stay awake so that if we are found he can alert the other two. Comrade Rose was to sleep until midday, then Gulden and then it was my turn at 0400 hours. We divide the food supply from the bread bags I retrieved earlier from the fallen. It was only a small ration of bread. I found 20 pieces in the bread bags. We also had some cigarettes.

The day goes by and still I suffer great pain. We want to be found and every hour we wait patiently for rescue.

We ration the bread even more to last a further two days in case we were not found. In the evening as it is getting dark we are suddenly startled by cries and roars. Fear begins to grip us and out of the darkness comes a donkey, which walks right past our position. Rose screams and does not want to live anymore like this, uncertain that he may live or die. He's crazy! During the night, all three of us fall asleep and I awake first at 0800 hours.

23 May 1941

We can hear grenade explosions and *MG* fire from the direction of the sea. It carries on until noon.

At midday, everything is quiet. At about 1300 hours we can hear heavy fire in the distance. It can only be *II/FJR1* near the city at Heraklion.[7] We see bombs fall on the airfield but cannot determine whether the aircraft are ours.

At 1610 hours we hear tanks drive past. They open fire wildly around us and we take cover behind a low concrete wall. At least 80 rounds pass our wooden hut but luckily for us all the impacts were over one metre above the ground.

Near evening we discover that our water supply is running low. I cannot move, so Gulden must get the water tonight. Just before 0100 hours, Gulden crawls into the darkness and returns just after 3am. However, the water can is only half full. Not slept very well the whole night, if salvation does not come soon we will perish miserably.

The uncertainty makes us despair, for it is already the third day and after the departure of our comrades we have seen no-one. We sleep through the rest of the night.

I wake up at 0730 hours and wake Gulden. Rose is still asleep; he is mentally exhausted.

24 May 1941

At 1100 hours we find ourselves caught between strong *MG* fire from both English [*sic*] and German guns. You can hear it in the firing sequence. We are in the middle of it, bullets fly all around our hiding place and we lie under cover until 1530 hours.

We see aircraft in the sky firing their weapons. We are scared and yelling at each other. The uncertainty about being found and how long it will take is driving us to despair. Our nerves are almost shattered.

It becomes night and none of us can sleep. Only from time to time do I hear Rose snoring. We wake him up again and again because it gets on our nerves and he often wakes himself due to his nerves.

We quietly talk to each other and try to keep each other's spirits up. We talk quietly about home and how beautiful it is there, and I try and instil some courage into Gulden and Rose. I am also suffering because I see no end to all this and I am frightened by the thought of captivity or death before me.

Our health, mentally and physically, is going downhill.

25 May 1941

The day starts with heavy *MG* fire; occasionally we can hear mortars or grenades. One lands in our area and a piece of the roof flies off. We see the clear sky and I realise again and again that it cannot go on like this.

I myself have no desire to live but I must not let the other two notice. I feign hopes of which I am not convinced of myself. In the sky flies a burning aircraft, [and] someone jumps with a parachute. I write a letter to my parents in the back of my book:

> Dear Parents and Siblings,
> If God desires and my loved ones should get this sheet of paper or my whole book, which is unlikely, then please remember me. I am far away, 3000km away from you in a foreign country. If not then I will already be dead and lying somewhere in the Cretan soil. Soil soaked with so much blood that even the grapes will have a red colour.

---

7   Bosshammer assumes it is his *Bataillon* when it may have been *II/FJR1*.

Today, May 25th 1941 I have spent five days lying badly wounded in a donkey stable. My left leg is shot up and I have lost a lot of blood. Our situation is hopeless because our comrades have not returned. It is possible that some of them have died or have been captured. Perhaps no-one knows that there are three wounded paratroopers still alive.

We cannot help each other because Rose, Gulden and I are all seriously wounded. We have not seen Doctors or comrades since the day we were wounded on 20 May.

Please also write few lines to Marga in Rückersdorf to say that she does not have to wait for me anymore. If I have ever wronged you then please forgive me because in my heart I did not want this. I cannot continue writing; I have to take cover due to shooting near our shack.

I greet you all to the core.

From your son and brother Bernd.

Goodbye dear ones. Written in the afternoon of 25 May 1941 on the Island of Crete

Night is breaking and we are still alive. We are still waiting for a miracle under very difficult conditions. That miracle is a rescue, but nothing is happening. It's already 0400 hours and I am still not sleeping.

Rose went crawling to fetch water again with his wounded leg and he has been away since 0100 hours. There are a few gunshots. He should have been back ages ago. The waterhole is 40–50m away from us.

At 0410 hours he comes back with about two litres of water. He had been shot again and had a new bandage on his left knee made from a piece of parachute. The tin container was also shot through, therefore [he has] only a small amount of water.

The night was cool and sleepless. Rose kept crying and moaning, and then he screamed out loud, he cannot calm down. The whining gets on the nerves.

There is now relatively little firing and quite far away from us.

26 May 1941

We managed to do it; we are still alive, though very tired and weary. I do not lose heart. I did not tell Rose and Gulden that I wrote a farewell letter. As far as they are concerned I keep only a diary.

At 1000 hours our aircraft fly around us for over two hours and bombard the enemy. Very strong *MG* fire from both sides. The uncertainty of where our comrades, where the Germans are, is terrible. We do not see any human beings. We are willing to endure one more day with our very last strength and tenacity, but then we must surely be found.

1200 hours, again lively rifle and *MG* fire from three sides. Not far from us mortars.

There is a plague of flies with us, an incredible number of flies in the shed.

From 1500 to 1530 hours occasional shots are heard, German judging by the direction.

1600 hours, everything is quiet again. Now and again we hear a cock crow. Has the enemy withdrawn?

Had a bowel movement for the first time at 1700 hours but very hard and painful. At 1800 hours, we all get a piece of *Knäckebrot*. We smoke the last cigarette and searched everywhere for more and found none. We collect the few butts that are lying around.

We can hear the battle noise coming from Heraklion but it remains quiet around us and we soon hope to be saved.

At night, Rose begins to rave. He is going insane and wishes to shoot us. I try to calm him down by telling him that I heard German voices and we might soon be saved. He gives me his pistol and a spare magazine. He will not get it back again. He screams and yells at me and then wants to kill us all with his pocket knife, so I also take that away from him. He cries and insults me over and over again, throwing all available objects at me, finally throwing his cup. It started one of the worst nights on Crete. I did not get any sleep as I had to pay close attention to Rose in case he snapped again.

27 May 1941

0600 hours. The night was very cold. I could not sleep because of Rose. I was constantly on guard in case he should lose his nerve again. He often raged, screamed and shouted at me, calling me a criminal. He was at the end of his strength.

Gulden and I despaired and scolded our comrades who have let us perish so shamelessly and miserably in this donkey stable.

At 0645 hours, two flares were fired from two locations, most likely by Germans at Heraklion. A wild dog barks and then strong rifle and *MG* fire.

At 0800 hours I once again rest. At 0845 hours through the hole in our roof I see several German aircraft.

Our wounds now stink, we have to re-dress them. There are maggots in the wound and it itches terribly. 0830 hours, and Gulden wants to fetch field dressings from our dead comrades. He crawls out of the shed and is immediately shot at. Luckily he crawls into a nearby ditch where he finds a field canteen of tea, three packets of *Knäckebrot*; one can of inedible meat and two field dressings.[8] In the ditch are three dead comrades and the smell is dreadful. He puts pieces of parachute over their faces and it is not clear who they are. I know that Hans Fiedler is out there and possibly Max Vogel.

1330 hours. Until now it has been amazingly quiet with only some short bursts of *MG* fire and very little rifle fire from the direction of the German positions.

The fly plague is very unpleasant and we cannot defend against it. We cut pieces from the parachute and cover our faces. Rose has calmed down; he speaks quietly and mutters incomprehensible words to himself. He has got it into his mind that he will not live much longer. Our hopes are dwindling day by day.

Our wounds continue to fester. We all have a high fever and chills, our faces are pale, the edges of our eyes are as red as blood. Seeing and recognising has become worse and our eyes are constantly watering. The eyelids fall but I do not want to sleep. I always think of Rose and I am afraid of his attacks, which come so suddenly and unexpectedly.

1730 hours. Exactly one week ago we jumped out of our aircraft. It is all very quiet. Our water supply is coming to an end. A German reconaissance plane flies over now and again. Mortar and *MG* fire, the war on Crete is still not over yet!

28 May 1941

The night was cold. At 0340 hours a white flare shot up into the sky and for a few seconds it lights up our stable. Gulden fetched water after we patched up the holes in the container. He comes back at 0700 hours and brings some field dressings with him.

I think of my brother Willi, who has his name day today.[9] I wonder if he is thinking of me.

1000 hours and everything is dead quiet. The whistling of the wind through the wood, the chirping of the birds and the buzz of the flies sounds like tender music in this miserable war. This cannot be bombed and destroyed. This is life!

---

8   The issued rations were completely unsuitable for Crete. They caused a mad thirst and also decomposed or melted in the heat. See Richter, p.83.

9   A Catholic tradition where a day associated to one's name is celebrated and were often more important than birthday celebrations.

I make a cross and on it write, Hans FIEDLER *5./Fallsch.Jg.Rgt.1* killed on 20.05.1941. I am anxious to put this cross by Fiedler so he can be identified. On a wooden board I write the names BOSSHAMMER – GULDEN – ROSE and make a cross behind it but do not write a date on it.

1130 hours. An aircraft engine can be heard far away. A single plane comes by and drops two bombs either on the airfield or close to it. Until 1600 hours there is rifle and *MG* fire followed by an eerie silence. I find another cigarette. Rose is sleeping so I am sharing the cigarette with Gulden. We only have eight matches left so we handle them carefully. All three of us have been ill these past few days, likely caused by the dirty water we are forced to drink.

1700–1800 hours. German bombers drop their loads on the north-west slope, probably on the airfield but we cannot see. Our stable roof is shaking and again a piece of the roof flies off and hits Rose on the head. He groans. We are all very bad and we see the end approaching. Can someone make it clear to the German fliers that we are down here and that they have to drop their bombs further toward the airfield.

Later it gets quieter. The night breaks in and nobody speaks a word. We will not fetch any more water. There is still about two cups each available. I take charge of the container and a sip will only be served in extreme emergency. I have not slept the night as Rose is incessantly hallucinating. I am afraid that he will take away the three pistols I have and try to shoot us all.

29 May 1941

Quite often during the night we can hear loud English voices quite close to us, possibly coming from the fortified mountainside. We expect capture at any moment. It is still very dark.

I keep my pistol ready because we do not want to give up that easily. Hopefully there are no partisans, which is the worst thing that could happen to us now. Each of us has a large sip of water, emptying one cup. I fall asleep and wake up only because of the snoring from Rose. Meanwhile it is light outside. Outside in the terrain I see movement, I hear voices!

0920 hours. RESCUE! I see two men through a crack in one of the boards. Both of them are bare-chested, with machine-pistols and pistols at the ready. I can hear voices but cannot determine whether they are German or English. I take hold of my pistol and give Gulden his. Rose remains asleep, he has a high fever.

Both men continue to approach. I look at one and can see a *Ritterkreuz* on a bare torso. I scream "Germans here", but it is not a scream, it's just a whisper. As hard as I try, the words come out quietly. They are now about 5m away. I scream "Germans!" Carefully the two men approach. I push a board away and they lower their weapons and come quickly to us. *Oberjäger* Racho (*2/ FJR1*) and *Oberleutnant* Alfred Schwarzmann (*8/FJR1*) have rescued us![10]

They fetch some medics who then carry us on an old table to the main dressing station. It is 1100 hours before we see a Doctor. Dr Bräuer puts a splint on my leg, gives me two injections, cleans out the wound and removes the maggots. I receive morphine.

At 1230 hours I am brought to the airfield. Here I receive another injection for wound fever and learn that the war on Crete is over. The enemy has left the island, we are saved.

1750 hours. I am taken to Athens aboard a Junkers JU-52 aircraft and sleep well during the flight. Rose and Gulden are not with me.

1930 hours. I arrive at the Olympia Military Hospital where I am checked over again and given more medicine. For what, I don't know!

2420 hours. I should get an anaesthetic but learn that the Doctors want to remove my left leg. I scream with rage. I still have a pistol on me and I threaten to shoot them. I am taken to an adjoining room, where I come across a physician who is sympathetic to my problem. I tell him my

---

10   Schwarzmann had been a medal-winning Olympic gymnast at the 1936 games in Berlin.

story and he puts me in a plaster cast, promises to help me and ensure that I am relocated as soon as possible.

I am stripped of my uniform, wrapped in a cloth and washed and then moved to a room with about 20 beds. I still have my pistol, a Belgian FN, which I brought back from Holland in May 1940. I hide it in my bed.

30 May 1941

Today the medics brought breakfast and more medicine. Then I was to be shaved, first with clippers and then with a razor. The beard hurts my face. Once finished, some small cuts on my face bleed heavily.

The Doctor makes a visit and he recognises me. He comes from Kamen in Westphalia. I don't know his name but he's a great buddy. He promises to help me and just wants me to stay calm. I trust him and consider how I can thank him. The plaster on my leg is cut open in the back near the exit wound. The wound hurts. It is cleaned, then I am given injections and then I sleep. I wake up to dinner and then sleep again.

31 May 1941

In the morning the Doctor comes alone to my bed. I offer him my pistol and place it in his hand. He is very surprised that I still have it and that it wasn't taken away from me. Details on how to get out of here are discussed. I have some money in my neck pouch so I give the cash to the Doctor.

At 1100 hours I receive a visit from *Oberjäger* Schatz and learn that *Oberleutnant* Harry Herrmann, *Leutnant* Fischer and *Leutnant* von Berlepsch are also here in the same hospital. *Leutnant* Ernst von Levetzow is not here and I fear he has been killed in action.[11] At 1400 hours *Feldwebel* Seeger, Fritz Katke, *Feldwebel* Geiselbrecht and *Gefreiter* Brockmann visit me.

1 & 2 June 1941

I felt very weak today with stomach ache and some vomiting. I spent most of the day sleeping.

3 June 1941

Before breakfast at around 0550 hours I was helped to a vehicle by a Doctor and two medics and driven to the airport in Athens. A JU-90 aircraft was ready and fully equipped for seven seriously injured men. An eighth man turned up so room was made for him. The flight was to Vienna with a stopover in Belgrade.

At 1910 hours the aircraft lands in Vienna but there are no spaces in the hospitals. During the night I am taken to the Reserve Hospital XIA on the Boerhaavegasse in the city.

4 June 1941

I am lying on a trolley in a long corridor waiting for a bed. Suddenly I see the bandaged head of an *Oberleutnant* coming up the stairs, assisted by a nurse. That swinging gait could only belong to Harry Herrmann. I called out to him and he answered: "Bosshammer, my son, what happened to you?" I briefly told him of my misfortune on Crete and he promised to help. A Doctor arrives and I am placed in a ward with many beds directly below the ward containing *Oberleutnant* Herrmann, *Leutnant* Fischer and *Leutnant* von Berlepsch. I am given a long broomstick so I can knock on the ceiling if something is wrong. Herrmann has arranged for my Mother to be informed and she actually visited some days later and stayed in Vienna for three days.

---

11   Von Levetzow was killed on 20 May and is buried in block 1, grave 884 at the cemetery in Maleme.

The days after

Harry Herrmann did a lot of work with the Doctors for the preservation of my left leg. After removing the heavy pelvic plaster-cast, my leg was covered with a stretch bandage and placed into a special leg splint. A steel wire was drilled through the left thigh just above the knee and connected to a rope laid over rollers and attached to some weights. X-rays showed that my left thigh bone was probably smashed by an explosive bullet. Everything was splintered. The leg had to be pulled so it could match the length of the other leg.

I have spent so much time on my back that every movement is painful. My weight at the hospital in Vienna was 34kg (68lb).

Whilst at the hospital, I received a visit from Marga Freifrau von Suttner. She was the mother of *Gefreiter* Suttner, who jumped ahead of me from our JU-52 over Crete. It was later discovered that he was shot through the heart in the doorway of the aircraft at the moment he was about to jump. She lived in Vienna and was accompanied by *Frau* Magda Hammer.

Staff physician Dr Schmidt took care of my treatment. Shortly before Christmas I was freed from the traction device and received a leg-pelvic plaster which went from the toes to the chest.

Harry Herrmann, Fischer and Berlepsch had since been released from hospital and had returned to duty. He wrote me a letter on 4 July 1941: "I was very delighted to hear that you came through for Rose and Gulden. I have recommended you all for the Iron Cross 1st Class. Most of the wounded are now back with us. I have stumbled across your expression that you are formerly a member of the *Kompanie*. You are still part of our old 5. *Kompanie* of *Regiment 1* and will remain so. It does not matter when you come back, just return to us healthy. Keep us up to date with your progress."

Von Berlepsch wrote on 29 November 1941: "*Oberjäger* Bienia and *Gefreiter* Neuen are back here and are employed in office work. In the next few days, *Gefreiter* Knögl will hand deliver a pay book, postal savings book, a combat report form, uniform blouse, trousers and a visor cap."

A few days after Christmas 1941 I was moved on request by hospital train to Cologne, then by ambulance to the home hospital 'Annaheim' near my home town of Düren.

At the end of 1942 I was sent for a few weeks' recovery firstly to Mariazell in Austria and then Ospedaletti in Italy. In the meantime I was able to move myself with the aid of crutches. Then at the beginning of 1943 I returned (on crutches) to the old *Kompanie* in Döberitz to take up office duties as a *Feldwebel*.

At the beginning of April 1943 we moved from Döberitz/Berlin to Laval/France where I became a transport officer.

My left leg had been preserved, albeit 2cm shorter than my right leg. The pain in my left knee joint has remained and will remind me of my combat service on Crete until my old age.

2

Heinrich Gömpel

The last days of the War on the Southern Front and the way home through the Alps. Diary and notes from April/May 1945

Heinrich Gömpel was born on 8 February 1920. He was a veteran of the early campaigns, serving with 9/FJR1 in Poland (Stawiszyn), Holland (Waalhaven) and Crete (Heraklion). He went on to serve in Russia in September 1941, before transferring to FJD4 at the end of 1943 and serving in Italy in the latter stages of the war. As the end of the war drew closer, Heini was attending a Führerschule *in Italy which was ordered to positions on the Po River to protect the withdrawal of German forces. In the following diary entries from 24 April to 29 May 1945, Heinrich recalls the final days of the war and his brief periods of captivity by Italian partisans and US forces during his exodus of almost 800km through the Alps in order to return home to his family.*

Unterfeldwebel Gömpel in tropical uniform, wearing a cloth version of the paratrooper's badge, a wound badge and the *Luftwaffe* ground assault badge. He also wears the *EK2* ribbon through his tunic buttonhole and *EK1* on his left breast pocket. (Heinrich Gömpel)

22 February 1944, with *Oberjäger* Gömpel preparing for a training jump, having been transferred to *FJD4*. The static line hook is tucked into the upper strap of the RZ20 parachute harness. (Heinrich Gömpel)

24 April 1945

The *Führerschule* at Bosca Chiesanuova is set to march to Gaiba and current positions on the northern bank of the River Po. We are to protect the retreat of the *Fallschirm-Armee* and Infantry units who have broken out of the pocket. I have post today, whilst in the foxhole. It is well camouflaged on top of an embankment.

On the opposite side of the wide river, the Americans keep hidden behind their high bank. They constantly keep us under cover with artillery salvos, *Jabos* and Iron Gustavs, who circle all day above our positions. Only with darkness do we get some respite. In spite of the continuous artillery fire we suffer no losses today.

25 April 1945

0100 hours. Alarm!

The Americans have broken through on the left and right of our well-developed line by means of amphibious tanks. We received a last-minute order to abandon our positions.

It became a serious situation; the enemy was already in the centre of Gaiba.

Under the cover of darkness, we crept through the American lines. During the day and under constant *Jabo* attacks and artillery fire, our small groups reached the relative safety of the foliage of some vineyards. In the evening we reached the south bank of the Adige River 20km to the north.

26 April 1945

In the night, our group crossed the Adige River at Badia Polesine by way of boats provided by a *Fallschirmjäger Pionier* unit. Our unit has been torn apart; there is no apparent front line anymore. Signs of disintegration amongst army units are noticeable everywhere.

27 April 1945

With a *Kampfgruppe* from the 26th *Panzer* Division, we reach Padua. The *Amis* should already be in Verona. We are constantly ambushed and fired upon by Partisans and we suffer many losses.

During the latter part of the morning on the march, I meet our *Oberfeldarzt* Dr Adolf Eiben, who is travelling with a mule column. He said to me: "The war is lost, it is over." In spite of delays near Padua, we spend the night in Nove, some 45km to the NW.

28 April 1945

In trucks, we drive on to Bassano. In the morning we come under fire from gangs of bandits, who take our last vehicles under fire from all sides. An accompanying four-barrel *Flak* gun creates hell. The journey ends in a position at the so-called Alpine Fortress at Primolano.

A General Staff Officer stands at a road junction and gives orders to all the units.

Under the command of an *Oberleutnant* from a *Nachrichtenzug*, our unit of 16 men are to march toward Feltre. We are to take up position at Fort Della Fragliati.

After half an hour we come under fire by Partisans with *MG* and rifle fire. We are caught on the slopes of the hill with hardly any cover. There are many losses. We were in the open, like being served on a platter. I save myself by jumping into a road attendant's house.

We answered the fire with our own infantry weapons; however, the bandits sat well camouflaged above us in amongst the rocks and trees. We received no assistance from the greater part of our forces in the valley below.

After we fired, large groups of partisans emerged from their cover and shouted in German for us to come out from our positions. We remained where we were.

A soldier suddenly began waving a handkerchief, our position could not be held. The Partisans came down to us and relieved us of our weapons and ammunition. After threatening to shoot us we were allowed to recover our casualties, eight wounded and one dead. We were then marched at the gallop to the north with many Partisan guards to watch over us. We climbed the steep rocks with their rifle barrels in our backs. When we were halfway up the slope, mortar fire began to come down on our former positions. Unfortunately it was too late.

After a toilsome march, we were allowed to stop for the night, but not until they had robbed us of everything.

29 April 1945

The Partisans marched with us towards Castello Tesino. Here, we were taken over by new guards. Near the De Brocon Pass, I saw an opportunity during a stop to remove myself from this Partisan custody. I hid myself beneath a rock in a nearby mountain brook and as soon as the '*Porko Dio*' [cursing] of the bandit group could not be heard anymore, I carefully continued on my own.

On the way, I met several soldiers from an Infantry unit, who had given up their position and were searching for any friendly forces.

We stayed overnight in a hay barn near Canale. We almost froze during the night. One man was always awake on guard duty. Local women would approach us and shout "Hitler will soon be dead" and "The Russians will soon be in Berlin."

30 April 1945

We were now in five groups, marching cautiously in the morning, more than ever on guard against Partisans. Since we were warned again and again to avoid roads and passes, we followed the advice of a German-speaking woman to use the drainage tunnel to the Lago di Paneveggio, which at that time was not full of water. Here we would be safe from the bandits who would shoot every German soldier on top of the passes.

After one hour we reached the tunnel entrance, which showed only a small amount of water. We had to bend over as the height of the initially bricked-up tunnel was only 1.3 metres. As we advanced down the tunnel we noticed that the shaft no longer reached this height and was carved into the rock. As the water sometimes reached our knees and it was also pitch dark, we worked forward very laboriously. After about an hour of crawling forward, three comrades gave up and went back.

Although I found it hard to carry on, I continued in the hope that we would soon reach the tunnel exit. An Infantry *Feldwebel* followed behind me. Due to exhaustion the breaks became longer and longer. After about six hours, which seemed like an eternity, we saw a light, the tunnel became wider and we stumbled over the sleepers of a small field railway.

The light finally came to us. Alerted by the sound of a vehicle, we realised that something was coming our way so we pressed ourselves close to the tunnel wall.

Then suddenly a small motor vehicle stopped in front of us and a voice from the darkness said would we like to ascend? Our saviour was an older man from South Tyrol who belonged to the staff of the water locks. He told us that he had heard us and that no-one had crawled through the drainage tunnel in such a time. The canal was 11km long. "Never again," said my comrade. We fell asleep where we had sat down. In the late evening we reached Moena, 10km to the north-west of the lake. We were warmly received by a South Tyrolean family living on the outskirts of the village. They too could not believe we had crawled through the tunnel. They marvelled at our courage and perseverance.

1 May 1945

Rest in Campitello di Fassa (80km south of the Austrian border) at a German Signals Unit HQ, which to our astonishment had begun to demobilise. Papers were burned and weapons were collected. I was able to fully equip myself with clothing, weapons and food. We also heard that Hitler was dead and that the war was over. This unit mixed with female staff lived, as we were told, for a long time in this peaceful area unaffected by the war. "They've had it good here," said the sergeant.

2 May 1945

The signals unit told me that the collection point for stragglers from *Fallschirmjäger Division 4* was supposed to be in the Brunneck area. Well fed, I marched on my own to finally reach my last unit. After a long ascent over the Pordoi Pass through metre-deep snow, I reached Pedratsches in the late evening, exhausted, but without being harassed by any partisans. Here I made contact with the Command of *O.B. Süd-West*. I was joyfully received and given the best food and accommodation in a posh hotel which was swarming with staff officers and their assistants.

It seemed to me that all these people were affected by a certain panic.

3 May 1945

After a good night's sleep, cash was distributed in the morning. I felt very rich, unsuspecting of the purpose of this so-called gift. I was also given many items from the canteen stores; my back-pack was stuffed. A *Zahlmeister* told me: "This way it will not fall into the hands of the Partisans." Suddenly there came the order: "Prepare for all-round defence, the Partisans are on the march."

I am allowed to position myself with a Beamte (an administrative official) on the south balcony with the only available aircraft machine gun. With the binoculars I could observe a good distance down the road.

At around 1000 hours we see them coming. Three trucks fully loaded with bandits. On the cab was a red flag with a hammer and sickle. My *MG* was ready to fire. I had the first truck nicely in my sights and only had to pull the trigger. The officer gave the alarm and then suddenly an order was heard: "Do not shoot, dismantle weapons and disable them." I was quite angry and shocked, but then I learned that Americans were with the partisans in order to negotiate our surrender.

The trucks with the partisans and Americans pulled up in front of the hotel with weapons ready to fire. There were about 100 men. Four Americans walked into the hotel and we had to sit in the yard. All vehicles including catering and staff cars were confiscated. My bulging backpack was still under the mattresses of a storage room. We are allowed to spend the night in the hotel.

4 May 1945

What I suspected happened today. The Partisans played up. Body searches and personal property such as watches, rings and the like were taken from the soldiers. I stayed in the basement whilst waiting for an opportunity to escape. But then something happened and we suddenly had to vacate the hotel. We were loaded onto two trucks and driven away under the protection of the Americans via Brunneck to Toblach. Here the entire staff of *O.B. Süd-West* was allowed to move into another hotel. We were interned, we were told. I had been able to take my full backpack with me.

5 May 1945

We were not allowed to leave the hotel so we played Skat.

6 May 1945

Boredom! American raid! How do we get out of here? None of the motley crew in the hotel room has any advice. One of them says: "We have it good here, let's wait, soon it will be the Americans against the Russians anyway."

7 May 1945

A detonation interrupted our lethargy this morning. We jumped to the windows and heard screaming Americans. They had been playing in the large square in front of the hotel with German

Panzerfäuste and one had gone off. We were allowed to get the injured guys out of the danger zone. An American officer sent word of thanks to the house and relaxed our confinement.

8 May 1945

News came today that Germany has capitulated. We were all ready for that news. Should everything have been in vain? The many dead and wounded comrades, the hardships, the endurance of the population? What else should we believe? We are now completely in the hands of our enemy!

Some of the staff officers begin to criticise the many mistakes made by the leadership.

11 May 1945

The collection staff of *General* Heidrich should be in the Bolzano area, which is where I want to go. Due to the help we gave the Americans on 7 May, I am given a travel pass and was therefore driven to Bolzano in a truck. In the evening I had to stay in a collection barracks, where I learned that my old unit was in the Trento area.

12 May 1945

My travel pass served me well. I am driven to Pergine Valsugana. Here I actually find the remains of the old unit, and even the two Italian kitchen girls are still here to my surprise. With a big hello and huge joy I am welcomed. My name had already been placed on the list of losses. We were considered internees and were allowed to move freely in the village.

In the place where the unit is encamped, I build myself – like the others – a shack and set up home. Then we begin to hear that the units are to move closer to the south. Close by I find a large pile of personnel data from the *Kompanie*, which was to be burned. I poked around in the pile and find some of my personal information, which was immediately tucked inside my jump trousers.

With the war over, my services are no longer required, yet I still have to hang around here. Technically we have been dismissed and I want to go home.

14 May 1945

I travel as a front-seat passenger on a catering truck so I can explore the area and assess the situation. The whole of the South Tyrol is like a large army camp. The Americans dominate the roads.

15 May 1945

Today we travel to Meran to get clothing. At one point I attempted to quietly slip away from the truck with my rucksack. Another passenger notices me, grins and says: "It's useless, you cannot get through, all roads and passes are blocked many times."

In Bolzano I jump off and in possession of my American travel pass I begin walking north on the Brenner road. At the town exit I stop an American truck and declare that I have to go to Toblach to join my unit. A German passenger translated for me and I am allowed to climb aboard. Near Mühlback in the Puster Valley we were allowed to dismount.

The Americans are having a snack break; white bread is distributed. I watch the Americans; they are brotherly and they impress me, they are not hateful.

At the railway siding on the street, two *Wehrmacht* train officers are sitting in front of a barrack building. I give them a piece of bread and casually ask them if they know of a getaway route. They point north toward Pfunders (Fundres).

The region is not yet fully occupied but there would be deep snow. The locals said that nobody could get through there. Now was the time. In an unguarded moment I pulled by backpack from the truck and crawled into the bushes. Still crawling, I reach the high forest and ran up the slope until I ran out of steam. I was out of sight and out of reach of the road.

At noon I passed close to a single farmstead. They had seen me approaching and called for me to wait. I was told there were still soldiers in the house and that a South Tyrolean man would take us across the border into Austria during the night. Hesitant and suspicious, I head for the house. There were over a dozen soldiers resting there waiting for darkness.

The South Tyrolean asked for payment in goods for the mountain tour, so I left him my spare shoes. We remained in the house all day until dark.

At dusk we begin to march in single file. At the beginning we made good progress, but then came the steep slopes, the first snowfields and deep snow. Tracks were sometimes visible and then lost again.

16 May 1945

Long after midnight we stopped at a snow-covered haystack. I am exhausted and take Pervitin tablets. Through deep snow we stomp in the direction of Hochfeiler on the Austrian border. At 0600 hours we are finally up in the Scharte at an altitude of around 2,900m. The South Tyrolean said that this was the limit and it would be downhill from here to Austria in the Zillertal (Ziller Valley).

On the way down, the man showed us the spot on a steep valley slope where days ago an avalanche broke loose, taking some soldiers with it.

We took a short break. The South Tyrolean said goodbye and I suddenly became alone when I accidentally slipped on the steep snowy surface. I slid down the valley for a few hundred metres on the seat of my pants until I was safe on a snowdrift. I was at the Pitscher-Joch [mountain pass in the Zillertal]. There was less snow here and the first hut appeared, which was fully inhabited by soldiers from all branches of the *Wehrmacht*. I spent the night in an Alpine hut not far from the village of Dorfamberg.

The first Austrians appeared wearing red and white armbands. They told me to report to the Americans down in the valley. They also told me to remove the dirty vulture [*Luftwaffe* eagle insignia] from my cap. I wanted to rough him up but a nice lady mediated. "He also wants to go home," she said!

17 May 1945

Along with a *Gebirgsjäger* who joined me in the morning, we went downhill to the actual Zillertal. We were warned by the local population that the Americans were everywhere and to stay away from the main roads. We bypassed Mayrhofen; the place was already occupied. We spent the night in the barn of a secluded farm. The farmer's wife cooked us jacket potatoes. She warned us that the Americans along with the Russians often patrolled the area at night. My *Gebirgs* comrade smiled and said: "They do not come out at night, they are afraid themselves." Before I crept into the straw I loosened some boards on the back wall of the barn, just in case. I was not very happy with the situation.

18 May 1945

During the night I was awakened by engine noise. Through the cracks in the wooden wall I saw that the yard outside was brightly lit. The dog barked and I heard "Hands Up!" The Americans were here. I woke my comrade, took my backpack and shoes in hand and climbed out through the hole in the boards and into the orchard on the other side. Here I dived over the fence and disappeared into the darkness. I could still hear the Americans screaming and shouting. Presumably they had just caught my comrade. A pity, but we were warned!

In the early morning I was already high on the plateau. Down in valley was a large town. I suspected it was Zeil and in the streets were Army vehicles. The plateau was intersected by cross valleys. I had to descend hundreds of metres and then ascend again. I found this very time-consuming, and with this detour you could not move forward. When I had descended again and tried to climb a rock face, I realised I had made a mistake. I had to conquer an overhanging rocky outcrop. I took off my backpack and tied a rope to it so I could pull the backpack up after overcoming this dangerous spot. When I pulled myself up to the rock with my last strength, the rope slipped out of my hands and the backpack tumbled down into the depths of the valley. Luckily it stopped 50m down on a mountain pine.

I was exhausted and powerless, but in a short time I was on the plateau. Since I knew that the Alpine huts up here were already partially farmed, I needed help to recover my backpack.

I saw the first hut nearby so I ventured out of the bush. Suddenly an American and a Russian were standing in front of me. They both smelled heavily of alcohol. The American had the Russian ask me where I had come from and if I had been registered in Zeil?

I quickly recovered from the shock and replied that I was from around here and I was on the way home. They demanded to know where the next Alpine hut was. I told them it was in the direction that I had just come from. They walked off and I was able to go. The two men were clearly on a *Schnapstour* [pub crawl].

I went to the nearest hut and I found frightened and trembling residents (an older grandma, a young woman and a boy of about 12 years). The American and the Russian had wanted alcohol and had threatened them with a pistol. Because they found nothing they had become ruthless and the woman had been beaten. I was able to soothe them and I asked if they would help me recover my backpack. By using hayloft cables, I could tie them together and slowly abseil down the rock face to rescue my backpack.

On my signal the rope tightened and I slowly edged myself over the rocky outcrop. The cable cut into my chest and I could hardly breathe. After many minutes I finally found ground under my feet and then began the climb back to the top of the rock face. I was exhausted, and so were the residents of the hut.

As it turned out, the rope had jammed in a rock crack. They quickly called grandma to help. With a heartfelt thank-you, I gave them two bars of soap and said goodbye to these helpful people.

I moved on and in the evening came to a remote farm. Here I was able to spend the night in the hayloft. I was dog sick and I could not sleep at all.

19 May 1945

I had slept for a long time. The Alpine farmers were already out on the meadow with their rakes. At the place where I had slept stood a pan of *mehlspeise* and a pot of milk.[1] I made myself breakfast, shaved, washed with running water, put on my rucksack and thanked their hospitality with a packet of tobacco.

The war was not quite over yet. I watched *Jabos* dropping bombs across the Inn Valley. A woman I met on the way explained to me the *SS* were still up in the Kartwendel Mountains and they did not want to surrender. Down in the Zillertal there were tank and truck columns. I was safe up here on the Wiederbergerhorn plateau, but I wanted to continue. I had to go through the Ziller and Inntal towards the German border.

In the afternoon I asked again for lodging at an alpine hut. Although she was fully booked, I was allowed to stay. Most of the residents were civilian soldiers and I noticed immediately that the brothers would not engage in any conversation and they disappeared into an adjoining room.

---

1   *Mehlspeise* is a flour-based sweet food such as pastries, cakes and dumplings.

20 May 1945

Bright spring weather today. There were long vehicle columns on the road down into the Zillertal. I have to get over to the other side. I spend half of the morning crawling through the meadows and take a short breather behind the bushes and then dare to cross the street during a gap in the columns. Here I reach the back door of a house and suddenly find myself standing in a large kitchen. A tall bearded man takes me by the arm and forces me into the pantry: "Stay here, the Americans are in front of the dining room, I'll bring you a *mehlspeise* right away." After a while the good man appears with a pancake and a measure of a beer-like drink and disappears back into the kitchen. With a ravenous appetite I quickly consumed the meal. Realising that I was starving, the man appeared with a second helping and asked me where I was heading. He showed me another safe route to the *Achensee* [Lake Achen].

Here I am in Fügen and I need to cross the River Inn. The man knew of a small boat. If need be I would have to bale it out and row to the opposite bank of the river. He handed me a marmalade jar and a piece of bread and said: "Make sure you get into the wooded area and keep to the path." Then he opened the door: "Go, the way is clear." There was not even time for me to say goodbye to this outstanding person.

I reached the main road through the forest in the Inn Valley. At lunchtime there was less traffic on the road. I crawled through the meadows and was soon standing on the southern bank of the broad flooded River Inn. After a long search I found the boat. I got my feet wet baling it out but it was soon ready to cast off; however, I found it very difficult to maintain control. Nevertheless, I reached the opposite bank, secured the boat and walked around Jenbach with wet and squeaky shoes. I met some young girls who gave me information about a shortcut to Pertisau and the *Achensee*. As I continued on my way I almost surprised an *Ami* patrol. I saw the soldiers with their jeep at the last moment behind an inn. For better or worse I had to leave the pre-planned path, walked along the uninhabited left bank of the lake and came to a road leading to the Kartwendel mountain range. I stopped at a managed alpine hut and a friendly young woman gave me plenty of *mehlspeise* and milk, and then I was allowed to sleep in a feather bed again.

21 May 1945

After a copious breakfast of *mehlspeise* and milk, I thanked the lovely landlady and said goodbye. An elderly man who was probably a resident showed me the way to the Plumsjoch. He told me that soldiers of the *Waffen-SS* could still be up there. After a long climb I reached the Plumsjoch Saddle in a dense snowstorm. A nearby hut offered shelter. I waited for the snowstorm to pass and then followed a narrow path. Suddenly I saw a *Waffen-SS* soldier standing behind a fir tree in full combat gear. He came over and asked me where I was going. I told him that I was going to cross the border during the night. He told me that I would not get away with it because the Americans in the valley had *Panzers* and it would be impossible to get through them. With his binoculars I could make out the *Ami* tanks. After a brief discussion with his comrades, who did not appear, I was allowed to go on, having given my word [to say] that I had not seen them.

Near Hinterriß I met women washing by the stream. I questioned them and they explained to me that the *Amis* were planning an action against the *SS*. No one would be able to leave at the moment. I was asked to stay with the farmers for a few days until the situation changed. This sounded like a good idea, so I went to the first of the larger farms and found that it was the Mayor's office. I only became aware of this later. In the corridor I met a man with a red and white armband and asked him if I could stay, and he told me to wait. Imagining that nothing could happen to me, I fell asleep in a chair.

I was suddenly and rudely awakened by American soldiers standing in front of me. I raised my hands and they marched me out to a three-quarter tonner already occupied by other members of the *Wehrmacht*. We were transported to Vorderriß in southern Germany. On the way I was searched; the guards were keen on my decorations and once they had finished they placed two packets of cigarettes on my backpack as compensation. I kicked them off with my foot and in return I received a slap. In Vorderriß I was locked alone in the basement of a house. A guard was always on watch. It was a bleak prospect for me.

22 May 1945

In the morning the door opened and I was handed cookies, a bar of chocolate and some tea. Then I had to stack gasoline canisters. The guard put two food rations in front of me. In the afternoon we were all taken to the big ice rink in Garmisch-Partenkirchen, where we were once again searched by the American Military Police. My watch was taken. There were already hundreds of *Wehrmacht* personnel in the stadium and it was filled to the last seat. Under the stairs I found two places to lie down with a like-minded person, and we reported to the so-called responsible prisoner in order to receive meals.

23 May 1945

The night was terrible. We could not sleep as men were constantly walking on the stairs above us. We looked for a new place to sleep and we were lucky. In the tower of the ice stadium my new friend gave out cigarettes and room was made for us to bed down. We again contacted the responsible prisoner for this part of the stadium. My clever comrade was able to get us double meals by registering us with the responsible person for our new abode and not telling the old one we had moved. Even with a double ration it was not enough. We were on hunger rations. Ten men were given a loaf of white bread to share, and whoever had a tin could receive a thinned-out tea. I could not stay here any longer. The comrades who had been here for some time were completely aphasic. We knew that we would starve here.

24 May 1945

Work parties were set up. I volunteered in the hope of getting out of the camp and evaluating the possibility of escape. On a fully loaded truck my work party was driven to Murnau. Here we had to fill bomb craters. At lunchtime two civilians walked by. One wore a carry basket on his back and a rake on his shoulder. He stared at me and turned to laugh. I felt uneasy and fingered my trousers on the assumption that he was amusing himself about a possible hole in my trousers. In an unguarded moment, the basket carrier came up to me, still laughing, and said: "Do you not recognise me? I am *Sanitäter-Feldwebel* Beutler, from your *Kompanie*!" I was speechless. He laughed at the fact that I had been captured. I wished him well, and since he was a former government official in Stade, I asked him to greet my fiancée in Fallingbostel, but that did not happen.

In the afternoon when we were brought back to camp, I saw my good friend Beutler standing with other fake civilians at the gate. They were being searched by the Military Police. I could have laughed at him, but I suddenly felt sorry for him.

25 May 1945

Today I was part of a working party at the American dental clinic. The Americans have everything. False teeth and dentures are made in this villa. We have to clean the trays of hardening material. We are fully catered for with this American unit and there is plenty of food. We are able to supplement our starving comrades, who are fully dependent on the poor camp rations. Not far from my sleeping place I became acquainted with Karl-Leo Schmitz from Aachen, who also worked in the dental clinic. Karl and I also made friends with a soldier who worked in the administration office of a warehouse, and we provide him with food and tobacco.

26 May 1945

We were actually quite satisfied: easy work, good food and well-meaning Americans at the dental clinic. A German-speaking American officer joined me today, asking about my unit and where I was from. He spoke with esteem about soldiers of the *Fallschirmtruppe*, and he also said we would all be home soon. On an errand to a neighbouring hotel I saw a wristwatch on the bedside table of an open *Ami* billet. It was quickly hidden in my shoe; that was revenge for the search at the stadium gate which cost me my own watch.

In the evening there was a kind of variety show in the stadium, which was performed by the ladies of the theatre and film group who were also incarcerated here. Among others, Gloria Astor sang 'Weekend and Sunshine' (*Wochenend und Sonnenschein*) with a good musical accompaniment.[2] She received a storming applause. The *Amis* also clapped!

27 May 1945

Today we are again required to work at the dental clinic. In the basement of a neighbouring house I obtain a civilian jacket. In the evening our friend from the camp administration, to whom we had informed of our escape plan, told us that we should try to get to the small ice rink next door early in the morning. From there a transport would be taking German soldiers to a special camp in Weilheim for interrogation.

We should try to join them and jump on the trucks, and at the first opportunity beyond the mountains jump off and escape.

28 May 1945

At 0700 hours, Karl and I stood with our rucksacks on the top seats of the stadium. From here we watched the *Ami* guards, and as soon as they turned around and took off we made our way into the ice stadium. We mingled unnoticed amongst the officers and soldiers.

We should have departed at 1000 hours, but at 1300 hours three trucks arrived. Karl and I climbed aboard the last truck. All of the trucks were overcrowded with men. Two *Ami* soldiers sat at the back by the tailgate and loaded their weapons. The vehicles set off, and after a two-hour drive through Garmisch, Oberammergau and Schongau we had our first stop. The American distributed two slices of white bread. We were allowed to sit down. In front of us we could hear chatter. The chief officer was probably comparing the road map with the driving order, and we kept overhearing "Weilheim, no Weilburg". They were confusing the two location names. They decided on Weilburg, and I told Karl. We did not need to jump off and escape just yet. It got dark and we noticed that the roadblocks in the villages were well controlled.

During the night we drove through the burnt-out and destroyed town of Würzburg. We were quietly chatting and the accompanying guards did not seem to be fully awake anymore. I also fell asleep, but was suddenly awakened by a blow to the back and I found my feet up in the air. Our truck now lay on its side in a ditch. I struggled to free myself from the tangle of swearing soldiers, but eventually had ground under my feet.

Karl came rushing over to me; he was fine. We were told that all men were to help right the truck. I took Karl aside and told him to get his pack, it's time! As both *Amis* and Germans struggled together to get the vehicle upright, Karl and I slipped away unnoticed into the darkness without any problems.

---

2   Born Gerda Mielke, Gloria Astor was a popular German singer throughout the war years.

29 May 1945

We had to be between the towns of Rhön and Knüll, because somewhere during the morning we had seen a signpost to Kassel. We marched into the sunny day without a break and kept away from the main traffic routes. Then the area suddenly seemed familiar to me! We took a short break near a stream. We were hungry and thirsty. In the afternoon we were on the road from Seigertshausen to Obergrenzebach, where we observed the hay harvest. Not far from the gravel road, underneath a bush, was a basket. I crept up to the basket when the two farmers were at the far end of the pasture. I found two beautiful *petzkuchen* [cakes] looking up at me. They helped to satisfy our hunger.

The closer we approached Ziegenhain, the more cautious we had to be. After circling Niedergrenzebach in the late afternoon, heading for Ziegenhain, we bumped into an American soldier who was standing behind the last house. In broken German he asked: "You want home? I also! War no good!" Then he gave both of us a cigarette, tapped his cap with his index finger and left. We both took a deep breath; we had been lucky.

We could not afford to be careless so close toward the end of our journey.

Twilight came and we ran through the Schwalm-Aue region and reached Treysa some four hours later. We sneaked through the Wagnergaße and reached the safety of my brother Hanerch's apartment in the Bahnhofstraße. My sister-in-law Christine welcomed us and took care of our physical wellbeing.

The next morning we arrived without difficulty in Florshain, which was only 5km away. My father, mother and siblings were overjoyed to finally see me, and I was glad that my long journey home was finally at an end.

When editing my journal notes I thought of all the hospitable and kind people who helped me on my long journey home. To them I will always be grateful.

(Heinrich Gömpel passed away on 9 December 2002, aged 82.)

Oberjäger Heinrich Gömpel (second left with goggles) prior to a training jump on 25 June 1943 at the military airfield at Orange in southern France. The men are from *1.Gruppe, 9.Kompanie, III/FJR1*. Heini has an MP40 SMG strapped to his chest with spare ammunition pouches. The rifle of the man in front is fitted with a cover to prevent the working parts of the rifle becoming entangled in the shroud lines of the parachute. All the men are wearing the RZ20 parachute and gas mask bags. (Heinrich Gömpel)

3

Franz Rzeha

Operations Hannibal and Mercury

Franz Rzeha was born on 28 November 1919 in Oderfurth (now Přívoz) in Moravian Ostrava, Czechoslovakia, close to the Polish border.

After graduation and subsequent vocational training, he joined Infantry Regiment 51 in 1939 and in March 1940 joined the Fallschirmtruppe. *After jump training at* Fallschirmschule II *Wittstock, Franz came to 5/FJR2 at the Hermann Göring Barracks in Berlin-Reinickendorf.*

Gefreiter Rzeha served with his Kompanie *through* Unternehmen *(Operation) Hannibal, the airborne assault on the Corinth Canal Bridge, and Unternehmen Merkur, the airborne invasion of Crete. After recovering from the hell of Crete, Franz Rzeha's* Kompanie *was sent to Russia in December 1941, serving on the Mius Front in the south followed by the Volkhov Front in the north. In the first six months of 1942, Franz suffered frostbite and was wounded three times. After treatment and recovery, he went on to become a jump instructor at the Wittstock* Fallschirmschule *and was promoted to* Feldwebel *in 1944.*

Gefreiter Franz Rzeha wearing the *EK1* and *EK2*. (Manfred Müller)

During his time as a Fallschirmjäger, *Franz conducted two combat jumps and 33 training jumps from various aircraft such as the Junkers W34, Heinkel He-111, JU-52, the Italian Savoya and the* Gigant *glider. He also made one jump from a tethered balloon due to a lack of fuel for training aircraft. Jump training at Wittstock was discontinued in March 1945.*

Franz Rzeha wrote of the following reports:

> "This documentation is intended to commemorate the comrades who lost their young lives in both Corinth and Crete. At the same time it should also be a reminder and a warning that such a destructive struggle must never be repeated."

Franz Rzeha in 2012.
(Manfred Müller)

5/FJR2 at the Sanssouci Palace in Potsdam in October 1940. The officers fourth from the left are: *Leutnant* Wirth, *Oberleutnant* Schrader (representing *Oberleutnant* Thiel), *Leutnant* Roland Krückeberg and *Leutnant* Amberger. *Der Kompanie Spieß*, *Hauptfeldwebel* Paul Baum, is fourth from right. Many of the men in this photo would be killed in the forthcoming operations at Corinth and Crete in 1941. Franz Rzeha is circled in the right of the photo (Manfred Müller)

Unternehmen Hannibal – The airborne assault on the Corinth Canal Bridge

At the beginning of April 1941 we were ready in all respects to conduct a jump operation. Located in the Plovdiv area of Bulgaria, we lay in tents around the Krumovo airfield surrounded by barbed wire.

The 'Establishment', April 1941

Krumovo was also home to a *Luftwaffe* squadron with its many fighter and bomber aircraft. Accompanying this squadron was an 'establishment' consisting of 25 girls! The establishment was open to us from 1900–2100 hours, no earlier and no later. An armed guard stood outside with orders to use his weapon if necessary. In addition to our monthly pay, we were given a 2 Mark coin with a hole in it. In military jargon it was known as 'hole money'. An older *Oberjäger* tried to gain admission outside of the prescribed time. After a brief discussion with the guard, a shot suddenly rang out and the *Oberjäger* was dead! His relatives were notified that he had died a hero's death. What should one write? He was shot in front of an establishment? After this incident the girls observed three days of mourning, which they strictly adhered to of course![1]

---

1   This may be the same incident witnessed by Sebastian Krug and retold through hearsay within the *Regiment*!

The upcoming Easter was celebrated with the Bulgarians. Until 24 April we did nothing much but play card games, and during the day we often watched the girls through the binoculars. They were sunning themselves on lounge chairs behind the barbed wire.

24 April 1941

A *Kompanie* briefing was held in the evening. Mission order! *FJR2* are to capture the retreating tide of English [*sic*] troops from the Balkans before they reach the Corinth Canal and escape the mainland by sea. We are to capture or destroy them! The main focus was to secure the bridge. Using aerial photos and ancient Greek maps, we memorised every metre of the terrain onto which our *Bataillon* will be dropped south of the bridge. Once again the parachutes and weapons are checked and we receive ammunition and hand grenades.

My *Zugführer* was *Leutnant* Amberger and I was assigned as his *Melder*, always running back and forth with his orders. For the mission he would jump first and I would be right behind him.

25 April 1941

Our *Regiment* and the other operational units are flown to Larissa in Greece. Here final preparations are made for the mission on the following day.

26 April 1941 – The airborne assault on the Corinth Canal Bridge

In beautiful weather with the sun rising behind us, we flew low above the water. The approach was without enemy contact, but just before the jump, as the aircraft pulled up to the jump height of 100m, we recieved strong defensive fire from *MGs* and a 2cm *Flak* position near the bridge.

We in the machine were quite relaxed and waited for the signal to 'get ready'. A few seconds later came the order 'ready to jump'. *Leutnant* Amberger stood in the door with me behind him. The defensive fire was getting stronger and we noticed bullet strikes in the aircraft. Amberger sank to his knees at the moment the signal came to 'jump'!

In a fraction of a second, using all my energy I pushed Amberger out of the doorway. He was deadweight and when he was clear we all followed him. There was no delay in the jump.

I landed just behind a position near the bridge occupied by three English [*sic*] soldiers who were probably expecting a *Stuka* attack as they had their hands up covering their faces. I stood, detached myself from the parachute harness, and with my pistol in hand shouted: "Hands up". I disarmed them and turned them over to comrade Skobranek. *Oberleutnant* Hans Thiel came over and ordered me to proceed to the bridge at once to take up a securing position.[2] Only five minutes had passed since the jump and I was already in position near the bridge. I saw our *Pioniers* removing the explosive charges and a war correspondent filming Von der Heyden on the bridge.[3] Ten minutes had passed since the jump, and suddenly there was a tremendous detonation. Instinctively I threw myself to the ground as fragments and debris flew through the air all around me. I did not know what was going on, but when I opened my eyes I saw the effect of the explosion. The bridge had been blown up. I immediately went to the train station, where *Oberleutnant* Hans Thiel was now located. On the way I passed *Leutnant* Amberger, lying on the ground, still attached to his parachute harness. I wanted to help him, and as I stood about 3 metres in front of him he screamed

---

2   The parachute assault was preceded minutes earlier by a glider landing by men from *2. Zug* of *3/Fallsch. Pi.Btl.7* under the command of *Leutnant* Norbert Häffner and a *Zug* from *6/FJR2* under the command of *Leutnant* Hans Teusen. Their mission was to secure the bridge and remove any demolition charges prior to the arrival of the parachute troops. (Schirmer)

3   *Sonderführer* Eberhard von der Heyden was a member of a *Propoganda Kompanie* and was present at Corinth to take photographs. He and several *Pioniers* happened to be on the bridge when it was destroyed. (Schirmer)

and waved his pistol in the air: "I will shoot anyone who approaches me." I left him and reported the incident to *Oberleutnant* Thiel.

Meanwhile, armed with a machine-pistol and hand grenades, I took part in the clean-up operation of the jump zone, where the enemy were still defending themselves. We combed the area; there were still dead and wounded men on the jump zone. After about four hours we had prevailed and only occasional single shots were heard. We then rested. We took many prisoners who were taken to the train station, where the dressing station had been established. There were more dead and wounded then we had expected.

At around 1030 hours I was ordered to secure the road from Athens to Corinth when I suddenly heard the sound of moving tanks. In the first *Panzer* was a young *SS* officer looking out of the hatch, who asked "What's going on here?", to which I replied: "Paratrooper operation to secure the bridge over the Corinth Canal but it went up in the air about 10 minutes after the jump!"

Epilogue

Hauptmann Gerhart Schirmer took over command of *II/FJR2* when *Major* Erich Pietzonka was injured during the jump. In a post-action report, *Hauptmann* Schirmer stated that at approximately 1900 hours on 26 April 1941, 72 English officers and 1,200 men went into captivity, many of whom were wounded. Casualties for *II/FJR2* were 47 killed, 47 seriously wounded, 73 lightly wounded and three missing.

Unternehmen Merkur – The airborne invasion of Crete

In memory of my comrades of *5/FJR2* who lost their lives in the murderous battle on Crete.

It was 21 May 1941, about 1500 hours, when the jump into hell began. Much has been written and spoken about Operation Mercury. I would like to add my own account of how I experienced the mission in my *Kompanie*. It is a factual report.

19 May 1941

5/FJR2 is billeted in tents near the airfield at Tanagra in Greece. There was a mood of excitement amongst my comrades. The tension of the upcoming mission did not allow us to rest. All thought back to the jump operation at Corinth on 26 April, and we were convinced that the upcoming mission would be short and sweet. Songs were sung and thoughts were with our loved ones at home.

A briefing took place later that night, and for the first time we heard that Crete will be our mission. The jump area will be at Heraklion. The mission of *II/FJR2* should take place on 20 May, and since *Major* Pietzonka was still in the military hospital, *Hauptmann* Schirmer would retain command of the *Bataillon*.

20 May 1941

The losses of JU-52 transport aircraft during the first wave of the operation meant that *5. Kompanie*, without the *Zug* 'Krückeberg', and *6. Kompanie* would have to stay behind.[4] Both units had been deployed to the Corinth Canal and had suffered heavy losses.

---

4   This *Zug* under the command of *Oberleutnant* Roland Krückeberg was dropped with *Hauptmann* Schirmer's *II/FJR2* west of Heraklion. He was killed on 23 May 1941 and his remains were not recovered. In a letter

There was a lot of activity at the Tanagra airfield. A huge dark cloud of dust spread across the runway. The landing JU-52s had to be laboriously refuelled by hand from barrels and reloaded with weapon containers. Many of the machines were covered in bullet holes, but flew on to new operations regardless. The situation on Crete was critical. By the evening of 20 May, none of the target airfields were in German hands. *General* Student ordered a decisive strike on 21 May to conquer the Maleme aerodrome and its hinterland.

By order of the *XI Fliegerkorps*, *Fallschirmjäger* formations that had remained on the mainland on 20 May would be dispatched as reinforcements for the *LL.St.Rgt* in the Maleme sector where they were desperately required. This ad hoc *Bataillon* would consist of 500 men from the *Fallschirm Panzerjäger Abteilung* under the command of *Major* Hannes Schmitz and a *Kompanie* from *FJR2* under the command of *Leutnant* Hans Klein. The remains of *II/FJR2*, namely 5. *Kompanie* under *Oberleutnant* Thiel and 6. *Kompanie* under *Oberleutnant* Nagele, with an assigned *Zug* from *Fallsch. San.Abt.7* under *Oberarzt* Dr Dieter Hartmann, would be dropped east of Pyrgos. An attack from the west by the reinforced *IV Bataillon* of the *Sturmregiment* under *Hauptmann* Gericke, and the departure of the Thiel/Nagele group behind enemy lines, was set for 1500 hours on 21 May.

21 May 1941

A new briefing was given in the early hours. Our 5. *Kompanie* would now jump to the west of Platanias, fight its way to the Maleme airfield, secure the airfield and make contact with the *Sturmregiment*. It was as simple as that!

In the meantime, bad news came from Crete. Not a good sign for us. Still, the mood was good and we knew we had to help our comrades. We inspected our weapons carefully but were only able to carry out an external inspection of our parachutes as they were packed and sealed, fresh from the factory. We trusted the parachute packer's skills; there was nothing more we could do.

I attached my machine-pistol to my chest strap and the spare magazines were attached to my body under the bonesack, just like the bread bag which was filled with iron rations and a few lemons. I also had my canteen and a pistol. I stowed as much as possible in the pockets of the bonesack, such as egg grenades, six Czech hand grenades with impact fuses (Model RG34) and a bandage pack. Everything else was stowed in the *Waffenbehälter*.

With beating hearts we climbed aboard the aircraft. The sun had reached its zenith when the aircraft began to taxi. The JU-52 took off and we flew towards Crete. After a short time we saw the sea below us, and we flew so low that it felt as though we were touching the water. Our ME-110 escorts flew past to the left and right of us.

Shortly before reaching Crete, we flew past the offshore island of Theodori where we began to encounter the enemy's murderous defensive fire. We heard and saw the impacts of light defensive weapons on the corrugated metal body of the JU-52. From the windows we saw two damaged machines fly back to the mainland. On one an engine burned and the second had a severely damaged tail. We, in our machine, looked at each other and wished each other '*Hals und Beinbruch*' (break a leg). We later learned that the English [*sic*] had established an observation position on the southern tip of Theodori where they could direct their defensive fire at every approach point to the Maleme airfield. It was not detected until 23 May, and by then it was too late.

The command 'get ready' rang out. Enemy *Flak* fired at the approaching JU-52s from all tubes. The signal to jump was salvation to us!

---

sent to Franz from Schirmer, the former *Bataillonskommandeur* stated that Krückeberg jumped with him at Heraklion and that he was killed on 22 May during the fighting in front of the western gate. Krückeberg's name is recorded on a panel at the Maleme memorial for those whose bodies were never recovered.

The jump from a height of approximately 70m was a jump into hell! We jumped in front of and into camouflaged positions of both English [*sic*] and New Zealand troops in a vineyard west of the Platanias River.[5] I could hear the hissing of the passing bullets. They directed a hail of bullets from their well-constructed positions as if they knew we were coming. Many, many comrades were already dead or seriously wounded, still attached to their parachutes. No sooner had we landed on the firm ground, we could hear the cries for help: "*Sanitäter!*" There were none. In the beginning the cries for help were quite loud, but later they became quieter and quieter until they finally fell silent.

The surviving comrades quickly identified the main area of resistance, so we pushed on towards the hill where the strongest defensive fire was coming from. On the right and on the left the enemy withdrew, taking along their dead and wounded to take up new positions on the hill.

One *MG* nest in particular located under two olive trees gave us a hard time, the New Zealanders' wide-brimmed hats still hanging on the branches. With two comrades I worked my way forward to within 10m of the *MG*, covered by the green grapevines. We were in a blind spot. At my command we threw our hand grenades and stormed the hill. The *MG* fell silent. The well-camouflaged enemy trenches were taken by 12 comrades who had come from another part of the hill, and we watched as the enemy retreated west, once again carrying their dead and wounded, which we allowed. On the hill we settled in to the trench positions recently vacated by the enemy.

Nothing moved in the jump area and I could only hear a faint call for a *Sani*. I moved toward the direction of the calling comrade. Hardly ten metres away I found a comrade lying on the ground. He was younger than me and I did not know him. I had to crawl to reach him, as no doubt somewhere out there was an enemy who could observe this spot of earth. His face was smeared with blood, his exposed thighs were wounded and the blood was heavily encrusted. I tried to dress the wounds as best as I could. His canteen was empty, so I tried to quench his thirst with a few drops from one of my lemons. I also tried to reassure him and calm him down. He looked up at me and said: "My head is so heavy!" I put my left arm under his head and lifted it slightly. With his big eyes he looked pleadingly at me and whispered "mother, mother!", words that his distant mother would never hear. Who could even guess that this young *Fallschirmjäger*, her son, would suffer such a miserable lonely death? So he died lying in my arm. I covered his sunken face with a cloth and crawled back to the hill.

At this time it was past 1800 hours. The *Kompanie* had lost all the *Portepee Unteroffiziere*. The *Kompaniechef*, *Oberleutnant* Thiel, had also been killed.

Oberleutnant Hans Thiel (right arrow) and *Leutnant* Roland Krückeberg (left arrow), taken in Plovdiv shortly before the invasion. (Jose Ramon Artaza Ibañez)

---

5   Positions held by the New Zealand 5th Infantry Brigade with attached 28th Maori Battalion.

5/FJR2 graves on Crete for men killed on 21 May. From left to right: *Hauptfeldwebel* Paul Baum, *Kompanieführer Oberleutnant* Hans Thiel, *Gefreiter* Rudolf Patzwahl and *Gefreiter* Josef Schink. (Manfred Müller)

The *Kompanie* had practically been destroyed. The sun was already low on the western horizon. Whenever one of us raised our heads too far, a well-camouflaged sniper, half left on the hill, had us in his sights.

At the bottom of our hill we spotted a gully. Two comrades tried to reach this waterhole, taking our water bottles with them. We could see them at the waterhole drinking, and then they filled up the water bottles and also their jump helmets. Then it happened! Suddenly we heard shots and saw both of them fall and topple into the gulley!

At dusk, two more comrades came from nowhere and joined us on the hill. We were now a total of 11 men. One group moved to the jump area to search for weapons and ammunition. They found some. We now had one MG as well as a few machine-pistols, ammo and hand grenades. No living comrades could be found and a link-up with the *Sturmregiment* or *6. Kompanie* did not materialise. We decided to wait until the morning and then push through to Maleme.

The night began, the stars shone and the crickets chirped. Somewhere in the direction of Maleme, we could hear a donkey braying. The enemy scanned the jump area with searchlights. We froze and avoided any sudden movements. It was terribly cold, we were thirsty and our cracked lips hurt. Our limbs were exhausted as we waited for the morning.

22 May 1941

At dawn, we were attacked by elements of the 28th New Zealand (Maori) Battalion. From the east, the enemy approached on two occasions to throw hand grenades. We struggled desperately.

The ammunition became less and less. The enemy retreated to their starting position, re-formed and attacked a third time. They used their mortars on our position again and again, and came closer and closer. We fired our last cartridge! They threw hand grenades and our *MG* shooter was mortally wounded by fragments to his abdomen. He was our last *Kompanie* casualty.

Now they stormed us with fixed bayonets. A drunken Maori rushed at me. I saw him coming, smelt his alcohol breath, my empty pistol in my hand. I already felt the Maori's bayonet on my stomach when at the last second a young English officer pushed the Maori's rifle aside, grabbed my shoulder and said: "Come on boy."[6] My life had been saved. After my remaining comrades were taken out of their holes, the enemy immediately gave us their water bottles. They could see that we were almost dying of thirst. Ten of us sat there and waited for what was coming. After a short while, the commanding officer came to look at our small group and said in German with an English accent: "Where are the others?" We shrugged our shoulders and a comrade replied: "There are no others." Then the officer stood in front of us, looked at us one by one with watering eyes and said "All right boys" and saluted. We took the path into captivity.

Barely two hours had passed. We were taken to the enemy positions at Modhion (1.5km south of Gerani), and we had not been there long when a group of our *Stukas* approached. They repeatedly bombed the enemy positions and we were in the midst of it, familiar with how deadly this weapon could be. It was a terrible mess. We took advantage of the chaos and confusion and fled to the west. Our two hours of captivity was over.

Back in the old jump area, we searched for weapons. We found some of what we needed. I also found my parachute, with 'RZ' for Rzeha which I had written on the cover whilst at the Tanagra airfield. There was over 30 bullet holes in the parachute silk; never was our greeting '*Glück Ab*' (Good luck) so apt! I made myself a scarf from a large piece of parachute silk. Everywhere around the jump area lay our dead comrades in the blazing sun, the sweetish smell of death, the swollen, bloodied bodies. It was a sight that will never be forgotten.

After a brief silent commemoration, we made our way in the direction of the Maleme aerodrome. In a nearby olive grove we came across *Oberleutnant* Raimund Nagele and reported in as the remnants of *5. Kompanie*. It was about 1600 hours. We were integrated into his unit and were designated as *Stoßtrupp Nagele*, part of *Kampfgruppe Gericke*. At this time the assault squad consisted of 30 men from *6. Kompanie* and 10 men from *5. Kompanie*.

23 May 1941

We attack toward Pyrgos and Gerani until we are close to Platanias. We move on the right side of the coastal road to Chania. There are a few isolated artillery rounds. We take up a rest position near Platanias during the night.

24 May 1941

Oberst Hermann Ramcke is with us in an olive grove.[7] We make a report about the fight of *5. Kompanie* and the many dead we suffered. He silently shook our hands. We continue to Platanias. Suddenly *Gebirgsjäger* are with us. Together we take Platanias. No breather. Continue towards Agia Marina. The night passes without incident.

---

6   Franz Rzeha informed *Hauptmann* Schirmer of this incident. Rzeha was ordered to find the officer at the POW camp. Rzeha recognised him, and through an English-speaking comrade they spoke about the incident. The officer was from London and asked Rzeha to send a letter to his mother via the Red Cross. After reporting back to Schirmer, he gave the order for the English officer to be transferred to a military hospital in Athens. (Schirmer)

7   *Oberst* Ramcke jumped near Tavronitis late in the afternoon on 21 May to take over command of the Sturmregiment from the wounded *Oberst* Eugen Meindl. See Golla, p.471.

25 May 1941

We attacked eastward along the coastal road towards Chania. Our planes are bombing the town. The enemy offers only isolated resistance.

26 May 1941

The English [*sic*] military hospital at Apostolei is captured without a fight. We sleep under mosquito nets for two hours then further on to Galatas. Isolated enemy fire.

27 May 1941

We attack on the right side of the coastal road towards the last heights west of Chania. We meet light resistance. This is music to our ears. At 1000 hours we attack Chania. A liaison officer arrived in the staging area. The *Führer* is willing to sign death warrants for plundering and rape. What was that all about? We were just happy to be alive! By the way, this was not one of our virtues. We knew how to behave properly!

The attack began with mortar fire but we met only weak resistance. At around 1630 hours we entered the town from the south-west. It had been severely damaged by the *Luftwaffe*.

28 May 1941

At 1600 hours the fight for Crete was over in our sector. I am billeted in a villa near Suda Bay.

3 June 1941

In a tented camp south-west of Chania I was awarded the *EK1* by *Hauptmann* Schirmer. From 3 June to 25 June we are recovering from the jump into hell!

26 June 1941

Return flight from Heraklion, Crete, to the Megara airfield near Athens in Greece, where I obtained lodgings.

27 June 1941

In Athens and we visit the Acropolis. I drink with my surviving comrades.

4 July 1941

Departure by truck via Theben, Lamia and Larissa to Saloniki.

9 July 1941

Departure from Thessaloniki by train via Skopje, Niche and Belgrade to Agram.

14 July 1941

We pass the Reich border and pass through Graz, Regensburg, Hof, Leipzig, and Bitterfeld to Berlin.

17 July 1941

Back to our barracks in Berlin-Reinickendorf. After some refreshment we are given a rapturous welcome by the population in a regimental parade on the Seestraße in Reinickendorf.

21 July 1941

We Crete veterans receive a 14-day special leave. When we return from leave there are dark clouds moving in the sky. Our next mission has already been planned. Russia!

Reflecting on Crete

One cannot complete the description of the battle without mentioning the unimaginable physical hardships that the paratroopers were exposed to during the bitter 10-day fighting. The sun burned in the sky, 35–38 degrees in the shade! The paratroopers had long since discarded their *Fliegerbluse* from beneath the bonesack. Every man had to crouch, crawl and run whilst burdened with weapons, ammunition and other military equipment. The emergency rations had long since been consumed or lost from the pockets. One rubbed the spikes of barley which grew here and there and chewed the hard grains in the dry mouth. In addition, [we had] constant thirst as there was nothing to drink for the whole long day beneath the burning sun. There were positions where you could not move from behind cover. So emaciated were the fighters and so indifferent, they often never took cover from potential enemy fire. At night the guard's eyes fell shut, even if they were only a few metres away from the enemy.

Epilogue

On that fateful afternoon of 21 May 1941, many men of *5./FJR2* jumped into an olive grove in the vicinity of the coast road between Gerani and the Platanias River and found themselves suspended in the trees. The greater part of the *Kompanie* jumped about 200m south of the road directly into the positions of the 5th New Zealand Brigade in a vineyard. From this hill the enemy had a clear field of view to the Maleme airfield to the west and Platanias to the east.

The casualty figures for *5. Kompanie* were 63 killed, including the *Kompaniechef*, *Oberleutnant* Hans Thiel, and the *Zugführer*, *Oberleutnant* Roland Krückeberg. Thirty-six men were wounded and two were captured upon landing, although many others were taken into captivity during the day.

The graves of *Oberleutnant* Hans Thiel and *Hauptfeldwebel* Paul Baum. (aretecrete.com)

The lucky ones: *Gefreite* and *Obergefreite* from *5/FJR5* who survived. Front row, left to right: Franz Rzeha, Zillgit, Lenz, Nowak, Kotzibik, Hamman. In short-sleeves is Klehe, to his left Fichter and Korbel on the railing. (Jean-Yves Nasse)

The end of the war for Franz Rzeha

In March 1945, *Fallschirmschule II* at Wittstock was evacuated. The Russians stood near Frankfurt on the Oder River. The training *Kompanie* was filled with non-jumpers, and as the newly designated *FJR58* we were moved to the Hook of Holland.[8] There I was assigned with my *Zug* of 48 men to a 900m-long coastal sector, which we had to defend. This was in Gravenzande. We had three heavy guns directed at the sea, with minefields and barbed wire behind us.

After the surrender in 1945, I was interred by the British and on 25 June 1945 registered by a British discharge office and released from captivity.

By the end of the war I had been awarded the following:

- *EK2* and *EK1*
- *Kreta*, *Fsch.Jg.Rgt 2* and *Fallschirm Division* cuff titles
- Reichs sport badge
- *Luftwaffe* Paratroopers badge
- Close combat clasp in silver
- Wound badge in silver
- Eastern Front medal 41/42

In 1964 I became a member of the New Zealand Crete Veterans Association.

(Franz Rzeha passed away in Bad Mergentheim on 6 November 2013, aged 93.)

---

8   Part of *FJD20*, formed on 5 April 1945 from *Fallschirmjäger-Ausbildungs-Regiment 2*.

Afterword

I hope you the reader have enjoyed these first-hand accounts and diaries as much as I have enjoyed collating them over the years. They provide a fascinating insight into the wartime service of a small cross-section of men who served as *Fallschirmjäger* during the Second World War.

Since my first contact with a *Fallschirmjäger* veteran back in 1999, I have been struck by their friendliness and generosity, the absence of animosity toward their former foe and their enthusiasm to see their stories published for others to read.

Sadly, many of these men have now passed away and oral histories such as these now belong to an ever-decreasing number of veterans.

I hope that you the reader can appreciate the historical value of this publication.

I think Kurt Schulz summed it up in a letter he once wrote to me:

> You must be quite an extraordinary person to bring up the positive side of your former enemy. An enemy that caused so much misery in an unnecessary war that caused so much suffering to both of our peoples. You had your 'Blitz' and we the terrible fire bombings of most of our major cities, of which Dresden, Hamburg and my own hometown of Königsberg are hard to forget. The only thing that we should and can do is forgive but not forget and remember to learn from our past mistakes.

Bibliography

Books

Adler, Rudolf, *Der verlorene Haufen: Erinnerungen eines Fallschirmjägers* (Norderstedt: Herstellung und Verlag, 2004).

Bender, James Roger & Petersen, George A, *Hermann Goring: From Regiment to Fallschirmpanzerkorps* (Atglen: Schiffer Publishing, 1993).

Bliss, Heinz & Bosshammer, Bernd, *Das Fallschirmjäger-Lehr-Regiment* (Witzenhausen: Feldmann Druck, 1999).

Davin, D.M., *Official History of New Zealand in the Second World War 1939–45: Crete* (London: Oxford University Press, 1953)

Davis, Brian L, *Uniforms and Insignia of the Luftwaffe Volume 1: 1933-1940* (London: Arms and Armour Press, 1991).

Department of the Army, *Airborne Operations: A German Appraisal* (Washington D.C.: Department of the US Army, 1951)

Foley, Charles, *Commando Extraordinary: Otto Skorzeny* (London: Cassel, 1998).

Golla, Karl-Heinz, *The German Fallschirmtruppe 1936–41: Its genesis and employment in the first campaigns of the Wehrmacht* (Solihull: Helion & Company, 2012).

Gonzalez, Oscar, Steinke, Thomas & Tannahill, Ian, *The Silent Attack* (Barnsley: Pen & Sword, 2015).

Frühbeißer, Rudi, *Opfergang Deutscher Fallschirmjäger* (Germany: self-published, 1966).

Janzyk, Stephan, *Operation Fall Weiss: German Paratroopers in the Poland Campaign 1939* (Barnsley: Pen & Sword Military, 2017).

Kammann, Willi, *Die Geschichte des Fallschirmjäger Regiment 2: 1939 bis 1945* (Scheinfeld: self-published, 1987).

Kiriakopoulos, C.G., *Ten Days to Destiny: The Battle for Crete, 1941* (New York: Franklin Watts, 1985).

Knoblauch, Karl, *Der Letzte Hieb* (self-published, 1992).

Kurowski, Franz, *Jump into Hell: German Paratroopers in World War II* (Barnsley: Pen & Sword Books, 2010).

Lucas, James, *Storming Eagles – German Airborne Forces in World War Two* (London: Arms & Armour Press, 1988).

Mansolas, Angelos, *Monte Cassino – January–May 1944 – The Legend of the Green Devils* (Stroud: Fonthill Media, 2017).

Mooney, David, *The Concise Guide to Axis Aircraft of World War II* (London: Chancellor Press, 1996).

Morris, Allen, *German Airlift during the Battle of Crete* (Great Britain: Amazon, 2014).

Mrazek, James, *The Fall of Eben Emael* (Novato: Presidio Press, 1999).

Mühleisen, Hans-Otto, *Kreta 1941: Das Unternehmen Merkur 20.5 bis 1.6.1941* (Freiburg: Verlag Rombach, 1977).

Nasse, Jean-Yves, *Fallschirmjäger in Crete* (Paris: Histoire & Collections, 2002).

Nasse, Jean-Yves, *Green Devils: German Paratroopers 1939–1945* (Paris: Histoire & Collections, 1997).

Nisbett, Adrian, *Heroes in Death: The Von Blücher Brothers in the Fallschirmjäger – Crete May 1941* (Atglen: Schiffer Publishing, 2014).

Peters, Klaus J, *Fallschirm-Jäger Rgt.3: Band 1; Vom SturmBataillon zum Regiment 1916/1941* (San Jose: R. James Bender Publishing, 1992).

Prekatsounakis, Yannis, *The Battle for Heraklion: Crete 1941* (Solihull: Helion & Company, 2017).

Quarrie, Bruce, *German Airborne Divisions: Mediterranean Theatre 1942–45* (Oxford: Osprey Publishing, 2005).

Ramcke, Hermann Bernhard, *Fallschirmjäger: Brest and beyond 1944–1951* (Bradford: Shelf Books, 2016).

Richter, Heinz A,, *Operation Merkur: Die Eroberung der Insel Kreta im Mai 1941* (Ruhpolding: Verlag Franz Phillip Rutzen, 2011).

Roppelt, Fritz, *Der Vergangenheit auf der Spur* (self-published, 1993).

Scherzer, Veit, *Die Träger des Deutschen Kreuzes in Gold der Luftwaffe 1941–1945* (Zweibrücken: Verlag Heinz Nickel, 1992).

Schirmer, Gerhart, *Geschichte des Fallschirmjäger Regimentes 16 Ost* (Sonderdruck Kameradschaft 'Weisse Spiegel', 1988).

Shulman, Milton, *Defeat in the West* (Chailey: Masquerade, 1995).

Stargardt, Nicholas, *The German War: A nation under arms 1939–45* (London: Penguin Random House, 2015).

Stimpel, Hans-Martin, *Die deutsche Fallschirmtruppe 1942–1945: Einsätze auf Kriegsschauplätzen in Osten und Westen* (Hamburg: Mittler, 2001).

Taylor, Brian, *Barbarossa to Berlin: A Chronology of the Campaigns on the Eastern Front 1941 to 1945: Volume One* (Staplehurst: Spellmount, 2003).

Taylor, Brian, *Barbarossa to Berlin: A Chronology of the Campaigns on the Eastern Front 1941 to 1945: Volume Two* (Staplehurst: Spellmount, 2004).

Unknown author, *Gefechtsbericht Kreta Kriegstagebuch XI Fliegerkorps.*

US War Department, *German Military Dictionary: German to English* (Buxton: MLRS, 2006).

Veltzé, Karl, *Deutsche Fallschirmjäger: Uniformierung und Ausrüstung 1936-1945 Band 2* (Berlin: Zeughaus Verlag, 2016).

Villahermosa, Gilberto, *Hitler's Paratrooper: The life and battles of Rudolf Witzig* (Barnsley: Frontline Books, 2010).

Reports & Documents

Koch, Willi & Neumann, Dr Heinrich, 'Die Geschichte der Fallschirm-Sanitätsabteilung XI.Fliegerkorps'.

Bosshammer, Bernd, 'Dokumentation über die Fallschirmtruppe'.

Gefechtsbericht Kreta Kriegstagebuch XI Fliegerkorps, XI Fliegerkorps Abt.Ia.Br.B.Nr 2980/41 g.kdos from 11.6.41.

Gemeinschaft der Fallschirmpioniere, 'Addresses of the relatives of the former Fallsch.Pi.Btl as of February 1967'.

Roth, Günter, 'Oberst a.D Gerhart Schirmer's 90th Birthday: a Portrait', *Der Deutsche Fallschirmjäger* (6/2002).

The War Office, Periodical *Notes on the German Army No.38: XI Air Corps and The Attack on Crete* (The War Office, 20 March 1942)

US Army, 'German Military Abbreviations' (US Army, 1943).

US Army, 'German Demolition Equipment' (US Army, 1944).

Internet

Bund Deutscher Fallschirmjäger e.V: http://www.fschjgbund.de (accessed 6 August 2018).

German Fallschirmjäger 1936–1945: <web.archive.org/web/20060303155610/http://www.eagle19.freeserve.co.uk/> (accessed 5 September 2018).

Pissin D.W. Numbered Air Force Study 162. The Battle of Crete. (1956) <https://www.afhra.af.mil/Information/Studies/Numbered-USAF-Historical-Studies-151-200/> (accessed 29 December 2019)

POW recapture stories: <http://www.islandfarm.wales> (accessed 31 October 2018).

Volksbund Deutsche Kriegsgräberfürsorge: <www.volksbund.de> (accessed 6 August 2018).

War History Online: Erich Koch: Nazi war criminal who tried to evade the consequences of his crimes <https://m.warhistoryonline.com/world-war-ii/erich-koch-war-criminal.html> (accessed 3 November 2018).

Index

Index of People

Index of Places

Index of Military Formations & Units

Index of Materiel